CWNA: Certified Wireless Netwo
Study Guide

W9-CSQ-170

CWNA Exam Objectives

Sybex®
An Imprint of

WILEY

NOTE Exam objectives are subject to change at any time without prior notice and at Planet3's sole discretion. Please visit Planet3's website (www.cwnp.com) for the most current listing of exam objectives.

Sybex®
An Imprint of
WILEY

CWNA®
Certified Wireless
Network Administrator™
Study Guide

CWNA®
Certified Wireless
Network Administrator™
Study Guide

David D. Coleman
David A. Westcott

Wiley Publishing, Inc.

Acquisitions and Development Editor: Jeff Kellum
Technical Editor: Sam Coyl
Production Editor: Martine Dardignac
Copy Editor: Judy Flynn
Production Manager: Tim Tate
Vice President and Executive Group Publisher: Richard Swadley
Vice President and Executive Publisher: Joseph B. Wikert
Vice President and Publisher: Neil Edde
Permissions Editor: Shannon Walters
Media Development Specialist: Kate Jenkins
Book Designers: Judy Fung and Bill Gibson
Compositor: Laurie Stewart, Happenstance Type-O-Rama
Illustrator: Jeffrey Wilson, Happenstance Type-O-Rama
Proofreader: Nancy Riddiough
Indexer: Nancy Guenther
Cover Designer: Ryan Sneed

Sybex®
An Imprint of
WILEY

To Our Valued Readers:

Thank you for looking to Sybex for your CWNA exam prep needs. We at Sybex are proud of our reputation for providing certification candidates with the practical knowledge and skills needed to succeed in the highly competitive IT marketplace. Certification candidates have come to rely on Sybex for accurate and accessible instruction on today's crucial technologies and business skills.

Just as Planet3 is committed to establishing measurable standards for certifying IT wireless administration professionals by means of the CWNA certification, Sybex is committed to providing those individuals with the knowledge needed to meet those standards.

The authors and editors have worked hard to ensure that this edition of the *CWNA: Certified Wireless Network Administrator Study Guide* you hold in your hands is comprehensive, in-depth, and pedagogically sound. We're confident that this book will exceed the demanding standards of the certification marketplace and help you, the CWNA certification candidate, succeed in your endeavors.

As always, your feedback is important to us. If you believe you've identified an error in the book, please send a detailed e-mail to support@wiley.com. And if you have general comments or suggestions, feel free to drop me a line directly at nedde@wiley.com. At Sybex we're continually striving to meet the needs of individuals preparing for certification exams.

Good luck in pursuit of your CWNA certification!

Neil Edde
Vice President & Publisher
Wiley Publishing, Inc.

We would like to dedicate this book to our parents, teachers, instructors, and mentors, who have helped us throughout our lives. We hope that through this book and through our teaching and mentoring we can help others achieve their goals.

Acknowledgments

David Coleman would like to thank his children, Brantley and Carolina, for their patience and understanding of their father throughout the writing of the book. I love you kids very much.

David Westcott would like to thank his wife, Gina, for her patience, understanding, and support and for the hours she spent reading and editing the book.

Writing the CWNA study guide has been a nine-month adventure that neither of us fully grasped from the start. We would like to thank all of the following individuals for their support and contributions during the entire process.

We must first thank Acquisitions and Developmental Editor Jeff Kellum of Sybex Publishing for initially finding us and bringing us on to this project. Jeff is an extremely patient and understanding editor who, despite our best efforts, needed to send us an occasional nasty e-mail message. We would also like to thank Project Editor Martine Dardignac of Wiley. Martine was an absolute pleasure to work with despite the fact that we drove her crazy. We would also love to thank our copyeditor, Judy Flynn; our proofreader, Nancy Riddiough; the illustrators; and our media development specialist, Shannon Walters.

We need to give a big shout out to our technical editor, Sam Coyle. Sam is a member of the IEEE with many years of practical experience in wireless communications. His contributions to the book were nothing short of invaluable. When Sam is not providing awesome technical editing, he is vice president of business development for Kandersteg\Netrepid (www.netrepid.com), a wireless solutions provider.

We would also like to thank Devin Akin, Kevin Sandlin, Scott Turner, and Scott Williams of the CWNP Program (www.cwnp.com). You gentlemen should be proud of the internationally renowned wireless certification program that you have developed. It has been a pleasure working with all of you the past four years.

Thanks to Proxim and to Ken Ruppel (kenruppel@gmail.com) for allowing us to include the video "Beam Patterns and Polarization of Directional Antennas" on the CD-ROM, and thanks to Andrew Potter for making himself available for our photography needs.

Special thanks goes to Andras Szilagyi, not only for creating the EMANIM software program, but also for all the extra assistance he provided by working with us to create a customized version of the program for the CD-ROM.

We would also like to think the following individuals and companies for their contributions to the book:

- Air Defense—Nico Darrow, Ralf Deltrap, and Bryan Harkins (www.airdefense.net)
- Air Magnet—Jonathan Bass and Chia Chee Kuan (www.airmagnet.com)
- AirWave (www.airwave.com)
- Andrew Potter Photography—Andrew Potter (www.andrewpotterphotography.com)
- Aruba Networks—Christopher Leach (www.arubanetworks.com)
- Cognio—William Flanagan and Margo Schlossberg (www.cognio.com)
- Cushcraft—Mark Miller (www.cushcraft.com)
- D-Link—(www.dlink.com)
- Ekahau—Jussi Kiviniemi (www.ekahau.com)
- Fortress Technologies—Andrea Shirley and Joe Tomasone (www.fortresstech.com)

- Helium Networks—Keith Borden, Ed Finn, and Walt Halasowski (www.heliumnetworks.com)
- Juniper Networks—Curt Hooper, Paul Levesque, and Matt Sweet (www.juniper.net)
- NetStumbler—Marius Milner (www.netstumbler.com)
- Ortronics—Jeff Davis, Arlene Franchini, and Irene Bammer (www.ortronics.com)
- Proxim—Ken Day, Pamela Valentine, and Amit Malhotra (www.proxim.com)
- SpectraLink—Melissa Aguirre, Ray Baum, Wayne McAllister, Wylee Post, and Robin Raulf-Sager (www.spectralink.com)
- Spectrotech—Mark Morgan (www.spectrotech.com.au)
- TamoSoft—Michael Berg (www.tamosoft.com)
- Times Microwave Systems—Joe Lanoue (www.timesmicrowave.com)
- Wi-Fi Alliance—Kelly Davis-Felner (www.wifi.org)
- Wildpackets—Stephanie Temple (www.wildpackets.com)

Foreword

Wireless LANs seem to be everywhere these days. The technology is advancing so rapidly that it seems almost impossible to stay abreast of all of the changes. The small office/home office (SOHO) sector is adopting new WLAN technologies well before there are ratified amendments or interoperability certifications in place for each technology. The small/medium business (SMB) sector is slightly more cautious but often serves as a test bed for many leading-edge technologies. The enterprise has adopted 802.11 technology slowly over the last five years, and adoption has often been due to driving factors such as saving money, as with VoWiFi and device tracking technologies, or being able to accomplish new business goals that could not be achieved without wireless technology.

Wireless has recently become wildly popular in the enterprise, and vendors are frantically releasing new products into the market. With a relentless stream of new technologies and products comes an increased demand for education and certification. The CWNP Program is dedicated strictly to staying abreast of all facets of 802.11 technology—with both standards and products. The CWNA certification is the first step in the CWNP line of certifications and is focused on administering an enterprise 802.11 WLAN. CWNA includes topics such as 802.11 standards, security, management, protocol analysis, QoS, site surveying, and radio frequency. Additional certifications focus more intensely on security, protocol analysis, QoS, and RF spectrum management.

David Coleman and David Westcott have worked as Certified Wireless Network Trainers (CWNTs) for as long as the CWNT certification has been available, and each was quick to pursue all CWNP certifications as they were released. Each has years of experience with a breadth of WLAN technologies and leading-edge products, which is obvious to their students and anyone working alongside them in the field. Having worked with each of these gentlemen for years, I can confidently say there could be no finer pair of seasoned trainers collaborating on a CWNA book. These WLAN veterans have devoted hundreds of hours to pouring their experience into this book, and the reader is assured to acquire a plethora of 802.11 knowledge. Mr. Coleman and Mr. Westcott have participated in the shaping of the CWNP Program as a whole since its earliest days and have each added tremendous value to the CWNA certification specifically. I would like to thank each of these fine gentlemen for their unwavering support of the CWNP Program, and I would like to congratulate them on their diverse accomplishments as engineers, trainers, and now authors.

Devin Akin
Chief Technology Officer
The CWNP Program

Contents at a Glance

Contents

Table of Exercises

Introduction

If you have purchased this book or if you are thinking about purchasing this book, then you probably have some interest in taking the CWNA® (Certified Wireless Network Administrator) certification exam or in learning more about what the CWNA certification exam is about. The authors would like to congratulate you on this first step, and we hope that our book can help you on your journey. Wireless networking is currently one of the hottest technologies on the market. As with many fast-growing technologies, the demand for knowledgeable people is often greater than the supply. The CWNA certification is one way to prove that you have the knowledge and skills to support this growing industry. This study guide was written with that goal in mind.

This book was written to help teach you about wireless networking so that you have the knowledge needed to not only pass the CWNA certification test, but to also be able to design, install, and support wireless networks. We have included review questions at the end of each chapter to help you test your knowledge and prepare for the test. We have also included labs, white papers, videos, and presentations on the CD to further facilitate your learning.

Before we tell you about the certification process and requirements, we must mention that this information may have changed by the time you are taking your test. We recommend that you visit www.cwnp.com as you prepare to study for your test to determine what the current objectives and requirements are.

Don't just study the questions and answers! The practice questions in this book are designed to test your knowledge of a concept or objective that is likely to be on the CWNA certification. The practice questions will be different than the actual certification questions. If you learn and understand the topics and objectives, you will be better prepared for the test.

About CWNA® and CWNP®

If you have ever prepared to take a certification test for a technology that you are unfamiliar with, you know that you are not only studying to learn a different technology, but you are probably also learning about an industry that you are unfamiliar with. Read on and we will tell you about the CWNP Program. *CWNP* is an abbreviation for *Certified Wireless Network Professional*. There is no CWNP test. CWNP is the umbrella for the certification program that is offered by Planet3 Wireless, Inc. (Planet3). Planet3 is a privately held Georgia (U.S.) company that created the CWNP certifications and courses. The CWNP certification program is a vendor-neutral program.

The objective of the CWNP Program is to certify people on wireless networking, not on a specific vendor's product. Yes, at times the authors of this book and the creators of the certification will talk about, demonstrate, or even teach how to use a specific product; however, the goal is the overall understanding of wireless, not the product itself. If you learned to drive a car, you had to physically sit and practice in one. When you think back and reminisce, you probably don't tell someone you learned to drive a Ford; you probably say you learned to drive using a Ford.

There are six wireless certifications offered by the CWNP Program:

Wireless#™ ("wireless sharp")   The Wireless# certification is an entry-level certification focusing on Wi-Fi, Bluetooth, WiMAX, ZigBee, RFID, VoWLAN, and infrared wireless networks. The Wireless# exam (PW0-050) covers a moderate level of detail on a broad base of wireless technologies.

CWNA®, Certified Wireless Network Administrator   The CWNA certification is a foundation-level Wi-Fi certification; however, it is not considered an "entry-level" technology certification. Individuals taking this exam (exam #PW0-100) typically have a solid grasp on network basics such as the OSI model, IP addressing, PC hardware, and network operating systems. Many of these candidates already hold other industry-recognized certifications, such as the CompTIA Network+ or Cisco CCNA, and are looking for the CWNA certification to enhance or complement existing skills.

CWSP®, Certified Wireless Security Professional   The CWSP certification exam (PW0-200) is focused on standards-based wireless security protocols, security policy, and secure wireless network design. This certification introduces candidates to many of the technologies and techniques that intruders use to compromise wireless networks and administrators use to protect wireless networks. With recent advances in wireless security, WLANs can be secured beyond their wired counterparts.

CWAP®, Certified Wireless Analysis Professional   The CWAP certification exam (PW0-205) measures your ability to analyze and troubleshoot wireless LANs. Before taking the exam, you should understand the frame structures and exchange processes for each of the 802.11 series of standards and how to use the tools that are available for analyzing and troubleshooting today's wireless LANs.

CWNE®, Certified Wireless Network Expert   The CWNE certification focuses on advanced WLAN analysis, design, troubleshooting, quality of service (QoS) mechanisms, spectrum management, and extensive knowledge of the IEEE 802.11 standard as amended. This certification is the pinnacle of the WLAN certification industry, and the exam is sure to be demanding.

CWNT®, Certified Wireless Network Trainer   Certified Wireless Network Trainers are qualified instructors certified by the CWNP Program to deliver CWNP training courses to IT professionals. CWNTs are technical and instructional experts in wireless technologies, products, and solutions. To ensure a superior learning experience for our customers, CWNP Education Partners are required to use CWNTs when delivering training using Official CWNP Courseware.

    Effective January 1, 2007, all material from the existing CWAP exam will be integrated into the CWNE certification.

How to Become a CWNA

To become a CWNA, you must do the following two things: agree that you have read and will abide by the terms and conditions of the CWNP Confidentiality Agreement, and pass the CWNA certification test.

 A copy of the CWNP Confidentiality Agreement can be found online at the CWNP website.

When you sit to take the test, you will be required to accept this confidentiality agreement before you can continue with the test. Once you have agreed, you will be able to continue with the test, and if you pass the test, you are then a CWNA.

The information for the exam is as follows:

- Exam Name: Wireless LAN Administrator
- Exam Number: PW0-100
- Cost: $175.00 (in U.S. dollars)
- Duration: 90 minutes
- Questions: 60
- Question Types: Multiple choice/multiple answer
- Passing Score: 70% (80% for instructors)
- Available Languages: English
- Availability: Register at Pearson VUE (www.vue.com/cwnp) or Thompson Prometric (www.2test.com)

When you schedule the exam, you will receive instructions regarding appointment and cancellation procedures, ID requirements, and information about the testing center location. In addition, you'll receive a registration and payment confirmation letter. Exams can be scheduled weeks in advance or, in some cases, even as late as the same day.

After you have successfully passed the CWNA exam, the CWNP Program will award you a certification that is good for three years. To recertify, you will need to pass the current PW0-100 exam, the CWSP exam, or the CWNE exam. If the information you provided the testing center is correct, you will receive an e-mail from CWNP recognizing your accomplishment and providing you with a CWNP certification number. After you earn any CWNP certification, you can request a certification kit. The kit includes a congratulatory letter, a certificate, and a wallet-sized personalized ID card. You will need to log in to the CWNP tracking system, verify your contact information, and request your certification kit.

Who Should Buy This Book?

If you want to acquire a solid foundation in wireless networking and your goal is to prepare for the exam, this book is for you. You will find clear explanations of the concepts you need to grasp and plenty of help to achieve the high level of professional competency you need in order to succeed.

If you want to become certified as a CWNA, this book is definitely what you need. However, if you just want to attempt to pass the exam without really understanding wireless, this study guide isn't for you. It's written for people who want to acquire hands-on skills and in-depth knowledge of wireless networking.

How to Use This Book and the CD

We've included several testing features in the book and on the CD-ROM. These tools will help you retain vital exam content as well as prepare to sit for the actual exam.

Before You Begin   At the beginning of the book (right after this introduction) is an assessment test you can use to check your readiness for the exam. Take this test before you start reading the book; it will help you determine the areas you may need to brush up on. The answers to the assessment test appear on a separate page after the last question of the test. Each answer includes an explanation and a note telling you the chapter in which the material appears.

Chapter Review Questions   To test your knowledge as you progress through the book, there are review questions at the end of each chapter. As you finish each chapter, answer the review questions and then check your answers—the correct answers appear on the page following the last review question. You can go back to reread the section that deals with each question you got wrong to ensure that you answer correctly the next time you're tested on the material.

Electronic Flashcards   You'll find flashcard questions on the CD for on-the-go review. These are short questions and answers, just like the flashcards you probably used in school. You can answer them on your PC or download them onto a Palm device for quick and convenient reviewing.

Test Engine   The CD also contains the Sybex Test Engine. With this custom test engine, you can identify weak areas up front and then develop a solid studying strategy that includes each of the robust testing features described previously. Our thorough readme file will walk you through the quick, easy installation process.

In addition to the assessment test and the chapter review questions, you'll find two sample exams. Use the test engine to take these practice exams just as if you were taking the actual exam (without any reference material). When you've finished the first exam, move on to the next one to solidify your test-taking skills. If you get more than 95 percent of the answers correct, you're ready to take the certification exam.

Full Text of the Book in PDF   The CD-ROM contains this book in PDF (Adobe Reader) format so you can easily read it on any computer. If you have to travel but still need to study for the exam, and you have a laptop with a CD-ROM drive, you can carry this entire book with you.

Labs and Exercises   Several chapters in this book have labs that use software, spreadsheets, and videos that are also provided on the CD-ROM that is included with this book. These labs and exercises will provide you with a broader learning experience by providing hands-on experience and step-by-step problem solving.

Extra CWNA certification practice test questions can be found at www.sybex.com.

Exam Objectives

The CWNA exam measures your understanding of the fundamentals of RF behavior, your ability to describe the features and functions of wireless LAN components, and your knowledge of the skills needed to install, configure, and troubleshoot wireless LAN hardware peripherals and protocols.

The skills and knowledge measured by this examination are derived from a survey of wireless networking experts and professionals. The results of this survey were used in weighing the subject areas and ensuring that the weighting is representative of the relative importance of the content.

The following chart provides the breakdown of the exam, showing you the weight of each section:

Subject Area	% of Exam
Radio Frequency (RF) Technologies	21%
802.11 Regulations and Standards	12%
802.11 Protocols and Devices	14%
802.11 Network Implementation	21%
802.11 Network Security	16%
802.11 RF Site Surveying	16%
Total	100%

Radio Frequency (RF) Technologies—21%

1.1. RF Fundamentals

1.1.1. Define and explain the basic concepts of RF behavior.

- Gain
- Loss
- Reflection
- Refraction
- Diffraction
- Scattering
- VSWR
- Return loss
- Amplification
- Attenuation
- Absorption

- Wave propagation
- Free space path loss
- Delay spread

1.2. RF Mathematics

1.2.1. Understand and apply the basic components of RF mathematics.

- Watt
- Milliwatt
- Decibel (dB)
- dBm
- dBi
- dBd
- RSSI
- System operating margin (SOM)
- Fade margin
- Link budget
- Intentional radiator
- Equivalent isotropically radiated power (EIRP)

1.3. RF Signal and Antenna Concepts

1.3.1. Identify RF signal characteristics, the applications of basic RF antenna concepts, and the implementation of solutions that require RF antennas.

- Visual LOS
- RF LOS
- The Fresnel zone
- Beamwidths
- Azimuth and elevation
- Passive gain
- Isotropic radiator
- Polarization
- Antenna diversity
- Wavelength
- Frequency
- Amplitude
- Phase

1.3.2. Explain the applications of basic RF antenna types and identify their basic attributes, purpose, and function.

- Omni-directional/dipole antennas
- Semi-directional antennas
- Highly-directional antennas
- Phased array antennas
- Sectorized antennas

1.3.3. Describe the proper locations and methods for installing RF antennas.

- Pole/mast mount
- Ceiling mount
- Wall mount

1.4. RF Antenna Accessories

1.4.1. Identify the use of the following wireless LAN accessories and explain how to select and install them for optimal performance within FCC regulations.

- Amplifiers
- Attenuators
- Lightning arrestors
- Grounding rods/wires
- RF cables
- RF connectors
- RF signal splitters

802.11 Regulations and Standards—12%

2.1. Spread Spectrum Technologies

2.1.1. Identify some of the uses for spread spectrum technologies.

- Wireless LANs
- Wireless PANs
- Wireless MANs
- Wireless WANs

2.1.2. Comprehend the differences between and explain the different types of spread spectrum technologies.

- FHSS
- DSSS
- OFDM

2.1.3. Identify the underlying concepts of how spread spectrum technology works.

- Modulation
- Coding

2.1.4. Identify and apply the concepts that make up the functionality of spread spectrum technology.

- Co-location
- Channels
- Carrier frequencies
- Dwell time and hop time
- Throughput vs. bandwidth
- Communication resilience

2.2. IEEE 802.11 Standard

2.2.1. Identify, explain, and apply the concepts covered by the IEEE 802.11 standard and the differences between the following 802.11 clauses.

- 802.11
- 802.11a
- 802.11b
- 802.11d
- 802.11e
- 802.11f
- 802.11g
- 802.11h
- 802.11i
- 802.11j
- 802.11n
- 802.11r
- 802.11s

2.3. 802.11 Industry Organizations and Their Roles

2.3.1. Define the roles of the following organizations in providing direction, cohesion, and accountability within the wireless LAN industry.

- FCC
- IEEE
- Wi-Fi Alliance

802.11 Protocols and Devices—14%

3.1. 802.11 Protocol Architecture

3.1.1. Summarize the processes involved in authentication and association.

- The 802.11 State Machine
- Open System and Shared Key authentication
- Association, reassociation, and disassociation
- Deauthentication
- Shared keys
- Certificates and PACs

3.1.2. Define, describe, and apply the following concepts associated with wireless LAN service sets.

- BSS and BSSID
- ESS and ESSID/SSID
- IBSS
- Roaming
- Infrastructure mode
- Ad-Hoc mode

3.1.3. Explain and apply the following power management features of wireless LANs.

- PSP mode
- CAM mode
- TIM/DTIM/ATIM

3.2. 802.11 MAC andPHY Layer Technologies

3.2.1. Describe and apply the following concepts surrounding wireless LAN frames.

- 802.11 frame format vs. 802.3 frame format
- Layer 3 protocol support by 802.11 frames

3.2.2. Identify methods described in the 802.11 standard for locating, joining, and maintaining connectivity with an 802.11 wireless LAN.

- Active scanning (probes)
- Passive scanning (beacons)
- Dynamic rate selection

3.2.3. Define, describe, and apply 802.11 modes and features available for moving data traffic across the RF medium.

- DCF vs. PCF modes
- CSMA/CA vs. CSMA/CD protocols

- RTS/CTS and CTS-to-Self protocols
- Fragmentation
- Wireless Multimedia (WMM) certification

3.3. Wireless LAN Infrastructure and Client Devices

3.3.1. Identify the purpose of the following wireless LAN infrastructure devices and describe how to install, configure, secure, and manage them.

- Access points
- Wireless LAN bridges
- Wireless LAN switches
- PoE injectors and PoE-enabled switches
- Residential Wireless Gateways
- Enterprise Wireless Gateways
- Enterprise Encryption Gateways
- Wireless LAN routers
- Remote office wireless switches
- Wireless LAN Mesh Routers

3.3.2. Describe the purpose of the following wireless LAN client devices and explain how to install, configure, secure, and manage them.

- PCMCIA cards
- USB, CF, and SD devices
- Serial and Ethernet converters
- PCI and Mini-PCI cards
- Card adapters
- Wireless workgroup bridges

802.11 Network Implementation—21%

4.1. 802.11 Network Design, Implementation, and Management

4.1.1. Identify technology roles for which wireless LAN technology is appropriate.

- Corporate data access and end-user mobility
- Network extension to remote areas
- Building-to-building connectivity (bridging)
- Last-mile data delivery (wireless ISP)
- Small office/ home office (SOHO) use
- Mobile office networking

- Educational/classroom use
- Industrial (warehousing and manufacturing)
- Healthcare (hospitals and offices)
- Hotspots (public network access)

4.2. 802.11 Network Troubleshooting

4.2.1. Identify and explain how to solve the following wireless LAN implementation challenges.

- Multipath
- Hidden nodes
- Near/far
- Narrowband and wideband RF interference
- System throughput
- Co-channel and adjacent-channel interference
- Weather

802.11 Network Security — 16%

5.1. 802.11 Network Security Architecture

5.1.1. Identify and describe the strengths, weaknesses, appropriate uses, and appropriate implementation of the following 802.11 security-related items.

- Shared Key authentication
- WEP
- WPA-PSK
- Encryption algorithms
- RC4
- AES
- Key management mechanisms
- TKIP
- CCMP
- Access control and authentication
- 802.1X/EAP framework
- EAP types commonly used with 802.11 WLANs
- WPA/WPA2
- AAA support
- RADIUS

- LDAP compliant/compatible
- Local authentication database
- MAC filters

5.1.2. Describe the following types of wireless LAN security attacks, and explain how to identify and prevent them where possible.

- Eavesdropping
- RF jamming (denial of service)
- Man-in-the-middle
- Management interface exploits
- Encryption cracking
- Hijacking

5.1.3. Describe, explain, and illustrate the appropriate applications for the following client-related wireless security solutions.

- Role based access control
- IPSec VPN
- PPTP VPN
- Profile-based firewalls
- Captive portal

5.1.4. Describe, explain, and illustrate the appropriate applications for the following wireless LAN system security and management features.

- Rogue AP detection and/or containment
- SNMPv3/HTTPS/SSH

5.2. 802.11 Network Security Analysis Systems, Devices

5.2.1. Identify the purpose and features of the following wireless analysis systems and explain how to install, configure, integrate, and manage them as applicable.

- Handheld and laptop protocol analyzers
- Distributed wireless intrusion prevention systems (WIPSs)
- Remote hardware and software sensors
- Handheld RF analyzers

5.3. 802.11 Network Security Policy Basics

5.3.1. Describe the following general security policy elements.

- Risk assessment
- Impact analysis
- Security auditing

5.3.2. Describe the following functional security policy elements.

- Baseline practices
- Design and implementation practices
- Physical security
- Social engineering
- Monitoring, response, and reporting

802.11 RF Site Surveying—16%

6.1. 802.11 Network Site Survey Fundamentals

6.1.1. Explain the importance and processes involved in conducting a complete RF site survey.

6.1.2. Explain the importance of and proprietary documentation involved in preparing for an RF site survey.

- Gathering business requirements
- Interviewing managers and users
- Defining security requirements
- Gathering site-specific documentation
- Documenting existing network characteristics
- Gathering permits and zoning requirements
- Indoor or outdoor-specific information

6.1.3. Explain the technical aspects and information collection procedures involved in an RF site survey.

- Interference sources
- Infrastructure connectivity and power requirements
- RF coverage requirements
- Data capacity requirements
- Client connectivity requirements

6.1.4. Describe site survey reporting procedures.

- Customer reporting requirements
- Reporting methodology
- Security-related reporting
- Graphical documentation
- Hardware recommendations and bills of material

6.2. 802.11 Network Site Survey Systems and Devices

6.2.1. Identify the equipment, applications, and system features involved in performing automated site surveys.

- Predictive analysis/simulation applications

- Integrated virtual site survey features

- Self-managing RF technologies

- Passive site survey verification tools and/or applications

6.2.2. Identify the equipment and applications involved in performing manual site surveys.

- Site survey hardware kits

- Active site survey tools and/or applications

- Passive site survey tools and/or applications

- Manufacturers' client utilities

Tips for Taking the CWNA Exam

Here are some general tips for taking your exam successfully:

- Bring two forms of ID with you. One must be a photo ID, such as a driver's license. The other can be a major credit card or a passport. Both forms must include a signature.

- Arrive early at the exam center so you can relax and review your study materials, particularly tables and lists of exam-related information.

- Read the questions carefully. Don't be tempted to jump to an early conclusion. Make sure you know exactly what the question is asking.

- There will be questions with multiple correct responses. When there is more than one correct answer, a message at the bottom of the screen will prompt you to either "choose two" or "choose all that apply." Be sure to read the messages displayed to know how many correct answers you must choose.

- When answering multiple-choice questions you're not sure about, use a process of elimination to get rid of the obviously incorrect answers first. Doing so will improve your odds if you need to make an educated guess.

- Do not spend too much time on one question. This is a form-based test; however, you cannot move forward and backward through the exam. You must answer the current question before you can move to the next question, and once you have moved to the next question, you cannot go back and change an answer on a previous question.

- Keep track of your time. Since this is a 90-minute test consisting of 60 questions, you have an average of 90 seconds to answer each question. You can spend as much or as little time on any one question, but when 90 minutes is up, the test is over. Check your progress. After 45 minutes, you should have answered at least 30 questions. If you have not, don't panic.

You will need to simply answer the remaining questions at a faster pace. If on average you can answer each of the remaining 30 questions 4 seconds quicker, you will recover 2 minutes. Again, don't panic; just pace yourself.

- For the latest pricing on the exams and updates to the registration procedures, visit CWNP's website at `www.cwnp.com`.

About the Authors

David D. Coleman is a wireless security/networking trainer and consultant. He teaches the CWNP classes that are recognized throughout the world as the industry standard for wireless networking certification and he also conducts vendor-specific Wi-Fi training. He has also taught numerous "train-the-trainer" classes and "beta" classes for the CWNP program. David has instructed IT professionals from around the globe in wireless networking administration, wireless security, and wireless frame analysis. His company, AirSpy Networks (`www.airspy.com`), specializes in corporate training and has worked in the past with SpectraLink and Dell Computers and Air Defense. AirSpy Networks also specializes in government classes and has trained numerous computer security employees from various law enforcement agencies, the U.S. Marines, the U.S. Army, the U.S. Navy, and other federal and state government agencies. David resides in Atlanta, Georgia, where he shares a home with his two teenage children, Carolina and Brantley, and his dog, Bo the WonderPuppy. He can be reached via e-mail at `david@airspy.com`.

David Westcott is an independent consultant and technical trainer with over 20 years of experience in information technology, specializing in computer networking and security. In addition to providing consulting advice and direction to his corporate clients, David has been a certified trainer for over 12 years, providing training to government agencies, corporations, and universities. David was an adjunct faculty member for Boston University's Corporate Education Center for over 10 years. David has developed courseware for Boston University and many other clients in the areas of networking and security.

Since installing his first wireless network in 1999, David has become a Certified Wireless Network Trainer, Administrator, Security Professional, and Analysis Professional. David has consulted with Planet3 Wireless, providing content and technical editing for the Planet3 Wireless courseware used in the CWNP wireless certification programs. David has also earned certifications from Cisco, Microsoft, EC-Council, CompTIA, and Novell. David lives in Concord, Massachusetts, with his wife, Gina. In his spare time, David is a licensed pilot and enjoys flying places with his wife. He can be reached via e-mail at `david@westcott-consulting.com`.

Assessment Test

1. Which of these frequencies has the longest wavelength?

    A. 750 KHz

    B. 2.4 GHz

    C. 252 GHz

    D. 2.4 MHz

2. Which of these terms can best be used to compare the relationship between two radio waves that share the same frequency?

    A. Multipath

    B. Multiplexing

    C. Phase

    D. Spread spectrum

3. While performing a site survey, you determine that the clients must receive a signal of −75 dBm, which already includes the fade margin of 10 dBm. What is the receive sensitivity of the wireless card?

    A. −65 dBm

    B. −75 dBm

    C. −85 dBm

    D. Cannot be determined with the information provided

4. Calculate the system operating margin given the following information: Signal received = −65 dBm, fade margin = 15 dBm, receive sensitivity = −85 dBm.

    A. 20 dBm

    B. 15 dBm

    C. −70 dBm

    D. −80 dBm

    E. Cannot be determined with the information provided

5. A bridge transmits at 10 mW. The cable to the antenna produces a loss of 3 dB and the antenna produces a gain of 20 dBi. What is the EIRP?

    A. 25 mW

    B. 27 mW

    C. 4 mW

    D. 1,300 mW

    E. 500 mW

6. What are some possible effects of voltage standing wave ratio (VSWR)? (Choose all that apply.)

  A. Increased amplitude

  B. Decreased signal strength

  C. Transmitter failure

  D. Erratic amplitude

  E. Out of phase signals

7. When installing a higher-gain omni-directional antenna, which of the following occurs?

  A. The horizontal coverage increases.

  B. The horizontal coverage decreases.

  C. The vertical coverage increases.

  D. The vertical coverage decreases.

8. 802.11a clause 17 radio cards are backward compatible with which devices?

  A. 802.11 clause 15 devices

  B. 802.11g clause 19 radio cards

  C. 802.11 clause 14 FHSS devices

  D. 802.11b HR/DSSS radio cards

  E. 802.11h radio cards

  F. None of the above

9. Which 802.11 amendment goal specifies for the use of the 5.850 to 5.925GHz frequency band?

  A. 802.11a

  B. 802.11h

  C. 802.11p

  D. 802.11g

  E. 802.11u

10. Which of the following are valid ISM bands? (Choose all that apply.)

  A. 902–928 MHz

  B. 2.4–2.4835 MHz

  C. 5.725–5.825 GHz

  D. 5.725–5.875 GHz

11. Choose two spread spectrum signal characteristics.

  A. Narrow bandwidth

  B. Low power

  C. High power

  D. Wide bandwidth

12. A Service Set Identifier is often synonymous with which of the following?

    A. IBSS

    B. ESSID

    C. BSSID

    D. Basic Service Set Identifier

    E. BSS

13. Which ESS design scenario is defined by the 802.11 standard?

    A. Two or more access points with overlapping coverage cells

    B. Two or more access points with overlapping disjointed coverage cells

    C. One access point with a single BSA

    D. Two basic service sets connected by a DS with co-located coverage cells

    E. None of the above

14. What CSMA/CA conditions must be met before an 802.11 radio card can transmit? (Choose all that apply.)

    A. The NAV timer must be equal

    B. The random backoff timer must have expired

    C. The CCA must be positive

    D. The proper interframe space must have occurred

    E. The access point must be in PCF mode

15. Beacon management frames contain which of the following information? (Choose all that apply.)

    A. Channel information

    B. Destination IP address

    C. Basic data rate

    D. Traffic indication map (TIM)

    E. Vendor proprietary information

    F. Time stamp

    G. Channel information

16. Anthony Dean was hired to perform a wireless packet analysis of your network. While performing the analysis, he noticed that many of the data frames were preceded by an RTS frame followed by a CTS frame. What could cause this phenomenon to occur? (Choose all that apply.)

    A. Due to high RF noise levels, some of the stations have automatically enabled RTS/CTS.

    B. Some stations were manually configured for RTS/CTS.

    C. A nearby 802.11a is causing some of the nodes to enable protection mechanism.

    D. The network is a mixed-mode environment.

17. Jeff Davis is running a mixed-mode 802.11b and 802.11g wireless network. Station 1 is an 802.11g device with RTS/CTS enabled for its protection mechanism. The AP has CTS-to-Self enabled as its protection mechanism. Station 2 is an 802.11b device. When station 1 sends a frame of data to station 2, how many total frames are required for the communication to be successful?

A. 4

B. 6

C. 7

D. 8

18. Which WLAN device uses self-healing and self-forming mechanisms and layer 2 routing protocols?

A. WLAN switch

B. WLAN controller

C. WLAN VPN router

D. WLAN mesh router

19. Which WLAN devices offer AP management, user management, intrusion detection, and spectrum management? (Choose all that apply.)

A. Wireless Network Management System (WNMS)

B. WLAN switch

C. WLAN controller

D. Enterprise Wireless Gateway (EWG)

E. All of the above

20. In most countries, what is the maximum cumulative speed for co-located 802.11b APs without subjecting the APs to channel overlap? (Choose all that apply.)

A. 11 Mbps

B. 33 Mbps

C. 54 Mbps

D. 162 Mbps

21. Wireless mesh routers often have two radio cards. One radio is used for client connectivity and the other is used for backhaul. Which of these statements bests meets this model. (Choose all that apply.)

A. A 2.4 GHz radio is used for distribution, while a 5 GHz radio is used for access

B. An 802.11b/g radio is used for client connectivity, while an 802.11b radio is used for backhaul

C. An 802.11b/g radio is used for client connectivity, while an 802.11a radio is used for backhaul

D. A 2.4 GHz radio is used for access, while a 5 GHz radio is used for distribution

22. If 802.1X/EAP security is in place, what type of roaming solution is needed for time-sensitive applications such as VoWiFi?

    A. Nomadic roaming solution

    B. Proprietary layer 3 roaming solution

    C. Seamless roaming solution

    D. Mobile IP solution

    E. Fast secure roaming solution

23. The hidden node problem occurs when one client station's transmissions are not heard by all the other client stations in the coverage area of a basic service set (BSS). What are some of the consequences of the hidden node problem? (Choose all that apply.)

    A. Retransmissions

    B. Inter-symbol interference (ISI)

    C. Collisions

    D. Increased throughput

    E. Decreased throughput

24. Which of these solutions would be considered strong WLAN security?

    A. SSID cloaking

    B. MAC filtering

    C. WEP

    D. Shared Key authentication

    E. CCMP/AES

25. Which security standard defines port-based access control?

    A. 802.11x

    B. 802.3b

    C. 802.11i

    D. 802.1X

    E. 802.11s

26. Which is the best tool for detecting an RF jamming denial of service attack?

    A. Mobile WIDS locater tool

    B. Distributed WIDS

    C. Spectrum analyzer

    D. Distributed WIPS

    E. Oscilloscope

27. Which of these attacks can be detected by a wireless intrusion detection system (WIDS)? (Choose all that apply.)

    A. Deauthentication spoofing

    B. MAC spoofing

    C. Rogue ad-hoc network

    D. Association flood

    E. Rogue AP

28. You have been hired by the XYZ Company based in the United States for a wireless site survey. What government agencies need to be informed before a tower is installed of a height that exceeds 200 feet above ground level? (Choose three.)

    A. RF regulatory authority

    B. Local municipality

    C. Fire department

    D. Tax authority

    E. Aviation authority

29. You have been hired by the ABC Corporation to conduct an indoor site survey. What information will be in the final site survey report that is delivered? (Choose two.)

    A. Security analysis

    B. Coverage analysis

    C. Spectrum analysis

    D. Routing analysis

    E. Switching analysis

30. Name potential sources of interference in the 5 GHz UNII band. (Choose all that apply.)

    A. Perimeter sensors

    B. Nearby 802.11a WLAN

    C. Cellular phone

    D. DSSS access point

    E. Bluetooth

31. Which of these measurements are taken for indoor coverage analysis? (Choose all that apply.)

    A. Received signal strength

    B. Signal-to-noise ratio

    C. Noise level

    D. Path loss

    E. Packet loss

Answers to Assessment Test

1. **A.** A 750 KHz signal has an approximate wavelength of 1312 feet, or 400 meters. A 252 GHz single has an approximate wavelength of less than .05 inches, or 1.2 millimeters. Remember, the higher the frequency of a signal, the smaller the wavelength property of an electromagnetic signal. To calculate the wavelength, use the formula $\lambda = c / f$. So $\lambda = 300{,}000{,}000 / 750{,}000$, which calculates to 400 meters. For more information, see Chapter 2.

2. **C.** Phase involves the positioning of the amplitude crests and troughs of two waveforms. For more information, see Chapter 2.

3. **C.** The receive sensitivity is the minimum amount of signal required for successful communications. If the desired signal level is –75 dBm, including the fade margin, then to determine the receive sensitivity, you must subtract the fade margin from the desired signal level. So –75 dBm minus 10 dBm equals –85 dBm. For more information, see Chapter 3.

4. **A.** The system operating margin is the difference between the signal received and the signal required. For more information, see Chapter 3.

5. **E.** The 10 mW of power is decreased by 3 dB, or divided by 2, giving 5 mW. This is then increased by 20 dBi, or multiplied by 10 twice, giving 500 mW. For more information, see Chapter 3.

6. **B, C, D.** Reflected voltage caused by an impedance mismatch may cause a degradation of amplitude, erratic signal strength, or even the worst-case scenario of transmitter burnout. See Chapter 4 for more information.

7. **A, D.** When the gain of an omni-directional antenna is increased, the vertical coverage area decreases while the horizontal coverage area is increased. See Chapter 4 for more information.

8. **F.** 802.11a clause 17 devices operate in the 5 GHz UNII bands and use OFDM technology at the Physical layer. They are not backward compatible with equipment from any other 802.11 standard. For more information, see Chapter 5.

9. **C.** The 802.11p draft amendment defines enhancements to the 802.11 standard to support communications between high-speed vehicles and roadside infrastructure in the licensed ITS band of 5.9GHz. For more information, see Chapter 5.

10. **A, D.** The ISM bands are 902–928 MHz, 2.4–2.4835 GHz, and 5.725–5.875 GHz. 5.725–5.825 is the upper UNII band. There is no ISM band that operates in a 2.4 MHz range. See Chapter 6 for more information.

11. **B, D.** A spread spectrum signal utilizes bandwidth that is wider than what is required to carry the data and has low transmission power requirements. See Chapter 6 for more information.

12. **B.** The network name of an Extended Service Set is often called an ESSID (Extended Service Set ID) and is essentially synonymous with an SSID network name in the most common deployments of an ESS. For more information, see Chapter 7.

13. E.   The scenarios described in options A, B, and D are all examples of how an Extended Service Set may be deployed. However, the 802.11 standard does not mandate any of the correct examples. For more information, see Chapter 7.

14. A, B, C, D.   Carrier Sense Multiple Access with Collision Avoidance is a medium access method that utilizes multiple checks and balances to try to minimize collisions. These checks and balances can also be thought of as several lines of defense. The various lines of defense are put in place to hopefully ensure that only one radio is transmitting while all other radios are listening. The four lines of defense include the network allocation vector, the random backoff timer, the clear channel assessment and interframe spacing. For more information, see Chapter 8.

15. A, C, D, E, F, G.   The only information not contained in the beacon management frame is the destination IP address. Since the beacon is a layer 2 frame, there is no layer 3 information included in the frame. For more information, see Chapter 8.

16. B, D.   Stations can be manually configured to use RTS/CTS for all transmissions. This is usually done to diagnose hidden node problems. This network could also be a mixed-mode 802.11b and 802.11g network and the 802.11g nodes have enabled RTS/CTS as their protection mechanism. For more information, see Chapter 9.

17. B.   Station 1 must first send the data frame to the AP using RTS/CTS. This will require four frames (RTS, CTS, Data, ACK). When the AP sends the frame to station 2, since station 2 is an 802.11b device, there is no need to use its protection mechanism. Therefore, the transmission from the AP to station 2 will require two frames (Data, ACK). For more information, see Chapter 9.

18. D.   WLAN mesh routers create a self-forming WLAN mesh network that automatically connects access points at installation and dynamically updates routes as more clients are added. Because interference may occur, a self-healing WLAN mesh network will automatically reroute data traffic in a Wi-Fi mesh cell using proprietary layer 2 routing protocols. For more information, see Chapter 10.

19. B, C.   WLAN switches, also known as WLAN controllers, use centralized management and configuration of thin access points. User management capabilities are available through the use of role-based access control (RBAC). Most WLAN switches also have internal Wireless Intrusion Detection Systems (WIDS) and also offer spectrum management capabilities. For more information, see Chapter 10.

20. B.   802.11b supports three non-overlapping channels, each with a maximum speed (not throughput) of 11 Mbps, providing a cumulative maximum speed of 33 Mbps. For more information, see Chapter 11.

21. C, D.   When installing a mesh router, it is best to use two radio cards. The 2.4 GHz or 802.11b/g radio is used for client connectivity, while the 5.8 GHz or 802.11a radio is used for mesh connectivity or backhaul. For more information, see Chapter 11.

22. E.   The 802.11i amendment defines an 802.1X/EAP security solution in the enterprise. The average time involved during the authentication process can be 700 milliseconds or longer. Voice over Wi-Fi (VoWiFi) requires a handoff of 50 milliseconds or less when roaming. A fast secure roaming (FSR) solution is needed if 802.1X/EAP security and time-sensitive applications are used together in a wireless network. Currently, FSR solutions are proprietary, although the 802.11i amendment defines optional FSR and the 802.11r draft will probably eventually standardize fast secure roaming. For more information, see Chapter 12.

23. A, C, E.   The stations that cannot hear the hidden node will transmit at the same time that the hidden node is transmitting. This will result in continuous transmission collisions in a half-duplex medium. Collisions will corrupt the frames and they will need to be retransmitted. Any time retransmissions are necessary, more overhead is added to the medium, resulting in decreased throughput. Inter-symbol interference is a result of multipath and not the hidden node problem. For more information, see Chapter 12.

24. E.   While you can hide your SSID to cloak the identity of your wireless network from script kiddies and non-hackers, it should be clearly understood that SSID cloaking is by no means an end-all wireless security solution. Because of spoofing and because of all the administrative work that is involved, MAC filtering is not considered a reliable means of security for wireless enterprise networks. WEP and Shared Key authentication are legacy 802.11 security solutions. CCMP/AES is defined as the default encryption type by the 802.11i security amendment. Cracking the AES cipher would take the lifetime of the sun using the current tools that are available today. For more information, see Chapter 13.

25. D.   The 802.1X IEEE standard is not specifically a wireless standard and often is mistakenly referred to as 802.11x. The 802.1X standard is a port-based access control standard. 802.1X provides an authorization framework that allows or disallows traffic to pass through a port and thereby access network resources. For more information, see Chapter 13.

26. C.   Although the wireless intrusion detection and prevention products might be able to detect some RF jamming attacks, the only tool that will absolutely identify an interfering signal is a spectrum analyzer. A spectrum analyzer is a frequency domain tool that can detect any RF signal in the frequency range that is being scanned. For more information, see Chapter 14.

27. A, B, C, D, E.   802.11 wireless intrusion detection systems can may be able to monitor for as many as 50 or more attacks. Any layer 2 DoS attack and spoofing attack and most rogue devices can be detected. For more information, see Chapter 14.

28. A, B, E.   In the United States, if any tower exceeds a height of 200 feet above ground level (AGL), you must contact both the FCC and FAA, which are communications and aviation regulatory authorities. Other countries will have similar height restrictions, and the proper RF regulatory authority and aviation authority must be contacted to find out the details. Local municipalities may have construction regulations and a permit may be required. For more information, see Chapter 15.

29. B, C.   The final site survey report, known as the deliverable, will contain spectrum analysis information identifying potential sources of interference. Coverage analysis will also define RF cell boundaries. The final report also contains recommended access point placement, configuration settings, and antenna orientation. Application throughput testing is often an optional analysis report included in the final survey report. Security, switching, and routing analysis are not included in a site survey report. For more information, see Chapter 15.

30. A, B.   A nearby 802.11a WLAN and perimeter sensors both transmit in the 5 GHz UNII bands. DSSS access points and Bluetooth transmit in the 2.4 GHz frequency space. Cellular phones transmit in licensed frequencies. For more information, see Chapter 16.

31. A, B, C and E.   RF coverage cell measurements that are taken during an indoor passive site survey include received signal strength, noise levels, signal-to-noise ratio (SNR), and data rates. Packet loss can be an additional measurement recorded during an active manual site survey. Packet loss is a calculation needed for an outdoor wireless bridging survey. For more information, see Chapter 16.

Chapter

1

Overview of Wireless Standards and Organizations

IN THIS CHAPTER, YOU WILL LEARN ABOUT THE FOLLOWING:

✓ **Standards Organizations**

- ▪ Federal Communications Commission
- ▪ International Telecommunication Union Radiocommunication Sector
- ▪ Institute of Electrical and Electronics Engineers
- ▪ Wi-Fi Alliance

✓ **Communications Fundamentals**

Learning a new technology can seem like a daunting task. There are so many new acronyms, abbreviations, terms, and ideas to become familiar with. One of the keys to learning any subject is to learn the basics. Whether you are learning to drive a car, fly an airplane, or install a wireless computer network, there are basic rules, principles, and concepts that, once learned, provide the building blocks for the rest of your education.

IEEE 802.11, also referred to as Wireless Fidelity (Wi-Fi), is the standard for providing local area network (LAN) communications using radio frequencies (RF). IEEE 802.11 is actually a group of standards that work together to provide wireless networking. There are numerous standards organizations and regulatory bodies that help govern and direct the IEEE 802.11 technology and industry. Having an understanding of these different organizations can help provide you with insight as to how IEEE 802.11 functions, and sometimes even how and why the standards have evolved the way they have.

As you become more knowledgeable about wireless networking, you may want to or need to read some of the standards that are created by the different organizations. Along with the information about the standards bodies, this chapter includes a brief overview of their documents.

In addition to reviewing the different standards organizations that guide and regulate Wi-Fi, this chapter will review some fundamentals of communications and data keying that are not part of the CWNA exam but may help you better understand wireless communications.

Identifying Standards Organizations

Each of the standards organizations discussed in this chapter help to guide a different aspect of the wireless networking industry.

The International Telecommunication Union Radiocommunication Sector (ITU-R) and local entities such as the Federal Communications Commission (FCC) set the rules for what the user can do with a radio transmitter. Frequencies, power levels, and transmission methods are managed and regulated by these organizations. These organizations work together to help guide the growth and expansion that is being demanded by wireless users.

The Institute of Electrical and Electronics Engineers (IEEE) creates standards for compatibility and coexistence between networking equipment. The IEEE standards must adhere to the rules of the communications organizations, such as the FCC.

The Wi-Fi Alliance performs certification testing to make sure wireless networking equipment conforms to IEEE standards.

The International Organization for Standardization (ISO) created the Open Systems Interconnection (OSI) model, which is an architectural model for data communications.

We will look at each of these organizations in the following sections.

Federal Communications Commission (FCC)

To put it simply, the *Federal Communications Commission (FCC)* regulates communications to and from the United States. The task of the FCC in wireless networking is to regulate the radio signals that are used for wireless networking. The FCC is an independent United States government agency that is answerable to the United States Congress. It was established by the Communications Act of 1934 and is responsible for regulating interstate and international communications by radio, television, wire, satellite, and cable. The FCC's jurisdiction covers all of the 50 states, the District of Columbia, and U.S. possessions. Most countries have governing bodies that function similarly to the FCC.

The FCC and the respective controlling agencies in the other countries typically regulate two categories of wireless communications: licensed and unlicensed. Whether the wireless communications is licensed or unlicensed, the user is still regulated on what they can do. The difference is that unlicensed users do not have to go through the license application procedures before they can install a wireless system. Both licensed and unlicensed communications are typically regulated in the following five areas:

- Frequency
- Bandwidth
- Maximum power of the intentional radiator
- Maximum equivalent isotropically radiated power (EIRP)
- Use (indoor and/or outdoor)

Essentially, the FCC and other regulatory bodies set the rules for what the user can do regarding the RF transmissions. From there, the standards organizations create the standards to work within these guidelines. These organizations work together to help meet the demands of the fast growing wireless industry.

The FCC rules are published in the Code of Federal Regulations (CFR). The CFR is divided into 50 titles that are updated yearly. The title that is relevant to wireless networking is Title 47, *Telecommunications*. Title 47 is divided into many parts; Part 15, "Radio Frequency Devices," is where you will find the rules and regulations regarding wireless networking related to 802.11. Part 15 is further broken down into subparts and sections. A complete reference will look like 47CFR15.3.

More information can be found at www.fcc.gov and wireless.fcc.gov.

International Telecommunication Union Radiocommunication Sector (ITU-R)

A global hierarchy exists for management of the RF spectrum worldwide. The United Nations has tasked the *International Telecommunication Union Radiocommunication Sector (ITU-R)* with global spectrum management. The ITU-R maintains a database of worldwide frequency assignments and coordinates spectrum management through five administrative regions.

The five regions are broken down:

Region A: North and South America   Inter-American Telecommunication Commission (CITEL)

www.citel.oas.org

Region B: Western Europe   European Conference of Postal and Telecommunications Administrations (CEPT)

www.cept.org

Region C: Eastern Europe and Northern Asia   Regional Commonwealth in the field of Communications (RCC)

www.rcc.org

Region D: Africa   African Telecommunications Union (ATU)

www.atu-uat.org

Region E: Asia and Australasia   Asia-Pacific Telecommunity (APT)

www.aptsec.org

Within each region, local government RF regulatory bodies such as the following manage the RF spectrum for their respective countries:

- Australia, Australian Communications Authority (ACA)
- Japan, Association of Radio Industries and Businesses (ARIB)
- New Zealand, Ministry of Economic Development
- United States, Federal Communications Commission (FCC)

More information about the ITU-R can be found at www.itu.int/ITU-R/.

Institute of Electrical and Electronics Engineers (IEEE)

The *Institute of Electrical and Electronics Engineers*, commonly known as the *IEEE*, is a global professional society with over 350,000 members. The IEEE's mission is to "promote the engineering process of creating, developing, integrating, sharing, and applying knowledge about electro and information technologies and sciences for the benefit of humanity and the profession." To networking professionals, that means creating the standards that we use to communicate.

The IEEE is probably best known for its LAN standards, the IEEE 802 project.

The 802 project is one of many IEEE projects; however, it is the only project that will be addressed in this book.

IEEE projects are subdivided into working groups to develop standards that address specific problems or needs. For instance, the IEEE 802.3 working group was responsible for the creation of a standard for Ethernet, and the IEEE 802.11 working group was responsible for creating the wireless standard. The numbers are assigned as the groups are formed, so 11 was assigned to the wireless group since it was the 11th working group that was formed under the IEEE 802 project.

As the need arises to revise existing standards created by the working groups, task groups are formed. These task groups are assigned a sequential single letter (multiple letters are assigned if all single letters have been used) that is added to the end of the standard number (for example, 802.11a, 802.11g, and 802.3af). Some letters such as *o* and *l* are not assigned. This is done to prevent confusion with the numbers 0 and 1. Other task group letters may not be assigned to prevent confusion with other standards. For example, 802.11x has not been assigned because it can be easily confused with 802.1X and because 802.11x has become a common casual reference to the 802.11 family of standards.

More information can be found at www.ieee.org.

It is important to remember that the IEEE standards, like many other standards, are written documents describing how technical processes and equipment should function. Unfortunately, this often allows for different interpretations when the standard is being implemented, so it is common for early products to be incompatible between vendors, as was the case with the early 802.11 products.

Wi-Fi Alliance

The *Wi-Fi Alliance* is a global, nonprofit industry trade association with over 200 member companies. The Wi-Fi Alliance is devoted to promoting the growth of wireless LANs (WLANs). One of the Wi-Fi Alliance's primary tasks is to ensure the interoperability of WLAN products by providing certification testing. During the early days of the 802.11 standard, the Wi-Fi Alliance further defined it and provided a set of guidelines to assure compatibility between different vendors. Products that pass the Wi-Fi certification process receive a Wi-Fi Certified certificate:

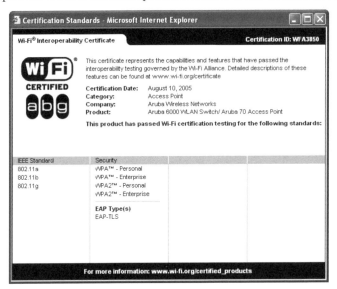

The Wi-Fi Alliance was founded in August 1999 and was known as the Wireless Ethernet Compatibility Alliance (WECA). In October 2002, the name was changed to what it is now, the Wi-Fi Alliance.

The Wi-Fi Alliance has certified over 1,500 Wi-Fi products for interoperability since testing began in April 2000. Certification includes three categories:

Wi-Fi products based on IEEE radio standards   802.11a, 802.11b, 802.11g in single-mode, dual-mode (802.11b and 802.11g), and multiband (2.4 GHz and 5 GHz) products

Wi-Fi wireless network security   Wi-Fi Protected Access (WPA), Personal and Enterprise; Wi-Fi Protected Access 2 (WPA2), Personal and Enterprise

Support for multimedia content over Wi-Fi networks   Wi-Fi Multimedia (WMM)

It is important to note that the Wi-Fi Alliance's WPA2 security standard mirrors the IEEE's 802.11i security standard. Additionally, the Wi-Fi Alliance's WMM standard mirrors the IEEE's 802.11e Quality of Service (QoS) standard.

More information can be found at www.wi-fi.org. Several white papers from the Wi-Fi Alliance are also included on the CD.

International Organization for Standardization

The *International Organization for Standardization*, commonly known as the *ISO*, is a global, nongovernmental organization that identifies business, government, and society needs and develops standards in partnership with the sectors that will put them to use. The ISO is responsible for the creation of the Open Systems Interconnection (OSI) model, which has been a standard reference for data communications between computers since the late 1970s.

The OSI model is the cornerstone of data communications, and learning to understand it is one of the most important and fundamental tasks a person in the networking industry can undertake.

The layers of the OSI model are as follows:

- Layer 7, Application
- Layer 6, Presentation
- Layer 5, Session
- Layer 4, Transport
- Layer 3, Network
- Layer 2, Data-Link
- Layer 1, Physical

You should have a working knowledge of the OSI model for both this book and the CWNA exam. Make sure you understand the seven layers of the OSI model and how communications take place at the different layers. If you are not comfortable with the concepts of the OSI model, spend some time reviewing it on the Internet or from a good networking fundamentals book prior to taking the CWNA test.

More information can be found at www.iso.org.

Why Is It ISO and not IOS?

ISO is not a mistyped acronym. It is actually a word derived from the Greek word *isos*, meaning *equal*. Since acronyms can be different from country to country due to varying translations, the ISO decided to use a word instead of an acronym for its name. With this in mind, it is easy to see why a standards organization would give itself a name that means equal.

Communications Fundamentals

Although the CWNA certification is considered one of the entry-level certifications in the Certified Wireless Network Professional (CWNP) wireless certification program, it is by no means an entry-level certification in the computing industry. Most of the candidates for the CWNA certificate have experience in other areas of information technology. However the background and experience of these candidates varies greatly.

Unlike professions for which knowledge and expertise is learned through years of structured training, most computer professionals have followed their own path of education and training.

When people are responsible for their own education, they typically will gain the skills and knowledge that are directly related to their interests or their job. The more fundamental knowledge is often ignored because it is not directly relevant to the tasks at hand. Later, as their knowledge increases and they become more technically proficient, people realize that they need to learn about some of the fundamentals.

Many people in the computer industry understand that in data communications, bits are transmitted across wires or waves. They even understand that some type of voltage change or wave fluctuation is used to distinguish the bits. When pressed, however, many of these same people have no idea what is actually happening with the electrical signals or the waves.

In the following sections, we will review some fundamental communications principles that directly and indirectly relate to wireless communications. Understanding these concepts will help you to better understand what is happening with wireless communications and to more easily recognize and identify the terms used in this profession.

Understanding Carrier Signals

Since data ultimately consists of bits, the transmitter needs a way of sending both 0s and 1s to transmit data from one location to another. An AC or DC signal by itself does not perform this task. However, if a signal is fluctuated or altered, even slightly, the data can be properly sent and received. This modulated signal is now capable of distinguishing between 0s and 1s and is referred to as a *carrier signal*.

Three components of a wave that can be fluctuated or modified to create a carrier signal are amplitude, frequency, and phase.

 This chapter will review the basics of waves as they relate to the principles of data transmission. Chapter 2, "Radio Frequency Fundamentals," will cover radio waves in much greater detail.

All radio-based communications use some form of modulation to transmit data. To encode the data in a signal sent by AM/FM radios, cellular telephones, and satellite television, some type of modulation is performed on the radio signal that is being transmitted.

The average person typically is not concerned with how the signal is modulated, only that the device functions as expected. However, to become a better wireless network administrator, it is useful to have a better understanding of what is actually happening when two stations communicate. The rest of this chapter will introduce you to the fundamentals of encoding data. Chapter 2 will provide much more detail about waves and wave propagation, whereas this chapter provides an introduction to waves as a basis for understanding carrier signals and data encoding.

Amplitude and Wavelength

RF communication starts when radio waves are generated from an RF transmitter and sent to a receiver at another location. RF waves are similar to the waves that you see in an ocean or lake. Waves are made up of two main components: wavelength and amplitude (see Figure 1.1). *Amplitude* is the height, force, or power of the wave. If you were standing in the ocean as the waves came to shore, you would feel the force of a larger wave much more than you would a smaller wave. Antennas do the same thing, but with radio waves. Smaller waves are not as noticeable as bigger waves. A bigger wave generates a much larger electrical signal in an antenna, making the signal received much more easily recognizable.

Wavelength is the distance between similar points on two back-to-back waves. When measuring a wave, the wavelength is typically measured from the peak of a wave to the peak of the next wave. Amplitude and wavelength are both properties of waves.

Frequency

Frequency describes a behavior of waves. Waves travel away from the source that generates them. How fast the waves travel, or more specifically, how many waves are generated over a 1-second period of time, is known as frequency. If you were to sit on a pier and count how often a wave hits it, you could tell someone how frequently the waves were coming to shore. Think of radio waves in the same way; however, they travel much faster than the waves in the ocean. If you were to try to count the radio waves that are used in wireless networking, in the time it would take for one wave of water to hit the pier, several billion radio waves would have also hit the pier.

FIGURE 1.1 This drawing shows the wavelength and amplitude of a wave.

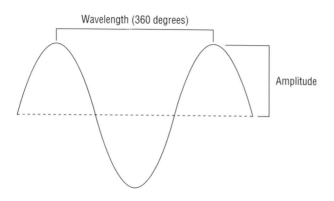

Phase

Phase is a relative term. It is the relationship between two waves with the same frequency. To determine phase, a wavelength is divided into 360 pieces referred to as degrees (see Figure 1.2). If you think of these degrees as starting times, then if one wave begins at the 0 degree point and another wave begins at the 90 degree point, these waves are considered to be 90 degrees out of phase.

In an ideal world, waves are created and transmitted from one station and received perfectly intact at another station. Unfortunately, RF communications do not occur in an ideal world. There are many sources of interference and many obstacles that will affect the wave in its travels to the receiving station. In Chapter 2, we'll introduce you to some of the outside influences that can affect the integrity of a wave and your ability to communicate between two stations.

FIGURE 1.2   This drawing shows two waves that are identical; however, they are 90 degrees out of phase with each other.

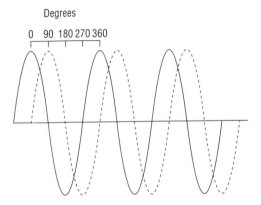

Time and Phase

Suppose you have two stopped watches and both are set to noon. At noon you start your first watch, and then you start your second watch 1 hour later. The second watch is 1 hour behind the first watch. As time goes by, your second watch will continue to be 1 hour behind. Both watches will maintain a 24-hour day, but they are out of synch with each other. Waves that are out of phase behave similarly. Two waves that are out of phase are essentially two waves that have been started at two different times. Both waves will complete full 360-degree cycles, but they will do it out of phase, or out of synch with each other.

Understanding Keying Methods

When data is sent, a signal is transmitted from the transceiver. In order for the data to be transmitted, the signal must be manipulated so that the receiving station has a way of distinguishing 0s and 1s. This method of manipulating a signal so that it can represent multiple pieces of data is known as a *keying method*. A keying method is what changes a signal into a carrier signal. It provides the signal with the ability to encode data so that it can be communicated or transported.

There are three types of keying methods that will be reviewed in the following sections: Amplitude Shift Keying (ASK), Frequency Shift Keying (FSK), and Phase Shift Keying (PSK). These keying methods are also referred to as *modulation* techniques. Keying methods use two different techniques to represent data:

Current State   With current state techniques, the current value (the current state) of the signal is used to distinguish between 0s and 1s. The use of the word *current* in this context does not refer to current as in voltage but rather to current as in the present time. Current state techniques will designate a specific or current value to indicate a binary 0 and another value to indicate a binary 1. At a specific point in time, it is the value of the signal that determines the binary value. For example, you can represent 0s and 1s using an ordinary door. Once a minute you can check to see if the door is open or closed. If the door is open it represents a 0, and if the door is closed it represents a 1. The current state of the door, open or closed, is what determines 0s or 1s.

State Transition   With state transition techniques, the change (or transition) of the signal is used to distinguish between 0s and 1s. State transition techniques may represent a 0 by a change in the phase of a wave at a specific time, whereas a 1 would be represented by no change in the phase of a wave at a specific time. At a specific point in time, it is the presence of a change or the lack of presence of a change that determines the binary value. The section on Phase Shift Keying will provide examples of this in detail, but a door can be used again to provide a simple example. Once a minute you check the door. In this case, if the door is moving (opening or closing), it represents a 0, and if the door is still (either open or closed), it represents a 1. In this example, the state of transition (moving or not moving) is what determines 0s or 1s.

Amplitude Shift Keying

Amplitude Shift Keying (ASK) varies the amplitude or height of the signal to represent the binary data. ASK is a current state technique, where one level of amplitude can represent a 0 bit and another level of amplitude can represent a 1 bit. Figure 1.3 shows how a wave can modulate an ASCII letter *K* using Amplitude Shift Keying. The larger amplitude wave is interpreted as a binary 1, and the smaller amplitude wave is interpreted as a binary 0.

This shifting of amplitude determines the data that is being transmitted. The way the receiving station performs this task is to first divide the signal being received into periods of time known as symbol periods. The receiving station then samples or examines the wave during this symbol period to determine the amplitude of the wave. Depending upon the value of the amplitude of the wave, the receiving station can determine the binary value.

FIGURE 1.3 An example of Amplitude Shift Keying (ASCII Code of an Upper Case K)

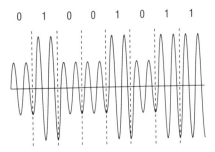

0 1 0 0 1 0 1 1

As you will learn later in this book, wireless signals can be unpredictable and also subject to interference from many sources. When noise or interference occurs, it usually affects the amplitude of a signal. Since a change in amplitude due to noise could cause the receiving station to misinterpret the value of the data, ASK has to be used cautiously.

Frequency Shift Keying

Frequency Shift Keying (FSK) varies the frequency of the signal to represent the binary data. FSK is a current state technique, where one frequency can represent a 0 bit and another frequency can represent a 1 bit (Figure 1.4). This shifting of frequency determines the data that is being transmitted. When the receiving station samples the signal during the symbol period, it determines the frequency of the wave, and depending upon the value of the frequency, the station can determine the binary value.

Figure 1.4 shows how a wave can modulate an ASCII letter *K* using Frequency Shift Keying. The faster frequency wave is interpreted as a binary 1, and the slower frequency wave is interpreted as a binary 0.

FSK is used in some of the earlier 802.11 standards. With the demand for faster communications, FSK techniques would require more expensive technology to support faster speeds, making it less practical.

FIGURE 1.4 An example of Frequency Shift Keying (ASCII Code of an Upper Case K)

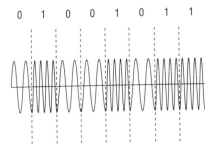

0 1 0 0 1 0 1 1

Phase Shift Keying

Phase Shift Keying (PSK) varies the phase of the signal to represent the binary data. PSK is a state transition technique, where one phase can represent a 0 bit and another phase can represent a 1 bit. This shifting of phase determines the data that is being transmitted. When the receiving station samples the signal during the symbol period, it determines the phase of the wave and the status of the bit.

Figure 1.5 shows how a wave can modulate an ASCII letter *K* using Phase Shift Keying. A phase change at the beginning of the symbol period is interpreted as a binary 1, and the lack of a phase change at the beginning of the symbol period is interpreted as a binary 0.

PSK is used extensively in the 802.11 standards. Typically, the receiving station samples the signal during the symbol period and compares the phase of the current sample with the previous sample and determines the difference. This degree difference, or differential, is used to determine the bit value. More advanced versions of PSK can encode multiple bits per symbol. Instead of using two phases to represent the binary values, four phases can be used. Each of the four phases is capable of representing two binary values (00, 01, 10, or 11) instead of one (0 or 1), thus shortening the transmission time. When more than two phases are used, this is referred to as Multiple Phase Shift Keying (MPSK). Figure 1.6 shows how a wave can modulate an ASCII letter *K* using a Multiple Phase Shift Keying method. Four possible phase changes can be monitored, with each phase change now able to be interpreted as 2 bits of data instead of just 1. Notice that there are fewer symbol times in this drawing than there are in the drawing in Figure 1.5.

FIGURE 1.5   An example of Phase Shift Keying (ASCII Code of an Upper Case K)

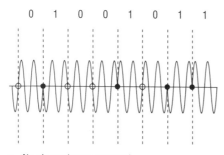

o No phase change occurred
● Phase change occurred

FIGURE 1.6   An example of Multiple Phase Shift Keying (ASCII Code of an Upper Case K)

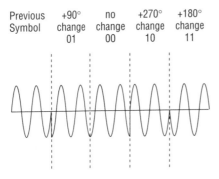

Summary

This chapter explained the roles and responsibilities of the three key organizations involved with the wireless networking industry:

- FCC
- IEEE
- Wi-Fi Alliance

To provide a basic knowledge of how wireless stations transmit and receive data, we introduced some of the components of waves and modulation:

- Carrier signals
- Amplitude
- Wavelength
- Frequency
- Phase
- Keying methods
- ASK
- FSK
- PSK

When troubleshooting RF communications, having a solid knowledge of waves and modulation techniques can help you understand the fundamental issues behind communications problems and hopefully assist with leading you to a solution.

Exam Essentials

Know the three industry organizations.   Understand the roles and responsibilities of the FCC, IEEE, and Wi-Fi Alliance.

Understand wavelength, frequency, amplitude, and phase.   Know the definitions of each RF characteristic.

Understand the concepts of modulation.   ASK, FSK, and PSK are three carrier signal modulation techniques.

Key Terms

Before you take the exam, be certain you are familiar with the following terms:

amplitude	International Telecommunication Union Radiocommunication Sector (ITU-R)
Amplitude Shift Keying (ASK)	keying method
carrier signal	modulation
Federal Communications Commission (FCC)	phase
frequency	Phase Shift Keying (PSK)
Frequency Shift Keying (FSK)	wavelength
Institute of Electrical and Electronics Engineers (IEEE)	Wi-Fi Alliance
International Organization for Standardization (ISO)	

Review Questions

1. IEEE is an abbreviation for what?

   A. International Electrical and Electronics Engineers

   B. Institute of Electrical and Electronics Engineers

   C. Institute of Engineers - Electrical and Electronic

   D. Industrial Electrical and Electronics Engineers

2. FCC is an abbreviation for what?

   A. Frequency Communications Commission

   B. Frequency Communications Chart

   C. Federal Communications Commission

   D. Federal Communications Corporation

3. ISO is the short name of which organization?

   A. International Standards Organization

   B. International Organization for Standards

   C. International Organization for Standardization

   D. Organization for International Standards

4. The 802.11 standard was created by which organization?

   A. IEEE

   B. OSI

   C. ISO

   D. Wi-Fi Alliance

   E. FCC

5. What organization ensures interoperability of WLAN products?

   A. IEEE

   B. ITU-R

   C. ISO

   D. Wi-Fi Alliance

   E. FCC

6. What type of signal is required to carry data?

    A. Communications signal

    B. Data signal

    C. Carrier signal

    D. Binary signal

    E. Digital signal

7. Which keying method is most susceptible to interference from noise?

    A. FSK

    B. ASK

    C. PSK

    D. DSK

8. Which keying method is used for some of the slower, earlier 802.11 standards but not used for the faster standards?

    A. FSK

    B. ASK

    C. PSK

    D. DSK

9. Which keying method is used extensively in the 802.11 standards?

    A. FSK

    B. ASK

    C. PSK

    D. DSK

10. The Wi-Fi Alliance is responsible for which of the following standards? (Choose all that apply.)

    A. WPA2

    B. WEP

    C. 802.11

    D. WMM

    E. PSK

11. Which wave properties can be modulated to encode data? (Choose all that apply.)

    A. Amplitude

    B. Frequency

    C. Phase

    D. Wavelength

12. EIRP is an abbreviation for what?

   A. Effective isotropically radiated power

   B. Electronic information regulatory panel

   C. Equivalent isotropic radiated power

   D. Equivalent isotropically radiated power

13. The height or power of a wave is known as what?

   A. Phase

   B. Frequency

   C. Amplitude

   D. Wavelength

14. Global spectrum management is tasked to what organization?

   A. FCC

   B. Wi-Fi Alliance

   C. ITU-R

   D. IEEE

15. A modulated signal capable of carrying data is known as what?

   A. Data transmission

   B. Communications channel

   C. Data path

   D. Carrier signal

16. Which of the following wireless communications parameters and usage are typically regulated? (Choose all that apply.)

   A. Frequency

   B. Bandwidth

   C. Maximum power

   D. Maximum EIRP

   E. Indoor/outdoor usage

17. The IEEE 802.11g name is broken down into three components. 802 is the _____, .11 is the _____, and g is the _____.

   A. Project, working group, task group

   B. Committee, project, group

   C. Project, working group, committee

   D. It is not broken into separate components. It is known solely as the 802.11g committee.

18. A wave is divided into degrees. How many degrees make up a complete wave?

    A. 100

    B. 180

    C. 212

    D. 360

19. RF noise usually affects which property of a wave?

    A. Amplitude

    B. Wavelength

    C. Frequency

    D. Phase

20. The OSI model consists of how many layers?

    A. 4

    B. 6

    C. 7

    D. 9

Answers to Review Questions

1. B. IEEE stands for Institute of Electrical and Electronics Engineers.

2. C. FCC stands for Federal Communications Commission.

3. C. Remember that ISO is not an abbreviation or an acronym. It is actually a word derived from the Greek word *isos*, meaning *equal*.

4. A. The IEEE is responsible for the creation of all of the 802 standards.

5. D. The Wi-Fi Alliance provides certification testing, and when a product passes the test, it receives a Wi-Fi Certified certificate.

6. C. A carrier signal is a modulated signal that is used to transmit binary data.

7. B. Due to the effects of noise on the amplitude of a signal, Amplitude Shift Keying (ASK) has to be used cautiously.

8. A. With the demand for faster communications, FSK techniques would require more expensive technology to support faster speeds, making it less practical.

9. C. Phase Shift Keying (PSK) is used extensively in the 802.11 standards. Amplitude Shift Keying (ASK) is not typically used due to the effects of noise on the amplitude of the signal. Frequency Shift Keying (FSK) would require expensive technology to support faster speeds. DSK does not exist.

10. A, D. 802.11 and WEP (Wired Equivalent Privacy) are part of the IEEE 802.11 standard. PSK is not a standard, it is an encoding technique.

11. A, B, C. The three keying methods that can be used to encode data are Amplitude Shift Keying (ASK), Frequency Shift Keying (FSK), and Phase Shift Keying (PSK).

12. D. Although some books define EIRP as effective isotropically radiated power, the proper term is equivalent isotropically radiated power.

13. C. Height or power are two terms that describe the amplitude of a wave. Frequency is how often a wave repeats itself. Wavelength is the actual length of the wave, typically measured from peak to peak. Phase refers to the starting point of a wave in relation to another wave.

14. C. The International Telecommunication Union Radiocommunication Sector (ITU-R) has been tasked with global spectrum management.

15. D. A carrier signal is a signal that has been modulated to carry data.

16. A, B, C, D, E. All of these are typically regulated by the local or regional RF regulatory body.

17. A. 802 is the project, which is subdivided into working groups. Working groups are further subdivided into task groups.

18. D. A wave is divided into 360 degrees.

19. A. RF noise typically affects the amplitude, or height, of a wave.

20. C. The OSI model is sometimes referred to as the seven layer model.

Chapter

2

Radio Frequency Fundamentals

IN THIS CHAPTER, YOU WILL LEARN ABOUT THE FOLLOWING:

✓ **Define a Radio Frequency Signal**

✓ **Define and Describe the Following RF Characteristics**

- Polarity
- Wavelength
- Frequency
- Amplitude
- Phase

✓ **Define and Describe the Following RF Behaviors**

- Wave Propagation
- Absorption
- Reflection
- Scattering
- Refraction
- Diffraction
- Loss (Attenuation)
- Free Space Path Loss
- Multipath
- Gain (Amplification)

To properly design, deploy, and administer an 802.11 wireless network, in addition to understanding the OSI model and basic networking concepts, you must broaden your understanding of many other networking technologies. For instance, when administering an Ethernet network, you typically need a comprehension of TCP/IP, bridging, switching, and routing. The skills to manage an Ethernet network will also aid you as a Wi-Fi administer because most 802.11 wireless networks act as "portals" into wired networks. The IEEE only defines the 802.11 technologies at the Physical layer and the MAC sublayer of the Data-Link layer.

In order to fully understand the 802.11 technology, it is necessary to have a clear concept of how wireless works at the first layer of the OSI model, and at the heart of the Physical layer is radio frequency (RF) communications.

In a wired LAN, the signal is confined neatly inside the wire and the resulting behaviors are anticipated. However, just the opposite is true for a wireless LAN. Although the laws of physics apply, RF signals move through the air in a sometimes very unpredictable manner. Since RF signals are not saddled inside an Ethernet wire, you should always try to envision a wireless LAN as an "ever changing" network.

Does this mean that you must be an RF engineer from Georgia Tech to perform an 802.11 site survey or monitor a Wi-Fi network? Of course not, but if you have a good grasp of the RF characteristics and behaviors that we will define in this chapter, your skills as a wireless network administrator will be ahead of the curve. Why does a wireless network perform differently in an auditorium full of people than it does inside an empty auditorium? Why does the performance of a wireless LAN seem to degrade in a storage area with metal racks? Why does the range of a 5 GHz radio transmitter seem shorter than the range of a 2.4 GHz radio card? These are the type of questions that can be answered with some basic knowledge of how RF signals work and perform.

Wired communications travel across what is known as *bounded medium*. Bounded medium contains or confines the signal (small amounts of signal leakage can occur). Wireless communications travel across what is known as *unbounded medium*. Unbounded medium does not contain the signal, which is free to radiate into the atmosphere in all directions (unless restricted or redirected by some outside influence).

In this chapter, we first define what an RF signal does. Then we will look at both the properties and the behaviors of RF.

What Is an RF (Radio Frequency) Signal?

An RF signal starts out as an electrical *alternating current (AC)* signal that is originally generated by a transmitter. This AC signal is sent through a copper conductor (typically a coaxial cable) and radiated out of an antenna element in the form of an electromagnetic wireless signal. Changes of electron flow in an antenna, otherwise known as current, produce changes in the electromagnetic fields around the antenna.

An alternating current is an electrical current with a magnitude and direction that varies cyclically, as opposed to direct current, the direction of which stays in a constant form. The shape and form of the AC signal—defined as the *waveform*—is what is known as a sine wave, as shown in Figure 2.1. Sine wave patterns can also be seen in light, sound, and the ocean.

FIGURE 2.1   A sine wave

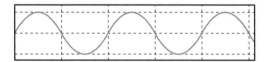

An RF signal radiates in a continuous pattern that is governed by certain properties such as wavelength, frequency, amplitude, phase, and polarity. Additionally, electromagnetic signals can travel through mediums of different materials or travel in a perfect vacuum. When an RF signal travels through a vacuum, it moves at the speed of light, which is approximately 300,000,000 meters per second, or 186,000 miles per second. RF signals travel using a variety or combination of movement behaviors. These movement behaviors are referred to as *propagation* behaviors. We will discuss some of these propagation behaviors in this chapter, including absorption, reflection, scattering, refraction, diffraction, amplification, and attenuation.

Identifying Radio Frequency Characteristics

In every RF signal exists characteristic that are defined by the laws of physics:

- Polarity
- Wavelength
- Frequency
- Amplitude
- Phase

We will look at each of these in more detail in the following sections.

Polarity

When the movement of the electron flow changes direction in an antenna, electromagnetic waves that change and move away from the antenna are also produced. The waves consist of two component fields: the electrical (E-field) and the H-field, which is magnetic.

Think of a wave as a physical disturbance that transfers energy back and forth between these two fields. These fields are at right angles to each other, and the transfer of energy between these fields is known as *oscillation*.

Polarization is the vertical or horizontal positioning of an antenna. The orientation of the antenna affects the *polarity* of the signal. The electric field always resides parallel in the same orientation (plane) of the antenna element. As shown in Figure 2.2, the parallel plane is called the E-plane and the plane that is perpendicular to the antenna element is known as the H-plane.

FIGURE 2.2   Polarity, E-plane, and H-plane

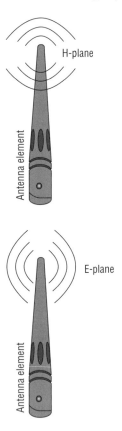

Wave polarity is defined as the position and direction of the electric field (E-field), as referenced to the surface of the earth. If an antenna element is positioned vertically, then the E-field is also vertical. Vertical polarization is when the E-field is perpendicular to the earth. If an antenna element is positioned horizontally, then the electric field is also horizontal.

Horizontal polarization is when the E-field is parallel to the earth. Antennas will often have polarity markings indicating which direction is vertical or horizontal.

Vertical, horizontal, and other types of polarization will be discussed in more detail in Chapter 4, "Radio Frequency Signal and Antenna Concepts."

Wavelength

As stated earlier, an RF signal is an alternating current (AC) that continuously changes between a positive and negative voltage. An oscillation, or cycle, of this alternating current is defined as a single change from up to down to up, or as a change from positive to negative to positive.

A *wavelength* is the distance between the two successive crests (peaks) or two successive troughs (valleys) of a wave pattern. In simpler words, a wavelength is the distance that a single cycle of an RF signal actually travels.

The Greek symbol λ (lambda) represents wavelength.

It is very important to understand the following statement: The higher the frequency, the less distance the propagated wave will travel. AM radio stations operate at much lower frequencies than wireless LAN radios. For instance, WSB-AM in Atlanta broadcasts at 750 KHz and has a wavelength of 1,312 feet, or 400 meters. That is quite a distance for one single cycle of an RF signal to travel. In contrast, some radio navigation satellites operate at a very high frequency, near 252 GHz, and a single cycle of the satellite's signal has a wavelength of less than .05 inches, or 1.2 millimeters. Figure 2.3 displays a comparison of these two extremely different types of RF signals.

Notice that the next time you hear a car coming down the street with loud music, the first thing you will hear will be the bass (lower frequencies). This is a practical example to show that lower frequencies travel farther than higher frequencies.

The majority of wireless LAN (WLAN) radio cards operate in either the 2.4 GHz frequency range or the 5 GHz range. In Figure 2.4, you see a comparison of a single cycle of the two different frequency WLAN radio cards.

Note that the length of a 2.45 GHz wave is about 4.8 inches, or 12 centimeters. The length of a 5.775 GHz wave is only a distance of about 2 inches, or 5 centimeters.

FIGURE 2.3   750 KHz wavelength and 252 GHz wavelength

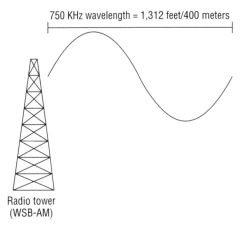

750 KHz wavelength = 1,312 feet/400 meters

Radio tower
(WSB-AM)

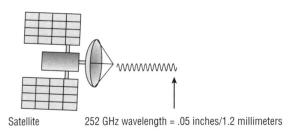

Satellite   252 GHz wavelength = .05 inches/1.2 millimeters

FIGURE 2.4   2.45 GHz wavelength and 5.775 GHz wavelength

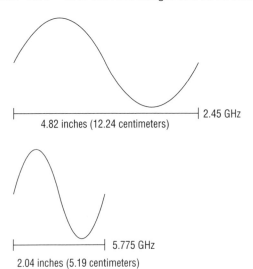

2.45 GHz
4.82 inches (12.24 centimeters)

5.775 GHz
2.04 inches (5.19 centimeters)

As you can see by these illustrations, the wavelengths of the different frequency signals are different because, although each signal only cycles one time, the waves travel dissimilar distances. In Figure 2.5, you see the formulas for calculating wavelength distance in either inches or centimeters.

FIGURE 2.5   Wavelength formulas

Inches: wavelength = 11.811/frequency (GHz)

Centimeters: wavelength = 30/frequency (GHz)

Throughout this study guide, you will be presented with various formulas. You will not need to know these formulas for the CWNA certification test. The formulas are in this study guide to demonstrate concepts and to be used as reference material.

Real World Scenario

How Does the Wavelength of a Signal Concern Me?

Because the wavelength property is shorter in the 5 GHz frequency range, Wi-Fi equipment using 5 GHz radio cards will have shorter range and coverage area than Wi-Fi equipment using 2.4 GHz radio cards.

Part of the design of the wireless LAN includes what is called a *site survey*. Part of the responsibility of the site survey is to determine zones, or cells, of usable signal coverage in your facilities. The 2.4 GHz access points will provide greater RF footprints than the higher-frequency equipment simply because of the wavelengths of the two different frequency signals. More 5 GHz access points may have to be installed to meet the same coverage needs that are achieved by a lesser number of 2.4 GHz access points.

Frequency

As previously mentioned, an RF signal cycles in an alternating current in the form of an electromagnetic wave. You also know that the distance traveled in one signal cycle is the wavelength. But what about how often an RF signal cycles?

Frequency is the number of times a specified event occurs within a specified time interval. A standard measurement of frequency is *hertz (Hz)*, which was named after the German physicist Heinrich Rudolf Hertz. An event that occurs once in 1 second is equal to 1 Hz. An event that occurs 325 times in 1 second is measured as 325 Hz. The frequency at which electromagnetic waves cycle is also measured in hertz. Thus, the number of times an RF signal cycles in 1 second is the frequency of that signal.

Different metric prefixes can be applied to the hertz (Hz) measurement of radio frequencies:

1 hertz (Hz) = 1 cycle per second

1 kilohertz (KHz) = 1,000 cycles per second

1 megahertz (MHz) = 1,000,000 (million) cycles per second

1 gigahertz (GHz) = 1,000,000,000 (billion) cycles per second

So when we are talking about 2.4 GHz WLAN radio cards, the RF signal is oscillating 2.4 billion times per second!

> **NOTE**   There is a direct relationship between frequency (f, measured in hertz, or Hz), wavelength (λ, measured in meters, or m), and speed of light (c, which is 300,000,000 m/sec). The following reference formulas illustrate the relationship: $\lambda = c/f$ and $f = c/\lambda$.

Amplitude

Another very important property of an RF signal is the amplitude, which simply can be characterized as the signal's strength or power. *Amplitude* can be defined as the maximum displacement of a continuous wave. With RF signals, the amplitude corresponds to the electrical field of the wave. When you look at an RF signal in an oscilloscope, the amplitude is represented by the positive crests and negative troughs of the sine wave.

In Figure 2.6, you can see that (λ) represents wavelength and (y) represents the amplitude. The first signal's crests and troughs have more magnitude, thus it has more amplitude. The second signal's crests and troughs have decreased, and therefore the signal has less amplitude.

Note that although the signal strength (amplitude) is different, the frequency of the signal remains constant. A variety of factors can cause an RF signal to lose amplitude, otherwise known as attenuation, which we will discuss later in this chapter in the section "Loss (Attenuation)."

Different types of RF technologies require varying degrees of transmit power. AM radio stations may transmit narrow band signals with as much power as 50,000 watts. The radio cards in most indoor 802.11 access points have a transmit power range between 1 milliwatt (mW) and 100 mW. You will learn later that Wi-Fi radio cards can actually receive signals with amplitudes as low as billionths of a milliwatt.

FIGURE 2.6 Amplitude

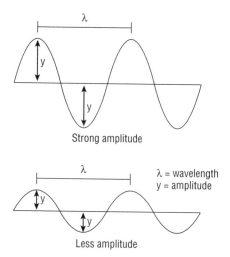

Strong amplitude

λ = wavelength
y = amplitude

Less amplitude

Phase

Phase is not a property of just one RF signal but instead involves the relationship between two or more signals that share the same frequency. The phase involves the relationship between the position of the amplitude crests and troughs of two waveforms.

Phase can be measured in distance, time, or degrees. If the peaks of two signals with the same frequency are in exact alignment at the same time, they are said to be *in phase*. Conversely, if the peaks of two signals with the same frequency are not in exact alignment at the same time, they are said to be *out of phase*. Figure 2.7 illustrates this concept.

What is important to understand is the effect that phase has on amplitude when radio cards receive multiple signals. Signals that have 0 (zero) degrees phase separation (in phase) actually combine their amplitude, which results in a received signal of much greater signal strength, or twice the amplitude. If two RF signals are 180 degrees out of phase (the peak of one signal is in exact alignment with the trough of the second signal), they cancel each other out and the effective received signal strength is null. Depending on the amount of phase separation of two signals, the received signal strength may be either cumulative or diminished.

On your CD is a freeware program called EMANIM. Toward the end of this chapter, you will use this program to execute Exercise 2.1, which will be a lab that demonstrates the effects of phase.

FIGURE 2.7   Phase

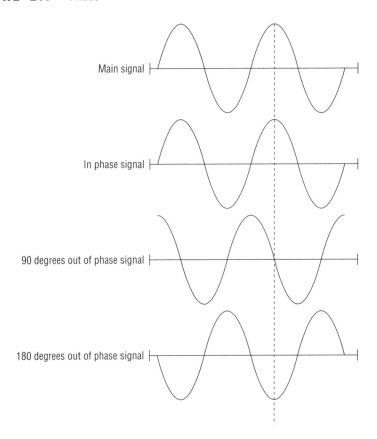

Identifying RF Behaviors

As an RF signal travels through the air and other different mediums, it can move and behave in different manners. RF propagation behaviors include absorption, reflection, scattering, refraction, diffraction, loss, free space path loss, multipath, attenuation, and gain.

Wave Propagation

Now that you have learned about some of the various characteristics of an RF signal, it is important to have an understanding of the way an RF signal behaves as it moves away from an antenna. As stated before, electromagnetic waves can move through a perfect vacuum or pass through materials or other media. The way in which the RF waves move—known as *wave propagation*—can vary drastically depending on the materials in the signal's path. Drywall will have a much different effect on an RF signal than metal.

What happens to an RF signal between two locations is a direct result of how the signal propagates. When we use the term *propagate*, try to envision an RF signal broadening or spreading as it travels farther away from the antenna. An excellent analogy is shown in Figure 2.8, which depicts an earthquake. Note the concentric seismic rings that propagate away from the epicenter of the earthquake. RF waves behave in much the same fashion. The manner in which a wireless signal moves is often referred to as propagation behavior.

FIGURE 2.8   Earthquake

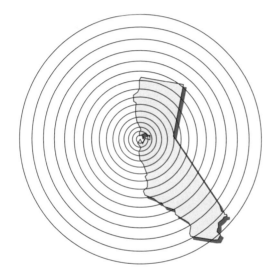

 As a WLAN engineer, it is important to have an understanding of RF propagation behaviors for making sure that access points are deployed in the proper location, for making sure the proper type of antenna is chosen, and for monitoring the health of the wireless network.

Absorption

The most common RF behavior is *absorption*. If the signal does not bounce off an object, move around an object, or pass through an object, then 100 percent absorption has occurred. As pictured in Figure 2.9, most materials will absorb some amount of an RF signal to varying degrees.

FIGURE 2.9   Absorption

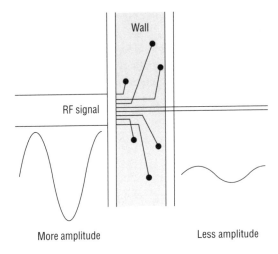

Brick and concrete walls will absorb a signal significantly, whereas drywall will absorb a signal to a lesser degree. Water is another example of a medium that can absorb a signal to a large extent. Absorption can be a leading cause of attenuation, which will be discussed later in this chapter.

 Real World Scenario

User Density

Mr. Akin performs a wireless site survey at a campus lecture hall. He determined how many access points are required and their proper placement so that he will have the necessary RF coverage. Ten days later, Professor Sandlin gives a heavily attended lecture on business economics. During this lecture, the signal strength and quality of the wireless LAN was less than desirable. What happened? Human bodies!

An average adult body is 50 to 65 percent water. Water causes absorption, which results in attenuation. User density is an important factor when designing a wireless network. One reason is the effects of absorption. Another reason is the amount of available bandwidth, which we will discuss in Chapter 15, "RF Site Survey Fundamentals."

Reflection

One of the most important RF propagation behaviors to be aware of is reflection. When a wave hits a smooth object that is larger than the wave itself, depending upon the media, the wave may bounce in another direction. This behavior is categorized as *reflection*. An analogous situation could be a child bouncing a ball off a sidewalk and the ball changing direction. Figure 2.10 depicts a laser beam pointed at a single small mirror. Depending on the angle of the mirror, the laser beam bounces or reflects off into a different direction. RF signals can reflect in the same manner depending on the objects or materials the signals encounter.

FIGURE 2.10   Reflection analogy

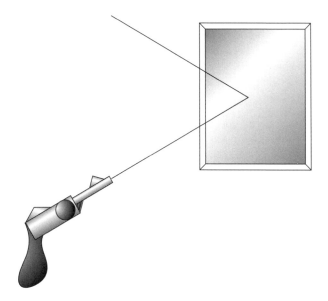

There are two major types of reflections: sky wave reflection and microwave reflection. Sky wave reflection can occur in frequencies below 1 GHz where the signal has a very large wavelength. The signal bounces off the surface of the charged particles of the ionosphere in the earth's atmosphere. This is why you can be in Charlotte, North Carolina, and listen to WLS-AM in Chicago on a clear night.

Microwave signals, however, exist between 1 GHz and 300 GHz. Because they are higher-frequency signals, they have much smaller wavelengths, thus the term *microwave*. Microwaves can bounce off of smaller objects like a metal door. Microwave reflection is what we are concerned about in wireless LAN environments. In an outdoor environment, microwaves can reflect off of large objects and smooth surfaces such as buildings, roads, bodies of water, and even the earth's surface. In an indoor environment, microwaves reflect off of smooth surfaces such as doors, walls, and file cabinets. Anything made of metal will absolutely cause reflection. Other materials such as glass and concrete may cause reflection as well.

Reflection Is a Major Source of Poor WLAN Performance

Reflection can be the cause of serious performance problems in a wireless LAN. As a wave radiates from an antenna, it broadens and disperses. If portions of this wave are reflected, new wave fronts will appear from the reflection points. If these multiple waves all reach the receiver, the multiple reflected signals cause an effect called multipath.

Multipath can degrade the strength and quality of the received signal or even cause data corruption or cancelled signals. (Further discussion of multipath occurs later in this chapter. Hardware solutions to compensate for the negative effects of multipath, such as directional antennas and antenna diversity, will be discussed in Chapter 4, "RF Signal and Antenna Concepts.")

Although reflection and multipath can be your number one enemy, new antenna technologies such as Multiple Input Multiple Output (MIMO) may become commonplace in the future to actually take advantage of reflected signals.

Scattering

Did you know that the color of the sky is blue because the wavelength of light is smaller than the molecules of the atmosphere? This blue sky phenomenon is known as Rayleigh scattering. The shorter blue wavelength light is absorbed by the gases in the atmosphere and radiated in all directions. This is another example of an RF propagation behavior called *scattering*, sometimes called scatter.

Scattering can most easily be described as multiple reflections. These multiple reflections occur when the electromagnetic signal's wavelength is larger than pieces of whatever medium the signal is passing through.

Scattering can happen in two different ways. The first type of scatter is on a smaller level and has a lesser effect on the signal quality and strength. This type of scatter may manifest itself when the RF signal moves through a substance and the individual electromagnetic waves are reflected off the minute particles within the medium. Smog in our atmosphere and sandstorms in the desert can cause this type of scattering.

The second type of scattering occurs when an RF signal encounters some type of uneven surface and is reflected into multiple directions. Chain link fences, tree foliage, and rocky terrain commonly cause this type of scattering. When striking the uneven surface, the main signal dissipates into multiple reflected signals, which can cause substantial signal downgrade and may even cause a loss of the received signal.

FIGURE 2.11   Scattering analogy

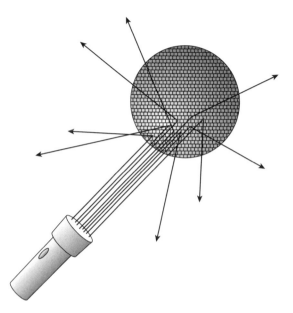

Figure 2.11 shows a flashlight being shined against a disco mirror ball. Note how the main signal beam is completely displaced into multiple reflected beams with less amplitude and into many different directions.

Refraction

In addition to RF signals being absorbed or bounced (via reflection or scattering), if certain conditions exist, an RF signal can be bent in a behavior known as *refraction*. A straightforward definition of refraction is the bending of an RF signal as it passes through a medium with a different density, thus causing the direction of the wave to change. RF refraction most commonly occurs as a result of atmospheric conditions.

 When you're dealing with long-distance outdoor bridge links, an instance of refractivity change that might be a concern is what is known as the *k-factor*. A k-factor of 1 means there is no bending. A k-factor of less than 1, such as 2/3, would represent the signal bending away from the earth. A k-factor of more than 1 represents bending toward the earth. Normal atmospheric conditions have a k-factor of 4/3, which is bending slightly toward the curvature of the earth.

The three most common causes of refraction are water vapor, changes in air temperature, and changes in air pressure. In an outdoor environment, RF signals typically refract slightly back down toward the earth's surface. However, changes in the atmosphere may cause the signal to bend away from the earth. In long-distance outdoor wireless bridge links, refraction can be an issue. An RF signal may also refract through certain types of glass and other materials that are found in an indoor environment. Figure 2.12 show several examples of refraction.

FIGURE 2.12   Refraction

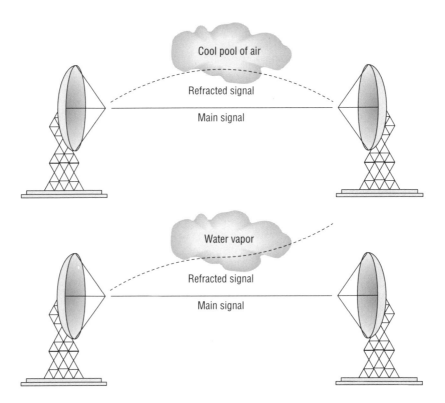

Diffraction

Not to be confused with refraction, another RF propagation behavior exists that also bends the signal; it's called *diffraction*. Diffraction is the bending of an RF signal around an object (whereas refraction, as you recall, is the bending of a signal as it passes through a medium). Diffraction is the bending and the spreading of an RF signal when it encounters an obstruction. The conditions that must be met for diffraction to occur depend entirely on the shape, size, and material of the obstructing object as well as the exact characteristics of the RF signal, such as polarization, phase, and amplitude.

Typically, diffraction is caused by some sort of partial blockage of the RF signal, such as a small hill or a building that sits between a transmitting radio and a receiver. The waves that encounter the obstruction slow down in speed, which causes them to bend around the object.

The waves that did not encounter the object maintain their original speed and do not bend. The analogy depicted in Figure 2.13 is a rock sitting in the middle of a river. Most of the current maintains the original flow; however, some of the current that encounters the rock will reflect off the rock and some will diffract around the rock.

Sitting directly behind the obstruction is the receiver radio that is now in an area known as the *RF shadow*. Depending upon the change in direction and velocity of the diffracted signals, the area of the RF shadow can become a dead zone of coverage or still possibly receive degraded signals.

FIGURE 2.13   Diffraction analogy

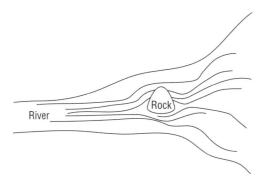

Loss (Attenuation)

Loss, also known as *attenuation*, is best described as the decrease of amplitude or signal strength. A signal may lose strength while on a wire or in the air. On the wired portion of the communications (RF cable), the AC electrical signal will lose strength due to the electrical impedance of coaxial cabling and other components such as connectors.

> In Chapter 4, we will discuss impendence, which is the measurement of opposition to the AC current. You will also learn about impendence mismatches, which can create signal loss on the wired side.

Attenuation is typically not desired, however, on rare occasions an RF engineer may even add a hardware attenuator device on the wired side of an RF system to introduce attenuation to remain compliant with power regulations.

Once the RF signal is radiated into the air via the antenna, the signal will attenuate due to absorption, distance, and the negative effects of multipath. You already know that as an RF signal passes through different mediums, the signal can be absorbed into the medium, which in turn causes a loss of amplitude. Different materials typically yield different attenuation results. As discussed earlier, water is a major source of absorption as well as dense materials such as cinder blocks, all of which lead to attenuation.

On your CD is a freeware program called EMANIM. Use this program to execute Exercise 2.1, which demonstrates the effects of absorption which results in attenuation.

EXERCISE 2.1

Visual Demonstration of Absorption

In this exercise, you will use a program called EMANIM to view the attenuation effect of materials due to absorption.

1. Insert the CD included with this book and install the EMANIM program and double-clicking emanim_setup.exe.

2. From the main EMANIM menu, click Phenomenon.

3. Click Sybex CWNA Study Guide.

4. Click Exercise 2.2. When a radio wave crosses matter, the matter absorbs part of the wave. As a result, the amplitude of the wave decreases. The extinction coefficient determines how much of the wave is absorbed by unit length of material. Vary the length of the material and the extinction coefficient for Wave 1 to see how it affects the absorption.

Both loss and gain can be gauged in a relative measurement of change in power called decibels (dB), which will be discussed extensively in Chapter 3. Table 2.1 shows the different attenuation values for several materials.

TABLE 2.1 Materials-Attenuation Comparison

Material	2.4 GHz
Foundation Wall	–15 dB
Brick, Concrete, Concrete Blocks	–15 dB
Elevator or metal obstacle	–10 dB
Metal Rack	–6 dB
Drywall or Sheetrock	–3 dB
Non-tinted Glass Windows or Door	–3 dB

TABLE 2.1   Materials-Attenuation Comparison *(continued)*

Material	2.4 GHz
Wood Door	–3 dB
Cubicle Wall	–2 dB

This chart is meant as a reference chart and is not information that will be covered on the CWNA exam.

It is important to understand that an RF signal will also lose amplitude merely as a function of distance in what is known as free space path loss. Also, reflection propagation behaviors can produce the negative effects of multipath and as a result cause attenuation in signal strength.

Free Space Path Loss

Due to the laws of physics, an electromagnetic signal will attenuate as it travels despite the lack of attenuation caused by obstructions, absorption, reflections, diffractions, and so on. *Free space path loss* is the loss of signal strength caused by the natural broadening of the waves, often referred to beam divergence. RF signal energy spreads over larger areas as the signal travels farther away from an antenna, and as a result, the strength of the signal attenuates.

One way to illustrate free space path loss is to use a balloon analogy. Before a balloon is filled with helium, it remains small but with a dense rubber thickness. After the balloon is inflated and has grown and spread in size, the rubber becomes very thin. RF signals will lose strength in much the same manner. Luckily, this loss in signal strength is logarithmic and not linear, thus the amplitude does not decrease as much in a second segment of equal length as it decreases in the first segment. A 2.4 GHz signal will change in power by about 80 dB after 100 meters but will only lessen another 6 dB in the next 100 meters.

Here are the formulas to calculate free space path loss:

$LP = 36.6 + (20\log 10F) + (20\log 10D)$

   LP = path loss in dB

   F = frequency in MHz

   D = distance in miles between antennas

$LP = 32.4 + (20\log 10F) + (20\log 10D)$

   LP = path loss in dB

   F = frequency in MHz

   D = distance in kilometers between antennas

NOTE Free space path loss formulas are provided as a reference and are not included on the CWNA exam. Many of the formulas in this book are provided in the form of spreadsheet calculators on the book's CD.

An even simpler way to estimate free space path loss is called the 6dB rule (remember for now that decibels are a measure of gain or loss, and further details of dB will be covered extensively in Chapter 3, "Radio Frequency Componets, Measurements, and Mathematics"). The 6dB rule states that doubling the distance will result in a loss of amplitude of 6 dB. Table 2.2 shows estimated path loss and confirms the 6dB rule. Also notice that the 5 GHz signal attenuates more than the 2.4 GHz signal. It should be noted that higher frequency signals attenuate faster because of the shorter wavelength.

TABLE 2.2   Attenuation Due to free space path loss

Distance [km]	Attenuation [dB]	
	2.4 GHz	5 GHz
1	100.4	106.4
2	106.4	112.4
4	112.4	118.5
8	118.5	124.5

Multipath

Multipath is a propagation phenomenon that results in two or more paths of a signal arriving at a receiving antenna at the same time or within nanoseconds of each other. Due to the natural broadening of the waves, the propagation behaviors of reflection, scattering, diffraction, and refraction will occur. A signal may reflect off an object or scatter, refract, or diffract.

In an indoor environment, reflected signals and echoes can be caused by walls, desks, floors, file cabinets, and numerous other obstructions. In an outdoor environment, it could be a flat road, large body of water, building, or atmospheric conditions. Therefore we have signals bouncing and bending in many different directions. The principal signal will still travel to the receiving antenna, but many of the bouncing and bent signals may also find their way to the receiving antenna. In other words, "multiple paths" of the RF signal arrive at the receiver, as seen in Figure 2.14.

It usually takes a little bit longer for the reflected signals to arrive at the receiving antenna because they must travel a longer distance than the principal signal. The time differential between these signals can be measured in millionths of a second (nanoseconds).

Real World Scenario

Why Is Free Space Path Loss Important?

All radio cards have what is known as a receiver sensitivity level. A radio card can properly interpret and receive a signal down to a certain fixed amplitude threshold. If a radio card receives a signal above its amplitude threshold, the card can differentiate between the signal and other RF noise that is in the background. The background noise is typically referred to as the *noise floor*.

Once the amplitude of a received signal falls below the radio card's threshold, the card can no longer make the distinction between the signal and the background noise. The concept of free space path loss also applies to road trips in your car. When you are in a car listening to AM radio, eventually you will drive out of range and will no longer be able to hear the music above the static noise.

When designing both indoor wireless LANS and outdoor wireless bridge links, you must make sure that the RF signal will not attenuate below the receiver sensitivity level of your wireless radio card simply due to free space path loss. You achieve this goal indoors during a site survey. An outdoor bridge link requires a series of calculations called a *link budget*. (Site surveys will be covered in Chapters 15 and 16 and link budgets will be covered in Chapter 3.)

The time differential between these multiple paths is known as the *delay spread*. You will learn later in the book that certain spread spectrum technologies are more tolerant than others of delay spread.

So what exactly happens when mutipath presents itself? In television signal transmissions, multipath causes a ghost effect with a faded duplicate image to the right of the main image. With RF signals, the effects of multipath can be either constructive or destructive. Quite often they are very destructive. Due to the differences in phase of the multiple paths, the combined signal will often attenuate, amplify, or become corrupted. These effects are sometimes called *Rayleigh fading* named after British physicist Lord Rayleigh.

The four results of multipath are as follows:

- **Downfade** This is decreased signal strength. When the multiple RF signal paths arrive at the receiver at the same time and are out of phase with the primary wave, the result is a decrease in signal strength (amplitude). Phase differences of between 121 and 179 degrees will cause downfade.

- **Upfade** This is increased signal strength. When the multiple RF signal paths arrive at the receiver at the same time and are in phase or partially out of phase with the primary wave, the result is an increase in signal strength (amplitude). Smaller phase differences of between 0 and 120 degrees will cause upfade. Please understand, however, that the final received signal can never be stronger than the original transmitted signal due to free space path loss.

- **Nulling** This is signal cancellation. When the multiple RF signal paths arrive at the receiver at the same time and are 180 degrees out of phase with the primary wave, the result can be a complete cancellation of the RF signal.

- **Data Corruption** Intersymbol interference can cause data corruption. Because of the difference in time between the primary signal and the reflected signals known as the delay spread, along with the fact that there may be multiple reflected signals, the receiver can have problems demodulating the RF signal's information. The delay spread time differential can cause bits to overlap with each other and the end result is corrupted data, as seen in Figure 2.15. This type of multipath interference is often known as *intersymbol interference (ISI)*.

The good news is that the receiving station will detect the errors through an 802.11 defined cyclic redundancy check (CRC) because the checksum will not calculate accurately. The 802.11 standard requires that all unicast frames must be acknowledged by a receiving station with an acknowledgment (ACK) frame; otherwise, the transmitting station will have to retransmit the frame. The receiver will *not* acknowledge a frame that has failed the CRC. Therefore, unfortunately, the frame must be retransmitted, but this is better than it being misinterpreted. Mutipath can have a very negative effect on the performance or throughput of your wireless LAN due to retransmissions that are a direct result of intersymbol interference.

So how is a hapless WLAN engineer supposed to deal with all these multipath issues? The use of unidirectional antennas will often reduce the amount of reflections, and antenna diversity can also be used to compensate for the negative effects of multipath.

On your CD is a freeware program called EMANIM. Use this program for Exercise 2.2, which demonstrates the effects of phase and multipath fading.

EXERCISE 2.2

Visual Demonstration of Multipath and Phase

In this exercise you will use a program called EMANIM to view the effect on amplitude due to various phases of two signals arriving at the same time.

1. Insert the CD included with this book and install the EMANIM program by double-clicking emanim_setup.exe.

2. From the main EMANIM, menu click Phenomenon.

3. Click Sybex CWNA Study Guide.

4. Click Exercise 2.1a.

5. Two identical, vertically polarized waves are superposed (you might not see both of them because they cover each other). The result is a wave having double the amplitude of the component waves.

6. Click Exercise 2.1b.

7. Two identical, 70 degrees out of phase waves are superposed. The result is a wave with an increased amplitude over the component waves.

8. Click Exercise 2.1c. Two identical, 140 degree out of phase waves are superposed. The result is a wave with a decreased amplitude over the component waves.

9. Click on Exercise 2.1d. Two identical, vertically polarized waves are superposed. The result is a cancellation of the two waves.

FIGURE 2.14   Multipath

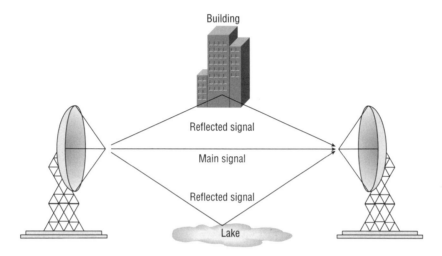

Building

Reflected signal

Main signal

Reflected signal

Lake

FIGURE 2.15   Data corruption ISI

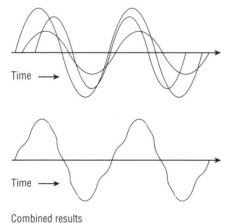

Multiple Received Signals

Time ⟶

Time ⟶

Combined results

Gain (Amplification)

Gain, also known as *amplification* , can best be described as the increase of amplitude or signal strength. The two types of gain are known as active gain and passive gain. A signal's amplitude can be boosted by the use of external devices. *Active gain* is usually caused by the use of an amplifier on the wire that connects the transceiver to the antenna. The amplifier is usually bidirectional, meaning that it increases the AC voltage both inbound and outbound. Active gain devices require the use of an external power source. *Passive gain* is accomplished by focusing the RF signal with the use of an antenna. Antennas are passive devices that do not require an external power source. Instead, the internal workings of an antenna focus the signal more powerfully in one direction than another.

 The proper use of RF amplifiers and antennas will be covered extensively in Chapter 4.

Despite the usual negative effects of multipath, it should be reiterated that when multiple RF signals arrive at the receiver at the same time and are in phase or partially out of phase with the primary wave, the result can be an increase or gain in amplitude.

There are two very different tools that can be used to measure the amplitude of a signal at even given point. The first, a frequency domain tool, can be used to measure amplitude in a finite frequency spectrum. The frequency domain tool used by WLAN engineers is also called a *spectrum analyzer*. The second tool, a time domain tool, can be used to measure how a signal's amplitude changes over time. The conventional name for a time domain tool is an *oscilloscope*. Figure 2.16 shows how both these tools can be used to measure amplitude.

FIGURE 2.16   RF signal measurement tools

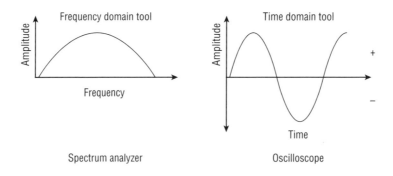

Summary

This chapter covered the meat and potatoes, the basics, of radio frequency signals. In order to properly design and administer a WLAN network, it is essential to have a thorough understanding of the following principles of RF properties and RF behaviors:

- Electromagnetic waves and how they are generated

- The relationship between wavelength, frequency, and the speed of light

- Signal strength and the various ways in which a signal can either attenuate or amplify

- The importance of the relationship between two or more signals

- How a signal moves by bending, bouncing, or absorbing in some manner

  When troubleshooting an Ethernet network, the best place to start is always at layer 1, the Physical layer. Wireless LAN troubleshooting should also begin at the Physical layer. Learning the RF fundamentals that exist at layer 1 is an essential step in proper wireless network administration.

Exam Essentials

Understand wavelength, frequency, amplitude, and phase.   Know the definition of each RF characteristic and how it can affect wireless LAN design

Remember all the RF propagation behaviors.   Be able to explain the differences in each RF behavior (such as reflection, diffraction, scattering, and so on) and the various mediums that are associated with each behavior.

Understand what causes attenuation.   Loss can occur either on the wire or in the air. Absorption, free space path loss, and multipath downfade are all causes of attenuation.

Define free space path loss.   Despite the lack of any obstructions, electromagnetic waves attenuate in a logarithmic manner as they travel away from the transmitter.

Remember the four results of multipath and their relationship to phase.   Multipath may cause downfade, upfade, nulling, and data corruption.

Know the results of intersymbol interference and delay spread.   The time differential between a primary signal and reflected signals may cause corrupted bits and affect throughput due to retransmissions.

Explain the difference between active and passive gain.   RF amplifiers are active devices, whereas antennas are passive devices.

Key Terms

Before you take the exam, be certain you are familiar with the following terms:

absorption	noise floor
active gain	oscillation
alternating current (AC)	oscilloscope
amplification	passive gain
amplitude	phase
attenuation	polarity
delay spread	propagation
diffraction	Rayleigh fading
free space path loss	reflection
frequency	refraction
gain	RF shadow
hertz (Hz)	scattering
intersymbol interference (ISI)	spectrum analyzer
loss	wavelength
multipath	wave propagation

Review Questions

1. What are some results of multipath interference? (Choose all that apply.)

   A. Cross polarization

   B. Upfade

   C. Excessive retransmissions

   D. Absorption

2. What term best defines the distance traveled in one positive to negative to positive oscillation of an electromagnetic signal?

   A. Crest

   B. Frequency

   C. Trough

   D. Wavelength

3. Which of the following statements are true about amplification? (Choose all that apply.)

   A. Some antennas require an outside power source.

   B. RF amplifiers inject an AC current into the wire.

   C. Antennas are passive gain amplifiers that focus the energy of a signal in one direction.

   D. RF amplifiers passively increase signal strength by focusing the AC current of the signal.

   E. Signal strength may passively increase due to multipath.

4. A standard measurement of frequency is called what?

   A. Hertz

   B. Milliwatt

   C. Nanosecond

   D. Decibel

   E. K-factor

5. When an RF signal bends around an object, this propagation behavior is known as what?

   A. Stratification

   B. Refraction

   C. Scattering

   D. Diffraction

   E. Attenuation

6. When the multiple RF signals arrive at a receiver at the same time and are _____ with the primary wave, the result can be _____.

A. out of phase, scattering

B. in phase, intersymbol interference

C. in phase, attenuation

D. 180 degrees out of phase, amplification

E. in phase, cancellation

F. 180 degrees out of phase, cancellation

7. Which of the following statements are true? (Choose all that apply.)

A. As a result of upfade, a final received signal will be stronger than the original transmitted signal.

B. As a result of downfade, a final received signal will never be stronger than the original transmitted signal.

C. As a result of upfade, a final received signal will never be stronger than the original transmitted signal.

D. As a result of downfade, a final received signal will be stronger than the original transmitted signal.

8. What is the frequency of an RF signal that cycles 2.4 million times per second?

A. 2.4 hertz

B. 2.4 MHz

C. 2.4 GHz

D. 2.4 kilohertz

E. 2.4 KHz

9. What is an example of a time domain tool that could be used by an RF engineer?

A. Oscilloscope

B. Spectroscope

C. Spectrum analyzer

D. Refractivity gastroscope

10. What are some objects or materials that may cause reflection? (Choose all that apply.)

A. Metal

B. Trees

C. Asphalt road

D. Lake

E. Carpet floors

11. Which one of these statements is correct?

    A. A lower-frequency signal travels less than a higher-frequency signal and attenuates faster.

    B. A higher-frequency signal travels farther than a lower-frequency signal but attenuates faster.

    C. A lower-frequency signal travels farther than a higher-frequency signal but attenuates faster.

    D. A higher-frequency signal travels less than a lower-frequency signal and attenuates faster.

12. Which behavior can be described as an RF signal encountering a chain link fence, causing the signal to bounce into multiple directions?

    A. Diffraction

    B. Scatter

    C. Reflection

    D. Refraction

    E. Multiplexing

13. What is another name for background noise?

    A. Noise ceiling

    B. Background interference

    C. Noise floor

    D. Background information

14. Which of the following can cause refraction of an RF signal traveling through it? (Choose all that apply.)

    A. Shift in air temperature

    B. Change in air pressure

    C. Humidity

    D. Smog

    E. Wind

    F. Lightning

15. Which of the following statements are true about free space path loss? (Choose all that apply.)

    A. RF signals will attenuate as they travel despite the lack of attenuation caused by obstructions.

    B. Path loss occurs at a constant rate.

    C. RF signals will attenuate as they travel because of obstructions.

    D. Path loss occurs at a logarithmic rate.

16. What term is used to describe the time differential between a primary signal and a reflected signal arriving at a receiver?

    A. Path delay

    B. Spread spectrum

    C. Multipath

    D. Delay spread

17. What is an example of a frequency domain tool that could be used by an RF engineer?

    A. Oscilloscope

    B. Spectroscope

    C. Spectrum analyzer

    D. Refractivity gastroscope

18. Using knowledge of RF characteristics and behaviors, which of the following options should a WLAN engineer be most concerned about during an indoor site survey? (Choose all that apply.)

    A. Firewall door

    B. Indoor temperature

    C. User density

    D. Drywall

19. Which three properties have an interrelated relationship?

    A. Frequency, wavelength, and the speed of light

    B. Frequency, amplitude, and the speed of light

    C. Frequency, phase, and amplitude

    D. Amplitude, phase, and the speed of sound

20. Which RF behavior best describes a signal striking a medium and bending in a different direction?

    A. Refraction

    B. Scattering

    C. Diffusion

    D. Diffraction

    E. Microwave reflection

Answers to Review Questions

1. B, C. Mutipath may result in attenuation, amplification, signal loss, or data corruption. If two signals arrive together in phase, the result is an increase in signal strength called upfade. The delay spread may also be too significant and cause data bits to be corrupted, resulting in excessive retransmissions.

2. D. The wavelength is the distance between the repeating crests (peaks) or repeating troughs (valleys) of a single cycle of a wave pattern.

3. C, E. Passive gain is typically created by antennas that focus the energy of a signal without the use of an outside power source. Passive gain may also result in the form of upfade, which is one effect of multipath.

4. A. The standard measurement of the number of times a signal cycles per second is hertz (Hz). One Hz is equal to one cycle in 1 second.

5. D. Often confused with refraction, the diffraction propagation is the bending of the wavefront around an obstacle. Diffraction is caused by some sort of partial blockage of the RF signal, such as a small hill or a building that sits between a transmitting radio and a receiver

6. F. Nulling or cancellation can occur when multiple RF signals arrive at the receiver at the same time and are 180 degrees out of phase with the primary wave.

7. B, C. When the multiple RF signals arrive at the receiver at the same time and are in phase or partially out of phase with the primary wave, the result is an increase in signal strength (amplitude). However, the final received signal, whether affected by upfade or downfade, will never be stronger than the original transmitted signal due to free space path loss.

8. B. 802.11 wireless LANS operate in the 5 GHz and 2.4 GHz frequency range. However 2.4 GHz is equal to 2.4 billion cycles per second. The frequency of 2.4 million cycles per second would be 2.4 MHz.

9. A. An oscilloscope is a time domain tool that be used to measure how a signal's amplitude changes over time. A spectrum analyzer is a frequency domain tool.

10. A, C, D. This is a tough question to answer because many of the same mediums can cause several different propagation behaviors. Metal will always bring about reflection. Water is a major source of absorption; however, large bodies of water can also cause reflection. Flat surfaces such as asphalt roads, ceiling, and walls will also result in reflection behavior.

11. D. Because of the wavelength property of an electromagnetic signal, the higher the frequency, the less distance the propagated wave will travel. Also, due to the smaller wavelength, high-frequency signals attenuate faster.

12. B. Scattering, or scatter, is defined as an RF signal reflecting in multiple directions when encountering an uneven surface.

13. C. The noise floor is a signal strength measurement of all unwanted sources of noise.

14. A, B, C. Air stratification is a leading cause of refraction of an RF signal. Changes in air temperature, changes in air pressure, and water vapor are all causes of refraction.

15. A, D. Due to the natural broadening of the wavefront, electromagnetic signals lose amplitude as they travel away from the transmitter. The rate of free space path loss is logarithmic and not linear.

16. D. The time difference due to reflected signals taking a longer path is known as the delay spread.

17. C. A spectrum analyzer is a frequency domain tool that can be used to measure amplitude in a finite frequency spectrum. An oscilloscope is a time domain tool.

18. A, C. Firewall doors are made of metal and will cause reflections, which can lead to multipath issues. People are composed primarily of water and a high user density could affect signal performance due to absorption.

19. A. There is a direct relationship between frequency (f), wavelength (λ), and speed of light (c). $\lambda = {}^{c}/{}_{f}$.

20. A. Refraction is the bending of an RF signal when it encounters a medium.

Chapter 3

Radio Frequency Components, Measurements, and Mathematics

IN THIS CHAPTER, YOU WILL LEARN ABOUT THE FOLLOWING:

- ✓ **The Components of RF Communications**
  - Transmitter
  - Receiver
  - Antenna
  - Isotropic Radiator
  - Intentional Radiator (IR)
  - Equivalent Isotropically Radiated Power (EIRP)

- ✓ **Units of Power and Comparison**
  - Watt
  - Milliwatt
  - Decibel (dB)
  - dBi
  - dBd
  - dBm

- ✓ **RF Mathematics**
  - Rule of 10s and 3s

- ✓ **Received signal strength indicator (RSSI)**

- ✓ **System Operating Margin (SOM)/Link Budget**

- ✓ **Fade Margin**

- ✓ **Inverse Square Law**

To put it simply, data communication is the transferring of information between computers. No matter what form of communication is being used, there are many components that are required to achieve a successful communication. Before we look at some of the individual components, let's initially keep things simple and look at the three basic requirements for successful communications:

- Two or more devices want to communicate.

- There must be a medium, a means, or a method for them to use to communicate.

- There must be a set of rules for them to use when they communicate. (This will be covered in Chapter 8, "802.11 Medium Access.")

These three basic requirements are the same for all forms of communication, whether a group of people are having a conversation at a dinner party, two computers are transmitting data via a dial-up modem, or many computers are communicating via a wireless network.

The existence of a computer network essentially implies that the first requirement is met. If we did not have two or more devices that wanted to share data, we wouldn't need to create the network in the first place. The CWNA certification program also assumes this and is therefore rarely if ever concerned specifically with the data itself. It is assumed that we have data, and our concern is to transmit it.

This chapter will focus on the second requirement for successful communications, the medium, means, or method to communicate. We will cover the components of radio frequency (RF), which make up what we refer to as the medium for wireless communications. Here we will be concerned with the transmission of the RF signal and the role of each of the devices and components along the transmission path. We will also look at how each device or component affects the transmission.

In Chapter 2, "Radio Frequency Fundamentals," you learned that there are many RF behaviors that affect the signal as it leaves the transmitter and travels toward the receiver. As the signal moves through the different components and through the air, its power changes. Some components increase the power of the signal (gain), while other components decrease the power (loss). In this chapter you will learn how to quantify and measure the power of the waves and calculate how the waves are affected by both internal and external influences. Through these calculations, you will be able to accurately determine whether you will have the means to communicate between devices.

RF Components

Many components contribute to the successful transmission and reception of an RF signal. Figure 3.1 shows the key components that will be covered in this section. In addition to understanding the function of the components, it is important to understand how the strength of the signal is specifically affected by each of the components.

Later in this chapter, when we discuss RF mathematics, we will show you how to calculate the effect each of the components has on the signal.

FIGURE 3.1   RF components

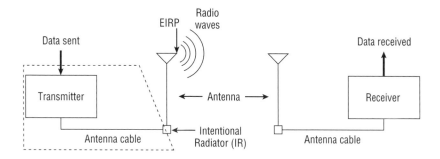

Transmitter

The transmitter is the initial component in the creation of the wireless medium. The computer hands the data off to the transmitter, and it is the transmitter's job to begin the RF communication.

In Chapter 1, "Overview of Wireless Standards and Organizations," you learned about carrier signals and modulation methods. When the transmitter receives the data, it will begin generating an alternating current (AC) signal. This AC signal determines the frequency of the transmission. For an 802.11, 802.11b, or 802.11g transmission, the AC signal will oscillate around 2.4 billion times per second. For an 802.11a transmission, the AC signal will oscillate around 5 billion times per second. This oscillation determines the frequency of the radio wave.

The exact frequencies used will be covered in Chapter 6, "Wireless Networks and Spread Spectrum Technologies."

The transmitter will take the data provided and modify the AC signal using a modulation technique to encode the data into the signal. This modulated AC signal is now a carrier signal, containing the data to be transmitted. The carrier signal is then transported either directly to the antenna or through a cable to the antenna.

In addition to generating a signal at a specific frequency, the transmitter is responsible for determining the amplitude, or what is more commonly referred to as the power level, of the signal. The higher the amplitude of the wave, the more powerful the wave is and the further it will travel. The power levels that the transmitter is allowed to generate are determined by the local regulatory body, such as the Federal Communications Commission (FCC) in the United States.

Although we are explaining the transmitter and receiver separately in this chapter, and although functionally they are different components, typically they are one device that is referred to as a transceiver (transmitter/receiver). Typical wireless devices that have transceivers built into them are access points, bridges, and client adapters.

Antenna

An antenna provides two functions in a communication system. When connected to the transmitter, it collects the AC signal that it receives from the transmitter and directs, or radiates, the RF waves away from the antenna in a pattern specific to the antenna type. When connected to the receiver, it takes the RF waves that it receives through the air and directs the AC signal to the receiver. The receiver converts the AC signal to bits and bytes. As you will see later in this chapter, the signal that is received is much less than the signal that is generated. This signal loss is analogous to two people trying to talk to each other from opposite ends of a football field. Due to distance alone (free space), the yelling from one end of the field may be heard as barely louder than a whisper on the other end.

The signal of an antenna is usually compared or referenced to an *isotropic radiator*. An isotropic radiator is a *point source* that radiates signal equally in all directions. The sun is probably one of the best examples of an isotropic radiator. It generates equal amounts of energy in all directions. Unfortunately, it is not possible to manufacture an antenna that is a perfect isotropic radiator. The structure of the antenna itself influences the output of the antenna, similar to the way the structure of a lightbulb affects the bulb's ability to emit light equally in all directions.

There are two ways to increase the power output from an antenna. The first is to generate more power at the transmitter, as stated in the previous section. The other is to direct, or focus, the RF signal that is radiating from the antenna. This is similar to how you can focus light from a flashlight. If you remove the lens from the flashlight, the bulb is typically not very bright and radiates in almost all directions. To make the light brighter, you could use more powerful batteries, or you could put the lens back on. The lens is not actually creating more light. It is focusing the light that was radiating in all different directions into a narrow area. Some antennas radiate waves as the bulb without the lens does, while some radiate focused waves as the flashlight with the lens does.

 In Chapter 4, "Radio Frequency Signal and Antenna Concepts," you will learn about the different types of antennas and how to properly and most effectively use them.

Receiver

The receiver is the final component in the wireless medium. The receiver takes the carrier signal that is received from the antenna and translates the modulated signals into 1s and 0s. It then takes this data and passes it to the computer to be processed. The job of the receiver is not always an easy one. The signal that is received is a much less powerful signal than what was transmitted due to the distance it has traveled and the effects of free space path loss. The signal is also often altered due to interference from other RF sources and multipath.

Intentional Radiator (IR)

The FCC Code of Federal Regulations (CFR) Part 15 defines an *intentional radiator (IR)* as "a device that intentionally generates and emits radio frequency energy by radiation or induction." Basically, it's something that is specifically designed to generate RF as opposed to something that generates RF as a byproduct of its main function, such as a motor that incidentally generates RF noise.

Regulatory bodies such as the FCC limit the amount of power that is allowed to be generated by an IR. The IR consists of all the components from the transmitter to the antenna but not including the antenna, as seen in Figure 3.1. The power output of the IR is thus the sum of all the components from the transmitter to the antenna, again not including the antenna. The components making up the IR include the transmitter, all cables and connectors, and any other equipment (grounding, lightning arrestors, amplifiers, attenuators, etc.) between the transmitter and the antenna. The power of the IR is measured at the connecter that provides the input to the antenna. Since this is the point where the IR is measured and regulated, we often refer to this point alone as the IR. Using the flashlight analogy, the IR is all of the components up to the lightbulb socket but not the bulb and lens. This is the raw power, or signal, that is provided, and now the bulb and lens can focus the signal.

Equivalent Isotropically Radiated Power (EIRP)

Equivalent isotropically radiated power (EIRP) is the highest RF signal strength that is transmitted from a particular antenna. To understand this better, think of our flashlight example for a moment. Let's assume that the bulb without the lens generates 1 watt of power. When you put the lens on the flashlight, it focuses that 1 watt of light. If you were to look at the light now, it would appear much brighter. If you were to measure the brightest point of the light that was being generated by the flashlight, due to the effects of the lens, it may be equal to the brightness of an 8 watt bulb. So by focusing the light, you are able to make the equivalent isotropically radiated power of the focused bulb equal to 8 watts.

> It is important for you to know that you can find other references to EIRP as equivalent isotropic radiated power and effective isotropic radiated power. The use of EIRP in this book is consistent with the FCC definition, "equivalent isotropically radiated power, the product of the power supplied to the antenna and the antenna gain in a given direction relative to an isotropic antenna." Even though the terms that the initials stand for differ, the definition of EIRP is consistent.

As you learned earlier in this chapter, antennas are capable of focusing or directing RF energy. This focusing capability can make the effective output of the antenna much greater than the signal entering the antenna. Because of this ability to amplify the output of the RF signal, regulatory bodies such as the FCC limit the amount of EIRP from an antenna.

In the next section of this chapter you will learn how to calculate how much power is actually being provided to the antenna (IR) and how much power is coming out of the antenna (EIRP).

Units of Power and Comparison

When an 802.11 wireless network is designed, two key components are coverage and performance. A good understanding of RF power, comparison, and RF mathematics can be very helpful during the network design phase.

In this section, we will introduce you to an assortment of units of power and units of comparison. It is important to know and understand the different types of units of measurement and how they relate to each other. Some of the numbers that you will be working with will represent actual units of power and others will represent relative units of comparison. Actual units are ones that represent a known or set value.

To say that a man is 6 feet tall is an example of an actual measurement. Since the man's height is a known value, in this case feet, you know exactly how tall he is. Relative units are comparative values comparing one item to a similar type of item. For example, if you wanted to tell someone how tall the man's wife is using comparative units of measurement, you could say that she is 5/6 his height. You now have a comparative measurement: if you know the actual height of either one, you can then determine how tall the other is.

Comparative units of measurement are useful when working with units of power. As you will see later in this chapter, we can use these comparative units of power to compare the area that one access point can cover versus another access point. Using simple mathematics, we can determine things such as how many watts are needed to double the distance of a signal from an access point.

Table 3.1 below categorizes the different units.

TABLE 3.1   Units of Measure

Units of Power	Units of Comparison
Watt (W)	Decibel (dB)
Milliwatt (mW)	dBi
dBm	dBd

Watt

A watt is the basic unit of power, named after James Watt, an eighteenth-century Scottish inventor. One watt is equal to 1 ampere (amp) of current flowing at 1 volt. To give a better explanation of a watt, we will use a modification of the classic water analogy.

Many of you are probably familiar with a piece of equipment known as a power washer. If you are not familiar with it, it is a machine that connects to a water source, such as a garden hose, and allows you to direct a stream of high-pressure water at an object, with the premise that the fast-moving water will clean the object. The success of a power washer is based upon two components: the pressure that is applied to the water and the volume of water that is used over a period of time, also known as flow. These two components provide the power of the water stream. If you increase the pressure, you will increase the power of the stream. If you increase the flow of the water, you will also increase the power of the stream. The power of the stream is equal to the pressure times the flow.

A watt is very similar to the output of the power washer. Instead of the pressure generated by the machine, electrical systems have voltage. Instead of water flow, electrical systems have current, which is measured in amps. So the amount of watts generated is equal to the volts times the amps.

Milliwatt (mW)

A milliwatt (mW) is also a unit of power. To put it simply, a milliwatt is 1/1,000 of a watt. The reason you need to be concerned with milliwatts is because most of the 802.11 equipment that you will be using transmits at power levels between 1 and 100 mW. Although regulatory bodies such as the FCC may allow power outputs of as much as 4 watts, only rarely in point-to-point communications, such as in building-to-building environments, would you use 802.11 equipment with more than 250 mW of power.

Decibel (dB)

The first thing you should know about the decibel (dB) is that it is a unit of comparison, not a unit of power. Therefore, it is used to represent a difference between two values. In wireless networking, decibels are often used to either compare the power of two transmitters or, more often, compare the difference or loss between the EIRP output of a transmitter and the amount of power received by the receiver.

Decibel is derived from the term *bel*. Employees at Bell Telephone Laboratories needed a way to represent power losses on telephone lines as power ratios. They defined a *bel* as the ratio of 10 to 1 between the power of two sounds. Let's look at an example: An access point transmits data at 100 mW. Laptop1 receives the signal at a power level of 10 mW, and laptop2 receives the signal at a power level of 1 mW. The difference between the signal from the access point (100 mW) to laptop1 (10 mW) is 100:10, or a 10:1 ratio, or 1 bel. The difference between the signal from laptop1 (10 mW) to laptop2 (1 mW) is 10:1, also a 10:1 ratio, or 1 bel. So the power difference between the access point and laptop2 is 2 bels.

Bels can be looked at mathematically using logarithms. Not everyone understands or remembers logarithms, so we will review them. First, we need to look at raising a number to a power. If you take 10 and raise it to the third power ($10^3 = y$), what you are actually doing is multiplying three 10s ($10 \times 10 \times 10$). If you do the math, you will calculate that y is equal to 1,000. So the completed formula is $10^3 = 1,000$. When calculating logarithms, you change the formula to $10^y = 1,000$. Here you are trying to figure out what power 10 needs to be raised to in order to get to 1,000. You know in this example that the answer is 3. You can also write this equations as $y = \log10(1,000)$ or $y = \log_{10}1,000$. So the complete equation is $3 = \log10(1,000)$. Here are some examples of power and log formulas:

$10^1 = 10$	$\log10(10) = 1$
$10^2 = 100$	$\log10(100) = 2$
$10^3 = 1,000$	$\log10(1,000) = 3$
$10^4 = 10,000$	$\log10(10,000) = 4$

Now let's go back and calculate the bels from the access point to the laptop2 example using logarithms. Remember that bels are used to calculate the ratio between two powers. So let's refer to the power of the access point as P_{AP} and the power of laptop1 as P_{L1}. So the formula for this example would be $y = \log10(P_{AP}/P_{L1})$. If you plug in the power values, the formula becomes $y = \log10(100/1)$, or $y = \log10(100)$. So this equation is asking 10 raised to what power equals 100. The answer is 2 bels ($10^2 = 100$).

OK, so this is supposed to be a section about decibels and so far we have just covered bels. In certain environments, bels are not exact enough, which is why we use decibels instead. To calculate decibels, all you need to do is multiply bels by 10. So the formulas for bels and decibels are as follows:

bels = $\log10(P_1/P_2)$

decibels = $10 \times \log10(P_1/P_2)$

Now let's go back and calculate the decibels of the access point to laptop2 example. So the formula now is $y = 10 \times \log10(P_{AP}/P_{L1})$. If you plug in the power values, the formula becomes $y = 10 \times \log10(100/1)$, or $y = 10 \times \log10(100)$. So the answer is 20 decibels.

You do not need to know how to calculate logarithms for the CWNA exam. These examples are only here to give you some basic understanding of what they are and how to calculate them. Later in this chapter you will learn how to calculate decibels without using logarithms.

Now that you have learned about decibels, you are probably still wondering why you can't just work with milliwatts. You can if you want, but since power changes are logarithmic, the differences between values can become extremely large and more difficult to deal with. It is easier to say that a 100 mW signal decreased by 70 decibels than to say that it decreased to .00001 milliwatts. Table 3.2 compares milliwatts and decibel change, using 1 mW as the reference point. Due to the scale of the numbers, you can see why decibels can be easier to work with.

TABLE 3.2   Comparison of Milliwatts and Decibel Change (relative to 1 mW)

milliwatts	decibel change
.0001	−40
.001	−30
.01	−20
.1	−10
1	0
10	+10
100	+20
1,000	+30
10,000	+40
100,000	+50

dBi

Earlier in this chapter, we compared an antenna to an isotropic radiator. Theoretically, an isotropic radiator can radiate an equal signal in all directions. An antenna cannot do this due to construction limitations. In other instances, you do not want an antenna to radiate in all

Real World Scenario

Why Should You Use Decibels?

In Chapter 2, you learned that there are many behaviors of waves that can adversely affect a wave. One of the behaviors that you learned about was free space path loss.

If an access point is transmitting at 100 mW and a laptop is 100 meters (.1 kilometer) away from the access point, the laptop is receiving only about .000001 milliwatts of power. The difference between the numbers 100 and .000001 is so large that it doesn't have much relevance to someone looking at it. Additionally, it would be easy for someone to accidentally leave out a zero when writing or typing .00001 (as we just did).

If you use the free space path loss formula to calculate the decibel loss for this scenario, the formula would be

decibels = 32.4 + (20log10(2400)) + (20log10(.1))

The answer is approximately 80 decibels of loss. This number is easier to work with and less likely to be miswritten or mistyped.

directions because you want to focus the signal of the antenna in a particular direction. Whichever the case may be, it is important to be able to calculate the radiating power of the antenna so that you can determine how strong a signal is at a certain distance from the antenna. You may also want to compare the output of one antenna to that of another.

The gain or increase of power from an antenna when compared to what an isotropic radiator would generate is known as decibels isotropic (dBi). Another way of phrasing this is "decibel gain relative to an isotropic radiator." Since you are comparing two antennas, and since antennas are measured in gain, not power, you can conclude that dBi is a comparative measurement and not a power measurement. The dBi value is measured at the strongest point or the focus point of the antenna signal. Since antennas always focus their energy more in one direction than another, the dBi value of an antenna is always a positive gain and not a loss.

A common antenna used on access points is the half-wave dipole antenna. The half-wave dipole antenna is a small, typically rubber-encased, general purpose antenna and has a dBi value of 2.14.

Any time you see dBi, think antenna gain.

dBd

The antenna industry uses two different dB scales to describe the gain of antennas. The first scale, which you just learned about, is dBi, which is used to describe the gain of an antenna relative to a theoretical isotropic antenna. The other scale used to describe antenna gain is decibels dipole (dBd), or "decibel gain relative to a dipole antenna." So a dBd value is the increase in gain of an antenna when it is compared to the signal of a dipole antenna. Like dBi, since dBd is comparing two antennas, and since antennas are measured in gain, not power, you can also conclude that dBd is a comparative measurement and not a power measurement. The definition of dBd seems simple enough, but what happens when you want to compare two antennas and one is represented with dBi and the other with dBd? This is actually quite simple. A standard dipole antenna has a dBi value of 2.14. If an antenna has a value of 3 dBd, this means that it is 3 dB greater than a dipole antenna. Since the value of a dipole antenna is 2.14 dBi, all you need to do is add 3 plus 2.14. So a 3 dBd antenna is equal to a 5.14 dBi.

 Don't forget that dB, dBi, and dBd are comparative, or relative, measurements and not units of power.

 **Real World Scenario**

The Real Scoop on dBd

When working with 802.11 equipment, it is not often that you will have an antenna with a dBd value. 802.11 antennas typically are measured using dBi. On the rare occasion that you do run into one, just add 2.14 and you now know the antenna's dBi value.

dBm

Earlier when you read about bels and decibels, you learned that they measured differences or ratios between two different signals. Regardless of the type of power that was being transmitted, all you really knew was that the one signal was greater or less than the other by a particular number of bels or decibels. dBm also provides a comparison, but instead of comparing a signal to another signal, it is used to compare a signal to 1 milliwatt of power. dBm means "decibels relative to 1 milliwatt." So what you are doing is setting dBm to 0 (zero) and equating that to 1 milliwatt of power. Since dBm is a measurement that is compared to a known value, 1 milliwatt, then dBm is actually a measure of power. You can now state that 0 dBm is equal to 1 milliwatt. Using the formula $dBm = 10 \times \log10(P_{mW})$, you can determine that 100 mW of power is equal to 20 dBm.

If you happen to have the dBm value of a device and want to calculate the corresponding milliwatt value, you can do that too. The formula is $P_{mW} = \log^{-1}(P_{dBm} \div 10)$. Another, easier way of looking at the formula, and an easier way of using it, is $P_{mW} = 10^{(PdBm \div 10)}$. Just divide the dBm value by 10, and raise 10 to that power. If you are given a value of 20 dBm, to convert it to mW, the formula is $P_{mW} = 10^{(20 \div 10)}$ or $P_{mW} = 10^2 = 100$ mW.

It might seem a little ridiculous to have to deal with both milliwatts and dBm. If milliwatts are a valid measurement of power, then why not just use them? Why do you have to, or want to, also use dBm? These are good questions that are asked often by students. A very practical reason to use dBm can be shown using the free space path loss formula again. Following are two free space path loss equations. The first equation calculates the decibel loss of a 2.4GHz signal at 100 meters (.1 kilometer) from the RF source, and the second calculates the decibel loss of a 2.4GHz signal at 200 meters (.2 kilometer) from the RF source:

$$fspl = 32.4 + (20\log10(2400)) + (20\log10(.1)) = 80.00422 \text{ dB}$$

$$fspl = 32.4 + (20\log10(2400)) + (20\log10(.2)) = 86.02482 \text{ dB}$$

In this example, by doubling the distance from the RF source, the signal decreased by about 6 dB. If you double the distance between the transmitter and the receiver, the received signal will decrease by 6 dB. No matter what numbers are chosen, if the distance is doubled, the decibel loss will be 6 dB. This rule also implies that if you increase the EIRP by 6 decibels, the usable distance will double. This "6 dB rule" is very useful for comparing cell sizes or estimating the coverage of a transmitter. Remember, if you were working with milliwatts, this rule would not be relevant. By converting milliwatts to dBm, you have a more practical way to compare signals.

Remember the "6 dB rule." +6 dB doubles the distance of the usable signal. −6 dB halves the distance of the usable signal

Using dBm also makes it very easy to calculate the effects of antenna gain on a signal. If a transmitter generates a 20 dBm signal and the antenna adds 6 dBi of gain to the signal, then the power that is radiating from the antenna (EIRP) is equal to the sum of the two numbers, which is 26 dBm.

RF Mathematics

When the topic of RF mathematics is discussed, most people cringe and panic because they expect formulas that have logarithms in them. Fear not. You are about to learn RF math, without having to use logarithms. If you want to refresh yourself on some of your math skills prior to going through this section, then review the following:

- Addition and subtraction using the numbers 3 and 10
- Multiplication and division using the numbers 2 and 10

No, we are not kidding. If you know how to add and subtract using 3 and 10 and if you know how to multiply and divide using 2 and 10, then you have all of the math skills you need to perform RF math. Read on, and we will teach you how.

Rule of 10s and 3s

Before you fully delve into the rule of 10s and 3s, it is important to know that this rule may not give you the exact same answers that you would get if you used the logarithmic formulas. The rule of 10s and 3s provides approximate values, not necessarily exact values. If you are an engineer creating a product that must conform to RF regulatory guidelines, you will need to use logarithms to calculate the exact values. However, if you are a network designer planning a network for your company, you will find that the rule of 10s and 3s will provide you with the numbers you need to properly plan your network.

This section will take you step-by-step through numerous calculations. All of the calculations will be based upon the following four rules:

- If you add 3 to the dBms, you must multiply the mWs by 2.
- If you subtract 3 from the dBms, you must divide the mWs by 2.
- If you add 10 to the dBms, you must multiply the mWs by 10.
- If you subtract 10 from the dBms, you must divide the mWs by 10.

Once you remember these rules, you will be able to quickly perform RF calculations. After reviewing these rules, continue reading this chapter for a step-by-step procedure for using the rule of 10s and 3s. As you work through the step-by-step procedures, remember that dBm is a unit of power and dB is a unit of change. dB is a value of change that can be applied to dBm. So if you have 10 dBm and it increases by 3 dB, you can add these two numbers together to get a result of 13 dBm.

EXERCISE 3.1

Step-by-Step Procedure

On a sheet of paper, create two columns. The header of the first column should be **dBm** and the header of the second column should be **mW**.

dBm	mW

Next to the dBm header place a **+** and **–** sign, and next to the mW header place a × and ÷ sign. These will help you to remember that all math performed on the dBm column is addition or subtraction and all math performed on the mW column is multiplication or division.

+			×
–	dBm	mW	÷

EXERCISE 3.1 *(continued)*

To the left of the + and − signs, write the numbers **3** and **10**, and to the right of the × and ÷ signs, write the numbers **2** and **10**. Any addition or subtraction to the dBm column can be performed using only the numbers 3 and 10. Any multiplication or division to the mW column can be performed using only the numbers 2 and 10.

$$
\begin{array}{ccccc}
3 & + & & & \times & 2 \\
10 & - & \underline{\hspace{2cm}} & \underline{\hspace{2cm}} & \div & 10 \\
 & & \text{dBm} & \text{mW} & &
\end{array}
$$

If there is a + on the left, then there needs to be a × on the right. If there is a − on the left, then there needs to be a ÷ on the right. If you are adding or subtracting a 3 on the left, you must be multiplying or dividing by a 2 on the right. If you are adding or subtracting a 10 on the left, you must be multiplying or dividing by a 10 on the right.

The last thing that needs to be done is to put a **0** under the dBm column and a **1** under the mW column. Remember that the definition of dBm is "decibels relative to 1 milliwatt." So now the chart shows that 0 dBm is equal to 1 milliwatt.

$$
\begin{array}{ccccc}
3 & + & & & \times & 2 \\
10 & - & \underline{\hspace{2cm}} & \underline{\hspace{2cm}} & \div & 10 \\
 & & \text{dBm} & \text{mW} & & \\
 & & 0 & 1 & &
\end{array}
$$

 From now on, any RF math examples will start with this chart. We suggest that when you take your CWNA exam, you create this chart on the note paper provided to you and use it as the starting point for any of the RF math questions.

 Real World Scenario

Rule of 10s and 3s

dBm + 3 = mW × 2

dBm − 3 = mW ÷ 2

dBm + 10 = mW × 10

dBm − 10 = mW ÷ 10

Before we continue with other examples, it is important to emphasize that a change of 3 dB equates to a doubling or halving of the power, no matter what power measurement is being used. In our usage of the rule of 10s and 3s, we are dealing with milliwatts because that is the typical measurement used by 802.11 equipment. However, it is important to remember that a 3 dB increase means a doubling of the power regardless of the power scale used. So a 3 dB increase of 1.21 gigawatts of power would result in 2.42 gigawatts of power.

NOTE   An animated explanation of the rule of 10s and 3s—as well as explanations of the following examples—has been created using PowerPoint and can be run from the CD that you received with your book. If you do not have PowerPoint on your computer, you can download from Microsoft's website a PowerPoint Viewer that will allow you to view any PowerPoint file.

EXERCISE 3.2

Rule of 10s and 3s Example 1

In this example, you will begin at 1 mW and double the power three times. In addition to calculating the new power level in milliwatts, you will calculate the power level in dBms.

1. The first thing to do is create the initial chart.

$$
\begin{array}{cc}
3 \;\; + & \times \quad 2 \\
10 \;\; - & \div \quad 10 \\
\underline{\text{dBm}} \quad \underline{\text{mW}} \\
0 \qquad\qquad 1
\end{array}
$$

2. Now you want to double the power for the first time. So to the right of the 1 mW and on the next line, write × **2**. Then below the 1, perform the calculation.

$$
\begin{array}{cc}
3 \;\; + & \times \quad 2 \\
10 \;\; - & \div \quad 10 \\
\underline{\text{dBm}} \quad \underline{\text{mW}} \\
0 \qquad\qquad 1 \\
= 2 \leftarrow \times 2
\end{array}
$$

3. You are not done yet with this new line. Remember that whatever is done to one side of the chart, there must be a correlative mathematical equation on the other side. Since you multiplied by 2 on the right side, you must add 3 to the left side. So you have just calculated that 3 dBm is equal to 2 mW.

$$
\begin{array}{cc}
3 \;\; + & \times \quad 2 \\
10 \;\; - & \div \quad 10 \\
\underline{\text{dBm}} \quad \underline{\text{mW}} \\
0 \qquad\qquad 1 \\
+3 \rightarrow = 3 \qquad = 2 \leftarrow \times 2
\end{array}
$$

EXERCISE 3.2 *(continued)*

4. You have just completed the first doubling of the power. Now you will double it two more times and perform the necessary mathematical commands. Since this is the first time using this process, all of the steps have been shown using arrows. Future examples will not contain these arrows.

$$
\begin{array}{cccc}
3 & + & & \times & 2 \\
10 & - & & \div & 10 \\
& \underline{\text{dBm}} & \underline{\text{mW}} & \\
& 0 & 1 & \\
& 3 & 2 & \\
+3 & = 6 & = 4 & \times 2 \\
+3 & = 9 & = 8 & \times 2 \\
\end{array}
$$

You have just calculated that 4 mW = 6 dBm and 8 mW = 9 dBm. If you had used the formula for dBm instead of the rule of 10s and 3s, the actual answers would be 4 mW = 6.0206 dBm and 8 mW = 9.0309 mW. As you can see, this set of rules is very accurate but not exact.

EXERCISE 3.3

Rule of 10s and 3s Example 2

You have a wireless bridge that generates a 100 mW signal. The bridge is connected to an antenna using cable that creates 3 dB of signal loss. The antenna provides 10 dBi of signal gain. In this example, calculate the IR and EIRP values.

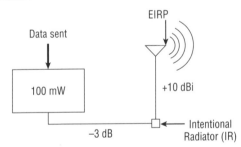

As a reminder, and as seen in the graphic, the IR is the signal up to but not including the antenna, and the EIRP is the signal radiating from the antenna.

EXERCISE 3.3 (continued)

1. The first step is to determine if using 10 or 2, and × or ÷, you can go from 1 mW to 100 mW. It is not too difficult to realize that multiplying 1 by 10 twice will give you 100. So the bridge is generating 100 mW or 20 dBm of power.

3 + 10 −	dBm	mW	× 2 ÷ 10
	0	1	
+ 10	10	10	× 10
+ 10	20	100	× 10

2. Next you have the antenna cable, which is introducing 3 dB of loss to the signal. Once you calculate the effect of the 3 dB loss, you know the value of the IR. You can represent the IR as either 17 dBm or 50 mW.

3 + 10 −	dBm	mW	× 2 ÷ 10
	0	1	
+ 10	10	10	× 10
+ 10	20	100	× 10
− 3	17	50	÷ 2

3. Now all that is left is to calculate the increase on the signal due to the gain from the antenna. Since the gain is +10 dBi, you add 10 to the dBm column and multiply the mW column by 10. This gives you an EIRP of 27 dBm or 500 mW.

3 + 10 −	dBm	mW	× 2 ÷ 10
	0	1	
+ 10	10	10	× 10
+ 10	20	100	× 10
− 3	17	50	÷ 2
+ 10	27	500	× 10

So far all of the numbers chosen in the examples have been very straightforward, using the values that are part of the template. However, in the real world, this is not going to be the case. Using a little creativity, you can calculate gain or loss for any integer. Unfortunately, the rule of 10s and 3s does not work for fractional or decimal numbers. For those numbers you will need to use the logarithmic formula.

dB gain or loss is cumulative. If, for example, you had three sections of cable connecting the transceiver to the antenna (we would never do this of course, but go with us on this for the moment) and each section of cable provided –2 dB of loss, all three cables would create 6 dB of loss. All you would have to do to calculate the loss is to subtract 3 twice. Decibels are very flexible. As long as you come up with the total that you need, they don't care how you do it.

Table 3.3 shows how to calculate all integer dB loss and gain from –10 to +10 using combinations of just 10s and 3s. Take a moment to look at these values and you will realize that with a little creativity, you can calculate the loss or gain of any integer.

TABLE 3.3 dB Loss and Gain (–10 through +10)

Loss or Gain (dB)	Combination of 10s and 3s
–10	–10
–9	–3 –3 –3
–8	–10 –10 +3 +3 +3 +3
–7	–10 +3
–6	–3 –3
–5	–10 –10 +3 +3 +3 +3 +3
–4	–10 +3 +3
–3	–3
–2	–3 –3 –3 –3 +10
–1	–10 +3 +3 +3
+1	+10 –3 –3 –3
+2	+3 +3 +3 +3 –10
+3	+3
+4	+10 –3 –3
+5	+10 +10 –3 –3 –3 –3 –3

TABLE 3.3 dB Loss and Gain (–10 through +10) *(continued)*

Loss or Gain (dB)	Combination of 10s and 3s
+6	+3 +3
+7	+10 –3
+8	+10 +10 –3 –3 –3 –3
+9	+3 +3 +3
+10	+10

EXERCISE 3.4

Rule of 10s and 3s Example 3

This example is going to be a little more complicated. You have an access point that is transmitting at 50 mW. The signal loss between the access point and the antenna is –1 dB, and the access point is using a 5 dBi antenna. In this example, calculate the IR and the EIRP values.

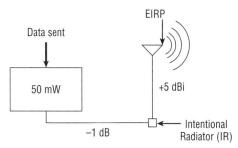

1. The first step after drawing up the template is to convert the 1 mW to 50 mW. This can be done by multiplying the 1 mW by 10 twice and then dividing by 2.

2. The dBm column then needs to be adjusted by adding 10 twice and subtracting 3. When the calculations are more complex, it's useful to separate and label the different sections.

3 + 10 –	dBm	mW	× 2 ÷ 10	
	0	1		
+ 10	10	10	× 10	
+ 10	20	100	× 10	Transmitter
– 3	17	50	÷ 2	

3. The signal loss between the access point and the antenna is –1 dB. Table 3.3 shows that –1 dB can be calculated by subtracting 10 and adding 3 three times.

4. The mW column will need to be adjusted by dividing by 10 and then multiplying by 2 three times. So the IR is either 16 dBm or 40 mW.

3 +			× 2	
10 –	dBm	mW	÷ 10	
	0	1		
+ 10	10	10	× 10	
+ 10	20	100	× 10	Transmitter
– 3	17	50	÷ 2	
– 10	7	5	÷ 10	
+ 3	10	10	× 2	
+ 3	13	20	× 2	Connector
+ 3	16	40	× 2	

5. The antenna adds a gain of 5 dBi. Table 3.3 shows that 5 dBi can be calculated by adding 10 twice and subtracting 3 five times.

6. The mW column will need to be adjusted by multiplying by 10 twice and dividing by 2 five times. The EIRP is therefore either 21 dBm or 125 mW.

3 +			× 2	
10 –	dBm	mW	÷ 10	
	0	1		
+ 10	10	10	× 10	
+ 10	20	100	× 10	Transmitter
– 3	17	50	÷ 2	
– 10	7	5	÷ 10	
+ 3	10	10	× 2	
+ 3	13	20	× 2	Connector
+ 3	16	40	× 2	
+ 10	26	400	× 10	
+ 10	36	4000	× 10	
– 3	33	2000	÷ 2	
– 3	30	1000	÷ 2	Antenna
– 3	27	500	÷ 2	
– 3	24	250	÷ 2	
– 3	21	125	÷ 2	

EXERCISE 3.5

Rule of 10s and 3s Example 4

In this example, you have an access point that is providing coverage to a specific area of a warehouse using an external directional antenna. The access point is transmitting at 30 mW. The cable and connector between the access point and the antenna creates –3 dB of signal loss. The antenna provides 20 dBi of signal gain. In this example, you will calculate the IR and EIRP values.

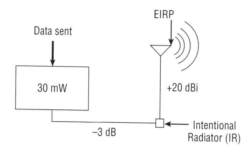

It's not always possible to calculate both sides of the chart using the rule of 10s and 3s. In some cases, no matter what you do, you cannot calculate the mW value using 10 or 2. This is one of those cases. You cannot set the mW and dBm values to be equal, but you can still calculate the mW values using the information provided.

7. Instead of creating the template and setting 0 dBm equal to 1 mW, enter the value of the transmitter, in this case 30 mW. In the dBm column, just write unknown. Even though you will not know the dBm value, you can still perform all of the necessary mathematics.

3 +
10 –
    dBm   mW   × 2
                       ÷ 10
    unknown   30

8. The cable and connectors introduce 3 dB of loss, so subtract 3 from the dBm column and divide the mW column by 2. So the output of the IR is 15 mW.

3 +
10 –
    dBm   mW   × 2
                       ÷ 10
    unknown   30
– 3   unknown – 3   15   ÷ 2

EXERCISE 3.5 *(continued)*

9. The 20 dBi gain from the antenna increases the dBm by 20, so add 10 twice to the dBm column, and multiply the mW column by 10 twice. So the output of the EIRP is 1,500 mW.

		dBm	mW		
3	+			×	2
10	−			÷	10
		unknown	30		
− 3		unknown − 3	15	÷ 2	
+ 10		unknown + 7	150	× 10	
+ 10		unknown + 17	1,500	× 10	

RF Math Summary

Many different concepts, formulas, and examples were covered in the RF mathematics section, so we will bring things together and summarize what was covered. It is important to remember that the bottom line is that you are trying to calculate the power at different points in the RF system and the effects caused by gain or loss. If you want to perform the RF math calculations using the logarithmic formulas, here they are:

$$dBm = 10 \times log10(mW)$$

$$mW = 10^{(dBm \div 10)}$$

If you want to use the rule of 10s and 3s, just remember the four simple rules, and you will not have a problem.

1. $dBm + 3 = mW \times 2$

2. $dBm - 3 = mW \div 2$

3. $dBm + 10 = mW \times 10$

4. $dBm - 10 = mW \div 10$

Received Signal Strength Indicator (RSSI)

The *received signal strength indicator (RSSI)* is an optional 802.11 parameter with a value from 0 to 255. It is designed to be used by the hardware manufacturer as a relative measurement of the RF power that is received. The RSSI is one of the indicators that is used by a wireless device to determine if another device is transmitting.

Although it is optional, most vendors appear to have implemented RSSI. The actual range of the RSSI value is from 0 to a maximum value (less than or equal to 255) that each vendor can choose on its own (known as RSSI_Max). The RSSI is also used as one of the factors when a client is determining whether it should roam to another access point.

There are two problems that exist when trying to compare RSSI values between different manufacturers' wireless cards. The first problem is that the manufacturers may have chosen two different values as the RSSI_Max. So manufacturer A may have chosen a scale from 0 to 100, whereas manufacturer B may have chosen a scale from 0 to 60. All other things being equal, vendor A may indicate a signal with an RSSI value of 25, whereas vendor B may indicate that same signal with an RSSI value of 15. If you were to compare these two cards without knowing any additional information, you may think that manufacturer A makes a more sensitive card.

The second problem with RSSI is that the manufacturers will take their range of RSSI values and compare them to a different range of dBm values. So manufacturer A may take its 100 number scale and relate it to dBm values of –110 dBm to –10 dBm, whereas manufacturer B will take its 60 number scale and relate it to dBm values of –95 dBm and –35 dBm. So not only do we have different numbering schemes, but we also have different ranges of values.

Given this information, RSSI values can assist with troubleshooting only if you are comparing information reported by different PCs using the same wireless card. If you attempt to compare values between manufacturers, you are definitely comparing apples and oranges.

System Operating Margin (SOM)/Link Budget

The system operating margin (SOM), also known as link budget, is the calculation of the amount of RF signal that is received minus the amount of signal required by the receiver. Figure 3.2 shows all of the components and their effects on the SOM of the receiver, known as the *receive sensitivity*. Manufacturers determine the receive sensitivity for each speed supported by the wireless card. Different speeds use different modulation techniques and encoding methods and some encoding methods are more susceptible to corruption.

FIGURE 3.2   Link budget components

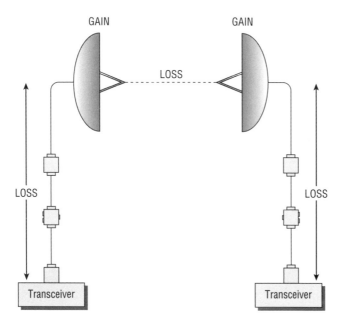

In order to determine the receive sensitivity of a card at a specific speed, data must be transmitted to the client at a high power level. If the bit error rate of the received data is below a predefined threshold, meaning the data was received properly, then this signal level is at or above the receive sensitivity of the receiver. The manufacturer then decreases the power level and checks the data received again. The decrease of power is repeated until the bit error rate is above the predefined threshold, meaning the data was not received properly. At this point, the receive sensitivity has been exceeded. The last power level test when the data was received properly is the receive sensitivity for that card at the speed tested. This procedure is repeated for each of the speeds that the card supports. Remember, the lower the number, the weaker the signal and the more reliable the card. A receive sensitivity chart of a client card may look something like this:

1 Mbps	–94 dBm
2 Mbps	–93 dBm
5.5 Mbps	–92 dBm
6 Mbps	–86 dBm
9 Mbps	–86 dBm
11 Mbps	–90 dBm
12 Mbps	–86 dBm
18 Mbps	–86 dBm
24 Mbps	–84 dBm
36 Mbps	–80 dBm
48 Mbps	–75 dBm
54 Mbps	–71 dBm

Remember that we are dealing with negative numbers here, so –71 dBm is the highest receive sensitivity on this list. Typically, the faster the speed, the higher the receive sensitivity. This is not always the case in instances where we compare different technologies, such as 802.11b at 11 Mbps (direct sequence spread spectrum, or DSSS) and 802.11g at 6 Mbps (Orthogonal Frequency Division Multiplexing, or OFDM).

You may be wondering why these numbers are negative when up till now most of the dBm numbers you have worked with have been positive. Figure 3.3 shows a simple summary of the gains and losses in an office environment. Until now you have worked primarily with calculating the IR and EIRP. It is the effect of free space path loss that makes the values negative, as you will see in the calculations based upon Figure 3.3. The link budget is equal to the received signal minus the receive sensitivity. In this example, the received signal is the sum of all components, which is

20 dBm + 5 dBi − 73.98 dB + 2.14 dBi = −46.84 dBm

If the receive sensitivity of the laptop's radio is −71 dBm, then the link budget is

−46.84 dBm − (−71 dBm) = 24.16 dBm

FIGURE 3.3   Office link budget gain and loss

Dipole antenna, 5 dBi

Free space path loss
50 meters
−73.98 dB

Access point,
TX = 20 dBm

Integrated antenna
2.14 dBi

Let's look at the SOM of a point-to-point wireless network, as seen in Figure 3.4. In this case, the two antennas are 10 kilometers apart. In addition to the effects of the antennas and cables, there are also lightning arrestors. Assume that the receiver sensitivity is −80 dBm. In this configuration, the calculation for the link budget is as follows:

Transceiver	10 dBm
10' LMR 600 cable	−.44 dB
Lightning arrestor	−.1 dB
50' LMR 600 cable	−2.21 dB
Parabolic antenna	+25 dBi
FSPL	−120 dB
Parabolic antenna	+25 dBi
50' LMR 600 cable	−2.21 dB
Lightning arrestor	−.1 dB
10' LMR 600 cable	−.44 dB
Total signal	−65.5 dBm

So the SOM is

−65.5 dBm − (−80 dBm) = 14.5 dBm

FIGURE 3.4   Point-to-point link budget gain and loss

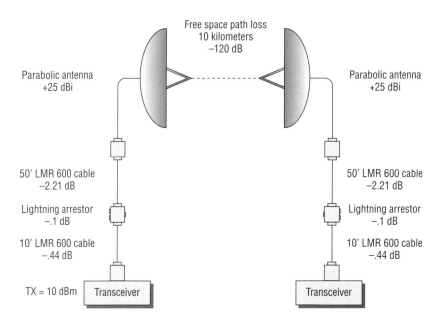

Fade Margin

Fade margin is a level of desired signal above what is required. A good way to explain fade margin is to think of it as a comfort zone. If a receiver has a receive sensitivity of –80 dBm, then as long as the signal received is greater than –80 dBm, the transmission will be successful. The problem is that the signal being received fluctuates due to many outside influences. In order to accommodate for the fluctuation, it is a common practice to add 10 to 20 dBs to the receive sensitivity value. The additional value that is added is known as the fade margin.

Let's say that a receiver has a sensitivity of –80 dBm and a signal is typically received at –76 dBm. Then under normal circumstances, this communication is successful. However, due to outside influences, the signal may fluctuate by ± 5 dBm. This means that most of the time, the communication is successful, but on those occasions that the signal has fluctuated to –81 dBm, the communication will be unsuccessful. By adding a fade margin of 10 dBm, you are now stating that for your needs, the receive sensitivity is –70 dBm, and you will plan your network so that the received signal is greater than –70 dBm. If the received signal fluctuates, you have already built in some padding, in this case 10 dBm. In some environments where RF performance is well documented, different fade margin values are associated with service levels and uptime statistics.

If you look back at Figure 3.4 and added a fade margin of 10 dBm to the receive sensitivity of –80 dBm, then the amount of signal required for the link would be –70 dBm. Since the signal is calculated to be received at –65.5 dBm, you will have a successful communication. However if you chose a fade margin of 15 dBm, the amount of signal required would be –65 dBm, and based upon the configuration in Figure 3.4, you would not have enough signal to satisfy the link budget plus the 15 dBm fade margin.

Since RF communications can be affected by many outside influences, it is common to have a fade margin to provide a level of link reliability. By increasing the fade margin, you are essentially increasing the reliability of the link.

Inverse Square Law

Earlier in this chapter you learned about the 6 dB rule, which states that a +6 dB change in signal will double the usable distance of a signal and a –6 dB change in signal will halve the usable distance of a signal. This rule and these numbers are actually based upon the Inverse Square Law, originally developed by Isaac Newton. This law states that the change in power is equal to 1 divided by the square of the change in distance.

What this means is that if you are receiving a signal at a certain power level and a certain distance (D) and you were to double the distance $(2 \times D)$, then the new power level will change by $1 \div (2 \times D)^2$. If at a distance of 1 feet (call this D) you were receiving a signal of 4 mW, then at a distance of 2 feet $(2 \times D)$ the power would change by $1 \div 2^2$, which is $1/4$. So the power at 2 feet is 4 mW $\times 1/4$, which is equal to 1 mW.

To see how this relates to the 6 dB rule, using the rule of 10s and 3s, consider that to change from 4 mW to 1 mW, you would need to divide the mW column by 2 twice. This would require you to subtract 3 twice from the dBm column, giving you a –6 dBm change caused by the doubling of the distance of the signal.

3 +			× 2
10 –	dBm	mW	÷ 10
	6	4	
– 3	3	2	÷ 2
– 3	0	1	÷ 2

Summary

This chapter covered three key areas of RF communications:

- RF components
- RF measurements
- RF mathematics

It is important to understand how each of the RF components affects the output of the transceiver. Whenever a component is added, removed, or modified, the output of the RF communications is changed. You need to understand these changes and make sure that the system conforms to regulatory standards. The following RF components were covered in this chapter:

- Transmitter
- Receiver
- Antenna
- Isotropic radiator
- Intentional radiator (IR)
- Equivalent isotropically radiated power (EIRP)

In addition to understanding the components and their effects on the transmitted signal, you must know the different units of power and comparison that are used to measure the output and the changes to the RF communications:

- Units of power
  - Watt
  - Milliwatt
  - dBm
- Units of comparison
  - dB
  - dBi
  - dBd

After you become familiar with the RF components and their effect on the RF communications and you know the different units of power and comparison, you need to understand how to perform the actual calculations and determine whether your RF communication will be successful. It is important to know how to perform the calculations and some of the terms and concepts involved with making sure that the RF link will work properly. These concepts and terms are as follows:

- Rule of 10s and 3s
- Received signal strength indicator (RSSI)
- Fade margin
- System operating margin (SOM)/link budget
- Inverse Square Law

Exam Essentials

Understand the RF components.   Know the function of each of the components and which components add gain and which components add loss.

Understand the units of power and comparison.   Make sure you are very comfortable with the difference between units of power and units of comparison. Know all of the units of power and comparison, what they measure, and how they are used.

Be able to perform RF mathematics.   There will be no logarithms on the test; however, you must know how to use the rule of 10s and 3s. You will need to be able to calculate a result based upon a scenario, power value, or comparative change.

Understand the practical uses of RF mathematics.   When all is said and done, the ultimate question is will the RF communication work. This is where an understanding of RSSI, SOM, fade margin, and link budget is important.

Key Terms

Before you take the exam, be certain you are familiar with the following terms:

6 dB rule	milliwatt
antenna	Newton's Inverse Square Law
dBd	point source
dBi	receive sensitivity
dBm	received signal strength indicator (RSSI)
decibel (dB)	receiver
equivalent isotropically radiated power (EIRP)	rule of 10s and 3s
fade margin	system operating margin (SOM)
gain	transmitter
intentional radiator (IR)	unit of comparison
isotropic radiator	unit of power
link budget	watt
loss	

Review Questions

1. What RF component is responsible for generating the AC signal?

    A. Antenna

    B. Receiver

    C. Transmitter

    D. Transponder

2. A point source that radiates signal equally in all directions is known as what?

    A. Omni-directional signal generator

    B. Omni-directional antenna

    C. Intentional radiator

    D. Nondirectional transmitter

    E. Isotropic radiator

3. A device that intentionally generates and emits radio frequency energy by radiation or induction is known as what?

    A. Isotropic radiator

    B. Intentional radiator

    C. Point source

    D. Signal generator

4. The sum of all the components from the transmitter to the antenna, not including the antenna, is known as what? (Choose two.)

    A. IR

    B. Isotropic radiator

    C. EIRP

    D. Intentional radiator

5. The highest RF signal strength that is transmitted from an antenna is known as what?

    A. Equivalent isotropically radiated power

    B. Transmit sensitivity

    C. Total emitted power

    D. Antenna radiated power

6. Select the units of power. (Choose three.)

   A. Watt

   B. Milliwatt

   C. Decibel

   D. dBm

   E. Bel

7. Select the units of comparison. (Choose four.)

   A. dBm

   B. dBi

   C. Decibel

   D. dBd

   E. Bel

8. 2 dBd is equal to how many dBi?

   A. 5 dBi

   B. 4.41 dBi

   C. 4.14 dBi

   D. The value cannot be calculated.

9. 23 dBm is equal to how many mW?

   A. 200 mW

   B. 14 mW

   C. 20 mW

   D. 23 mW

   E. 400 mW

10. A wireless bridge is configured to transmit at 100 mW. The antenna cable and connectors produce a 3 dB loss and are connected to a 16 dBi antenna. What is the EIRP?

   A. 20 mW

   B. 30 dBm

   C. 2,000 mW

   D. 36 dBm

   E. 8 W

11. RSSI is an abbreviation of what?

   A. Receiver source strength indicator

   B. Received strength signal indication

   C. Received signal status indicator

   D. Received signal strength indicator

12. The minimum sensitivity point of a receiver is known as what?

   A. Receive sensitivity

   B. Minimum reception level

   C. Receive failure level

   D. Minimum receive sensitivity point

13. The amount of RF signal that is received minus the amount of signal required by the receiver is known as what? (Choose two.)

   A. Link budget

   B. RSSI

   C. Receive sensitivity

   D. System operating margin

   E. Fade margin

14. dBi is a measure of what?

   A. The output of the transmitter

   B. The signal increase caused by the antenna

   C. The signal increase caused by the intentional transmitter

   D. The comparison between an isotropic radiator and the transceiver

15. Which of the following are valid calculations when using the rule of 10s and 3s? (Choose all that apply.)

   A. Multiply dBm by 3 and add 2 to mW.

   B. Add 10 to dBm and multiply mW by 10.

   C. Add 3 to dBm and multiply mW by 3.

   D. Subtract 10 from dBm and divide mW by 10.

   E. Divide dBm by 10 and subtract 10 from mW.

16. You are comparing two wireless cards. Card 1 has a receive sensitivity of –75 dBm, and card 2 has a receive sensitivity of –80 dBm. What would typically be true about these cards? (Choose all that apply.)

   A. Card 1 can receive a weaker signal.

   B. Card 2 can receive a weaker signal.

   C. Card 1 is likely to be more reliable.

   D. Card 2 is likely to be more reliable.

17. In a normal wireless bridged network, the greatest loss of signal is caused by what component?

  A. Receive sensitivity

  B. Antenna cable loss

  C. Lightning arrestor

  D. Free space path loss

18. To double the distance of a signal, the EIRP must be increased by how many dBs?

  A. 3 dB

  B. 6 dB

  C. 10 dB

  D. 20 dB

19. To increase the uptime or service level of a wireless link, which value would you want to increase?

  A. System operating gain

  B. Fade margin

  C. Link budget

  D. Free space path loss

20. Which value should not be used to compare wireless network cards manufactured by different companies?

  A. Receive sensitivity

  B. Transmit power range

  C. Antenna dBi

  D. RSSI

Answers to Review Questions

1. C. The transmitter generates the AC signal and modifies it using a modulation technique to encode the data into the signal.

2. E. An isotropic radiator is also known as a point source.

3. B. An intentional radiator is a device that is specifically designed to generate RF signal.

4. A, D. IR is an abbreviation of intentional radiator. It is the sum of power provided to the antenna, not including the antenna.

5. A. Equivalent isotropically radiated power, also known as EIRP, is a measure of the strongest signal that is radiated from an antenna.

6. A, B, D. Decibel and bel are units of comparison.

7. B, C, D, E. dBm is a unit of power.

8. C. To convert any dBd value to dBi, simply add 2.14 to the dBd value.

9. A. To convert to mW, first calculate how many 10s and 3s are needed to add up to 23, which is $0 + 10 + 10 + 3$. To calculate the mW, you must multiply $1 \times 10 \times 10 \times 2$, which calculates to 200 mW.

    Note: The CD has a PowerPoint presentation that also explains this answer.

10. C. To reach 100 mW, you can use 10s and 2s and multiplication and division. Multiplying by two 10s will accomplish this. This means that on the dBm side, you must add two 10s, which equals 20 dBm. Then subtract the 3 dB of cable loss for a dBm of 17. Since you subtracted 3 from the dBm side, you must divide the 100 mW by 2, giving you a value of 50 mW. Now add in the 16 dBi by adding a 10 and two 3s to the dBm column, giving a total dBm of 33. Since you added a 10 and two 3s, you must multiply the mW column by 10 and two 2s, giving a total mW of 2,000, or 2 W.

    Note: The CD has a PowerPoint presentation that also explains this answer.

11. D. The received signal strength indicator (RSSI) is an optional 802.11 parameter designed to be used by the hardware manufacturer as a relative measurement of the RF power that is received.

12. A. The amount of the signal required is the minimum sensitivity point of the receiver, known as the receive sensitivity.

13. A, D. Fade margin is an arbitrary value that is added to the receive sensitivity as padding to help guarantee that the RF communication stays up.

14. B. dBi is the measurement of the signal increase caused by the antenna relative to an isotropic radiator.

15. B, D. The only valid calculations are as follows:

Add 3 to dBm and multiply mW by 2.

Subtract 3 from dBm and divide mW by 2.

Add 10 to dBm and multiply mW by 10.

Subtract 10 from dBm and divide mW by 10.

16. B, D. The numbers are negative, and the card with the lower number can receive a weaker signal, therefore also making it more reliable.

17. D. A distance of as little as 100 meters will cause free space path loss of 80 dB, far greater than any other component.

18. B. An increase of 6 dB will increase the distance of the RF signal by approximately two times.

19. B. The larger the fade margin, the less likely that the link will lose its connection.

20. D. The RSSI should not be used to compare different cards because there is no standard for the range of values or a consistent scale.

Chapter

4

Radio Frequency Signal and Antenna Concepts

IN THIS CHAPTER, YOU WILL LEARN ABOUT THE FOLLOWING:

- ✓ **Active and Passive Gain**
- ✓ **Azimuth and Elevation Chart**
- ✓ **Beamwidth**
- ✓ **Antenna Types**
    - ▪ Omni-directional
    - ▪ Semi-directional
    - ▪ Highly-directional
    - ▪ Phased Array
    - ▪ Sector
- ✓ **Visual Line of Sight**
- ✓ **RF Line of Sight**
- ✓ **Fresnel Zone**
- ✓ **Earth Bulge**
- ✓ **Antenna Polarization**
- ✓ **Antenna Diversity**
- ✓ **Multiple-Input-Multiple-Output (MIMO)**
- ✓ **Antenna Connection and Installation**
    - ▪ Voltage Standing Wave Ratio (VSWR)
    - ▪ Antenna Mounting

✓ **Antenna Accessories**

- Cables
- Connectors
- Splitters
- Amplifiers
- Attenuators
- Lightning Arrestors
- Grounding Rods and Wires

In order to be able to communicate between two or more transceivers, the radio frequency (RF) signal must be radiated from the antenna of the transmitter with enough power so that it is received and understood by the receiver. The installation of antennas has the greatest ability to affect whether the communication is successful or not. Antenna installation can be as simple as placing an access point in the middle of a small office, providing full coverage for your company, or it can be as complex as installing an assortment of directional antennas, kind of like piecing together a jigsaw puzzle. Do not look at this as something to be afraid of; on the contrary, with proper understanding of antennas and how they function, successfully planning for and installing them in a wireless network will become a skillful and rewarding task.

This chapter will focus on the different categories and types of antennas and the different ways that they can direct an RF signal. Choosing and installing antennas is like choosing and installing lighting in a home. When installing home lighting, you have many choices: table lamps, ceiling lighting, narrow or wide beam directional spotlights. In Chapter 3, "Radio Frequency Components, Measurements, and Mathematics," you were introduced to the concept of antennas focusing RF signal. In this chapter, you will learn about the different types of antennas and their radiation patterns and how to use the different antennas in different environments.

You will also learn that even though we often use light to explain RF radiation, there are differences between the way the two behave. You will learn about aiming and aligning antennas, and you will learn that what you see is not necessarily what you will get.

In addition to learning about antennas, you will learn about the accessories that may be needed for proper antenna installation. In office environments you may only need to connect the antenna to the access point, and you are done installing the antenna. In outdoor installations you will need special cable and connectors, lightning arrestors and special mounting brackets. In this chapter, we will introduce you to the components necessary for successfully installing an antenna.

To summarize, in this chapter you will gain the knowledge that will allow you to properly select, install, and align antennas. These skills will help you successfully implement a wireless network, whether it is a point-to-point network between two buildings or a network providing wireless coverage throughout an office building.

Active and Passive Gain

In the previous chapter, you learned that you can increase the signal that is radiated out of the antenna (EIRP) by increasing the output of the transmitter, which in turn increases the amount of power provided to the antenna (Intentional Radiator) and thus the amount of power from the antenna (EIRP). When the power is increased by some type of electrical device, such as the transmitter or—as you will learn later in this chapter—an amplifier, the increase is referred to as *active gain.*

Another method of increasing power that you also learned about in the previous chapter is to direct or focus the power. When power is focused, the amount provided to the antenna does not change. It is the antenna acting like a lens on a flashlight that increases the power output by concentrating the RF signal in a specific direction. Since the gain from the antenna was created by shaping or concentrating the signal, and not by increasing the overall power, this increase is referred to as *passive gain.*

Passive gain is caused by focusing the existing power, while active gain is caused by adding more power.

When trying to decide whether gain is active or passive, determine whether the gain is due to a total increase in power caused by an electronic device (active gain) or whether it is due to the power being focused or directed (passive gain).

Azimuth and Elevation Chart

There are many types of antennas designed for many different purposes, just as there are many types of lights designed for many different purposes. When purchasing lighting for your home, it is easy to compare two lamps by turning them on and looking at the way each disperses the light.

Unfortunately, it is not possible to compare antennas in the same way. Actual side-by-side comparison requires you to walk around the antenna with an RF meter, take numerous signal measurements, and then plot the measurements either on the ground or on a piece of paper that represents the environment. Besides the fact that this is a time-consuming task, the results could be skewed by outside influences on the RF signal, such as furniture or other RF signals in the area. To assist potential buyers with their purchasing decision, antenna manufacturers create *azimuth charts* and *elevation charts*, commonly known as radiation patterns, for their antennas. These radiation patterns are created in controlled environments where the results cannot be skewed by outside influences and represent the signal pattern that is radiated by a particular model of antenna.

Figure 4.1 shows the azimuth and elevation charts of an antenna. The azimuth chart, labeled H-plane, shows the top-down view of the radiation pattern of the antenna. The elevation chart, labeled E-plane, shows the side view of the radiation pattern of the antenna. There is no standard that requires the antenna manufacturers to align the degree marks of the chart with the direction that the antenna is facing, so unfortunately it is up to the reader of the chart to understand and interpret it.

FIGURE 4.1   Azimuth and elevation charts

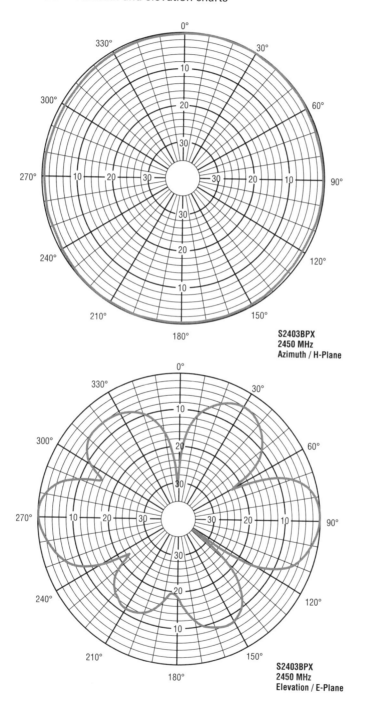

S2403BPX
2450 MHz
Azimuth / H-Plane

S2403BPX
2450 MHz
Elevation / E-Plane

Here are a few statements that will help you interpret the radiation charts:

- In either chart, the antenna is placed at the middle of the chart.
- Azimuth chart = H-plane = top-down view
- Elevation chart = E-plane = side view

The outer ring of the chart usually represents the strongest signal of the antenna. The chart does not represent distance or any level of power or strength. It only represents the relationship of power between different points on the chart.

One way to think of the chart is to consider the way a shadow behaves. If you were to move a flashlight closer or farther from your hand, the shadow of your hand would grow larger or smaller. The size of the shadow does not represent the size of the hand. The shadow only shows the relationship between the hand and the fingers. With an antenna, the radiation pattern will grow larger or smaller depending upon how much power the antenna receives, but the shape and the relationships represented by the patterns will always stay the same.

Beamwidth

Many flashlights have adjustable lenses, allowing the user to widen or tighten the concentration of light that is radiating from them. RF antennas are capable of focusing the power that is radiating from them, but unlike flashlights, antennas are not adjustable. The user must decide how much focus is desired prior to the purchase of the antenna.

Beamwidth is the measurement of how broad or narrow the focus of an antenna is and is measured both horizontally and vertically. It is the measurement from the center, or strongest point, of the antenna signal to each of the points along the horizontal and vertical axes where the signal decreases by half power (–3 dB), as seen in Figure 4.2. These –3 dB points are often referred to as half power points. The distance between the two half power points on the horizontal axis is measured in degrees, giving the horizontal beamwidth measurement. The distance between the two half power points on the vertical axis is also measured in degrees, giving the vertical beamwidth measurement.

It is important to realize that even though the majority of the RF signal that is generated is focused within the beamwidth of the antenna, there is still a significant amount of signal that radiates from outside of the beamwidth and from what is known as the antennas side or rear lobes. As you look at the azimuth charts of different antennas, you will notice that some of these side and rear lobes are fairly significant. Although the signal of these lobes is much less than the signal of the main beamwidth, they are dependable, and in certain implementations very functional. It is important when aligning point-to-point antennas that you make sure they are actually aligned to the main lobe and not a sidelobe.

Table 4.1 shows the different types of antennas that are used in 802.11 communications.

NOTE   Table 4.1 will provide reference information that will be useful as you learn about the antennas in this chapter.

FIGURE 4.2   Antenna beamwidth

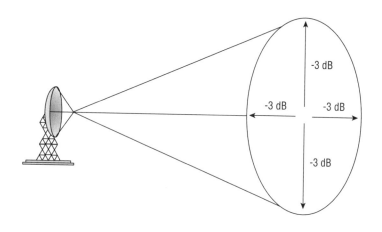

TABLE 4.1   Antenna Beamwidth

Antenna Types	Horizontal Beamwidth (in degrees)	Vertical Beamwidth (in degrees)
Omni-directional	360	7 to 80
Patch/panel	30 to 180	6 to 90
Yagi	30 to 78	14 to 64
Sector	60 to 180	7 to 17
Parabolic dish	4 to 25	4 to 21

Antenna Types

There are three main categories of antennas:

Omni-directional   Omni-directional antennas radiate RF in a fashion similar to the way a table or floor lamp radiates light. They are designed to provide general coverage in all directions.

Semi-directional   Semi-directional antennas radiate RF in a fashion similar to the way a wall sconce is designed to radiate light away from the wall or the way a street lamp is designed to shine light down on a street or a parking lot, providing a directional light across a large area.

Highly-directional   Highly-directional antennas radiate RF in a fashion similar to the way a spotlight is designed to focus light on a flag or a sign. Each type of antenna is designed with a different objective in mind.

It is important to keep in mind that this section is discussing the different types of antennas and not lighting. Although it is very useful to refer to lighting to provide antenna analogies, it is critical to remember that unlike lighting, RF signal can travel through solid objects like walls and floors.

In addition to antennas acting as radiators and focusing signals that are being transmitted, it is often overlooked that they also focus signals that are received. If you were to walk outside and look up at a star, it would appear fairly dim. If you were to look at that same star through binoculars, it would appear brighter. If you were to use a telescope, it would appear even brighter. Antennas function in a similar way. Not only do they amplify signal that is being transmitted, they also amplify signal that is being received. High gain microphones work in the same way, allowing us to not only watch the action of our favorite sport on television, but to also hear the action.

Antennas or Antennae?

Although it's not a matter of critical importance, many are often curious whether the plural of *antenna* is *antennas* or *antennae*. The simple answer is both, but the complete answer is it depends. When *antenna* is used as a biological term, the plural is *antennae*, such as the antennae of a bug. When it is used as an electronics term, the plural is *antennas*, such as the antennas on an access point.

Omni-directional Antennas

Omni-directional antennas radiate RF signal in all directions. The small rubber *dipole antenna*, often referred to as a "rubber duck" antenna, is the classic example of an omni-directional antenna and is the default antenna of most access points. A perfect omni-directional antenna would radiate RF signal like the theoretical isotropic radiator from Chapter 2, "Radio Frequency Fundamentals." The closest thing to an isotropic radiator is the omni-directional dipole antenna.

An easy way to explain the radiation pattern of a typical omni-directional antenna is to hold your index finger straight up (this represents the antenna) and place a bagel on it as if it were a ring (this represents the RF signal). If you were to slice the bagel in half horizontally, as if you were planning to spread butter on it, the cut surface of the bagel would represent the azimuth chart, or H-plane, of the omni-directional antenna. If you took another bagel and sliced it vertically instead, essentially cutting the hole that you are looking through in half, the cut surface of the bagel would now represent the elevation, or E-plane, of the omni-directional antenna.

In Chapter 3, you learned that antennas can focus or direct the signal that they are transmitting. It is important to know that the higher the dBi or dBd value of an antenna, the more focused the signal. When discussing omni-directional antennas, it is not uncommon to initially question how it is possible to focus a signal that is radiated in all directions. With higher-gain omni-directional antennas, the vertical signal is decreased and the horizontal power is increased. Figure 4.3 shows the elevation view of three theoretical antennas. Notice that the signal of the higher-gain antennas is elongated, or more focused horizontally. The horizontal beamwidth of omni-directional antennas is always 360 degrees, and the vertical beamwidth ranges from 7 to 80 degrees, depending upon the particular antenna.

Because of the narrower vertical coverage of the higher-gain omni-directional antennas, it is important to carefully plan how they are used. Placing one of these higher-gain antennas on the first floor of a building may provide good coverage to the first floor, but because of the narrow vertical coverage, the second and third floors may receive minimal signal. In some installations you may want this; in others you may not. Indoor installations typically use low-gain omni-directional antennas with gain of about 2.14 dBi.

Antennas are most effective when the length of the element is an even fraction (such as $1/4$ or $1/2$) or a multiple of the wavelength (λ). A 2.4 GHz half-wave dipole antenna (see Figure 4.4) consists of two elements, each $1/4\lambda$ in length (about 1 inch), running in the opposite direction from each other. Although this drawing of a dipole is placed horizontally, the antenna is always placed in a vertical orientation. Higher-gain omni-directional antennas are typically constructed by stacking multiple dipole antennas on top of each other and are known as *collinear antennas*.

FIGURE 4.3 Vertical radiation patterns of omni-directional antennas

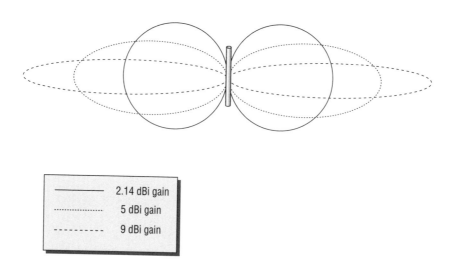

————————	2.14 dBi gain
··················	5 dBi gain
- - - - - - - -	9 dBi gain

FIGURE 4.4   Half-wave dipole antenna

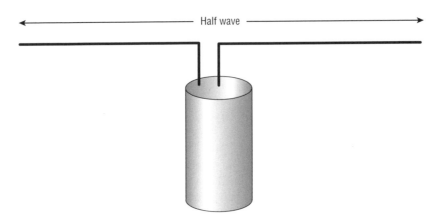

Omni-directional antennas are typically used in point-to-multipoint environments. The omni-directional antenna is connected to a device (such as an access point) that is placed at the center of a group of client devices, providing central communications capabilities to the surrounding clients. High-gain omni-directional antennas can also be used outdoors to connect multiple buildings together in a point-to-multipoint configuration. A central building would have an omni-directional antenna on its roof, and the surrounding buildings would have directional antennas aimed at the central building. In this configuration, it is important to make sure that the gain of the omni-directional antenna is high enough to provide the coverage necessary but not so high that the vertical beamwidth is too narrow to provide an adequate signal to the surrounding buildings. Figure 4.5 shows an installation where the gain is too high. The building to the left will be able to communicate, but the building on the right is likely to have problems.

FIGURE 4.5   Improperly installed omni-directional antenna

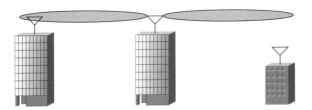

Semi-directional Antennas

Unlike omni-directional antennas that radiate RF signals in all directions, semi-directional antennas are designed to direct a signal in a specific direction. Semi-directional antennas are used for short- to medium-distance communications, with long-distance communications being served by highly-directional antennas.

It is common to use semi-directional antennas to provide a network bridge between two buildings in a campus environment or down the street from each other. Longer distances would be served by highly-directional antennas.

There are three types of antennas that fit into the semi-directional category:

- *Patch*

- *Panel*

- *Yagi* (pronounced "YAH-gee")

Patch and panel antennas, as seen in Figure 4.6, are more accurately classified or referred to as planar antennas. *Patch* refers to a particular way of designing the radiating elements inside the antenna. Unfortunately, it has become common practice to use the terms *patch* and *panel* interchangeably. If you are unsure of the antenna's specific design, it is better to refer to it as a planar antenna. These antennas can be used for outdoor point-to-point communications up to about a mile but are more commonly used as a central device for indoor point-to-multipoint communications. It is common for patch or panel antennas to be connected to access points to provide directional coverage within a building. Planar antennas can be used effectively in libraries, warehouses, and retail stores with long aisles of shelves. Due to the tall, long shelves, omni-directional antennas often have difficulty providing RF coverage effectively. In contrast, planar antennas can be placed high on the side walls of the building, aiming through the rows of shelves. The antennas can be alternated between rows with every other antenna being placed on the opposite wall. Since planar antennas have a horizontal beamwidth of 180 degrees or less, a minimal amount of signal will radiate outside of the building. With the antenna placement alternated and aimed from opposite sides of the building, the RF signal is more likely to radiate down the rows, providing the necessary coverage.

Planar antennas are also often used to provide coverage for long hallways with offices on each side or hospital corridors with patient rooms on each side. A planar antenna can be placed at the end of the hall and aimed down the corridor. A single planar antenna can provide RF signal to some or all of the corridor and the rooms on each side and some coverage to the floors above and below. How much coverage will depend upon the power of the transmitter, the gain and beamwidth (both horizontal and vertical) of the antenna, and the attenuation properties of the building.

Using semi-directional antennas indoors often reduces reflections, thus minimizing some of the negative effects of multipath such as data corruption.

Yagi antennas, as seen in Figure 4.7, are not as unusual as they sound. The traditional television antenna that is attached to the roof of a house or apartment is a yagi antenna. The television antenna looks quite different because it is designed to receive signals of many different frequencies (different channels) and the length of the elements vary according to the wavelength of the different frequencies. A yagi antenna that is used for 802.11 communications is designed to support a very narrow range of frequencies, so the elements are all about the same length. Yagi antennas are commonly used for short- to medium-distance point-to-point communications of up to about 2 miles, although high-gain yagi antennas can be used for longer distances.

Another benefit of semi-directional antennas is that they can be installed high on a wall and tilted downward toward the area to be covered. This cannot be done with an omni-directional antenna without causing the signal on the other side of the antenna to be tilted upward. Since the only RF signal that radiates from the back of a semi-directional antenna is incidental, the ability to aim it vertically is an additional benefit. Figure 4.8 shows the radiation patterns of a typical semi-directional panel antenna that was discussed in this section. Remember that these are actual azimuth and elevation charts from a specific antenna and that every manufacturer and model of antenna will have a slightly different radiation pattern.

FIGURE 4.6 The exterior of a patch antenna and the internal antenna element

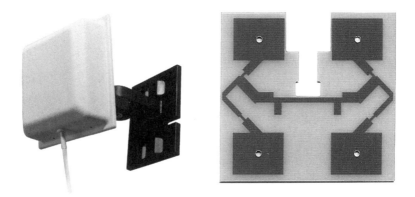

FIGURE 4.7 The exterior of a yagi antenna and the internal antenna element

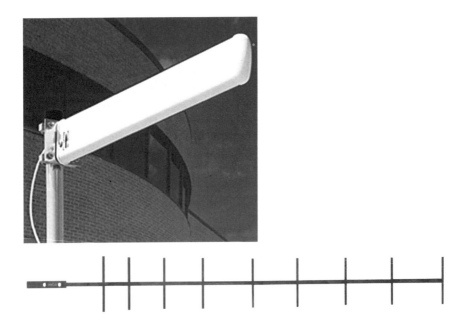

FIGURE 4.8   Radiation pattern of a typical semi-directional panel antenna

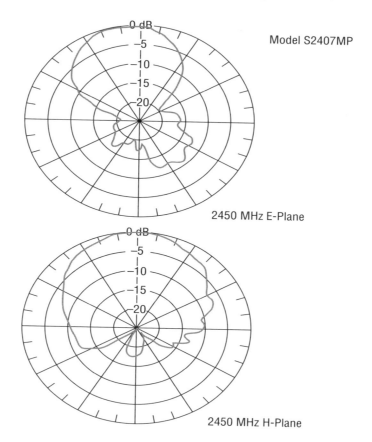

Model S2407MP

2450 MHz E-Plane

2450 MHz H-Plane

Highly-directional Antennas

Highly-directional antennas are strictly used for point-to-point communications, typically to provide network bridging between two buildings. They provide the most focused, narrow beamwidth of any of the antenna types. There are two types of highly-directional antennas: *parabolic dish* and *grid* antennas. The parabolic dish antenna is similar in appearance to the small digital satellite TV antennas that can be seen on the roofs of many houses. The grid antenna resembles the rectangular grill of a barbecue, with the edges slightly curved inward. The spacing of the wires on a grid antenna is determined by the wavelength of the frequencies that the antenna is designed for. Because of the high gain of highly-directional antennas, they are ideal for long-distance communications as far as 35 miles (58 km). Due to the long distances and narrow beamwidth, highly-directional antennas are affected more by antenna wind loading, which is antenna movement or shifting caused by wind. Even slight movement of a highly-directional antenna can cause the RF beam to be aimed away from the receiving antenna, interrupting the communications. In high-wind environments, grid antennas, due to the spacing between the wires, are less susceptible to wind load and may be a better choice. Another option in high-wind environments is to choose an antenna with a wider beamwidth. In this situation, if the antenna were to shift slightly, due to its wider coverage area, the signal would still be received. No matter which type of antenna is installed, the quality of the mount and antenna will have a huge effect in reducing wind load.

Phased Array

A *phased array antenna* is actually an antenna system and is made up of multiple antennas that are connected to a signal processor. The processor feeds the individual antennas with signals of different relative phases, creating a directed beam of RF signal aimed at the client device. Because it is capable of creating narrow beams, it is also able to transmit multiple beams to multiple users simultaneously. Phased array antennas do not behave like other antennas since they can transmit multiple signals at the same time. Because of this unique capability, they are often regulated differently by the local RF regulatory agency.

Phased array antennas are extremely specialized, expensive, and not commonly used in the 802.11 market. In fact, the leading manufacturer of 802.11 phase array antenna systems recently went out of business. It is an interesting and very capable technology; however, time will tell whether it has a future in the 802.11 market.

Sector Antennas

Sector antennas are a special type of high-gain, semi-directional antennas that provide a pie-shaped coverage pattern. These antennas are typically installed in the middle of the area where RF coverage is desired and placed back to back with other sector antennas. Individually, each antenna services its own piece of the pie, but as a group, all of the pie pieces fit together and provide omni-directional coverage for the entire area.

Unlike other semi-directional antennas, a sector antenna generates very little RF signal behind the antenna (*back lobe*) and therefore does not interfere with the other sector antennas that it is working with. The horizontal beamwidth of a sector antenna is from 60 to 180 degrees, with a narrow vertical beamwidth of from 7 to 17 degrees. Sector antennas typically have a gain of at least 10 dBi.

Installing a group of sector antennas to provide omni-directional coverage for an area provides many benefits over installing a single omni-directional antenna. To begin with, sector antennas can be mounted high over the terrain and tilted slightly downward, with the tilt of each antenna at an angle appropriate for the terrain it is covering. Omni-directional antennas can also be mounted high over the terrain; however, if an omni-directional antenna is tilted downward on one side, the other side will be tilted upward.

Since each antenna covers a separate area, each antenna can be connected to a separate transceiver and can transmit and receive independently of the other antennas. This would provide the capability for all of the antennas to be transmitting at the same time, providing much greater throughput. A single omni-directional antenna would be capable of transmitting to only one device at a time. The last benefit of the sector antennas over a single omni-directional antenna is that the gain of the sector antennas is much greater than the gain of the omni-directional antenna, providing a much larger coverage area.

Sector antennas are used extensively for cellular telephone communications and are starting to be used for 802.11 networking.

 Real World Scenario

Cellular Sector Antennas Are Everywhere

As you walk or drive around your town or city, look for radio communications towers that are around your neighborhood. Many of these towers have what appear to be rings of antennas around them. These rings of antennas are sector antennas. If a tower has more than one grouping or ring around it, then there are multiple cellular carriers using the same tower.

Visual Line of Sight

When light travels from one point to another, it travels across what is perceived to be an unobstructed straight line, known as visual *line of sight (LOS)*. For all intents and purposes, it is a straight line, but due to the possibility of light refraction, diffraction, and reflection, there is a slight chance that it is not. If you have been outside on a summer day and looked across a hot parking lot at a stationary object, you may have noticed that because of the heat rising from the pavement, the object that you were looking at seemed to be moving. This is an example of how visual LOS is sometimes altered slightly. When it comes to RF communications, visual LOS has no bearing on whether the RF transmission is successful or not.

RF Line of Sight

Point-to-point RF communication also needs to have an unobstructed line of sight between the two antennas. So the first step for installing a point-to-point system is to make sure that from the installation point of one of the antennas, you can see the other antenna. Unfortunately, for RF communications to work properly, this is not sufficient. An additional area around the visual LOS needs to remain clear of obstacles and obstructions. This area around the visual LOS is known as the Fresnel zone and is often referred to as RF line of sight.

Fresnel Zone

The *Fresnel zone* (pronounced "FRUH-nel"; the *s* is silent) is an imaginary football-shaped area (American football) that surrounds the path of the visual LOS between two point-to-point antennas. Figure 4.9 shows an illustration of the Fresnel zone's football-like shape.

Theoretically, there are an infinite number of Fresnel zone's, or concentric ellipsoids (the football shape), that surround the visual LOS. The closest ellipsoid is known as the first Fresnel zone, the next one is the second Fresnel zone, and so on, as seen in Figure 4.9. For simplicity's sake, and since they are the most relevant for this section, only the first two Fresnel zones are displayed in the figure. The subsequent Fresnel zones have very little effect on the communications.

If the first Fresnel zone becomes even partly obstructed, the obstruction will negatively influence the integrity of the RF communication. In addition to the obvious reflection and scattering that can occur if there are obstructions between the two antennas, the RF signal can be diffracted or bent as it passes an obstruction of the Fresnel zone. This diffraction of the signal decreases the amount of RF energy that is received by the antenna and may even cause the communications link to fail.

Figure 4.10 illustrates a link that is 1 mile long. The top solid line is a straight line from the center of one antenna to the other. The dotted line shows 60 percent of the bottom half of the Fresnel zone. The bottom solid line shows the bottom half of the first Fresnel zone. The trees are potential obstructions along the path.

Under no circumstances should you allow an object or objects to encroach more than 40 percent into the Fresnel zone of an outdoor point-to-point bridge link. Anything more than 40 percent is likely to make the communications link unreliable. Even less than 40 percent obstruction is likely to impair the performance of the link. Therefore, it is recommended that you try not to allow more than 20 percent obstruction of the Fresnel zone, particularly in wooded areas where the growth of trees may obstruct the Fresnel zone further in the future.

The typical obstacles that you are likely to encounter are trees and buildings. It is important to periodically visually check your link to make sure that trees have not grown into the Fresnel zone or that buildings have not been constructed that encroach into the Fresnel zone. Do not forget that the Fresnel zone exists below, to the sides, and above the visual LOS. If the Fresnel zone does become obstructed, you will need to either move the antenna (usually raise it) or remove the obstacle (usually with a chain saw—just kidding).

To determine if an obstacle is encroaching into the Fresnel, you will need to learn a few formulas that will allow you to calculate its radius. Do not fret; you will not be tested on these formulas.

The first formula will allow you to calculate the radius of the first Fresnel zone at the midpoint between the two antennas. This is the point where the Fresnel zone is the largest. This formula is as follows:

$$\text{radius} = 72.2 \times \sqrt{(D \div (4 \times F))}$$

D = distance of the link in miles

F = transmitting frequency in GHz

This is the optimal clearance that you want along the signal path. Although this is the ideal radius, it is not always feasible or practical. Therefore, the next formula will be very useful. It can be used to calculate the radius of the Fresnel zone that will allow you to have 60 percent of the Fresnel zone unobstructed. This is the minimum amount of clearance you need at the midpoint between the antennas. Here is this formula:

radius (60%) = $43.3 \times \sqrt{(D \div (4 \times F))}$

D = distance of the link in miles

F = transmitting frequency in GHz

FIGURE 4.9   Fresnel zone

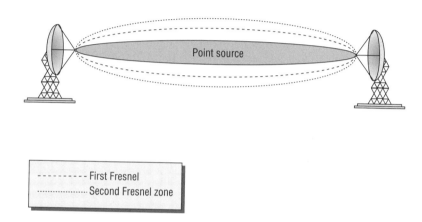

Point source

- - - - - - - - - First Fresnel

· · · · · · · · · · · Second Fresnel zone

FIGURE 4.10   60 percent and 100 percent Fresnel zone clearances

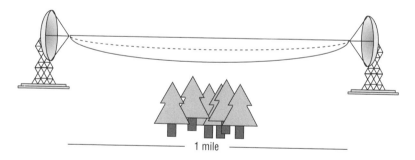

1 mile

Both of these formulas are very useful, but they have major benefits and shortcomings. These formulas calculate the radius of the Fresnel zone at the midpoint between the antennas. Since this is the point where the Fresnel zone is the largest, these numbers can be used to determine the minimum height the antennas need to be above the ground. Without knowing this number, if you place the antennas too low, the ground would be encroaching on the Fresnel zone and cause degradation to the communications. The problem with these formulas is that if there is a known object somewhere other than the midpoint between the antennas, it is not possible to calculate the radius of the Fresnel zone at that point. The following formula can be used for this purpose. It can be used to calculate the radius of any Fresnel zone at any point between the two antennas:

radius $= 72.2 \times \sqrt{((N \times d1 \times d2) \div (F \times D))}$

N = which Fresnel Zone you are calculating (usually 1 or 2)

d1 = distance from one antenna to the location of the obstacle in miles

d2 = distance from the obstacle to the other antenna in miles

D = total distance between the antennas in miles (D = d1 + d2)

F = frequency in GHz

To look at an example, Figure 4.11 shows a point-to-point communications link that is 10 miles long. There is an obstacle that is 3 miles away and 40 feet tall. So the values and the formula to calculate the radius of the Fresnel zone at a point 3 miles from the antenna are as follows:

N = 1 (for first Fresnel zone)

d1 = 3 miles

d2 = 7 miles

D = 10 miles

F = 2.4 GHz

radius at 3 miles $= 72.2 \times \sqrt{((1 \times 3 \times 7) \div (2.4 \times 10))}$

radius at 3 miles $= 72.2 \times \sqrt{((21 \div 24))}$

radius at 3 miles = 67.53 feet

So if the obstacle is 40 feet tall and the Fresnel zone at that point is 67.53 feet tall, then the antennas will need to be mounted at least 108 feet (40' + 67.53' = 107.53', we rounded up) above the ground to have complete clearance. If we are willing to allow the obstruction to encroach up to 40 percent into the Fresnel zone, we need to keep 60 percent of the Fresnel zone clear. So 60 percent of 67.53 feet is 40.52 feet. The absolute minimum height of the antennas will need to be 81 feet (40' + 40.52' = 80.52', we again rounded up). In the next section, you will learn that due to the curvature of the earth, you will actually need to raise the antennas even higher to compensate for the earth's bulge.

FIGURE 4.11 · Point-to-point communication with potential obstacle

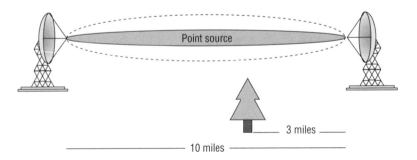

When highly-directional antennas are used, the beamwidth of the signal is smaller, causing a more focused signal to be transmitted. Many people think that a smaller beamwidth would decrease the size of the Fresnel zone. This is not the case. The size of the Fresnel zone is a function of the frequency being used and the distance of the link. Since the only variables in the formula are frequency and distance, the size of the Fresnel zone will be the same regardless of the antenna type or beamwidth. The first Fresnel zone is technically the area around the point source, where the waves are in phase with the point source signal. The second Fresnel zone is then the area beyond the first Fresnel zone, where the waves are out of phase with the point source signal. All of the odd-numbered Fresnel zones are in phase with the point source signal, and all of the even-numbered Fresnel zones are out of phase.

If an RF signal of the same frequency but out of phase with the primary signal intersects the primary signal, the out-of-phase signal will cause degradation or even cancellation of the primary signal (this was covered in Chapter 2 and demonstrated using the EMANIM software). One of the ways that an out-of-phase signal can intercept the primary signal is by reflection. It is therefore important to consider the second Fresnel zone when evaluating point-to-point communications. If the height of the antennas and the layout of the geography are such that the RF signal from the second Fresnel zone is reflected toward the receiving antenna, it can cause degradation of the link. Although this is not a common occurrence, the second Fresnel zone should be considered when planning or troubleshooting the connection, especially in flat, arid terrain like a desert.

Please understand that the Fresnel zone is three-dimensional. Can something impede upon the Fresnel zone from above? Although trees do not grow from the sky, a point-to-point bridge link could be shot under a railroad trestle or a freeway. In these rare situations, consideration would have to be given to proper clearance of the upper radius of the first Fresnel zone. A more common scenario would be the deployment of point-to-point links in an urban city environment. Very often building-to-building links must be shot between other buildings. In these situations, other buildings have the potential of impeding the side radiuses of the Fresnel zone. Until now, all of the discussion about the Fresnel zone has related to point-to-point communications. The Fresnel zone exists in all RF communications; however, it is in outdoor point-to-point communications where it can be most detrimental. Indoor environments have so many walls and other obstacles where there is already so much reflection, refraction, diffraction, and scattering that the Fresnel zone does not play a very big part in the success or failure of the link.

Earth Bulge

When you are installing long distance point-to-point RF communications, another variable that must be considered is the curvature of the earth, also known as the *earth bulge*. Since the landscape varies throughout the world, it is impossible to specify an exact distance for when the curvature of the earth will affect a communications link. The recommendation is that if the antennas are more than seven miles away from each other, you should take into consideration the earth bulge, since after seven miles, the earth itself begins to impede upon the Fresnel zone.

The following formula can be used to calculate the additional height that the antennas will need to be raised to compensate for the earth bulge:

$H = D^2 ÷ 8$

H = height of the earth bulge in feet

D = distance between the antennas in miles

You now have all of the pieces to estimate how high the antennas need to be installed. Remember, this is an estimate that is being calculated since it is assumed that the terrain between the two antennas does not vary. You need to know or calculate the following three things:

- The 60 percent radius of the first Fresnel zone

- The height of the earth bulge

- The height of any obstacles that may encroach into the Fresnel zone, and the distance of those obstacles from the antenna

Taking these three pieces and adding them together gives you the following formula, which can be used to calculate the antenna height:

H = obstacle height + earth bulge + Fresnel zone

$H = OB + (D^2 ÷ 8) + (43.3 \times \sqrt{(D ÷ (4 \times f))})$

OB = obstacle height

D = distance of the link in miles

F = transmitting frequency in GHz

As an example, Figure 4.12 shows a point-to-point link that spans a distance of 12 miles. In the middle of this link is an office building that is 30 feet tall. A 2.4 GHz signal is being used to communicate between the two towers. Using the formula, we calculate that each of the antennas needs to be installed at least 96.4 feet above the ground.

$H = 30 + (12^2 ÷ 8) + (43.3 \times \sqrt{(12 ÷ (4 \times 2.4))})$

$H = 30 + 18 + 48.4$

$H = 96.4$

FIGURE 4.12 Calculating antenna height

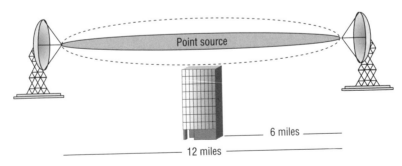

Antenna Polarization

Another consideration when installing antennas is *antenna polarization*. Although it is a lesser-known concern, it is extremely important for successful communications. Proper polarization alignment is vital when installing any type of antennas. Whether the antennas are installed with horizontal or vertical polarization is irrelevant, as long as both antennas are aligned with the same polarization. Polarization is not as important for indoor communications because the polarization of the RF signal often changes when it is reflected, which is a common occurrence indoors. Most access points use low-gain omni-directional antennas and they should be polarized vertically when mounted from the ceiling. Laptop manufacturers build diversity antennas into the sides of the monitor. When the laptop monitor is in the upright position, the internal antennas are vertically polarized as well.

On the CD that is included with this book is an excellent video, *Beam Patterns and Polarization of Directional Antennas*. This three-minute video explains and demonstrates the effects of antenna sidelobes and polarization. The filename of the video is `Antenna Properties.wmv`.

Antenna Diversity

Wireless networks, especially indoor networks, are prone to multipath signals. To help compensate for the effects of multipath, antenna diversity, also called space diversity, is commonly implemented in wireless networking equipment such as access points (APs). *Antenna diversity* is when an access point has two antennas and receivers functioning together to minimize the negative effects of multipath. Figure 4.13 shows a picture of an access point that uses antenna diversity. Since the wavelengths of 802.11 wireless networks are less than 5 inches long, the antennas can be placed very near each other and be effective. When the access point senses an RF signal, it compares the signal that it is receiving on both antennas and uses whichever antenna has the higher signal strength to receive the frame of data. This sampling is performed on a frame-by-frame basis, choosing whichever antenna has the higher signal strength.

Note that when an access point has two antenna ports for antenna diversity, the antennas should be installed in the same location. You should not be running antenna cables to antennas in opposite directions to provide better coverage.

Since the antennas are so close to each other, it is not uncommon to doubt that antenna diversity is actually beneficial. If you recall from Chapter 3, the amount of RF signal that is received is often less than .000001 milliwatts. At this level of signal, the slightest difference between the signals that each antenna receives can be significant. Other factors to remember are that the access point is often communicating with multiple client devices at different locations. These clients are not always stationary, thus further affecting the path of the RF signal.

The access point has to handle transmitting data differently than receiving data. When the access point needs to transmit data back to the client, it has no way of determining which antenna the client would receive from the best. The way the access point can handle transmitting data is to transmit using the antenna that it used most recently to receive data. This is often referred to as transmission diversity. Not all access points are equipped with this capability.

There are many different kinds of antenna diversity. The most common implementation of antenna diversity utilizes one radio card, two connectors, and two antennas. The question often gets asked why client cards seem to have only one antenna. In reality, PCMCIA client cards typically have two diversity antennas encased inside the card. Laptops with internal cards have diversity antennas mounted inside the laptop monitor. Remember that due to the half-duplex nature of the RF medium, when antenna diversity is used, only one antenna is operational at any given time. In other words, a radio card transmitting a frame with one antenna cannot be receiving a frame with the other antenna at the same time.

FIGURE 4.13   Access point with antenna diversity

Multiple Input Multiple Output (MIMO)

Multiple input multiple output (MIMO, pronounced "MY-moh") is another, more sophisticated form of antenna diversity. Unlike conventional antenna systems, where multipath propagation is an impairment, MIMO systems take advantage of multipath. There is much research and development currently happening with this technology and thus much disagreement about MIMO. There currently are no official or de facto standards for the technology. MIMO can safely be described as any RF communications system that has multiple antennas at both ends of the communications link being used concurrently. How the antennas are to be used has not yet been standardized. There are multiple vendors providing different current and proposed solutions. Complex signal processing techniques known as Space Time Coding (STC) are often associated with MIMO. These techniques send data using multiple simultaneous RF signals and the receiver then reconstructs the data from those signals. The proposed 802.11n standard will include MIMO technology.

Antenna Connection and Installation

In addition to the physical antenna being a critical component in the wireless network, the installation and connection of the antenna to the wireless transceiver is critical. If the antenna is not properly connected and installed, any benefit that the antenna introduces to the network can be instantly wiped out. Three key components associated with the proper installation of the antenna are voltage standing wave ratio (VSWR), return loss, and the actual mounting of the antenna.

Voltage Standing Wave Ratio (VSWR)

Voltage standing wave ratio (VSWR) is a measurement of the change in impedances to an AC signal. Voltage standing waves exist due to impedance mismatches or variations between devices in an RF communications system. Impedance is a value of ohms of electrical resistance to an AC signal. A standard unit of measurement of electrical resistance is the ohm, named after German physicist Georg Ohm. When the transmitter generates the AC radio signal, the signal travels along the cable to the antenna. Some of this incident (or forward) energy is reflected back toward the transmitter because of impedance mismatch.

Mismatches may occur anywhere but are usually due to abrupt impedance changes between the radio transmitter and cable and between the cable and the antenna. The amount of energy reflected depends on the level of mismatch between the transmitter, cable, and antenna. The ratio between the voltage of the reflected wave and the voltage of the incident wave, *at the same point along the cable,* is called the voltage reflection coefficient, usually designated by the Greek letter ρ (rho). When this quantity is expressed in dB, it is called return loss. So in an ideal system, where there are no mismatches (the impedance is the same everywhere), all of the incident energy will be delivered to the antenna (except for resistive losses in the cable) and there will be no reflected energy. The cable is said to be *matched*, and the voltage reflection coefficient is exactly zero and the return loss, in dB, is infinite. The combination of incident and reflected waves traveling back and forth along the cable creates a resulting *standing wave* pattern along the length of the line. The standing wave pattern is periodic (it repeats) and exhibits multiple peaks and troughs of voltage, current, and power.

VSWR is a numerical relationship between the measurement of the maximum voltage along the line (what is generated by the transmitter) and the measurement of the minimum voltage along the line (what is received by the antenna). VSWR is therefore a ratio of impedance mismatch, with 1:1 (no impedance) being optimal but unobtainable and typical values from 1.1:1 to as much as 1.5:1. VSWR military specs are 1.1:1.

$$\text{VSWR} = V_{max} \div V_{min}$$

When the transmitter, cable, and antenna impedances are matched (i.e., there are no standing waves), the voltage along the cable will be constant. This matched cable is also referred to as a *flat* line since there are no peaks and troughs of voltage along the length of the cable. In this case, VSWR is 1:1. As the degree of mismatch increases, the VSWR increases with a corresponding decrease in the power delivered to the antenna. Table 4.2 shows this effect.

If VSWR is large, this means that there is a large amount of voltage that is being reflected back toward the transmitter. This of course means a decrease in power or amplitude (loss) of the signal that is supposed to be transmitted. This loss of forward amplitude is known as return loss and can be measured in dB. Additionally, the power that is being reflected back is then directed back into the transmitter. If the transmitter is not protected from excessive reflected power or large voltage peaks, it can overheat and fail. Understand that VSWR may cause decreased signal strength, erratic signal strength, or even transmitter failure.

The first thing that can be done to minimize VSWR is to make sure that the impedance of all of the wireless networking equipment is matched. Most wireless networking equipment has an impedance of 50 ohms; however, you should check the manuals to confirm this. When attaching the different components, make sure that all connectors are installed and crimped properly and that they are snugly tightened.

TABLE 4.2   Signal loss caused by VSWR

VSWR	Radiated Power	Lost Power	dB power loss
1:1	100%	0%	0 dB
1.5:1	96%	4%	Nearly 0 dB
2:1	89%	11%	< 1 dB
6:1	50%	50%	3 dB

Antenna Mounting

As was stated earlier in this chapter, proper installation of the antenna is one of the most important tasks to ensure an optimally functioning network. The following are key areas to be concerned with when installing antennas:

- Placement
- Mounting
- Appropriate use
- Orientation
- Alignment
- Safety
- Maintenance

Placement

The proper placement of an antenna is dependent upon the type of antenna. When installing omni-directional antennas, it is important to place the antenna at the center of the area where you want coverage. Remember that lower-gain omni-directional antennas provide broader vertical coverage while higher-gain omni-directional antennas provide a wider but much flatter coverage. Be careful not to place high-gain omni-directional antennas too high above the ground because the narrow vertical coverage may cause the antenna to provide insufficient signal to clients located on the ground.

When installing directional antennas, make sure that you know both the horizontal and vertical beamwidths so that you can properly aim the antennas. Also make sure that you are aware of the amount of gain that the antenna is adding to the transmission. If the signal is too strong, it will overshoot the area that you are looking to provide coverage to. This is a security risk, and you should decrease the amount of power that the transceiver is generating to reduce the coverage area. Not only is it a security risk, overshooting your coverage area is considered rude.

If you are installing an outdoor directional antenna, in addition to concerns regarding the horizontal and vertical beamwidths, make sure that you have correctly calculated the Fresnel zone and mounted the antenna accordingly.

Mounting

After deciding where to place the antenna, the next step is to decide how to mount it. Many antennas, especially outdoor antennas, are mounted on masts or towers. It is common to use mounting clamps and U-bolts to attach the antennas to the masts. For mounting directional antennas, specially designed tilt-and-swivel mounting kits are available to make it easier to aim and secure the antenna. If the antenna is being installed in a windy location (what rooftop or tower isn't windy?), make sure that you take into consideration wind load and that you properly secure the antenna.

There are numerous ways of mounting antennas indoors. Two common concerns are aesthetics and security. Many organizations, particularly ones that provide hospitality-oriented services such as hotels and hospitals, are concerned about the aesthetics of the installation of the antennas. Specialty enclosures and ceiling tiles can help to hide the installation of the access points and antennas. Other organizations, particularly schools and public environments, are concerned with securing the access points and antennas from theft or vandalism. An access point can be locked in a secure enclosure, with a short cable connecting it to the antenna. There are even ceiling tiles with antennas built into them, invisible to anyone walking by. If security is a concern, mounting the antenna high on the wall or ceiling can also minimize unauthorized access.

Appropriate Use

Make sure that indoor antennas are not used for outdoor communications. Outdoor antennas are specifically built to withstand a wide range of temperatures that they may be exposed to. Outdoor antennas are also built to stand up to other elements, such as rain, snow, and fog. In addition to installing the proper antenna, make sure that the mounts that you use are designed for the environment in which you are installing them.

Alignment

Before installing an antenna, make sure you read the manufacturer's recommendations for mounting it. This suggestion is particularly important when installing directional antennas. Since directional antennas may have different horizontal and vertical beamwidths, and since directional antennas can be installed with different polarization, proper alignment can make the difference between being able to communicate or not.

The first step is to make sure you have decided on a polarization. Next, decide on the mounting technique and ensure that it is compatible with the mounting location. Then the antennas can be aligned. Once that occurs, the cables and connectors can be weatherproofed and secured from movement.

Safety

We can't emphasize enough the importance of being careful when installing antennas. Most of the time, the installation of an antenna involves climbing ladders, towers, or rooftops. Gravity and wind have a way of making an installation difficult for both the climber and the people below helping.

Plan the installation before you begin, making sure you have all of the tools and equipment that you will need to install the antenna. Unplanned stoppages of the installation and relaying forgotten equipment up and down the ladder add to the risk of injury.

Be careful when working with your antenna or near other antennas. Highly-directional antennas are focusing high concentrations of RF energy. This large amount of energy can be dangerous to your health. Do not power on your antenna while you are working on it, and do not stand in front of other antennas that are near where you are installing your antenna.

When installing antennas (or any device) on ceilings, rafters, or masts, make sure they are properly secured. Even a 1-pound antenna can be deadly if it falls from the rafters of a warehouse.

If you will be installing antennas as part of your job, we recommend that you take an RF health and safety course. These courses will teach you the FCC and the U.S. Department of Labor Occupational Safety and Health Administration (OSHA) regulations and how to be safe and compliant with the standards.

If you need an antenna installed on any elevated structure, such as a pole, tower, or even a roof, consider hiring a professional installer. Professional climbers and installers are trained and in some places certified to perform these types of installations. In addition to the training, they have the necessary safety equipment and proper insurance for the job.

If you are planning to install wireless equipment as a profession, you should develop a safety policy that is blessed by your local occupational safety representative. You should also receive certified training on climbing safety in addition to RF safety training. First aid and CPR training is also highly recommended.

Maintenance

There are two types of maintenance: preventative and diagnostic. When installing an antenna, it is important to prevent problems from occurring in the future. This seems like simple advice, but since antennas are often difficult to get to after they have been installed, it is especially prudent advice. Two key problems that can be minimized with proper preventative measures are wind damage and water damage. When installing the antenna, make sure all of the nuts, bolts, screws, and so on are tightened. Also make sure all of the cables are properly secured so that they are not thrashed about in the wind.

To help prevent water damage, cold shrink tubing or coaxial sealant can be used to minimize the risk of water getting into the cable or connectors.

WARNING   Heat shrink tubing should not be used because the cable can be damaged by the heat that is necessary to shrink the wrapping. Silicone should also not be used as air bubbles can form under the silicone and moisture can collect.

Another cabling technique is the drip loop. A drip loop prevents water from flowing down the cable and onto a connector or into the hole where a cable exits the building. Any water that is flowing down the cable will continue to the bottom of the loop and then drip off.

Antennas are typically installed and forgotten about until they break. It is advisable to periodically perform a visual inspection of the antenna. If the antenna is not easily accessible, a pair of binoculars or a camera with a very high zoom lens can make this a simple task.

Antenna Accessories

In Chapter 3, the components of RF communications were introduced. In that chapter, the main components were reviewed; however, there are other components that are either not as significant or not always installed as part of the communications link. Important specifications for all antenna accessories include frequency response, impedance, VSWR, maximum input power, and insertion loss. This section will discuss some of these components and accessories.

Cables

Improper installation or selection of cables can detrimentally affect the RF communications more than just about any other component or outside influence. It is important to remember this when installing antenna cables. The following list addresses some concerns when selecting and installing cables:

- Make sure you select the correct cable. The impedance of the cable needs to match the impedance of the antenna and transceiver. If there is an impedance mismatch, the return loss from VSWR will affect the link.

- Make sure the cable you select will support the frequencies that you will be using. Typically, cable manufacturers will list cutoff frequencies, which are the lowest and highest frequencies that the cable supports. This is often referred to as frequency response. For instance, LMR 1200 will not work with 5 GHz transmissions. LMR 900 is the highest you can use. However, you can use LMR 1200 for 2.4 GHz operations.

- Cables introduce signal loss into the communications link. To determine how much loss, cable vendors provide charts or calculators to assist you. Figure 4.14 is an attenuation chart for a type of cable produced by Times Microwave Systems. LMR cable is a popular brand of coaxial cable used in RF communications. The left side of the chart lists different types of LMR cable. The farther you move down the list, the better the cable is. The better cable is typically thicker, stiffer, more difficult to work with, and of course, more expensive. The chart shows how much decibel loss the cable will add to the communications link. The column headers list the frequencies that may be used with the cable. For example, 100 feet of LMR-400 cable used on a 2.5 GHz network (2,500 MHz) would decrease the signal by 6 dB.

- Attenuation increases with frequency. If you convert from 802.11b to 802.11a, the loss caused by the cable will be greater.

- Either purchase the cables precut and preinstalled with the connectors or hire a professional cabler to install the connections. Improperly installed connectors will add more loss to the communications link, which can nullify the extra money you just spent for the better-quality cable. It can also introduce return loss in the cable due to reflections.

FIGURE 4.14   Coaxial cable attenuation chart

Times Microwave Systems

LMR Cable	30	50	150	220	450	900	1,500	1,800	2,000	2,500	5,800
100A	3.94	5.10	8.95	10.90	15.83	22.84	30.08	33.22	35.19	39.81	64.10
195	1.97	2.55	4.44	5.40	7.78	11.13	14.53	15.99	16.90	19.02	29.90
195UF	2.34	3.03	5.28	6.42	9.25	13.23	17.28	19.01	20.10	22.62	35.57
200	1.77	2.29	3.98	4.83	6.96	9.92	12.92	14.21	15.01	16.87	26.35
200UF	2.12	2.74	4.78	5.80	8.35	11.91	15.51	17.05	18.01	20.24	31.62
240	1.34	1.73	3.01	3.66	5.28	7.56	9.87	10.87	11.49	12.93	20.35
240UF	1.60	2.07	3.62	4.40	6.34	9.07	11.85	13.04	13.78	15.52	24.42
300	1.06	1.37	2.40	2.92	4.22	6.06	7.93	8.74	9.24	10.42	16.53
300UF	1.27	1.65	2.88	3.50	5.06	7.26	9.51	10.48	11.08	12.50	19.81
400	0.68	0.88	1.54	1.87	2.71	3.90	5.13	5.66	5.99	6.76	10.82
400UF	0.81	1.05	1.84	2.25	3.25	4.68	6.15	6.79	7.19	8.12	12.99
500	0.54	0.70	1.22	1.49	2.17	3.13	4.13	4.57	4.84	5.48	8.86
500UF	0.64	0.84	1.47	1.79	2.60	3.76	4.96	5.48	5.81	6.58	10.64
600	0.42	0.55	0.96	1.18	1.72	2.50	3.32	3.67	3.90	4.43	7.26
600UF	0.51	0.66	1.16	1.41	2.06	3.00	3.98	4.41	4.68	5.31	8.71
900	0.29	0.37	0.66	0.80	1.17	1.70	2.25	2.48	2.64	2.99	4.87
900UF	0.35	0.45	0.79	0.96	1.41	2.04	2.70	2.98	3.16	3.59	5.85
1200	0.21	0.27	0.48	0.59	0.87	1.27	1.69	1.87	1.99	2.27	not supported
1700	0.15	0.20	0.35	0.43	0.63	0.94	1.27	1.41	1.50	1.72	not

UF = Ultraflex (more flexible cable)

Connectors

There are many types of connectors that are used to connect antennas to 802.11 equipment. Part of the reason for this is that the FCC Report & Order 04-165 requires that amplifiers have either unique connectors or electronic identification systems to prevent the use of noncertified antennas. This was done to prevent people from connecting higher-gain antennas, either intentionally or unintentionally, to a transceiver. An unauthorized high-gain antenna could exceed the maximum EIRP that is allowed by the FCC or other regulatory body. In response to this regulation, cable manufacturers sell "pigtail" adapter cables. These pigtail cables are usually short segments of cable (typically about 2 feet long) with different connectors on each end. They act as adapters, changing the connector, and allowing a different antenna to be used. The use of these adapter cables typically violates the rules of the local regulatory body. They are typically used by Wi-Fi hobbyists or network installers for testing purposes. Remember that these pigtails usually violate RF regulations and are not recommended or condoned.

Many of the same principles of cables apply to the connectors and also many of the other accessories. RF connectors need to be of the correct impedance to match the other RF equipment. They also support specific ranges of frequencies. The connectors add signal loss to the RF link, and lower-quality connectors are more likely to cause connection or VSWR problems. RF connectors on average add about $1/2$ dB of insertion loss.

Splitters

Splitters are also known as signal splitters, RF splitters, power splitters, and power dividers. A splitter takes an RF signal and divides it into two or more separate signals. Only under an unusually special or unique situation would you have a need to use an RF splitter. One such situation would be if you were connecting sector antennas to one transceiver. If you had three 120 degree antennas aimed away from a central point to provide 360 degree coverage, you could connect each antenna to its own transceiver or you could use a three-way splitter and equal-length cables to connect the antennas to a single transceiver. When you're installing a splitter in this type of configuration, not only will the signal be degraded because it is being split three times, known as through loss, but also each connector will add its own insertion loss to the signal. There are so many variables and potential problems with this configuration that we would recommend only that this type of installation be attempted by a very RF knowledgeable person and for temporary installations.

A more practical, but again rare, use of a splitter is to monitor the power that is being transmitted. The splitter can be connected to the transceiver and then split to the antenna and a power meter. This would allow you to actively monitor the power that is being sent to the antenna.

Amplifiers

An RF *amplifier* takes the signal that is generated by the transceiver, increases it, and sends it to the antenna. Unlike the antenna providing an increase in gain by focusing the signal, an amplifier provides an overall increase in power by adding electrical energy to the signal, which is referred to as active gain.

Amplifiers can be purchased as either unidirectional or bidirectional devices. Unidirectional amplifiers perform the amplification in only one direction, either when transmitting or when receiving. Bidirectional amplifiers perform the amplification in both directions.

The amplifier's increase in power is created using one of two methods: fixed gain or fixed output. With the fixed-gain method, the output of the transceiver is increased by the amount of the amplifier. A fixed-output amplifier does not add to the output of the transceiver. The fixed-output amplifier simply generates a signal equal to the output of the amplifier regardless of the power generated by the transceiver. Adjustable variable-gain amplifiers also exist, but it is a recommended practice not to use adjustable-gain amplifiers. Unauthorized adjustment of a variable-rate amplifier may result either in violation of power regulations or insufficient transmission amplitude.

Since most regulatory bodies have a maximum power regulation of 1 watt or less at the Intentional Radiator (IR), the main purpose of using amplifiers is to compensate for cable loss as opposed to boosting the signal for range. Therefore, when installing an amplifier, install it as close to the antenna as possible. Since the antenna cable adds loss to the signal, the shorter antenna cable will produce less loss and allow more signal to the antenna.

NOTE   Amplifiers must be certified with the system in use according to regulatory bodies like the FCC. It is far better to further engineer the system than to use an amp.

Attenuators

In some situations, it may be necessary to decrease the amount of signal that is radiating from the antenna. You could be installing a short point-to-point link and want to reduce the output to minimize interference to other RF equipment in the area. In some instances, even the lowest power setting of the transceiver may generate more signal than you want. In this situation, you can add a fixed-loss or a variable-loss *attenuator*. Attenuators are small devices about the size of a C-cell battery, with cable connectors on both sides. Attenuators absorb energy, decreasing the signal as it travels through. A variable-loss attenuator has a dial on it that allows you to adjust the amount of energy that is absorbed. Fixed-loss attenuators provide a set amount of loss. Variable-loss attenuators are also often used during outdoor site surveys to simulate loss caused by various grades of cabling and different lengths.

Another interesting use of a variable attenuator is to test the actual fade margin on a point-to-point link. By gradually increasing the attenuation until there is no more link, you can use that number to determine the actual fade margin of the link.

Lightning Arrestors

The purpose of a *lightning arrestor* is to redirect (shunt) transient currents caused by nearby lightning strikes or ambient static away from your electronic equipment and into the ground. Lightning arrestors are used to protect electronic equipment from the sudden surge of power that a nearby lightning strike or static buildup can cause. You may have noticed the use of the phrase "nearby lightning strike." This wording is used because lightning arrestors are not capable of protecting against a direct lightning strike. Lightning arrestors can typically protect against surges of up to 5,000 amperes at up to 50 volts. The IEEE specifies that lightning arrestors should be capable of redirecting the transient current in less than 8 microseconds. Most lightning arrestors are capable of doing it in less than 2 microseconds.

The lightning arrestor is installed between the transceiver and the antenna. Any devices that are installed between the lightning arrestor and the antenna will not be protected by the lightning arrestor. Therefore, the lightning arrestor is typically placed closer to the antenna, with all other communications devices (amplifiers, attenuators, etc.) installed between the lightning arrestor and the transceiver. Figure 4.15 shows a properly grounded radio, cabling, and antenna. After a lightning arrestor has performed its job by protecting the equipment from an electrical surge, it will have to be replaced, or it may have a replaceable gas discharge tube (like a fuse).

Fiber-optic cable can also be used to provide additional lightning protection. A short piece of fiber-optic cable can be inserted into the Ethernet cable that connects the wireless bridge to the rest of the network. Ethernet-to-fiber adapters, known as transceivers, convert the electrical Ethernet signal to a light-based fiber signal and then back to Ethernet. Since fiber-optic cable is constructed of glass and it uses light and not electricity to transmit data, it does not conduct electricity.

FIGURE 4.15 Installation of lightning protection equipment

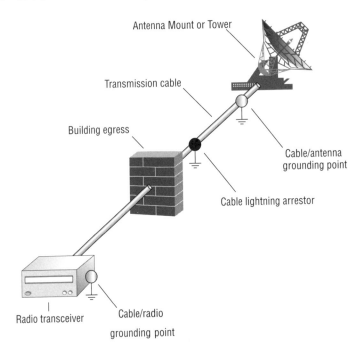

The fiber-optic cable acts as a kind of safety net should the lightning arrestor fail due to a much higher transient current or even a direct lightning strike. Realize that if there is a direct lightning strike to the antenna, you can plan on replacing all of the components from the fiber-optic cable to the antenna. Furthermore, a direct lightning strike may also arc over the fiber link and still cause damage to equipment on the opposite side of the fiber link. Grounding the RF cables as well can help prevent this from happening.

 Real World Scenario

Not Only Is lightning Unpredictable, the Results Are Too!

A business in a 5-story, 200-year-old brick brownstone in the North End neighborhood of Boston had a lightning strike, or a nearby lightning strike. This building was not even one of the tallest buildings in the area, and it was at the bottom of a small hill and surrounded by other similar buildings. An electrical current traveled down the water vent pipe, past a bundle of Ethernet cables. A transient current on the Ethernet cables damaged the transceiver circuits on the Ethernet cards in the PCs and on the individual ports on the Ethernet hub. About half of the Ethernet devices in the company failed, and about half of the ports on the hub were no longer functioning. Yet, all of the software recognized the cards, and all of the power and port lights worked flawlessly. The problem appeared to be cabling related.

You often will not know that the problem is lightning related, and the symptoms may be misleading. Testing the lightning arrestors can help with your diagnosis.

Grounding Rods and Wires

When lightning strikes an object, it is looking for the path of least resistance, or more specifically, the path of least impedance. This is where lightning protection and grounding equipment come in to play. A grounding system, which is made up of a grounding rod and wires, provides a low-impedance path to the ground. This low-impedance path is installed to encourage the lightning to travel through it instead of through your expensive electronic equipment.

Grounding rods and wires are also used to create what is referred to as a common ground. One way of creating a common ground is to drive a copper rod into the ground and connect your electrical and electronic equipment to this rod using wires or straps (grounding wires). The grounding rod should be at least 6 feet long and should be fully driven into the ground, leaving enough of the rod accessible to attach the ground wires to it. By creating a common ground, you have created a path of least impedance for all of your equipment should lightning cause an electrical surge.

On tower structures, a ground rod should be placed off of each leg with a No. 2 tinned copper wire. These connections should be exothermically welded to the tower legs. A No. 2 tinned copper wire should also form a ring around the grounding rods. The following diagram illustrates a proper grounding ring. The dashed lines are No. 2 tinned copper wire and the circles are grounding rods. Ice bridges and building grounds should also be bonded to this ring to provide equal grounding potentials.

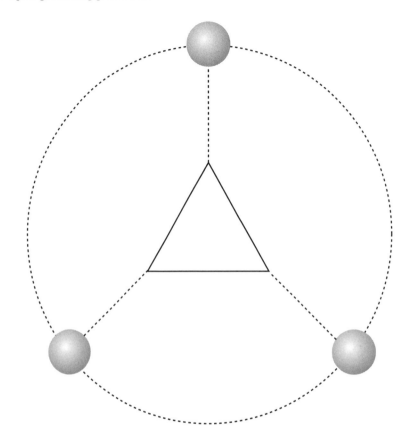

    Section 12.2.2 of the EIA/TIA 222F standard states that "a minimum ground shall consist of two $5/8$" diameter galvanized steel rods driven not less than 8 feet into the ground.... The ground rods shall be bonded with a lead of not smaller than No. 6 tinned bare copper to the nearest leg or to the metal base of the structure."

Summary

This chapter focused on RF signal and antenna concepts. The antenna is a key component of successful RF communications. There are five types of antennas that are used with 802.11 networks:

- Omni-directional (dipole, collinear)
- Semi-directional (patch, panel, yagi)
- Highly-directional (parabolic dish, grid)
- Phased array
- Sector

The antenna types produce different signal patterns, which can be viewed on the azimuth and elevation charts.

This chapter also reviewed some of the key concerns when installing point-to-point communications:

- Visual LOS
- RF LOS
- Fresnel zone
- Earth bulge
- Antenna polarization

The final section of this chapter covered VSWR and antenna mounting issues, along with antenna accessories and their roles.

Exam Essentials

Understand passive and active gain.   Understand how antennas provide passive gain and how transceivers and amplifiers provide active gain.

Know the different categories and types of antennas, how they radiate signals, and what type of environment they are used in.   Make sure you know the three main categories of antennas and the different types of antennas. Know the similarities and differences between them, and understand when and why you would use one antenna over another. Make sure that you understand azimuth and elevation charts, beamwidth, antenna polarization, and antenna diversity.

Fully understand Fresnel zone.   Make sure you understand all of the issues and variables involved with installing point-to-point communications. You are not required to memorize the Fresnel zone or earth bulge formulas; however, you will need to know all aspects regarding these topics and when and why you would use the formulas.

Understand the concerns associated with connecting and installing antennas and the antenna accessories.   Every cable, connector, and device between the transceiver and the antenna affects the signal that gets radiated from the antenna. Understand which devices provide gain and which devices provide loss. Understand what VSWR is and what values are good or bad. Know the different antenna accessories, what they do, and why and when you would use them.

Key Terms

Before you take the exam, be certain you are familiar with the following terms:

active gain	lightning arrestor
amplifier	line of sight (LOS)
antenna diversity	multiple input multiple output (MIMO)
antenna polarization	omni-directional antenna
attenuator	panel antenna
azimuth charts	parabolic dish antenna
back lobe	passive gain
beamwidth	patch antenna
dipole antenna	phased array antenna
earth bulge	sector antennas
elevation charts	semi-directional antenna
Fresnel zone	splitters
grid	voltage standing wave ratio (VSWR)
highly-directional antenna	yagi

Review Questions

1. Which of the following devices produce active gain? (Choose all that apply.)

   A. RF transceiver

   B. Parabolic dish

   C. Amplifier

   D. Sector antenna

2. The azimuth chart represents a view of an antenna's radiation pattern from which direction?

   A. Top

   B. Side

   C. Front

   D. Both top and side

3. What is the definition of the horizontal beamwidth of an antenna?

   A. The measurement of the angle of the main lobe as represented on the azimuth chart

   B. The distance between the two points on the horizontal axis where the signal decreases by a third. This distance is measured in degrees.

   C. The distance between the two −3 dB power points on the horizontal axis, measured in degrees

   D. The distance between the peak power and the point where the signal decrease by $1/2$. This distance is measured in degrees.

4. Which antennas are highly-directional? (Choose all that apply.)

   A. Yagi

   B. Patch

   C. Panel

   D. Parabolic dish

   E. Grid

   F. Sector

5. Semi-directional antennas are often used for which of the following purposes? (Choose all that apply.)

   A. Providing short-distance point-to-point communications

   B. Providing long-distance point-to-point communications

   C. Connecting to an access point for indoor point-to-multipoint communications

   D. Reducing reflections and the negative effects of multipath

6. The Fresnel zone should not be blocked by more than what percentage to maintain a reliable communications link?

    A. 20 percent

    B. 40 percent

    C. 50 percent

    D. 60 percent

7. The size of the Fresnel zone is controlled by what factors? (Choose all that apply.)

    A. Antenna beamwidth

    B. RF line of sight

    C. Distance

    D. Frequency

8. When a long-distance point-to-point link is installed, earth bulge should be considered beyond what distance?

    A. 5 miles

    B. 7 miles

    C. 10 mile

    D. 30 mile

9. A network administrator replaced some coaxial cabling used in an outdoor bridge deployment after water damaged the cabling. After replacing the cabling, the network administrator noticed that the EIRP increased drastically and is possibly violating the maximum EIRP power regulation mandate. What are the possible causes of the increased amplitude? (Choose all that apply.)

    A. The administrator installed a shorter cable.

    B. The administrator installed a lower-grade cable.

    C. The administrator installed a higher-grade cable.

    D. The administrator installed a longer cable.

    E. The administrator used a different color cable.

10. Which of the following are true for antenna diversity? (Choose all that apply.)

    A. The transceiver combines the signal from both antennas to provide better coverage.

    B. Transceivers can transmit from both antennas at the same time.

    C. The transceiver samples both antennas and only receives data from one antenna at a time.

    D. Transceivers can transmit from only one of the antennas at a time.

11. Which of the following are true for multiple input multiple output (M) devices? (Choose all that apply.)

A. M devices have multiple antennas at both ends of the communications link.

B. M devices transmit from one antenna at a time.

C. M devices transmit from both antennas at the same time.

D. M devices alternate between the antennas to provide better signal diversity.

12. The ratio between the maximum peak voltage and minimum voltage on a line is known as what?

A. Signal flux

B. Return loss

C. VSWR

D. Signal incidents

13. Voltage standing wave ratio is cause by what?

A. Signal reflection

B. Blockage of the Fresnel zone

C. Resistance between RF components

D. Mismatched impedance between RF components

14. When determining the mounting height of a long-distance point-to-point antenna, which of the following needs to be considered? (Choose all that apply.)

A. Frequency

B. Distance

C. Visual line of sight

D. Earth bulge

E. Antenna beamwidth

F. RF line of sight

15. Which of the following are true about cables? (Choose all that apply.)

A. They cause impedance on the signal.

B. They work regardless of the frequency.

C. Attenuation decreases as frequency increases.

D. They add loss to the signal.

16. Amplifiers can be purchased with which of the following features? (Choose all that apply.)

A. Bidirectional amplification

B. Unidirectional amplification

C. Fixed gain

D. Fixed output

17. The signal between the transceiver and the antenna will be reduced by which of the following methods? (Choose all that apply.)

  A. Adding an attenuator

  B. Increasing the length of the cable

  C. Shortening the length of the cable

  D. Using cheaper-quality cable

18. Lightning arrestors will defend against which of the following?

  A. Lighting strikes

  B. Power surges

  C. Transient currents

  D. Improper common grounding

19. The radius of the second Fresnel zone is _____. (Choose all that apply.)

  A. Out of phase with the point source

  B. In phase with the point source

  C. Smaller than the first Fresnel zone

  D. Larger than the first Fresnel zone

20. While aligning a directional antenna, you notice that the signal drops as you turn the antenna away from the other antenna, but then it increases a little. This increase in signal is cause by what?

  A. Signal reflection

  B. Frequency harmonic

  C. Side band

  D. Sidelobe

Answers to Review Questions

1. A, D. A parabolic dish and a sector antenna are both antennas that are capable of producing only passive gain.

2. A. The azimuth is the top-down view of an antenna's radiation pattern, also known as the H-plane.

3. C. The beamwidth is the distance in degrees between the −3 dB ($1/2$ power) point on one side of the main signal and the −3 dB point on the other side of the main signal, measured along the horizontal axis.

4. D, E. A parabolic dish and a grid are highly-directional. The rest of the antennas are semi-directional, and the sector antenna is a special type of semi-directional antenna.

5. A, C, D. Semi-directional antennas provide too wide of a beamwidth to support long-distance communications but will work for short distances. They are also useful for directing an RF signal in indoor point-to-multipoint environments.

6. B. Any more than 40 percent encroachment into the Fresnel zone is likely to make a link unreliable. The clearer the Fresnel zone the better.

7. C, D. The distance and frequency determine the size of the Fresnel zone.

8. B. The distance when the curvature of the earth should be considered is 7 miles.

9. A, C. Installing a shorter cable using the same grade will result in less loss and thus more amplitude being transmitting out the antenna. A higher-grade cable rated for less dB loss will have the same result.

10. C, D. A transceiver using antenna diversity can only transmit from one antenna at a time. If it transmitted from both antennas, the two signals would interfere with each other. A transceiver can also only interpret one signal at a time, so it samples the signals received by both antennas and chooses the better signal to be received.

11. A, C. MIMO devices must have multiple antennas at both ends of the communications link, and are capable of transmitting from both antennas at the same time.

12. C. Voltage standing wave ratio is the difference between these voltages and is represented as, for example, 1.5:1.

13. D. Impedance is a measurement of resistance on an AC signal, whereas resistance is a measurement on a DC signal.

14. A, B, D, F. Frequency and distance are needed to determine the Fresnel zone. Visual line of sight is not needed as long as you have RF line of sight. You may not be able to see the antenna due to fog, but the fog will not prevent RF line of sight. Earth bulge will need to be considered. The beamwidth is not needed to determine the height.

15. A, D. Cables must be selected that support the frequency you are using. Attenuation actually increases with frequency.

16. A, B, C, D. All of these are capabilities of amplifiers.

17. A, B, D. Adding an attenuator is an intentional act to add loss to the signal. Since cable adds loss, increasing the length will add more loss, whereas shortening the length will reduce the loss. Better-quality cables produce less signal loss.

18. C. Lightning arrestors will not stand up to a direct lightning strike, only transient currents caused by nearby lightning strikes.

19. A, D. The first Fresnel zone is in phase with the point source. The second Fresnel zone begins at the point where the signals transition from being in phase to being out of phase. Since the second Fresnel zone begins where the first Fresnel zone ends, the radius of the second Fresnel zone is larger than the radius of the first Fresnel zone.

20. D. Sidelobes are areas of coverage (other than the coverage provided by the main signal) that have a stronger signal than would be expected when compared with the areas around them. Sidelobes are best seen on an azimuth chart.

Chapter 5

IEEE 802.11 Standards

IN THIS CHAPTER, YOU WILL LEARN ABOUT THE FOLLOWING:

✓ **IEEE 802.11 Standard**

✓ **IEEE 802.11 Ratified Amendments**

- 802.11b
- 802.11a
- 802.11g
- 802.11d
- 802.11F
- 802.11h
- 802.11i
- 802.11j
- 802.11e

✓ **IEEE 802.11 Draft Amendments**

- 802.11k
- 802.11m
- 802.11n
- 802.11p
- 802.11r
- 802.11s
- 802.11T
- 802.11u
- 802.11v
- 802.11w

As discussed in Chapter 1, "Overview of Wireless Standards and Organizations," the Institute of Electrical and Electronics Engineers (IEEE) is the professional society that creates and maintains standards that we use for communications, such as the 802.3 Ethernet standard for wired networking. The IEEE has assigned working groups for several wireless communication standards. For example, the 802.15 working group is responsible for personal area network (PAN) communications using radio frequencies. Some of the technologies defined within the 802.15 standard include Bluetooth and ZigBee. Another example is the 802.16 standard, which is overseen by the Broadband Wireless Access Working Group; the technology is often referred to as WiMAX. The focus of this book is the technology as defined by the IEEE 802.11 standard, which provides for local area network (LAN) communications using radio frequencies (RF).

The 802.11 Working Group comprises 250+ wireless companies and has over 650 active members. It consists of standing committees, study groups, and numerous *task groups*. For example the Standing Committee-Publicity (PSC) is in charge of finding means to better publicize the 802.11 standard. The 802.11 Study Group (SG) is in charge of investigating the possibility of putting something new into the 802.11 standard.

A quick guide to the IEEE 802.11 Working Group can be found at http://grouper.ieee.org/groups/802/11/QuickGuide_IEEE_802_WG_and_Activities.htm.

Various 802.11 task groups are in charge of revising and amending the original standard that was developed by the MAC Task Group (MAC) and the PHY Task Group (PHY). Each group is assigned a letter from the alphabet, and it is common to hear the term "802.11 alphabet soup" when referring to all the amendments created by the multiple 802.11 task groups. Quite a few of the 802.11 task group projects have been completed and amendments to the original standard have been ratified. Other 802.11 task group projects still remain active and exist as draft amendments.

In this chapter, we will discuss the original 802.11 standard, the ratified amendments, and draft amendments of various 802.11 task groups.

Overview of the IEEE 802.11 Standard

The original 802.11 standard was published in June 1997 as IEEE Std. 802.11-1997, and it is often referred to as 802.11 Prime because it was the first WLAN standard. The standard was revised in 1999, reaffirmed in 2003, and published as IEEE Std. 802.11-1999 (R2003).

The IEEE specifically defines 802.11 technologies at the Physical layer and the MAC sublayer of the Data-Link layer. By design, the 802.11 standard does not address the upper layers of the OSI model, although there are interactions between the 802.11 MAC layer and the upper layers for parameters such as quality of service (QoS). The PHY Task Group (PHY) worked in conjunction with the MAC Task Group (MAC) to define the original 802.11 standard. The PHY Task Group (PHY) developed three Physical layer specifications:

Infrared (IR) Infrared technology uses a light-based medium. Although an infrared medium was indeed defined in the original 802.11 standard, the implementation is obsolete. More information about modern implementations of infrared can be found at the Infrared Data Association's website at www.irda.org. The scope of this book focuses on the 802.11 radio frequency (RF) mediums.

Frequency Hopping Spread Spectrum (FHSS) Radio frequency signals can be defined as narrowband signals or as spread spectrum signals. An RF signal is considered spread spectrum when the bandwidth is wider than what is required to carry the data. Frequency Hopping is a spread spectrum technology that was first patented during World War II. Frequency Hopping 802.11 radio cards are often called clause 14 devices due to the clause that referenced them in the original 802.11 standard.

Direct sequence spread spectrum (DSSS) Direct sequence is another spread spectrum technology that is frequently used and easiest to implement. DSSS 802.11 radio cards are often known as clause 15 devices.

As defined by 802.11 Prime, the frequency space in which either FHSS or DSSS radio cards can transmit is the license free 2.4 GHz *Industrial, Scientific, and Medical (ISM)* band. DSSS 802.11 radio cards can transmit in channels subdivided from the entire 2.4 to 2.4835 GHz ISM band. The IEEE is more restrictive for FHSS radio cards, which are permitted to transmit on 1 MHz subcarriers in the 2.402 to 2.480 GHz range of the 2.4 GHz ISM band.

Chances are that you will not be working with older legacy 802.11 equipment since most WLAN deployments use technologies as defined by newer 802.11 amendments. WLAN companies had the choice of manufacturing either clause 14 FHSS radio cards or clause 15 DSSS radio cards. Because spread spectrum technologies differ, they cannot communicate with each other and often have a hard time coexisting. Spread spectrum signals are analogous to oil and water because they do not mix well. Therefore, it is important to understand that an 802.11

DSSS radio cannot communicate with an 802.11 FHSS radio. The majority of legacy WLAN deployments used frequency hopping, but some DSSS solutions were available as well.

What about bandwidth? *Data rates* defined by the original 802.11 standard were 1 Mbps and 2 Mbps. Keep in mind that a data rate is the available *bandwidth* and not actual *throughput*. Due to medium access methods, aggregate throughput is typically 1/2 or less of the available data rate bandwidth.

FHSS and DSSS will be discussed in more detail in Chapter 6, "Wireless Networks and Spread Spectrum Technologies."

IEEE 802.11 Ratified Amendments

In the years that followed the publishing of the original 802.11 standard, new task groups were assembled to address potential enhancements to the standard. So far, nine amendments to the standard have been ratified and published by the distinctive task groups. These ratified supplements will now be discussed in a somewhat chronological order.

802.11b Amendment

Although Wi-Fi consumer market continues to grow at a tremendous rate, 802.11b compatible WLAN equipment gave the industry the first needed huge shot in the arm. In 1999, the IEEE Task Group b (TGb) published the IEEE Std. 802.11b-1999, and it was later amended and corrected as IEEE Std. 802.11b-1999/Cor1-2001. The Physical layer medium that is defined by 802.11b is strictly direct sequence spread spectrum (DSSS). The frequency space in which 802.11b radio cards can operate is the unlicensed 2.4 to 2.4835 GHz ISM band.

 Real World Scenario

Will 802.11b Devices Work with Legacy 802.11 Devices?

802.11b radio cards are known as clause 18 devices. The 802.11b amendment only specifies the use of a DSSS physical medium and does not specify FHSS. Since a good portion of the legacy 802.11 deployments used FHSS, 802.11b radio cards will not be backward compatible with those systems and cannot be used. However, 802.11b clause 18 radio cards should be backward compatible with the legacy 802.11 DSSS clause 15 devices. 802.11b WLAN equipment can communicate with legacy 802.11 DSSS WLAN equipment.

The TGb Task Group's main goal was to achieve higher data rates within the 2.4 GHz ISM band. 802.11b radio cards accomplish this feat by using a different spreading/coding technique called *Complementary Code Keying (CCK)* and modulation methods using the phase properties of the RF signal. 802.11 cards used a spreading technique called the *Barker Code*. The end result is that 802.11b radio cards support data rates of 1, 2, 5.5 and 11 Mbps. 802.11b systems are backward compatible with the 802.11 DSSS data rates of 1 Mbps and 2 Mbps. The transmission data rates of 5.5 and 11 Mbps are known as *High-Rate DSSS (HR-DSSS)*. Once again, understand that the supported data rates refer to available bandwidth and not aggregate throughput.

The Barker Code and CCK spreading techniques as well as applicable modulation methods will be discussed further in Chapter 6.

802.11a Amendment

During the same year the 802.11b amendment was approved, another very important amendment was also ratified and published as IEEE Std. 802.11a-1999. The engineers in the TGa Task Group set out to define how 802.11 technologies would operate in the newly allocated *Unlicensed National Information Infrastructure (UNII)* frequency bands. 802.11a radio cards can transmit in three different 100 MHz unlicensed frequency bands in the 5 GHz range, as shown in Table 5.1.

The 2.4 GHz ISM band is a much more crowded frequency space than the 5 GHz UNII bands. Microwave ovens, Bluetooth, cordless phones, and numerous other devices all operate in the 2.4 GHz ISM band and are potential sources of interference. In addition, the sheer number of 2.4 GHz WLAN deployments has often been a problem in environments such as multi-tenant office buildings.

One big advantage of using 802.11a WLAN equipment is that it operates in the less crowded 5 GHz UNII bands. Eventually the three UNII bands will also become crowded. Regulatory bodies such as the FCC are opening up more frequency space in the 5 GHz range.

TABLE 5.1   Unlicensed National Information Infrastructure

Band Frequency range
UNII-1 (lower) 5.150 GHz – 5.250 GHz
UNII-2 (middle) 5.250 GHz – 5.350 GHz
UNII-3 (upper) 5.725 GHz – 5.825 GHz

Further discussion about both the ISM and UNII bands will occur in Chapter 6.

802.11a radio cards operating in the 5 GHz UNII bands are classified as clause 17 devices. As defined by the 802.11a amendment, these devices are required to support data rates of 6, 12, and 24 Mbps with a maximum of 54 Mbps. With the use of a spread spectrum technology called *Orthogonal Frequency Division Multiplexing (OFDM)*, data rates of 6, 9, 12, 18, 24, 36, 48, and 54 Mbps are supported in most manufacturers' radio cards. It should be noted that an 802.11a radio does not have to support all of these rates and a vendor may have a different implementation of data rates that is not compatible with another vendor.

 OFDM will be discussed further in Chapter 6.

It should also be noted that 802.11a radio cards cannot communicate with 802.11 or 802.11b radio cards for two reasons. First, 802.11a radio cards use a different spread spectrum technology than 802.11/802.11b devices. Second, 802.11a devices transmit in the 5 GHz UNII bands, while the 802.11/802.11b cards operate in the 2.4 GHz ISM band. The good news is that 802.11a can coexist with 802.11 or 802.11b/g cards in the same physical space because these cards transmit in separate frequency ranges. In Figure 5.1, you see an access point (AP) with both a 2.4 GHz 802.11b/g radio and a 5 GHz 802.11a radio. Many enterprise wireless deployments run both 802.11a and 802.11b/g networks simultaneously.

FIGURE 5.1 Access point, dual radio cards

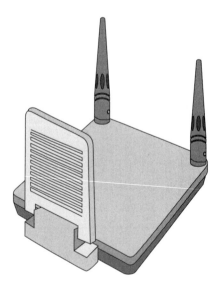

802.11g

Another amendment that generated a lot of excitement in the Wi-Fi marketplace was published as IEEE Std. 802.11g-2003. The IEEE defines 802.11g cards as clause 19 devices, which transmit in the 2.4 to 2.4835 GHz ISM frequency band.

The main goal of the TGg Task Group was to enhance the 802.11b Physical layer to achieve greater bandwidth yet remain compatible with the 802.11 MAC. To achieve the higher data rates, *Extended Rate Physical OFDM (ERP-OFDM)* technology is used exactly as defined in the 802.11a amendment. Therefore, data rates of 6, 9, 12, 18, 24, 36, 48, and 54 Mbps are possible using OFDM technology, although once again the IEEE only requires the data rates of 6, 12, and 24 Mbps. To maintain backward compatibility, the DSSS data rates of 1, 2, 5.5, and 11 are supported as well.

What Are the Operational Modes of an 802.11g Access Point and What Is the Effective Throughput?

While the 802.11g amendment mandates support for both DSSS and ERP-OFDM, Wi-Fi vendors typically allow an 802.11g access point to be configured in three very distinct modes:

B Only Mode   When an 802.11g AP is running in this operational mode, support for DSSS technology is solely enabled. Effectively, the access point has been configured to be an 802.11b access point and only DSSS clients will be able to communicate with the AP. Aggregate throughput will be the same as achieved in an 802.11b network.

G Only Mode   AP's configured as "G only" will communicate with other 802.11g client stations using only OFDM technology. Support for DSSS is disabled and therefore 802.11b clients will not be able to associate with the access point. Aggregate throughput will be equivalent to what can be achieved in an 802.11a network. For example, the aggregate throughput of an AP with a data rate of 54 Mbps might be about 19 to 20 Mbps. A "G Only" wireless LAN is sometimes referred to as a "Pure G" network.

B/G Mode   This is the default operational mode of most 802.11g access points and is often called *mixed mode*. Support for both DSSS and OFDM is enabled, therefore both 802.11b and 802.11g clients can communicate with the access point. However, a price must be paid for this coexistence of these two very different technologies. As soon as the first 802.11b DSSS station attempts to associate, the access point signals to all the 802.11g stations to enable "protection." While the protection mechanism does allow for 802.11b and 802.11g clients to coexist, the result is an immediate and significant degradation in throughput. An 802.11b/g access point with a data rate of 54 Mbps might see a decrease in aggregate throughput from 20 Mbps down to as little as 8 Mbps the instant the protection mechanism is enabled. A very thorough discussion of the protection mechanism can be found in Chapter 9, "802.11 MAC Architecture."

The 802.11g amendment defines the use of several PHYs but requires support for both DSSS and ERP-OFDM. The good news is that an 802.11g AP can communicate with 802.11g client stations as well as 802.11b stations. The ratification of the 802.11g amendment triggered monumental sales of Wi-Fi gear in both the small office, home office (SOHO) and enterprise markets because of both the higher data rates and the backward compatibility with older equipment. As mentioned earlier in this chapter, spread spectrum technologies cannot communicate with each other, yet the 802.11g amendment mandates support for both DSSS and ERP-OFDM. In other words, ERP-OFDM and DSSS technologies can coexist, yet they cannot speak to each other. Therefore, the 802.11g amendment calls out for a *protection mechanism* that allows the two technologies to coexist. The goal of the 802.11g "protection mechanism" is to prevent ERP-OFDM radio cards from transmitting at the same time as DSSS radio cards.

The 802.11g amendment also specifies other optional technologies, including *Packet Binary Convolutional Coding (PBCC)*. This technology is optional and is rarely used.

 A brief examination of PBCC can be found in Chapter 6.

Table 5.2 shows a brief overview and comparison of 802.11, 802.11b, 802.11g, and 802.11a.

TABLE 5.2   802.11 Standard/Amendment Comparison

	802.11	802.11b	802.11g	802.11a
Frequency	2.4 GHz ISM band	2.4 GHz ISM band	2.4 GHz ISM band	5 GHz UNII bands
Spread Spectrum Technology	FHSS or DSSS	DSSS only	ERP-OFDM and DSSS are mandatory. PBCC is optional.	ERP-OFDM
Data Rates	1, 2 Mbps	1, 2, 5.5, and 11 Mbps	DSSS: 1, 2, 5.5, and 11 Mbps OFDM: 6, 12 and 24 Mbps are mandatory. Also supported are 9, 18, 36, 48, and 54 Mbps. PBCC: 22 and 33 Mbps	6, 12 and 24 Mbps are mandatory. Also supported are 9, 18, 36, 48, and 54 Mbps.

TABLE 5.2 802.11 Standard/Amendment Comparison *(continued)*

	802.11	802.11b	802.11g	802.11a
Backward Compatabilty	N/A	802.11 DSSS only	802.11b and 802.11 DSSS	none
Ratified	1997	1999	2003	1999

802.11d

The original 802.11 standard was written for compliance with the regulatory domains of the United States, Canada, and Europe. Regulations in other countries might define different limits on allowed frequencies and transmit power. The 802.11d amendment, which was published as IEEE Std. 802.11d-2001, added requirements and definitions necessary to allow 802.11 WLAN equipment to operate in areas not served by the original standard.

Country code information is delivered in fields inside two wireless frames called beacons and probe requests. This information is then used by 802.11d compliant devices to ensure that they are abiding by a particular country's frequency and power rules. Figure 5.2 shows an AP configured for use in Mongolia and a capture of a beacon frame containing the country code, frequency, and power information.

The 802.11d amendment also defines other information specific to configuration parameters of a Frequency Hopping (FHSS) access point. FHSS parameters such as hopping patterns might vary from country to country, and the information needs to be once again delivered via the beacon or probe response frames. This information would only be useful in legacy deployments using FHSS spread spectrum technology.

A detailed discussion of beacons, probes and other wireless frames can be found in Chapter 8, "802.11 Medium Access."

FIGURE 5.2 802.11d Settings

802.11F

The IEEE Task Group F (TGF) published IEEE Std. 802.11F-2003 as a *recommended practice* in 2003.

NOTE   The uppercase *F* in the name IEEE Task Group F indicates that this amendment is considered a recommended practice and not a standard.

The original published 802.11 standard mandated that vendor access points support *roaming*. A mechanism is needed to allow client stations that are already communicating through one access point to be able to jump from the coverage area of the original AP and continue communications through a new access point. A perfect analogy is the roaming that occurs when using a cellular telephone. When you are talking to your best friend on the cell phone while driving in your car, your telephone will roam between cellular towers to allow for seamless communications and hopefully an uninterrupted conversation. Seamless roaming allows for mobility, which is the heart and soul of true wireless networking and connectivity.

In Figure 5.3, you see a station downloading a file through AP-1 from an FTP server residing on a wired network backbone. Please note that the access points have overlapping areas of coverage. As the station moves closer to AP-2, which has a stronger signal, the station may roam to access point 2 and continue the FTP transfer through the portal supplied by the new access point.

Although the handover that occurs during roaming can be measured in milliseconds, data packets intended for delivery to the station that has roamed to a new access point might still be buffered at the original access point. In order for the buffered data packets to find their way to the station, two things must happen:

1.   The new access point must inform the original access point about the station that has roamed and request any buffered packets.

2.   The original access point must forward the buffered packets to the new access point via the distribution system for delivery to the client who has roamed.

Figure 5.4 illustrates these two needed tasks.

Although the original 802.11 standard calls for the support of roaming, it fails to dictate how roaming should actually transpire. The IEEE initially intended for vendors to have flexibility with implementing proprietary AP-to-AP roaming mechanisms. The 802.11F amendment was an attempt to standardize how roaming mechanisms work behind the scene on the distribution system medium, which is typically an 802.3 Ethernet network using TCP/IP networking protocols. 802.11F addresses "vendor interoperability" for AP-to-AP roaming. The final result was a recommended practice to use the *Inter Access Point Protocol (IAPP)*. The IAPP protocol uses announcement and handover processes that result in how APs inform other APs about roamed clients as well as define a method of delivery for buffered packets.

FIGURE 5.3   Roaming

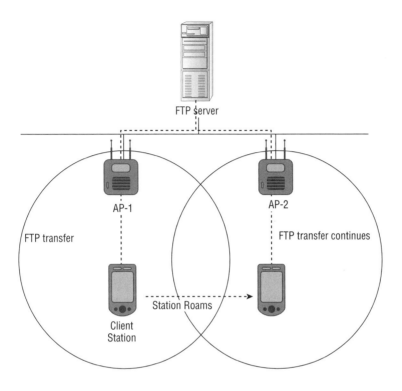

Will Roaming Work If I Mix and Match Different Vendors' Access Points?

The answer is maybe. If the access points of different vendors both support IAPP, then roaming handover should indeed work. However, the reason that the 802.11F amendment became only a recommended practice is that a vendor wants customers to purchase only the brand of AP that the vendor sells and not the competition's brand of AP. As a matter of fact, the use of the Inter Access Point Protocol is not required for certification with the Wi-Fi Alliance. It is therefore the "recommended practice" of this book not to mix different vendors' access points on the same wired network segment. Roaming will be discussed in further detail in both Chapter 7 and Chapter 8.

FIGURE 5.4 Roaming-distribution system medium

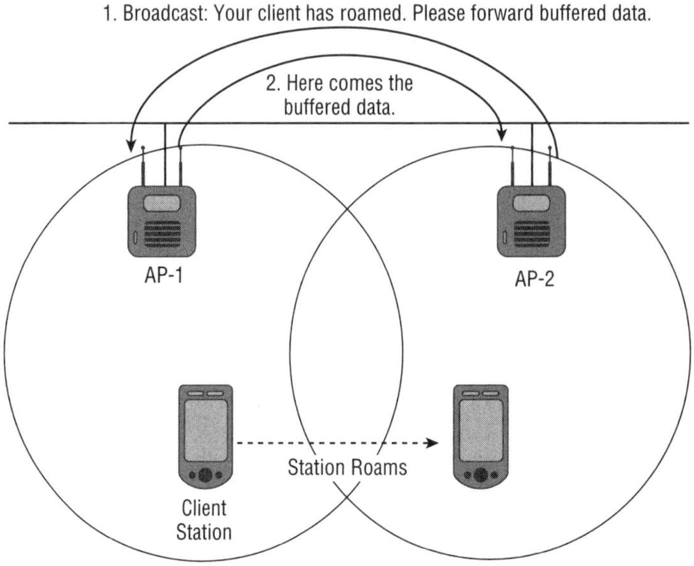

802.11h

Published as IEEE Std. 802.11h-2003, this amendment defines mechanisms for *dynamic frequency selection (DFS)* and *transmit power control (TPC)* that may be used to satisfy regulatory requirements for operation in the 5 GHz band in Europe.

DFS is used for spectrum management of 5 GHz channels for 802.11a radio cards. The European Radiocommunications Committee (ERC) mandates that radio cards operating in the 5 GHz band implement a mechanism to avoid interference with radar systems as well as provide equable use of the channels. The DFS service is used to meet the ERC regulatory requirements.

The dynamic frequency selection (DFS) service provides for the following:

- An AP will allow client stations to associate based on the supported channel of the access point. The term *associate* means that a station has become a member of the AP's wireless network.

- An AP can quiet a channel to test for the presence of radar.

- An AP may test a channel for the presence of radar before using the channel.

- An AP can detect radar on the current channel and other channels.

- An AP can cease operations after radar detection to avoid interference.

- When interference is detected, the AP may choose a different channel to transmit on and inform all the associated stations.

TPC is used to regulate the power levels used by 802.11a radio cards. The ERC mandates that radio cards operating in the 5 GHz band use TPC to abide by a maximum regulatory transmit power and are able to alleviate transmission power to avoid interference. The TPC service is used to meet the ERC regulatory requirements.

The transmit power control (TPC) service provides for the following:

- Stations can associate with an AP based on their transmit power.

- Designation of the maximum transmit power levels permitted on a channel as permitted by a regulations.

- An AP can specify the transmit power of any or all stations that are associated with the access point.

- An AP can change transmission power on stations based on factors of the physical RF environment such as path loss.

The information used by both DFS and TPC is exchanged between stations and access points inside of management frames. Although the 802.11h amendment was ratified specially to address compliance with European regulations in the 5 GHz band, many vendors have also applied TPC and DFS-like services to radio cards operating in the 2.4 GHz ISM band.

Later in this chapter we will discuss the 802.11k draft which could further enhance and develop TPC and DFS service capabilities.

802.11i

From 1997 to the year 2004, there really was not much defined in regard to security in the 802.11 standard. Two key components of any wireless security solution are data privacy (encryption) and authentication (identity verification). For seven years, the only defined method of encryption in an 802.11 network was the use of 64-bit static encryption called *Wired Equivalent Privacy (WEP)*.

WEP encryption has long been cracked and is not considered to be an acceptable means of providing data privacy. The 802.11 standard defined two methods of authentication. The default method is *Open System authentication*, which verifies the identity of everyone regardless. Another defined method is called *Shared Key authentication*, which opens up a whole new can of worms and potential security risk.

The 802.11i amendment, which was ratified and published as IEEE Std. 802.11i-2004, has finally defined stronger encryption and better authentication methods. The intended goal was to better hide the data flying through the air while at the same time place a bigger guard at the front door. The 802.11i security amendment is without a doubt one of the most important enhancements to the original 802.11 standard due to the seriousness of properly protecting a wireless network. The major security enhancements addressed in 802.11i are as follows:

Data privacy   Confidentiality needs have been addressed in 802.11i with the use of a stronger encryption method call *Counter Mode with Cipher Block Chaining Message Authentication*

Code Protocol (CCMP), which uses the *Advanced Encryption Standard (AES)* algorithm. The encryption method is often abbreviated as CCMP/AES, AES CCMP, or often just CCMP. The 802.11i supplement also defines an optional encryption method known as *Temporal Key Integrity Protocol (TKIP)*, which uses the RC-4 stream cipher algorithm and is basically an enhancement of WEP encryption.

Authentication   802.11i defines two methods of *authentication* using either an IEEE *802.1X* authorization framework or *preshared keys (PSKs)*. An 802.1X solution requires the use of an *Extensible Authentication Protocol (EAP)*, although the 802.11i amendment does not specify what EAP method to use.

Robust Security Network (RSN)   This is a method of establishing authentication, negotiating security associations, and dynamically generating encryption keys for clients and access points.

The Wi-Fi Alliance also has a certification known as *Wi-Fi Protected Access (WPA2)*, which is a mirror of the IEEE 802.11i security amendment. WPA version 1 was considered a preview of 802.11i and WPA version 2 is fully compliant with 802.11i.

Wi-Fi security is the top priority when deploying any wireless LAN and that is why there is another valued certification called Certified Wireless Security Professional (CWSP). At least 16 percent of the CWNA test will involve questions regarding Wi-Fi security. Therefore, wireless security topics such as 802.1X, EAP, AES CCMP, TKIP, WPA, and more will be described in more detail in Chapters 13 and 14.

802.11j

The main goal set out by the IEEE Task Group j (TGj) was to obtain Japanese regulatory approval by enhancing the 802.11 MAC and 802.11a PHY to additionally operate in Japanese 4.9 GHz and 5 GHz bands. The 802.11j amendment was approved and published as IEEE Std. 802.11j-2004.

In Japan, 802.11a radio cards can transmit in the lower UNII band at 5.15 GHz to 5.25 GHz as well as a Japanese licensed/unlicensed frequency space of 4.9 GHz to 5.091 GHz.

802.11a radio cards use OFDM technology with required channel spacing of 20 MHz. When 20 MHz channel spacing is used, data rates of 6, 9, 12, 18, 24, 36, 48, and 54 Mbps are possible using OFDM technology. Japan also has the option of using OFDM channel spacing of 10 MHz, which results in available bandwidth data rates of 3, 4.5, 6, 9, 12, 18, 24, and 27 Mbps. The data rates of 3, 6, and 12 Mbps are mandatory when using 10 MHz channel spacing.

Japanese regulatory guidelines and the regulatory information of other nations may be found in the appendix of this study guide.

802.11e

Since the adoption of the original 802.11 standard, there has not been any adequate *quality of service (QoS)* procedures defined for the use of time-sensitive applications like *Voice over IP (VoIP)*. *Voice over Wireless IP (VoWIP)* is also known as *Voice over Wirless Lan (VoWLAN)* and as *Voice over Wi-Fi (VoWiFi)*. Although deployments so exist, the QoS capabilities are typically handled at upper layers using proprietary solutions. Application traffic such as voice, audio, and video has a lower tolerance for latency and jitter and requires priority before data traffic. The newly approved IEEE Std. 802.11e-2005 amendment defines the layer 2 MAC methods needed to meet the QoS requirements for time-sensitive applications over IEEE 802.11 wireless LANs.

The original 802.11 standard defined two methods in which an 802.11 radio card may gain control of the half-duplex medium. The default method, *Distributed Coordination Function (DCF)*, is a completely random method of who gets to transmit on the wireless medium next. The original standard also defines another medium access control method called *Point Coordination Function (PCF)*, where the access point briefly takes control of the medium and polls the clients.

Chapter 8 describes the DCF and PCF methods of medium access in greater detail.

The 802.11e amendment defines enhanced medium access methods to support QoS requirements. *Hybrid Coordination Function (HCF)* is an additional coordination function that is applied in an 802.11e QoS wireless network. HCF has two access mechanisms to provide QoS. *Enhanced Distributed Channel Access (EDCA)* is an extension to DCF. The EDCA medium access method will provide for the "prioritization of frames" based on upper-layer protocols. Application traffic such as voice or video will be transmitted in a timely fashion on the 802.11 wireless medium, meeting the necessary latency requirements.

Hybrid Coordination Function Controlled Access (HCCA) is an extension to PCF. HCF gives the access point the ability to provide for "prioritization of stations." In other words, certain client stations will be given a chance to transmit before others.

The Wi-Fi Alliance also has a certification known as *Wi-Fi Multimedia (WMM)*. The WMM standard is a "mirror" of 802.11e and defines traffic prioritization in four access categories with varying degrees of importance.

802.11e and WMM will be covered in more detail in Chapter 9.

IEEE 802.11 Draft Amendments

What does the future hold in store for us with 802.11 wireless networking? The draft amendments are a looking glass into the future of the enhancements and new capabilities that might be available soon for 802.11 wireless networking devices. Greater throughput, client control, improved roaming, mesh networking, and more all await us on the wireless horizon.

Draft amendments are proposals that have yet to be ratified. Therefore, although some vendors are already selling products that have some of the capabilities described in the following sections, these features are still considered proprietary. For example, if you buy a "pre-802.11n" access point from vendor #1, then the promised increase in throughput capabilities will only be achieved using a "pre-802.11n" client card from that same vendor. Vendor #2's radio will most likely not be able to communicate in the same manner with vendor #1's radio. Also, even though a vendor might be marketing these preratified capabilities, there is no guarantee that the current products will work with future products that are "certified" as compliant with the forthcoming final ratified 802.11n amendment.

The recent ratification of the 802.11e QoS amendment combined with the future approval of the 802.11k, 802.11n, and 802.11r drafts is expected to spark a major convergence of data, voice, and video over the wireless medium. The remaining pages of this chapter will give you a glimpse into more sophisticated Wi-Fi products with more advanced capabilities.

Once again, please understand that because these are still draft amendments, the final amendments may be different.

802.11k

The goal of the 802.11 Task Group k (TGk) is to provide a means of radio resource measurement. The draft amendment calls for measurable Physical layer 1 and MAC sublayer of the Data-Link layer 2 client statistical information in the form of requests and reports. 802.11k defines mechanisms in which client station resource data is gathered and processed by an access point or WLAN switch. (WLAN switches will be covered in Chapter 10, "Wireless Devices." For now, think of a WLAN switch as a central controller that manages many access points.) In some instances, the client may also request information from an access point or WLAN switch. The following are some of the key resource measurements defined under 802.11k:

Transmit power control (TPC)   The 802.11h amendment defined the use of TPC for the 5 GHz band in Europe to reduce interference. Under 802.11k, transmit power control will also be used in other frequency bands and in areas governed by other regulatory agencies.

Client statistics   Physical layer information such as signal-to-noise ratio, signal strength, and data rates can all be reported back to the access point or WLAN switch. MAC information such as frame transmissions, retries, and errors may all be reported back to the access point or WLAN switch as well.

Channel statistics   Clients may assemble noise floor information based on any RF energy in the background of the channel and report back to the access point. Channel load information may also be collected and sent to the AP. The access point or WLAN switch may use this information for channel management decisions.

Roaming site reports   Mobile Assisted Hand-Over (MAHO) is a technique used by digital phones and cellular systems working together to provide better handover between cells. 802.11k gives access points or WLAN switches the ability to direct stations to perform the sort of tasks that a cellular network requires its handhelds to do when using Mobile Assisted Hand-Over.

Using proprietary methods, client stations keep a table of "known access points" and make decisions on when to roam to another access point. As defined by 802.11k, the access point or WLAN switch will request a station to listen for access points on other channels and gather information. The current AP or WLAN switch will then process that information and generate a "site report" detailing available access points from best to worst. Before a station roams, it will request the site report from the current AP and then roam to the best access point on the site report. The 802.11k draft in conjunction with the 802.11r "fast roaming" draft have the potential to greatly improve roaming performance in 802.11 wireless networks.

802.11m

The IEEE Task Group m (TGm) started an initiative in 1999 for internal maintenance of technical documentation of the 802.11 standard. 802.11m is often referred to as "802.11 house-keeping," with a mission of clarification and correction to the 802.11 standard. Unless you are a member of Task Group M, this amendment is of little significance to readers of this book.

802.11n

An event that is sure to have a major impact on the Wi-Fi marketplace will be the passage of the 802.11n amendment. Since the year 2004, the 802.11 Task Group n (TGn) has been working on improvements to the 802.11 standard to provide for greater throughput. The IEEE 802.11 standards in the past have always addressed bandwidth data rate; however, the objective of the 802.11n supplement is to increase the throughput in both the 2.4 GHz and 5 GHz frequency band. The baseline minimum throughput goal is 100 Mbps, although throughput of as much as 600 Mbps may be possible under the right conditions.

802.11n makes use of *multiple-input-multiple-output (MIMO)* technology in unison with Orthogonal Frequency Division Multiplexing (OFDM) technology. MIMO uses multiple receiving and transmitting antennas and actually capitalizes on the effects of multipath as opposed to compensating or eliminating them. The beneficial consequences of using MIMO are increased throughput and even greater range.

Further discussion about MIMO technology can be found in Chapter 4, "RF Signal and Antenna Concepts."

Currently two competing proposals are vying for 802.11n ratification, with companies aligning themselves into two separate consortiums called World-Wide Spectrum Efficiency (WWiSE) and Task Group n-Sync (TGn Sync). The WWiSE group has the backing of Airgo, Broadcom, Motorola, Nokia, and others. The TGn Sync group includes membership from Atheros, Cisco, Intel, Philips, Symbol, and others.

Issues being debated include OFDM channel sizes of possibly 10 MHz, 20 MHz, or 40 MHz and the use of one to four antennas. Other Physical layer issues such as transmit beamforming as well as MAC layer issues still have these two groups in disagreement. Thankfully, another group called the Enhanced Wireless Consortium (EWC) was formed to help speed up the IEEE 802.11n development process as well as promote the forthcoming 802.11n technology. Final ratification of the 802.11n amendment is expected in 2007. Passage of the 802.11n draft will give 802.11 enterprise deployments the desired throughput needed by a multiple-user and application-intensive environment.

> More information about Enhanced Wireless Consortium (EWC) can be found at www.enhancedwirelessconsortium.org.

802.11p

The mission of the 802.11 Task Group p (TGp) is to define enhancements to the 802.11 standard to support Intelligent Transportation Systems (ITS) applications. Data exchanges between high-speed vehicles will be possible in the licensed ITS band of 5.9 GHz. Additionally, communications between vehicles and roadside infrastructure will be supported in the 5 GHz bands, specifically the 5.850 to 5.925 GHz band within North America.

Communications may be possible at speeds of up to 200 kilometers per hour (124 mph) and within a range of 1,000 meters (3281 feet). Very short latencies will also be needed as some applications must guarantee data delivery within 4 to 50 milliseconds.

802.11p is also known as Wireless Access and Vehicular Environment (WAVE) and is the possible foundation for a U.S. Department of Transportation project called Dedicated Short Range Communications (DSRC). The DSRC project envisions a nationwide vehicle and roadside communication network utilizing applications such as vehicle safety services, traffic jam alarms, toll collections, vehicle collision avoidance, and adaptive traffic light control. 802.11p will also be applicable to marine and rail communications.

802.11r

The 802.11r draft is often referred to as the *fast roaming* amendment because the 802.11 Task Group r (TGr) is currently working on a protocol that will define faster handoffs when roaming occurs between cells in a wireless LAN. 802.11r was proposed primarily because of the time constraints of applications such as VoIP. Average time delays of hundreds of milliseconds occur when a client station roams from one access point to another access point.

Roaming can be especially troublesome when using an 802.11i enterprise security solution, which requires the use of a RADIUS server for authentication and often takes several hundred milliseconds. VoIP requires a handoff of 50 milliseconds or less to avoid a degradation of the quality of the call or, even worse, a loss of connection.

Under 802.11r, a station will be able to establish a QoS stream and set up security associations with a new access point before actually roaming to the new access point. The station can achieve these tasks either over the wire via the original access point or through the air. Eventually the station will complete the roaming process and move to the new access point. The time saved from prearranging security associations and QoS services will drastically speed up the handoffs between WLAN cells.

802.11s

A high-tech story that receives a lot of attention in the media describes blanketing entire cities with Wi-Fi coverage with the goal of citywide wireless access to the Internet. For the most part, the equipment being used for these large-scale 802.11 deployments is proprietary wireless mesh routers or mesh access points. The 802.11s Task Group has set forth the pursuit of standardizing *mesh networking* using the IEEE 802.11 MAC/PHY layers.

802.11 access points typically act as portal devices to a distribution system (DS) that is a wired 802.3 Ethernet medium. However, the 802.11 standard does not mandate that the *distribution system* use a wired medium. Access points can therefore act as portal devices to a *wireless distribution system (WDS)*. The 802.11s amendment proposes a protocol for adaptive, autoconfiguring systems that support broadcast, multicast, and unicast traffic over multihop mesh topologies in a WDS.

Further discussion on the DS and WDS can be found in Chapter 7, "Wireless LAN Topologies." Further discussion on 802.11 mesh networking can be found in Chapter 10.

Initially 15 different mesh proposals were submitted for 802.11s, although proposals from 2 major vendor alliances seem to have taken the lead. One consortium called Simple, Efficient and Extensible Mesh (SEEMesh) is backed by companies such as Intel, Motorola, Nokia, Texas Instruments, and others. The other major consortium is the Wi-Mesh Alliance (WiMA), whose membership includes Extreme Networks, Nortel, NextHop Technologies, Philips, Thomson, and more.

802.11T

The goal of the IEEE 802.11T Task Group (TGT) is to develop performance metrics, measurement methods, and test conditions to measure the performance of 802.11 wireless networking equipment.

The uppercase *T* in the name IEEE 802.11T Task Group indicates that this amendment will be considered a "recommended practice" and not a standard.

The 802.11T draft is also called Wireless Performance Prediction (WPP), with the final objective being consistent and universally accepted WLAN measurement practices. These 802.11 performance benchmarks and methods could be used by independent test labs, manufacturers, and even end users.

802.11u

The primary objective of the 802.11 Task Group u (TGu) is to address interworking issues between an IEEE 802.11 access network and any external network to which it is connected. A common approach is needed to integrate IEEE 802.11 access networks with external networks in a generic and standardized manner. 802.11u is also often referred to as Wireless InterWorking with External Networks (WIEN). This amendment may well address seamless handoff and session persistence with other external networks such as the Internet, cellular networks, and WiMAX.

Proprietary equipment such as hybrid telephones that allows for roaming between an enterprise WLAN and the wide area cellular networks are currently being developed. The 802.11u draft may one day standardize the procedures needed for the interworking between two very different networks.

 Real World Scenario

Are Throughput Results the Same with Different Vendors?

Multiple factors can affect throughput in a wireless network, including the physical environment, range, type of encryption, and more. One factor that can affect throughput is simply the vendor radio card that is being used for transmissions. Even though the 802.11 standards clearly define bandwidth data rates and medium access methods, throughput results vary widely from vendor to vendor. A throughput performance test using two radio cards from vendor #1 will most often yield very different results than the same throughput performance test using two radio cards from vendor #2. Typically, you will see better throughput results when sticking with one vendor as opposed to mixing vendor equipment. However, sometimes mixing vendor equipment will actually produce the unexplained consequence of increased throughput. Ratification of the 802.11T amendment will at the very least provide a more accurate means of performance testing.

802.11v

While 802.11k defines methods of retrieving information from client stations, 802.11v will give us the ability to configure client stations wirelessly from a central point of management. The main goal of the IEEE Task Group v (TGv) is for WLAN infrastructure (access points and wireless switches) to take improved control of wireless client stations. The following list includes some of the 802.11v proposals currently being discussed:

Wireless client control   SNMP Management Information Bases (MIBs) for client station attributes are currently being defined under 802.11v. This will give the ability to configure and manage clients wirelessly from a WLAN infrastructure device.

Load balancing   Enterprise WLAN deployments often encounter disproportionate associations of client stations between access points. This can cause an uneven distribution of available bandwidth and result in throughput problems. Currently, vendors implement proprietary load-balancing procedures to alleviate these problems. 802.11v may standardize and simplify load balancing.

Network selection   In order to join a wireless network, a client station radio card must be preconfigured with a profile that matches all the security credentials on the infrastructure side. 802.11v may provide mechanisms to implement client-side security settings from the WLAN infrastructure.

802.11w

One common type of attack on an 802.11 wireless LAN is a denial of service attack (DoS attack). There are a multitude of DoS attacks that can be launched against a wireless network; however, a very common DoS attack occurs at layer 2 using 802.11 management frames. Currently it is very simple for an attacker to edit deauthenication or disassociation frames and then retransmit the frames into the air, effectively shutting down a wireless network.

The IEEE Task Group w (TGw) is working on a "protected" management frame amendment with a goal of delivering management frames in a secure manner. The end result will hopefully prevent many of the layer 2 denial of service attacks that currently exist.

A discussion about both layer 1 and layer 2 DoS attacks can be found in Chapter 14, "Wireless Attacks, Intrusion Monitoring and Policy."

Neither 802.11l nor 802.11o amendments exist because they are considered typologically problematic. Also, it should be noted that there is no amendment with the name of 802.11x. The term 802.11x sometimes is used to refer to all the 802.11 standards. The IEEE 802.1X standard, which is a "port-based access control" standard, is often incorrectly called 802.11x.

Summary

This chapter covered the original 802.11 standard as well as the many ratified enhancements to the 802.11 standard and possible future enhancements. We covered the following:

- All the defined PHY and MAC layer requirements of the original 802.11 Prime standard

- All the approved enhancements to the 802.11 standard in the form of ratified amendments, including higher data rates, different spread spectrum technologies, quality of service, and security

- The future capabilities and improvements as proposed in the 802.11 drafts, including better throughput, mesh networking, faster roaming, and more

Although many proprietary Wi-Fi solutions exist and will continue to exist in the foreseeable future, standardization brings stability to the marketplace. The 802.11 standard and all the enhanced supplements provide a much needed foundation for vendors, network administrators, and end users alike.

The CWNA exam will test your knowledge of the original 802.11 standard, the ratified amendments, and all the related technologies very extensively. Technologies discussed in the draft proposals, such as MIMO and mesh networking, are also covered in the CWNA exam. Your primary focus should be on the original 802.11 standard and the ratified amendments. However, please understand that when 802.11 draft amendments become approved, they will be weighted heavier in future versions of the CWNA exam.

Exam Essentials

Know the defined PHYs of the original 802.11 standard and the amendments. Although the original 802.11 defined infrared, FHSS, and DSSS, later amendments used specific spread spectrum technologies.

Remember both the required data rates and supported data rates of each standard. 802.11 requires and supports data rates of 1 and 2 Mbps. Other standards offer a wider support for data rates. For example, 802.11a supports rate of 6, 9, 12, 18, 24, 36, 48, and 54 Mbps but only the rates of 6, 12 and 24 Mbps are mandatory. Please understand that data rates are considered bandwidth and not aggregate throughput.

Know the frequency bands defined by each standard. While 802.11a equipment operates in the 5 GHz UNII bands, 802.11, 802.11b and 802.11g devices transmit and receive in the 2.4 GHz ISM band.

Explain the three operational modes of 802.11g and the consequences of each mode. An 802.11g access point may be configured as B only mode, G only mode, or B/G mixed mode. The three modes have different support for different spread spectrum technologies and have different aggregate throughput results.

Define transmit power control and dynamic frequency selection.   TPC and DFS are mandated for use in Europe for the 5 GHz band. Both technologies are used as a means to avoid interference.

Explain the defined wireless security standards both pre-802.11i and post-802.11i.   Before the passage of 802.11i, WEP encryption and either Open System or Shared Key authentication were defined. The 802.11i amendment calls for the use of CCMP/AES for encryption. For authentication, 802.11i defines either an 802.1X/EAP solution or the use of preshared keys.

Define the Inter Access Point Protocol and why it was originally proposed.   IAPP is a "vendor interoperability" roaming protocol that is outlined in the 802.11F recommended practice.

Explain the purpose of the 802.11e amendment and the medium access methods it requires.   The 802.11e amendment addresses quality of service (QoS) issues by mandating the use of Enhanced Distributed Channel Access Function (EDCAF) and Hybrid Coordination Function (HCF).

Understand the purpose of each 802.11 draft proposal.   The 802.11s draft outlines mesh networking. 802.11n proposes throughput enhancements using MIMO technology. Each draft has a specific intended goal.

Key Terms

Before you take the exam, be certain you are familiar with the following terms:

802.1X	dynamic frequency selection (DFS)
Advanced Encryption Standard (AES)	Enhanced Distributed Channel Access (EDCA)
authentication	Extended Rate Physical OFDM (ERP-OFDM)
bandwidth	Extensible Authentication Protocol (EAP)
Barker Code	fast roaming
Complementary Code Keying (CCK)	frequency hopping spread spectrum (FHSS)
Counter Mode with Cipher Block Chaining Message Authentication Code Protocol (CCMP)	High-Rate DSSS (HR-DSSS)
data privacy	Hybrid Coordination Function (HCF)
data rates	Hybrid Coordination Function Controlled Access (HCCA)
direct sequence spread spectrum (DSSS)	Industrial, Scientific, and Medical (ISM)
Distributed Coordination Function (DCF)	infrared (IR)
distribution system (DS)	Inter Access Point Protocol (IAPP)

mesh networking

mixed mode

multiple-input-multiple-output (MIMO)

Open System authentication

Orthogonal Frequency Division
Multiplexing (OFDM)

Packet Binary Convolutional
Coding (PBCC)

Point Coordination Function (PCF)

preshared keys (PSKs)

protection mechanism

quality of service (QoS)

recommended practice

roaming

Robust Security Network (RSN)

Shared Key authentication

task groups

Temporal Key Integrity Protocol (TKIP)

throughput

transmit power control (TPC)

Unlicensed National Information
Infrastructure (UNII)

Voice over IP (VoIP)

Wi-Fi Protected Access (WPA2)

Wired Equivalent Privacy (WEP)

wireless distribution system (WDS)

Voice over Wi-Fi (VoWiFi)

Voice over Wireless IP (VoWIP)

Voice over Wireless LAN (VoWLAN)

Wi-Fi Multimedia (WMM)

Review Questions

1. The 802.11g amendment mandates support for which spread spectrum technologies? (Choose all that apply.)

   A. Orthogonal Frequency Division Multiplexing

   B. Frequency hopping spread spectrum

   C. Packet Binary Convolutional Coding

   D. Direct sequence spread spectrum

   E. Carrier Sense Multiple Access Collision Avoidance

2. Which 802.11 amendment defines quality of service (QoS) at the MAC sublayer?

   A. 802.11f

   B. 802.11d

   C. 802.11q

   D. 802.11e

   E. 802.11F

3. Which type devices may be used in an 802.11 WLAN network? (Choose all that apply.)

   A. Clause 17 OFDM

   B. Clause 15 DSSS

   C. Clause 18 DSSS

   D. Infrared

   E. Clause 14 FHSS

   F. Clause 18 DSSS/OFDM

4. The 802.11F recommended practice requires the use of which protocol?

   A. TPC

   B. EDCAF

   C. IAPP

   D. CSMA/CA

   E. DFS

5. The 802.11i amendment calls out for the use of which security enhancements? (Choose all that apply.)

   A. 802.11x

   B. WEP

   C. IPSec

   D. CCMP/AES

   E. CKIP

   F. 802.1X

6. An 802.11a radio card can transmit on _____ frequency and uses _____ spread spectrum technology.

   A. 5 MHz, OFDM

   B. 2.4 GHz, DSSS

   C. 2.4 GHz, OFDM

   D. 5 GHz, OFDM

   E. 5 GHz, DSSS

7. What are the required data rates of the 802.11a amendment?

   A. 3, 6, and 12 Mbps

   B. 6, 9, 12, 18, 24, 36, 48, and 54 Mbps

   C. 6, 12, 24, and 54 Mbps

   D. 6, 12, and 24 Mbps

   E. 1, 2, 5.5, and 11 Mbps

8. Which 802.11 draft is known as the "fast roaming" amendment?

   A. 802.11T

   B. 802.11r

   C. 802.11F

   D. 802.11k

   E. 802.11f

9. The 802.11 standard requires which bandwidth rates?

   A. 1, 2, 5.5, and 11 Mbps

   B. 6, 12, and 24 Mbps

   C. 1 and 2 Mbps

   D. 6, 9, 12, 18, 24, 36, 48, and 54 Mbps

   E. 3, 6, and 12 Mbps

10. What is the primary reason that 802.11a radio cards cannot communicate with 802.11g radio cards?

    A. 802.11a uses OFDM and 802.11g uses DSSS.

    B. 802.11a uses DSSS and 802.11g uses OFDM.

    C. 802.11a uses OFDM and 802.11g uses CCK.

    D. 802.11a operates at 5 GHz and 802.11g operates at 2.4 GHz.

    E. 802.11a requires Dynamic Frequency Selection and 802.11g does not.

11. The 802.11h amendment defines the use of which technologies? (Choose all that apply.)

    A. Dynamic Frequency Selection

    B. Enhanced Distributed Channel Access Function

    C. Direct sequence spread spectrum

    D. Temporal Key Integrity Protocol

    E. Transmit Power Control

12. Which 802.11 amendment gives network administrators the ability to configure client stations wirelessly from a central point of management?

    A. 802.11k

    B. 802.11v

    C. 802.11u

    D. 802.11w

    E. 802.11s

    F. None of the above

13. As defined by the various 802.11 amendments, which equipment is compatible? (Choose all that apply.)

    A. 802.11g and 802.11b

    B. 802.11b and 802.11/FHSS

    C. 802.11a and 802.11g

    D. 802.11a and 802.11h

    E. 802.11/DSSS and 802.11b

14. Maximum bandwidth rates of _____ are permitted under the 802.11a supplement.

    A. 108 Mbps

    B. 22 Mbps

    C. 24 Mbps

    D. 54 Mbps

    E. 11 Mbps

15. What are the security options available as defined in IEEE Std. 802.11-1999 (R2003)? (Choose all that apply.)

    A. CCMP/AES

    B. Open System authentication

    C. Preshared keys

    D. Shared Key authentication

    E. WEP

    F. TKIP

16. The 802.11u draft amendment is also known as _____ .

   A. Wireless InterWorking with External Networks (WIEN)

   B. Wireless Local Area Networking (WLAN)

   C. Wireless Performance Prediction (WPP)

   D. Wireless Access and Vehicular Environment (WAVE)

   E. Wireless Access Protocol (WAP)

17. The 802.11e supplement defines the use of which technologies? (Choose all that apply.)

   A. EDCA

   B. PCF

   C. Hybrid Coordination Function Channel Access

   D. VoIP

   E. Distributed Coordination Function

   F. VoWIP

18. Which technology was designed to avoid interference with radar in the 5GHz frequency range?

   A. Transmit Power Control

   B. IAPP

   C. Dynamic Frequency Selection

   D. Transmit Frequency Avoidance

   E. Frequency hopping spread spectrum

19. The 802.11b amendment defines the _____ PHY.

   A. HR/DSSS

   B. FHSS

   C. OFDM

   D. PBCC

   E. EIRP

20. Which layers of the OSI model are referenced in the 802.11 standard? (Choose all that apply.)

   A. Application

   B. Data-Link

   C. Presentation

   D. Physical

   E. Transport

   F. Network

Answers to Review Questions

1. A, D. Support for both direct sequence spread spectrum (DSSS) and Orthogonal Frequency Division Multiplexing (OFDM) is required under the 802.11g amendment. Support for Packet Binary Convolutional Coding (PBCC) is optional in the 802.11g amendment.

2. D. IEEE Std. 802.11e-2005 defines the layer 2 MAC methods needed to meet the quality of service (QoS) requirements for time-sensitive applications over IEEE 802.11 wireless LANs.

3. B, D, E. The original 802.11 standard defines three Physical layer specifications. An 802.11 legacy network could use FHSS, DSSS, or infrared. FHSS 802.11 radio cards are often known as clause 14 devices. DSSS 802.11 radio cards are often known as clause 15 devices.

4. C. The 802.11F recommended practice addresses "vendor interoperability" for AP-to-AP roaming. The Inter Access Point Protocol (IAPP) uses announcement and handover processes that result in how APs inform other APs about roamed clients that define a method of delivery for buffered packets.

5. D, F. The default encryption method defined by the 802.11i security amendment is Counter Mode with Cipher Block Chaining Message Authentication Code Protocol (CCMP), which uses the Advanced Encryption Standard (AES) algorithm. An optional choice of encryption is the Temporal Key Integrity Protocol (TKIP). The 802.11i amendment also requires the use of an 802.1X/EAP authentication solution or the use of preshared keys.

6. D. 802.11a radio cards operate in the 5 GHz Unlicensed National Information Infrastructure (UNII) frequency bands using Orthogonal Frequency Division Multiplexing (OFDM).

7. D. The IEEE Std. 802.11a-1999 requires data rates of 6, 12, and 24 Mbps. Data rates of 6, 9, 12, 18, 24, 36, 48, and 54 Mbps are typically supported. 54 Mbps is the maximum defined rate.

8. B. The 802.11r draft is often referred to as the fast roaming amendment because the 802.11 Task Group r (TGr) is currently working on a protocol that will define faster handoffs when roaming occurs between cells in a wireless LAN.

9. C. The legacy 802.11 standard, also known as 802.11 Prime, specified data rates of 1 and 2 Mbps.

10. D. Because 802.11a and 802.11g operate at different frequencies, they cannot communicate with each other. 802.11a equipment operates in the 5 GHz UNII bands, while 802.11g equipment operates in the unlicensed 2.4 GHz ISM band.

11. A, E. The IEEE Std. 802.11h-2003 defines mechanisms for dynamic frequency selection (DFS) and transmit power control (TPC) that may be used to satisfy regulatory requirements for operation in the 5 GHz band in Europe.

12. B. The 802.11v draft amendment defines SNMP-like Management Information Bases (MIBs), which could give administrators the ability to configure client stations wirelessly from a central point of management.

13. A, D, E. 802.11g requires the use of OFDM and DSSS in the unlicensed 2.4GHz ISM band and is backward compatible with 802.11b DSSS equipment. 802.11b uses DSSS in the 2.4 GHz ISM band and is backward compatible with only 802.11 DSSS equipment and not 802.11 FHSS equipment. The 802.11h amendment defines use of TPC and DFS in the 5 GHz UNII bands and is an enhancement to the 802.11a amendment.

14. D. The IEEE Std. 802.11a-1999 requires data rates of 6, 12, and 24 Mbps. Data rates of 6, 9, 12, 18, 24, 36, 48, and 54 Mbps are typically supported. 54 Mbps is the maximum defined rate.

15. B, D, E. The original 802.11 standard defined the use of WEP for encryption. The 802.11 standard defined two methods of authentication: Open System authentication and Shared Key authentication.

16. A. The 802.11u draft amendment defines integration of IEEE 802.11 access networks with external networks in a generic and standardized manner. 802.11u is also often referred to as Wireless InterWorking with External Networks (WIEN).

17. A, C. The 802.11e amendment defines two enhanced medium access methods to support quality of service (QoS) requirements. Enhanced Distributed Channel Access (EDCA) is an extension to DCF. Hybrid Coordination Function Channel Access(HCCA) is an extension to PCF.

18. C. The European Radiocommunications Committee (ERC) mandates that radio cards operating in the 5GHz band implement a mechanism to avoid interference with radar systems as well as provide equable use of the channels. Dynamic Frequency Selection as defined in 802.11h is used to meet the ERC regulatory requirements.

19. A. The 802.11b amendment defines systems that can transmit at data rates of 1, 2, 5.5, and 11 Mbps using High-Rate DSSS (HR-DSSS).

20. B, D. The IEEE specifically defines 802.11 technologies at the Physical layer and the MAC sub-layer of the Data-Link layer. By design, anything that occurs at the upper layers of the OSI model is insignificant to 802.11 communications.

Wireless Networks and Spread Spectrum Technologies

IN THIS CHAPTER, YOU WILL LEARN ABOUT THE FOLLOWING:

✓ **Industrial, Scientific, and Medical Bands (ISM)**

  ▪ 900 MHz ISM Band

  ▪ 2.4 GHz ISM Band

  ▪ 5.8 GHz ISM Band

✓ **Unlicensed National Information Infrastructure Bands (UNII)**

  ▪ Lower Band (UNII-1)

  ▪ Middle Band (UNII-2)

  ▪ Upper Band (UNII-3)

✓ **Narrowband and Spread Spectrum**

✓ **Frequency Hopping Spread Spectrum (FHSS)**

  ▪ Hopping Sequence

  ▪ Dwell Time

  ▪ Hop Time

  ▪ Modulation

✓ **802.11/b/g Channels**

✓ **Direct Sequence Spread Spectrum (DSSS)**

  ▪ DSSS Data Encoding

  ▪ Modulation

✓ **Packet Binary Convolutional Code (PBCC)**

✓ **Orthogonal Frequency Division Multiplexing (OFDM)**

  ▪ Convolutional Coding

✓ **802.11a Channels**

✓ **Throughput vs. Bandwidth**

✓ **Communication Resilience**

In this chapter you will learn about the different spread spectrum transmission technologies and frequency ranges that are supported by the 802.11 standard and amendments. You will learn how these frequencies are divided into different channels and some of the proper and improper ways of using the channels. Additionally, you will learn about spread spectrum and the different types of spread spectrum. You will also learn about Orthogonal Frequency Division Multiplexing (OFDM) and the similarities and differences between OFDM and spread spectrum.

Industrial, Scientific, and Medical (ISM) Bands

The IEEE 802.11 standard and the subsequent 802.11b and 802.11g amendments all define communications in the frequency range between 2.4 GHz and 2.4835 GHz. This frequency range is one of three frequency ranges known as the Industrial, Scientific, and Medical (ISM) bands. The ISM bands are as follows:

- 902–928 MHz (26 MHz wide)
- 2.4000–2.4835 GHz (83.5 MHz wide)
- 5.725–5.875 GHz (150 MHz wide)

The ISM bands are defined by the ITU Telecommunication Standardization Sector (ITU-T) in S5.138 and S5.150 of the Radio Regulations. Although the FCC governs the use of the ISM bands defined by the ITU-T in the United States, their usage in other countries may be different due to local regulations. The 900 MHz band is known as the Industrial band, the 2.4 GHz band is known as the Scientific band, and the 5.8 GHz band is known as the Medical band.

It should be noted that all three of these bands are license-free bands and there are no restrictions on what types of equipment can be used in any of them. For example, a radio card used in medical equipment can be used in the 900 MHz Industrial band.

900 MHz ISM Band

The 900 MHz ISM band is 26 MHz wide and spans from 902 MHz to 928 MHz. In the past, this band was used for wireless networking; however, most wireless networking now uses higher frequencies, which are capable of higher throughput. Another factor limiting the use of the 900 MHz ISM band is that in many parts of the world, part of the 900 MHz frequency range has already been allocated to the Global System for Mobile Communications (GSM) cellular phones.

Although the 900 MHz ISM band is rarely used for networking, many products such as baby monitors, wireless home telephones, and wireless headphones make use of this frequency range. 802.11 radio cards do not operate in the 900 MHz ISM band, but many older legacy deployments of wireless networking did operate in the 900 MHz ISM band. Some vendors still manufacture non-802.11 wireless networking devices that operate in the 900 MHz ISM band. This is a particularly popular frequency that is used for wireless ISPs due to its superior foliage penetration.

2.4 GHz ISM Band

The 2.4 GHz ISM band is currently the most common band used for wireless networking communications. The 2.4 GHz ISM band is 83.5 MHz wide and spans from 2.4000 GHz to 2.4835 GHZ. Use of the 2.4 GHz ISM is defined under the original 802.11 standard as well as two of the three major 802.11 networking amendments:

- 802.11
- 802.11b
- 802.11g

In addition to being used by networking equipment, the 2.4 GHz ISM band is also used by microwave ovens, cordless home telephones, baby monitors, and wireless video cameras. The 2.4 GHz ISM band currently is heavily used and one of the big disadvantages of using 802.11b/g radios is the potential for interference.

5.8 GHz ISM Band

The 5.8 GHz ISM band is 150 MHz wide and spans from 5.725 GHz to 5.875 GHz. As with the other ISM bands, the 5.8 GHz ISM band is used by many of the same types of consumer products: baby monitors, cordless telephones, and cameras. It is not uncommon for novices to incorrectly assume that the 5.8 GHz ISM band is the frequency space defined for use by the 802.11a amendment.

The IEEE 802.11a amendment actually defines the use of the 5 GHz Unlicensed National Information Infrastructure (UNII) Bands. Due to the different FCC power requirements, the 5.8 GHz ISM band is a preferred spectrum for long distance wireless bridging.

Unlicensed National Information Infrastructure Bands (UNII)

The IEEE 802.11a amendment designates data transmissions within the frequency space of the 5 GHz UNII bands. The 802.11a amendment uses three groupings, or bands, of UNII frequencies, often known as the lower, middle, and upper UNII bands. These three bands are typically designated as UNII-1 (lower), UNII-2 (middle), and UNII-3 (upper). All three of these bands are 100 MHz wide, which is a useful fact when trying to remember their frequency ranges. Although we use UNII as the abbreviation, many documents will show U-NII as the abbreviation. Both abbreviations are common and acceptable. The commonly used UNII bands are as follows:

UNII-1	Lower	5.15–5.25 GHz
UNII-2	Middle	5.25–5.35 GHz
UNII-3	Upper	5.725–5.825 GHz

In 2004, the FCC revised the UNII frequency specifications, adding an additional 11 new channels between the frequencies of 5.470 GHz and 5.725 GHz. Most hardware manufacturers are capable of transmitting in these 11 new channels without additional hardware modifications, and some Wi-Fi vendors in the United States are in the process of receiving permission from the FCC to transmit in the new channels. In these cases, it is likely that you will have to perform a firmware upgrade on your wireless device in order to take advantage of this new spectrum.

Lower Band (UNII-1)

The lower UNII band is 100 MHz wide and spans from 5.150 GHz to 5.250 GHz. This band is allowed to be used for indoor communications only (to prevent interference with mobile satellite services), with a maximum allowed output power of 40 mW at the intentional radiator (IR) as defined by the IEEE. Prior to 2004, the FCC required that all UNII-1–capable devices must have permanently attached antennas. This meant that any 802.11a device that supported UNII-1 could not have a detachable antenna, even if the device supported other frequencies or standards.

In 2004, the FCC changed the regulations to allow detachable antennas providing that the antenna connector is unique. This requirement is similar to the antenna requirements for the other UNII bands and the 2.4 GHz ISM band. Some access point manufacturers allow the ability to configure the device as a bridge and to work in the lower UNII band. Care must be taken to make sure that you do not exceed the limitations of your local regulatory body.

Middle Band (UNII-2)

The middle UNII band is 100 MHz wide and spans from 5.250 GHz to 5.350 GHz. This band is allowed to be used for indoor or outdoor communications, with a maximum allowed output power of 200 mW at the intentional radiator (IR) as defined by the IEEE. Local regulatory agencies may impose other restrictions that you will need to comply with.

Upper Band (UNII-3)

The upper UNII band is 100 MHz wide and spans from 5.725 GHz to 5.825 GHz. This band is typically used for outdoor point-to-point communications but can also be used indoors in some countries. The maximum allowed output power by the IEEE is 800 mW at the intentional radiator (IR).

The three commonly used UNII bands are each 100 MHz wide:

UNII-1	Lower	5.15–5.25 GHz
UNII-1	Lower	5.15–5.25 GHz
UNII-3	Upper	5.725–5.825 GHz

Notice that the starting frequency of UNII-3 is the same as the 5.8 GHz ISM band. Remember that the UNII-3 band is 100 MHz wide and the 5.8 GHz ISM band is 150 MHz wide.

Narrowband and Spread Spectrum

There are two primary radio frequency (RF) transmission methods: narrowband and spread spectrum. A narrowband transmission uses very little bandwidth to transmit the data that it is carrying, whereas a spread spectrum transmission uses more bandwidth than is necessary to carry its data. Spread spectrum technology takes the data that is to be transmitted and spreads it across the frequencies that it is using. For example, a narrowband radio might transmit data on 2 MHz of frequency space at 80 watts while a spread spectrum radio might transmit data over a 22 MHz frequency space at 100 milliwatts.

Figure 6.1 shows a rudimentary comparison of how a narrowband and spread spectrum signal relate to each other. Because narrowband signals take up a single or very narrow band of frequencies, intentional jamming or unintentional interference of this frequency range is likely to cause disruption in the signal. Because spread spectrum uses a wider range of frequency space, it is typically less susceptible to intentional jamming or unintentional interference from outside sources, unless the interfering signal was also spread across the range of frequencies used by the spread spectrum communications.

Narrowband signals are transmitted using much higher power than spread spectrum signals. Typically, the FCC or other local regulatory body requires that narrowband transmitters are licensed to minimize the risk of two narrowband transmitters interfering with each other. AM and FM radio stations are examples of narrowband transmitters that are licensed to make sure that two stations in the same or nearby market are not transmitting on the same frequency.

Spread spectrum signals are transmitted using very low power levels. Since the power levels are so low, they are less likely to cause interference with other systems and therefore are typically not required to be licensed by the local regulatory body.

One of the problems that occur with RF communications is multipath interference. Multipath occurs when a reflected signal arrives at the receiving antenna after the primary signal. This is similar to the way an echo is heard after the original sound.

FIGURE 6.1   Overlay of narrowband and spread spectrum frequency use

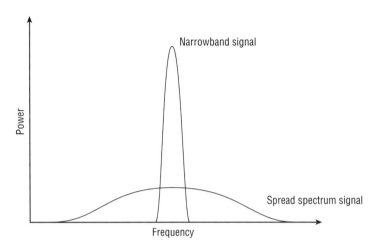

Let's use an example of yelling to a friend across a canyon. Let's assume you are going to yell, "Hello, how are you?" to your friend. To make sure that your friend understood your message, you might pace your message and yell each word 1 second after the previous word. If your friend heard the echo (multipath reflection of your voice) $1/2$ second after the main sound arrived, your friend would hear "HELLO hello HOW how ARE are YOU you" (echoes are represented by lowercase). Your friend would be able to interpret the message because the echo arrived between the main signals, or the sound of your voice. However, if the echo arrived 1 second after the main sound, the echo for the word *hello* would arrive at the same time the word *HOW* arrives. With both sounds arriving at the same time, it may not be possible to understand the message.

 Real World Scenario

Who Invented Spread Spectrum?

Spread spectrum was originally patented on August 11, 1942, by Hedy Kiesler Markey (Hedy Lamarr) and George Antheil and was originally designed to be a radio guidance system for torpedoes, for which it was never used. Lamarr was a famous actress and Antheil was a famous composer. The idea of spread spectrum was ahead of its time. It was not until 1957 that further development on spread spectrum occurred, and in 1962 frequency hopping spread spectrum was used for the first time between the U.S. ships at the blockade of Cuba during the Cuban Missile Crisis. If you would like to learn more about the interesting history of spread spectrum, search the Internet for "Lamarr" and "Antheil." There are many websites with articles about these two inventors and even copies of the original patent. Neither inventor ever made any money from their patent since it expired before the technology was ever developed.

RF data communications behave the same way as the sound example. The delay between the main signal and the reflected signal is known as the *delay spread*. If the delay spread is long enough that the reflected signal interferes with the next piece of data from the main signal, this is referred to as *inter-symbol interference (ISI)*. Spread spectrum systems are not as susceptible to ISI because they spread their signals across a range of frequencies. These different frequencies produce different delays in multipath, such that some wavelengths may be affected by ISI whereas others may not. Because of this behavior, spread spectrum signals are typically more tolerant of multipath interference than narrowband signals.

802.11b and 802.11g are tolerant of delay spread only to a certain extent. 802.11b can tolerate delay spread of up to 500 nanoseconds. Even though the delay spread can be tolerated, performance is much better when the delay spread is lower. The 802.11b transmitter will drop to a lower data rate when the delay spread increases. Longer symbols are used when transmitting at the lower data rates. When longer symbols are used, longer delays can occur before ISI occurs. According to some of the 802.11b vendors, 65 nanoseconds or lower delay spread is required for 802.11b at 11 Mbps.

Because of OFDM's greater tolerance of delay spread, an 802.11g transmitter can maintain 54 Mbps with a delay spread of up to about 150 nanoseconds. This depends upon the 802.11g chipset that is being used in the transmitter and receiver. Some chipsets are not as tolerant and switch to a lower data rate at a lower delay spread value.

Frequency Hopping Spread Spectrum (FHSS)

Frequency hopping spread spectrum (FHSS) was used in the original 802.11 standard and provided 1 and 2Mbps RF communications using the 2.4 GHz ISM band. The IEEE specified that in North America, 802.11 FHSS would use 79 MHz of frequencies, from 2.402 GHz to 2.480 GHz. Generally, the way FHSS works is it transmits data using a small frequency carrier space, then hops to another small frequency carrier space and transmits data, then to another frequency, and so on, as illustrated in Figure 6.2. More specifically, frequency hopping spread spectrum transmits data using a specific frequency for a set period of time, known as the dwell time. When the dwell time expires, the system changes to another frequency and begins to transmit on that frequency for the duration of the dwell time. Each time the dwell time is reached, the system changes to another frequency and continues to transmit.

Hopping Sequence

FHSS radios use a predefined *hopping sequence* (also called a hopping pattern or hopping set) comprising a series of small carrier frequencies, or "hops." Instead of transmitting on one set channel or finite frequency space, an FHSS radio card transmits on a sequence of sub-channels called hops. Each time the hop sequence is completed, it is repeated. Figure 6.2 shows a make-believe hopping sequence that consists of five hops.

FIGURE 6.2   FHSS components

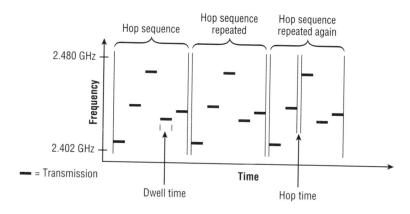

The IEEE 802.11 standard mandates that each hop is 1 MHz in size. These individual hops are then arranged in predefined sequences. In North America and most of Europe, the hopping sequences contain at least seventy-five 1 MHz hops, but no greater than seventy-nine 1 MHz hops. Other countries have different requirements; for example, France uses 35 hops, while Spain and Japan use 23 hops in a sequence. For successful transmissions to occur, all FHSS transmitters and receivers must be synchronized on the same carrier hop at the same time. The 802.11 standard defines hopping sequences that can be configured on an FHSS access point and the hopping sequence information is delivered to client stations via the beacon management frame.

Dwell Time

Dwell time is a defined amount of time that the FHSS system transmits on a specific frequency before it switches to the next frequency in the hop set. The local regulatory body typically limits the amount of dwell time. For example, the FCC specifies a maximum dwell time of 400 milliseconds (ms) per carrier frequency during any 30-second period of time. Typical dwell times are around 100 to 200 ms. The IEEE 802.11 standard specifies that a hopping sequence must consist of at least 75 frequencies, 1 MHz wide. Since the standard specifies a maximum bandwidth of 79 MHz, the maximum number of hops possible for a hop set would be 79. With an FHSS hop sequence consisting of 75 hops and a dwell time of 400 ms, it would take about 30 seconds to complete the hop sequence. Once the hop sequence is complete, it is repeated.

Hop Time

Hop time is not a specified period of time but rather a measurement of the amount of time it takes for the transmitter to change from one frequency to another. Hop time is typically a fairly small number, often about 200 to 300 microseconds (μs). With typical dwell times of 100 to 200 ms, hop times of 200 to 300 μs are insignificant. Insignificant or not, the hop time is essentially wasted time, or overhead, and takes up the same amount of time regardless of the dwell time. The longer the dwell time, the less often the transmitter has to waste time hopping to another frequency, thus greater throughput. If the dwell time is shorter, the transmitter has to hop more frequently, thus decreasing throughput.

Modulation

FHSS uses Gaussian Frequency Shift Keying (GFSK) to encode the data. 2-level GFSK (2GFSK) uses two frequencies to represent a 0 or a 1 bit. 4-level GFSK (4GFSK) uses four frequencies, with each frequency representing 2 bits (00, 01, 10, or 11). Because it takes cycles before the frequency can be determined, the symbol rate (rate that the data is sent) is only about 1 or 2 million symbols per second, a fraction of the 2.4 GHz carrier frequency.

What Is the Significance of the Dwell Time?

Since FHSS transmissions jump inside a frequency range of 79 MHz, a narrowband signal or noise would disrupt only a small range of frequencies and would produce only a minimal amount of throughput loss. Decreasing the dwell time can further reduce the effect of interference. Conversely, because the radio card is transmitting data during the dwell time, the longer the dwell time, the greater the throughput.

802.11/b/g Channels

In order to have a better understanding of how 802.11, 802.11b, and 802.11g are used, it is important to understand how the IEEE 802.11 standard divides the 2.4 GHz ISM band into 14 separate channels, as listed in Table 6.1. Although the 2.4 GHz ISM band is divided into 14 channels, the FCC or local regulatory body designates which channels are allowed to be used. Table 6.1 also shows what channels are supported in a sample of a few countries. As you can see, the regulations can vary greatly between countries.

Channels are designated by their center frequency. Each channel is 22 MHz wide and is often referenced by the frequency ± 11 MHz. For example, channel 1 is 2.412 GHz ± 11 MHz, which means that channel 1 spans from 2.401 GHz to 2.423 GHz. Since each channel is 22 MHz wide, and since the separation between channels is only 5 MHz, the channels will overlap.

Figure 6.3 shows an overlay of all of the channels and how they overlap. Channels 1, 6, and 11 have been highlighted because, as you can see, they are separated from each other by enough frequencies that they do not overlap. In order for two channels to not overlap, they must be separated by at least five channels or 25 MHz. Channels, such as 2 and 9, do not overlap, but by selecting 2 and 9, there is no additional legal channel that can be chosen that does not overlap either 2 or 9. In the U.S. and Canada, the only three simultaneously non-overlapping channels are 1, 6, and 11. In regions where channels 1 through 13 are allowed to be used, there are different combinations of three non-overlapping channels, although channels 1, 6, and 11 are usually chosen.

TABLE 6.1   DSSS Frequency Channel Plan

Channel ID	Center Frequency (GHz)	U.S. (FCC)	Canada (IC)	Europe (ETSI)	Japan (MKK)	Spain	France
1	2.412	X	X	X	X		
2	2.417	X	X	X	X		
3	2.422	X	X	X	X		
4	2.427	X	X	X	X		
5	2.432	X	X	X	X		
6	2.437	X	X	X	X		
7	2.442	X	X	X	X		
8	2.447	X	X	X	X		
9	2.452	X	X	X	X		
10	2.457	X	X	X	X	X	X
11	2.462	X	X	X	X	X	X
12	2.467			X	X		X
13	2.472			X	X		X
14	2.484						

X = supported channel

FIGURE 6.3 IEEE 802.11b/g channel overlay diagram

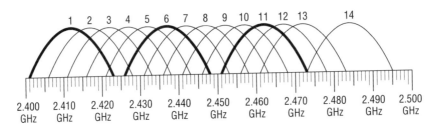

Although it is very common to represent the RF signal of a particular channel with an arch-type line, this is not a true representation of the signal. To explain it simply, in addition to the main *carrier frequency* or main lobe, sidebands are also generated, as shown in Figure 6.4. The IEEE defines a *transmit spectrum mask*, specifying that the first sideband lobe (–11 MHz to –22 MHz from the center frequency, and +11 MHz to +22 MHz from the center frequency) must be at least 30 dB less than the main lobe. The mask also specifies that any additional sideband lobes (–22 MHz from the center frequency and beyond and +22 MHz from the center frequency and beyond) must be at least 50 dB less than the main lobe.

The IEEE 802.11 definition of *non-overlapping DSSS channels* is changed by 802.11b. 802.11g OFDM uses the same channel numbering scheme as HR-DSSS found in 802.11b and therefore must deal with the channel overlap problem. 802.11a OFDM channels theoretically never overlap. The following graphic shows 802.11b HR-DSSS channels 1, 6, and 11 with 25 MHz of spacing between the center frequencies. These are the most commonly used non-overlapping channels in North America and most of the world for 802.11b.

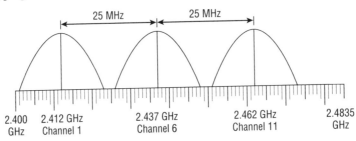

What exactly classifies DSSS or HR-DSSS channels as non-overlapping? According to the original 802.11 standard, DSSS channels had to have at least 30 MHz of spacing between the center frequencies to be considered non-overlapping. In a deployment of DSSS equipment using a channel pattern of 1, 6, and 11, the channels were considered overlapping because the center frequencies were only 25 MHz apart.

HR-DSSS was introduced under the 802.11b amendment, which states that channels need a minimum of 25 MHz of separation between the center frequencies to be considered non-overlapping. Therefore, when 802.11b was introduced, channels 1, 6, and 11 were considered non-overlapping.

The 802.11g amendment, which allows for backward compatibility with 802.11b HR-DSSS, also requires 25 MHz of separation between the center frequencies of HR-DSSS channels to be considered non-overlapping. 802.11g Extended Rate Physical – OFDM (ERP-OFDM) channels require only 20 MHz of separation between the center frequencies to be considered non-overlapping because the channel widths comply with 802.11a OFDM channel parameters. Under the 802.11g amendment, channels 1, 6, and 11 are considered non-overlapping for both HR-DSSS and ERP-OFDM.

The transmit spectrum mask is defined to minimize interference between devices on different frequencies. Even though the sideband lobes are mere whispers of signal compared to the main lobe, even a whisper is noticeable when the person whispering is close to you. This is true for RF devices too. Figure 6.5 represents RF signals on channels 1, 6, and 11. A signal level line indicates an arbitrary level of reception by the access point on channel 6. At level 1, meaning the AP on channel 6 receives only the signals above the level 1 line, the signals from channel 1 and channel 11 do not intersect (interfere) with the signals on channel 6. However, at the level 2 line, the signals from channel 1 and channel 11 do intersect (interfere) slightly with the signals on channel 6. At the level 3 line, there is significant interference from the signals from channel 1 and channel 11. Because of the potential for this situation, it is important to separate RF devices (usually 5 to 10 feet is sufficient for 802.11 devices) so that interference from sideband lobes does not occur. This is important both horizontally and vertically.

FIGURE 6.4 IEEE 802.11b transmit spectrum mask

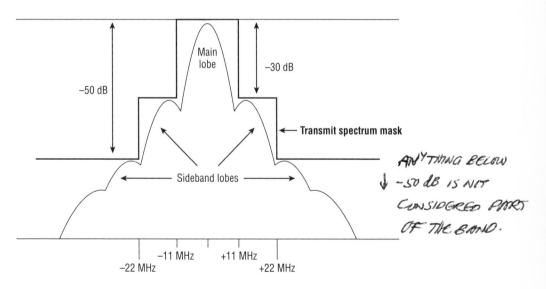

FIGURE 6.5   Sideband lobe interference

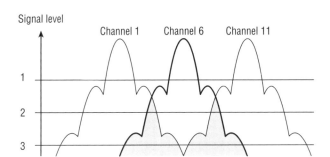

Direct Sequence Spread Spectrum (DSSS)

Direct sequence spread spectrum (DSSS) was originally specified in the primary or root 802.11 standard and provides 1 and 2 Mbps RF communications using the 2.4 GHz ISM band. DSSS was also specified in the 802.11b addendum and provides 5.5 and 11 Mbps RF communications using the same 2.4 GHz ISM band. The 802.11b 5.5 and 11 Mbps speeds are known as *High-Rate DSSS (HR-DSSS)*.

802.11b devices are backward compatible with 802.11 DSSS devices. This means that an 802.11b device can transmit using DSSS at 1 and 2 Mbps and using HR-DSSS at 5.5 and 11 Mbps. However, 802.11b devices are not capable of transmitting using FHSS; therefore, they are not backward compatible with 802.11 FHSS devices.

NOTE   DSSS 1 and 2 Mbps were specified in the original 802.11 standard. HR-DSSS 5.5 and 11 Mbps were specified in the 802.11b amendment.

Unlike FHSS where the transmitter jumped between frequencies, DSSS is set to one channel. The data that is being transmitted is spread across the range of frequencies that make up the channel. The process of spreading the data across the channel is known as data encoding.

DSSS Data Encoding

In Chapter 2, "Radio Frequency Fundamentals," you learned about many ways that RF signals can get altered or corrupted. Because 802.11 is an unbounded medium with a huge potential for RF interference, it had to be designed to be resilient enough that data corruption could be minimized. In order to achieve this, each bit of data is encoded and transmitted as multiple bits of data.

The task of adding additional, redundant information to the data is known as *processing gain*. In this day and age of data compression, it seems strange that we would use a technology that adds data to our transmission, but by doing so the communication is more resistant to data corruption. The system converts the 1 bit of data into a series of bits that are referred to as *chips*. To create the chips, a Boolean XOR is performed on the data bit and a fixed-length bit sequence pseudo-random number (PN) code. Using a PN code known as the Barker Code, the binary data 1 and 0 are represented by the following chip sequences:

Binary data 1 = 1 0 1 1 0 1 1 1 0 0 0

Binary data 0 = 0 1 0 0 1 0 0 0 1 1 1

This sequence of chips is then spread across a wider frequency space. While 1 bit of data might need only 2 MHz of frequency space, the 11 chips will require 22 MHz of frequency carrier. The process of converting a single data bit into a sequence of bits known as chips is often called "spreading" or "chipping." The receiving radio card converts, or "de-spreads," the chip sequence back into a single data bit. When the data is converted to multiple chips and some of the chips are not received properly, the radio will still be able to interpret the data by looking at the chips that were received properly. When the Barker Code is used, as many as 9 of the 11 chips can be corrupted, yet the receiving radio card will still be able to interpret the sequence and convert them back into a single data bit. This chipping process also makes the communication less likely to be affected by inter-symbol interference (ISI) since it uses more bandwidth.

> After the Barker Code is applied to data, a series of 11 bits, referred to as chips, represent the original single bit of data. This series of encoded bits makes up 1 bit of data. To help prevent confusion, it is best to think of and refer to the encoded bits as chips.

The Barker Code uses an 11-chip PN; however, the length of the code is irrelevant. To help provide the faster speeds of HR-DSSS, another more complex code, *Complementary Code Keying (CCK)*, is utilized. CCK uses an 8-chip PN, along with using different PNs for different bit sequences. CCK can encode 4 bits of data with 8 chips (5.5 Mbps) and can encode 8 bits of data with 8 chips (11 Mbps). Although it is interesting to learn about, a thorough understanding of CCK is not required for the CWNA exam.

Modulation

Once the data has been encoded using a chipping method, the transmitter needs to modulate the signal to create a carrier signal containing the chips. Differential Binary Phase Shift Keying (DBPSK) utilizes two phase shifts, one that represents a 0 chip and another that represents a 1 chip. To provide faster throughput, Differential Quaternary Phase Shift Keying (DQPSK) utilizes four phase shifts, allowing each of the four phase shifts to modulate two chips (00, 01, 10, 11) instead of just one chip, doubling the speed.

Table 6.2 shows a summary of the data encoding and modulation techniques used by 802.11 and 802.11b.

TABLE 6.2 802.11 and 802.11b Encoding and Modulation Overview

Standard	Data Rate (Mbps)	Encoding	Chip Length	Bits Encoded	Modulation
802.11	1	Barker Coding	11	1	DBPSK
802.11	2	Barker Coding	11	1	DQPSK
802.11b	5.5	CCK Coding	8	4	DQPSK
802.11b	11	CCK Coding	8	8	DQPSK

Packet Binary Convolutional Code (PBCC)

Packet Binary Convolutional Code (PBCC) is a modulation technique that supports data rates of 5.5, 11, 22, and 33 Mbps; however, both the transmitter and receiver must support the technology to achieve the higher speeds. PBCC was developed by Alantro Communications, which was purchased by Texas Instruments. During the development of the 802.11g addendum, PBCC was adopted as an optional modulation technique.

Orthogonal Frequency Division Multiplexing (OFDM)

Orthogonal Frequency Division Multiplexing (OFDM) is one of the most popular communications technologies, used in both wired and wireless communications. As part of 802.11 technologies, OFDM is specified in the 802.11a and 802.11g amendments and can transmit at speeds of up to 54 Mbps. OFDM is not a spread spectrum technology, even though it has similar properties to spread spectrum, such as low transmit power and using more bandwidth than is required to transmit data. Because of these similarities, OFDM is often referred to as a spread spectrum technology even though technically that reference is incorrect. OFDM actually transmits across 52 separate, closely and precisely spaced frequencies, often referred to as subcarriers, as illustrated in Figure 6.6.

FIGURE 6.6 802.11 Channels and OFDM subcarriers

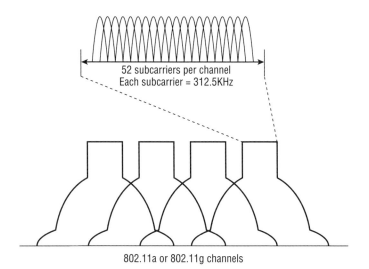

52 subcarriers per channel
Each subcarrier = 312.5KHz

802.11a or 802.11g channels

The frequency width of each subcarrier is 312.5 KHz. The subcarriers are also transmitted at lower data rates, but since there are so many subcarriers, overall data rates are higher. Also, because of the lower subcarrier data rates, delay spread is a smaller percentage of the symbol period, which means that ISI is less likely to occur. In other words, OFDM technology is more resistant to the negative effects of multipath than DSSS and FHSS. Figure 6.7 represents four of the 52 subcarriers. One of the subcarriers is highlighted so that you can more easily understand the drawing. Notice that the frequency spacing of the subcarriers has been chosen so that the harmonics overlap and provide cancellation of most of the unwanted signals.

FIGURE 6.7 Subcarrier signal overlay

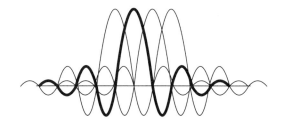

The 52 subcarriers are numbered from −26 to +26. Forty-eight of the subcarriers are used to transmit data. The other four, numbers −21, −7, +7, and +21, are known as pilot carriers. These four are used as reference for phase and amplitude by the demodulator, allowing the receiver to compensate for distortion of the OFDM signal.

Convolution Coding

In order to make OFDM more resistant to narrowband interference, a form of error correction known as *convolution coding* is performed. Convolution coding is not part of OFDM but rather part of 802.11a and 802.11g. It is a *forward error correction (FEC)* that allows the receiving system to detect and repair corrupted bits. There are many levels of convolution coding. Convolution coding uses a ratio between the bits transmitted vs. the bits encoded to provide these different levels. The lower the ratio, the less resistant the signal is to interference and greater the data rate will be. Table 6.3 displays a comparison between the technologies used to create the different data rates of 802.11a and 802.11g. Notice that the data rates are grouped by pairs based upon modulation technique and that the difference between the two speeds is caused by the different levels of convolution coding. A detailed explanation of convolution coding is extremely complex and far beyond the knowledge needed for the CWNA exam.

TABLE 6.3   802.11a and 802.11g Technology Comparison Chart

Data Rates (Mbps)	Modulation Method	Bits Transmitted	Transmitted	Bits Encoded	Ratio
6	DBPSK	1	1	2	1/2
9	DBPSK	1	3	4	3/4
12	DQPSK	2	1	2	1/2
18	DQPSK	2	3	4	3/4
24	16-QAM	4	1	2	1/2
36	16-QAM	4	3	4	3/4
48	64-QAM	6	2	3	2/3
54	64-QAM	6	3	4	3/4

802.11a Channels

The 802.11a amendment specifies the three 5 GHz UNII bands; lower UNII, middle UNII, and upper UNII. Each of these three UNII bands is 100 MHz wide. The centers of the outermost channels in the lower and middle UNII bands must be 30 MHz from the band's edge and 20 MHz for the upper UNII band. Each of the UNII bands has four non-overlapping channels with 20 MHz separation between the center frequencies. Figure 6.8 shows the valid lower and middle UNII channels in the top graphic and the valid upper UNII channels in the bottom graphic. Channel 36 is highlighted so that it is easier to distinguish a single carrier and its sideband lobes. The IEEE defines the center frequency of each channel as follows, where n_{ch} is all values from 0 through 200:

$$5{,}000 + 5 \times n_{ch} \; (MHz)$$

The IEEE does not specify a channel width.

As seen in Figure 6.9, the 802.11a spectrum mask, the sideband lobes do not drop off very quickly, and therefore the sideband lobes of two adjacent valid channels overlap and are more likely to cause interference. Due to the number of channels and the channel spacing of 802.11a, it is easier to separate adjacent channels and prevent interference.

FIGURE 6.8   UNII channel overview

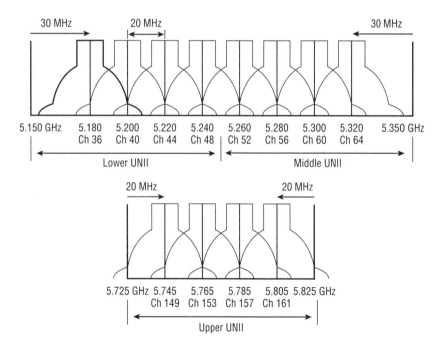

FIGURE 6.9   802.11a spectrum mask

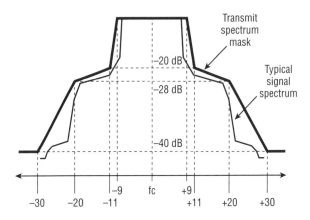

Throughput vs. Bandwidth

Wireless communication is typically performed within a constrained set of frequencies known as a frequency band. This frequency band is the bandwidth. Bandwidth does play a part in the speed of the signal and the throughput of the data, but there are many other factors that do too. In addition to bandwidth, data encoding and modulation also play a large part. Simply look at 802.11g and OFDM as an example. 802.11g can transmit at 6, 9, 12, 18, 24, 36, 48, or 54 Mbps, yet the bandwidth is the same for all of these speeds. What changes between all of these speeds is the modulation and coding technique.

One of the surprising facts when explaining wireless networking to a layperson is the actual throughput speed that an 802.11 wireless network provides. When a novice walks through a computer store and sees the packages of 802.11 devices, they usually assume that a device that is labeled as 54 Mbps is going to provide throughput of 54 Mbps. A medium access method known as Carrier Sense Multiple Access/Collision Avoidance (CSMA/CA) helps to ensure that only one radio card can be transmitting on the medium at any given time. Because of the half-duplex nature of the medium and the overhead generated by CSMA/CA, the actual aggregate throughput is typically 50 percent or less of the data rate. In addition to the throughput being affected by the half-duplex nature of 802.11 communication, the throughput is affected differently based upon the frequency used. Both 802.11a and 802.11g use OFDM; however, 802.11g does not perform as well due to the higher level of RF noise in the 2.4 GHz ISM band. It is also very important to understand that the 802.11 RF medium is a "shared" medium, meaning that in any discussion of throughput, it should be thought of as "aggregate throughput." For example, if a data rate is 54 Mbps, due to CSMA/CA the aggregate throughput might be about 20 Mbps. If five client stations were all downloading the same file from an FTP server at the same time, the perceived throughput for each client station would be about 4 Mbps under ideal circumstances.

There are many other things that add overhead and can affect the throughput. Security and encryption can both add additional processing requirements to encrypt and decrypt the data along with increasing the frame size, thus increasing the communication overhead. Fragmentation of frames creates additional overhead by forcing the system to transmit smaller frames, each with a complete set of 802.11 headers. RTS/CTS (which you will learn about in Chapter 9, "802.11 MAC Architecture") can also affect throughput by adding communication overhead. In some environments, though, fragmentation and RTS/CTS can actually increase throughput if the actual throughput was low due to communication problems.

There are variables at almost all layers of the OSI model that can affect the throughput of 802.11 communications. It is important to understand the different causes, their effects, and what can be done (if anything) to minimize their effect on overall data throughput.

Communication Resilience

There are many technologies that have been covered in this chapter that either directly or indirectly provide resilience to 802.11 communications. Spread spectrum spreads the data across a range of frequencies, making it less likely for a narrowband RF signal to cause interference. FHSS is inherently more resilient to narrowband interference than OFDM, and OFDM is more resilient to narrowband interference than DSSS. Since spread spectrum technology uses a range of frequencies, this inherently adds resilience because delay spread and ISI will vary between the different frequencies. Additionally, data encoding provides error recovery methods, helping to reduce the need for retransmission of the data.

Summary

This chapter focused on the technologies that make up wireless networking and spread spectrum. 802.11, 802.11b, and 802.11g use 2.4 GHz ISM bands, while 802.11a uses 5 GHz UNII bands. The ISM and UNII bands discussed in this chapter are:

- ISM 902–928 MHz

- ISM 2.4000–2.4835 GHz

- ISM 5.725–5.875 GHz

- Lower UNII 5.150–5.250 GHz

- Middle UNII 5.250–5.350 GHz

- Upper UNII 5.725–5.825 GHz

Spread spectrum technology was introduced and described in detail along with OFDM and convolutional coding. Key spread spectrum technologies and terms discussed are:

- FHSS
- Dwell time
- Hop time
- DSSS

This chapter ended with a comparison of throughput and bandwidth and a review of the communication resilience of the technologies used in 802.11.

Exam Essentials

Know the technical specifications of all of the ISM and UNII bands.   Make sure that you know all of the frequencies, bandwidth uses, channels, center channel separation rules, and power limits of these two bands.

Know spread spectrum.   Spread spectrum can be complicated and has different flavors. Understand FHSS, DSSS, and OFDM (yes, OFDM is not a spread spectrum technology, but it has similar properties and you have to know it). Understand how coding and modulation work with spread spectrum and OFDM.

Understand the similarities and differences between the transmission methods discussed in this chapter.   There are differences and similarities between many of the topics in this chapter. Carefully compare and understand them. Minor subtleties can be difficult to recognize when taking the test.

Key Terms

Before you take the exam, be certain you are familiar with the following terms:

bandwidth

carrier frequency

chips

co-location

Complementary Code Keying (CCK)

convolution coding

data encoding

delay spread

direct sequence spread spectrum (DSSS)

dwell time

forward error correction (FEC)

frequency hopping spread spectrum (FHSS)

High-Rate DSSS (HR-DSSS)

hop time

hopping sequence

Industrial, Scientific, and Medical (ISM)

inter-symbol interference (ISI)

Orthogonal Frequency Division Multiplexing (OFDM)

Packet Binary Convolutional Code (PBCC)

processing gain

spread spectrum

throughput

Unlicensed National Information Infrastructure (UNII)

Review Questions

1. Which of the following are valid ISM bands? (Choose all that apply.)

   A. 902–928 MHz

   B. 2.4–2.4835 GHz

   C. 5.725–5.825 GHz

   D. 5.725–5.875 GHz

2. Which of the following are valid UNII bands? (Choose all that apply.)

   A. 5.150–5.250 GHz

   B. 5.250–5.350 GHz

   C. 5.725–5.825 GHz

   D. 5.725–5.825 GHz

3. Which IEEE standards use ISM bands? (Choose all that apply.)

   A. 802.11

   B. 802.11a

   C. 802.11b

   D. 802.11g

4. What is the maximum IR allowed for the upper UNII band as defined by the IEEE?

   A. 40 mW

   B. 200 mW

   C. 800 mW

   D. 1,000 mw

5. In North America, the 802.11 standard designates what frequency space for use of FHSS transmissions?

   A. 2.4 GHz–2.4835 GHz

   B. 2.402 GHz–2.480 GHz

   C. 5.725 GHz–5.825 GHz

   D. 5.725 GHz–5.875 GHz

   E. None of the above

6. The original 802.11 standard requires how much separation between center frequencies for DSSS channels to be considered non-overlapping?

   A. 22 MHz

   B. 25 MHz

   C. 30 MHz

   D. 35 MHz

   E. 40 MHz

7. The 802.11b amendment requires how much separation between center frequencies for HR-DSSS channels to be considered non-overlapping?

   A. 22 MHz

   B. 25 MHz

   C. 30 MHz

   D. 35 MHz

   E. 40 MHz

8. What best describes hop time?

   A. The period of time that the transmitter waits before hopping to the next frequency

   B. The period of time that the standard requires when hopping between frequencies

   C. The period of time that the transmitter takes to hop to the next frequency

   D. The period of time the transmitter takes to hop through all of the FHSS frequencies

9. A neighbor has an 802.11b system that is using channel 5. What 802.11g channels will not cause RF interference? (Choose all that apply.)

   A. 1

   B. 6

   C. 10

   D. 11

10. As defined by the 802.11g amendment, how much separation between center frequencies is needed for HR-DSSS channels to be considered non-overlapping and how much separation between center frequencies is needed for ERP-OFDM channels to be considered non-overlapping?

   A. 25 MHz and 20 MHz

   B. 30 MHz and 20 MHz

   C. 22 MHz and 25 MHz

   D. 20 MHz and 25 MHz

   E. 20 MHz and 30 MHz

11. Which spread spectrum technology specifies data rates of 22 Mbps and 33 Mbps?

   A. DSSS

   B. PBCC

   C. OFDM

   D. PPtP

12. If data is corrupted by previous data from a reflected signal, this is known as what?

   A. Delay spread

   B. ISI

   C. Forward error creation

   D. Bit crossover

13. Assuming all IEEE channels are supported by an access point, how many channels does 802.11a support?

   A. 4

   B. 8

   C. 12

   D. 14

14. 802.11g supports which of the following? (Choose all that apply.)

   A. FHSS

   B. DSSS

   C. HR-DSSS

   D. OFDM

15. The 802.11b amendment calls for data rates of 1 Mbps, 2 Mbps, 5.5 Mbps, and 11 Mbps. What is the average amount of aggregate throughput percentage at any data rate?

   A. 80 percent

   B. 75 percent

   C. 50 percent

   D. 100 percent

16. In an FHSS system, throughput can be increased by which of the following?

   A. Shortening the dwell time and lengthening the hop time

   B. Shortening the dwell time and shortening the hop time

   C. Lengthening the dwell time and shortening the hop time

   D. Lengthening the dwell time and lengthening the hop time

17. With the center frequency of channel 1 at 2.412 GHz, what is the center frequency of channel 2?

- **A.** 2.444 GHz
- **B.** 2.417 GHz
- **C.** 2.424 GHz
- **D.** 2.422 GHz

18. HR-DSSS refers to which speeds? (Choose all that apply.)

- **A.** 1 Mbps
- **B.** 2 Mbps
- **C.** 5.5 Mbps
- **D.** 11 Mbps
- **E.** 54 Mbps

19. The Barker Code converts a bit of data into a series of bits that are referred to as what?

- **A.** Chipset
- **B.** Chips
- **C.** Convolutional code
- **D.** Complementary code

20. OFDM uses how many 312.5 KHz subcarriers for transmitting data?

- **A.** 54
- **B.** 52
- **C.** 48
- **D.** 36

Answers to Review Questions

1. A, B, D. The ISM bands are 902–928 MHz, 2.4–2.4835 GHz, and 5.725–5.875 GHz. 5.725–5.825 GHz is the upper UNII band.

2. A, B, C. Remember that the lower, middle, and upper UNII bands are 100 MHz wide.

3. A, C, D. The 802.11a amendment defines the use of the 5 GHz UNII bands. The IEEE 802.11 standard and the subsequent 802.11b and 802.11g amendments all define communications in the frequency range between 2.4 GHz and 2.4835 GHz.

4. C. As defined by the IEEE, the lower UNII has a maximum IR of 40 mw. The middle UNII has a maximum IR of 200 mW. The upper UNII has a maximum IR of 800 mW.

5. B. The IEEE specified that in North America, 802.11 FHSS would use 79 MHz of frequencies, from 2.402 GHz to 2.480GHz.

6. C. According to the original 802.11 standard, DSSS channels had to have at least 30 MHz of spacing between the center frequencies to be considered non-overlapping.

7. B. HR-DSSS was introduced under the 802.11b amendment, which states that channels need a minimum of 25 MHz of separation between the center frequencies to be considered non-overlapping.

8. C. The time that the transmitter waits before hopping to the next frequency is known as the dwell time. The hop time is not a required time but rather a measurement of how long the hop takes.

9. C, D. In order for two channels to not interfere, they must have at least a five-channel separation. The simplest way to determine what channels are valid is to add or subtract 5 from the channel from which you are trying to maintain separation. This answer will be the number of the closest allowed channel(s).

10. A. The 802.11g amendment, which allows for backward compatibility with 802.11b HR-DSSS, also requires 25 MHz of separation between the center frequencies of HR-DSSS channels to be considered non-overlapping. 802.11g ERP-OFDM channels require only 20 MHz of separation between the center frequencies to be considered non-overlapping because the channel widths comply with 802.11a OFDM channel parameters.

11. B. Packet Binary Convolutional Code (PBCC) is the optional modulation technique that specifies data rates of 22 and 33 Mbps.

12. B. The cause of the problem is delay spread resulting in inter-symbol interference (ISI), which causes data corruption.

13. C. Each of the lower, middle, and upper UNII bands are made up on 4 channels, giving a total of 12 channels. The FCC has specified another group of channels for unlicensed use, but currently the IEEE has not added it to its standard.

14. B, C, D. Most people associate 802.11g with OFDM. However, it must be backward compatible with 802.11b (DSSS and HR-DSSS) and 802.11 (DSSS).

15. C. A medium access method known as Carrier Sense Multiple Access/Collision Avoidance (CSMA/CA) helps to ensure that only one radio card can be transmitting on the medium at any given time. Because of the half-duplex nature of the medium and the overhead generated by CSMA/CA, the actual aggregate throughput is typically 50 percent or less of the data rate.

16. C. Lengthening the dwell time decreases the amount of hopping, and shortening the hop time decreases overhead. Increasing the dwell time increases throughput.

17. B. Each channel is 5 MHz above the previous channel.

18. C, D. HR-DSSS is short for High-Rate DSSS. When the 802.11b addendum was ratified, the two speeds that were added, 5.5 Mbps and 11 Mbps, were known as HR-DSSS.

19. B. When a data bit is converted to a series of bits, these bits that represent the data are known as chips.

20. C. OFDM uses 52 subcarriers, but only 48 of them are used to transport data. The other 4 subcarriers are used as pilot carriers.

Chapter 7

Wireless LAN Topologies

IN THIS CHAPTER, YOU WILL LEARN ABOUT THE FOLLOWING:

✓ **Wireless Networking Topologies**

- ▪ Wireless Wide Area Network (WWAN)
- ▪ Wireless Metropolitan Area Network (WMAN)
- ▪ Wireless Personal Area Network (WPAN)
- ▪ Wireless Local Area Network (WLAN)

✓ **802.11 Topologies**

- ▪ Access Point
- ▪ Client Station
- ▪ Distribution System (DS)
- ▪ Wireless Distribution System (WDS)
- ▪ Service Set Identifier (SSID)
- ▪ Basic Service Set (BSS)
- ▪ Basic Service Set Identifier (BSSID)
- ▪ Basic Service Area (BSA)
- ▪ Extended Service Set (ESS)
- ▪ Independent Basic Service Set (IBSS)
- ▪ Nonstandard 802.11 Topologies

✓ **802.11 Configuration Modes**

- ▪ Access Point Modes
- ▪ Client Station Modes

A computer network is a system that provides communications between computers. Computer networks can be configured as peer to peer, as client/server, or as centralized Central Processing Units (CPUs) with distributed dumb terminals. A networking *topology* is defined simply as the physical and/or logical layout of nodes in a computer network. Any individual who has taken a networking basics class is already familiar with bus, ring, star, mesh, and hybrid topologies that are often used in wired networks.

All topologies have advantages and disadvantages. A topology may cover very small areas or can exist as a worldwide architecture. Wireless topologies also exist as defined by the physical and logical layout of wireless hardware. Many wireless technologies exist and can be arranged into four major wireless networking topologies. The 802.11 standard defines one specific type of wireless communications. Within the 802.11 standard exists three types of topologies, known as service sets. Over the years, vendors have also made use of 802.11 hardware using nonstandard topologies to meet specific wireless networking needs. This chapter covers the topologies used by a variety of wireless technologies and covers 802.11-specific topologies, both standard and nonstandard.

Wireless Networking Topologies

While the main focus of this study guide is 802.11 wireless networking, which is a local area technology, other wireless technologies and standards exist in which wireless communications span either smaller or larger areas of coverage. Examples of other wireless technologies are cellular telephone, Bluetooth, and ZigBee. All of these different wireless technologies may or may not be arranged into four major wireless topologies:

- Wireless Wide Area Network (WWAN)
- Wireless Metropolitan Area Network (WMAN)
- Wireless Personal Area Network (WPAN)
- Wireless Local Area Network (WLAN)

Additionally, although the 802.11 standard is a WLAN standard, the same technology can sometimes be deployed in different wireless network architectures, discussed in this section.

Wireless Wide Area Network (WWAN)

A wide area network (WAN) covers a vast geographical area. A WAN might traverse an entire state, region, or country or even span worldwide. The best example of a WAN is the Internet. Many private and public corporate WANs consist of hardware infrastructure such T1 lines, fiber optics, and routers. Protocols used for wired WAN communications include Frame Relay, ATM, MPLS, and others.

A *wireless wide area network (WWAN)* also covers broad geographical boundaries but obviously uses a wireless medium instead of a wired medium. Wireless wide area networks typically use cellular telephone technologies. Cellular providers such as T-Mobile, Verizon, and Vodaphone use a variety of competing technologies to carry data. Some examples of these cellular technologies are GPRS, CDMA, TDMA, and GSM. Data can be carried to a variety of devices such as cell phones, PDAs, and cellular networking cards, as pictured in Figure 7.1.

Data rates and bandwidth using these technologies are relatively slow when compared to other wireless technologies, such as 802.11. However, as cellular technologies improve, so will cellular data transfer rates. It is important to understand that 802.11 wireless networking infrastructure cannot be deployed as a WWAN.

FIGURE 7.1   A cellular networking card

Wireless Metropolitan Area Network (WMAN)

A *wireless metropolitan area network (WMAN)* provides coverage to a metropolitan area such as a city and the surrounding suburbs. WMANs have been created for some time by matching different wireless technologies, and recent advancements have made this more practical. The wireless technology that is newly associated with a WMAN is defined by the 802.16 standard. The 802.16 standard defines broadband wireless access and is sometimes referred to as Worldwide Interoperability for Microwave Access (WiMAX). The WiMAX Forum is responsible for compatibility and interoperability testing of wireless broadband equipment such as 802.16 hardware.

802.16 technologies are viewed as a direct competition to other broadband services such as DSL and cable. Although 802.16 wireless networking is normally thought of as a last mile data delivery solution, the technology might also be used to provide access to users over citywide areas. Currently most 802.16 and WiMAX deployments are still in the testing phase; however, widespread practical wireless broadband deployments are possible in the foreseeable future.

> **NOTE** More information about the 802.16 standard can be found at http://ieee802.org/16. Information about WiMAX can be located at www.wimaxforum.org.

A lot of press has recently been generated about the possibility of citywide deployments of Wi-Fi networks, giving city residents access to the Internet throughout a metropolitan area. Although 802.11 technology was never intended to be used to provide access over such a wide area, at the time this book was written, cities such as Philadelphia and San Francisco had initiatives to achieve this very feat. The equipment being used for these large-scale 802.11 deployments is proprietary wireless mesh routers or mesh access points. It remains to be seen if 802.11 wireless networking can be scaled successfully in WMAN topology. Currently some 802.11 WMAN deployments do exist; however, they have not been running long enough to determine scalability.

Wireless Personal Area Network (WPAN)

A *wireless personal area network (WPAN)* is a wireless computer network used for communication between computer devices within close proximity of a user. Devices such as laptops, personal digital assistants (PDAs), and telephones can communicate with each other using a variety of wireless technologies. WPANs can be used for communication between devices or as portals to higher-level networks such as a local area networks (LANs) and/or the Internet. The most common technologies in wireless personal area networks are Bluetooth and infrared. Infrared is a light-based medium, while Bluetooth is a radio frequency medium that uses frequency hopping spread spectrum (FHSS) technology. Figure 7.2 pictures a headset and a cellular telephone that use Bluetooth radios to provide wireless connectivity between the two devices.

The IEEE 802.15 Working Group focuses on technologies used for WPANs such as Bluetooth and ZigBee. ZigBee is another RF medium that has the potential of low-cost wireless networking between devices in a WPAN architecture.

> **NOTE** Further information about the 802.15 WPAN standards can be found at www.ieee802.org/15. Information about Bluetooth can be located at www.bluetooth.com. The ZigBee Alliance provides information about ZigBee technology at www.zigbee.org. The Infrared Data Association offers data about infrared communications at www.irda.org.

The best example of 802.11 radios being used in a wireless personal area networking scenario would be as peer-to-peer connections.

FIGURE 7.2   Bluetooth communications

    More information about 802.11 peer-to-peer networking can be found later in this chapter in the section "independent basic service set (IBSS)."

Wireless Local Area Network (WLAN)

As you learned in earlier chapters, the 802.11 standard is defined as a *wireless local area network (WLAN)* technology. Local area networks provide networking for a building or campus environment. The 802.11 wireless medium is a perfect fit for local area networking simply due to the range and speeds that are defined by the 802.11 standard and its amendments. The majority of 802.11 wireless network deployments are indeed local area networks (LANs) that provide access at businesses and homes.

WLANs typically make use of multiple 802.11 access points connected by a wired network backbone. In enterprise deployments, WLANs are typically used to provide end users access to network resources and network services and a gateway to the Internet. Although 802.11 hardware can be used in other wireless topologies, the majority of Wi-Fi deployments are indeed WLANs, which is how the technology is defined by the IEEE 802.11 Working Group. The discussion of WLANs usually refers to 802.11 hardware; however, other proprietary and competing WLAN technologies do exist.

802.11 Topologies

The main component of an 802.11 wireless network is the radio card, which is referred to by the 802.11 standard as a *station (STA)*. The radio card can reside inside an access point or be used as a client station. The 802.11 standard defines three separate 802.11 topologies, known as service sets, that describe how these radio cards may be used to communicate with each other. These three 802.11 topologies are known as a basic service set (BSS), extended service set (ESS), and independent basic service set (IBSS). 802.11 radio cards can also be used in topologies not defined under the 802.11 standard. Some examples of these nonstandard topologies are bridging, repeating, workgroup bridging, and mesh networking.

Before we discuss the different 802.11 topologies, we need to review a few basic networking terms that are often misunderstood: simplex, half-duplex, and full-duplex. These are three dialog methods that are used as communications methods between people and also between computer equipment.

In simplex communications, one device is capable of only transmitting and the other device is capable of only receiving. FM radio is an example of simplex communications. Simplex communications are rarely used on computer networks.

In half-duplex communications, both devices are capable of transmitting and receiving; however, only one device can transmit at a time. Walkie-talkies, or two-way radios, are examples of half-duplex devices. IEEE 802.11 wireless networks use half-duplex communications.

In full-duplex communications, both devices are capable of transmitting and receiving at the same time. A telephone conversation is an example of a full-duplex communication. Most IEEE 802.3 equipment is capable of full-duplex communications. The only way to accomplish full-duplex communications in a wireless environment is to have a two-channel setup where all transmissions in one direction are receiving while all transmissions in the other direction are transmitting.

In this section we will cover all the componets that make up the three 802.11 service sets as well as componets in nonstandard 802.11 toplogies.

Access Point

The CWNP definition of an *access point (AP)* is a half-duplex device with switchlike intelligence. A wired infrastructure device typically associated with half-duplex communications is an Ethernet hub. A wired hub is effectively a shared medium in which only one host device can transmit data a time. Access points are half-duplex devices because the RF medium uses half-duplex communications that allows for only one radio card to be transmitting at any given time. In reality, an access point is simply a hub with a radio card and an antenna. The radio card inside an access point must contend for the half-duplex medium in the same fashion that the client station radio cards must contend for the medium.

Access points do have some switchlike cleverness that a wired hub simply does not possess. For example, although not defined by the 802.11 standard, an access point can support virtual local area networks (VLANs) that can be created on managed wired or wireless switches. VLANs are used to reduce the size of broadcast domains and to segregate the network for security purposes. Wired hubs do not support VLANs.

Another example of switchlike intelligence used by access points is the ability to address and direct wireless traffic. Managed switches maintain dynamic MAC address tables that can direct packets to ports based upon the destination MAC address of the packet. Similarly, an access point is a portal device that directs traffic either to the network backbone or back into the wireless medium. The 802.11 header of a wireless frame typically has three MAC addresses, but it can have as many as four in certain situations. The access point uses the complicated layer 2 addressing scheme of the wireless frames to forward the upper-layer information either to the distribution system medium or to another wireless client station. The upper-layer information that is contained in the body of an 802.11 wireless data frame is called a MAC Service Data Unit (MSDU). The 802.11 standard considers the radio card in an access point to be a unique station (STA) that provides connectivity between mobile 802.11 STAs (client stations) and a network infrastructure that may be either wired or wireless. It is beyond the scope of this book to offer a complete explanation of how this process occurs, but an access point directs traffic to ports much as a switch does. In the case of an AP, the traffic is directed to either the Ethernet portal or the radio card portal.

Because an access point operates in a half-duplex shared medium and possesses some switch-like intelligence, an AP is a hybrid device that might be humorously characterized as a wireless SWUB (half switch/half hub).

Client Stations

A radio card that is not used in an access point is typically referred to as a *client station*. Client station radio cards can be used in laptops, PDAs, scanners, phones, and many other mobile devices. Client stations must contend for the half-duplex medium in the same manner that an access point radio card contends for the RF medium. When client stations have a layer 2 connection with an access point, they are known as associated.

Distribution System (DS)

Access points by their very nature are portal devices. Wireless traffic can be destined back onto the wireless medium or forwarded onto what is called the *distribution system (DS)*. The DS consists of two main components:

Distribution System Medium (DSM)   A logical physical medium used to connect access points

Distribution System Services (DSS)   System services built inside an access point usually in the form of software

A single access point or multiple access points may be connected to the same distribution system medium. The majority of 802.11 deployments use an AP as a portal into an 802.3 Ethernet backbone, which serves as the distribution system medium. Access points are usually connected to a switched Ethernet network, which often also offers the advantage of supplying power to the access points via Power over Ethernet (PoE).

An access point may also act as a portal device into other wired and wireless mediums. The 802.11 standard by design does not care, nor does it define onto which medium an access point translates and forwards data. Therefore, an access point can be characterized as a "translational bridge" between two mediums. The AP translates and forwards data between the 802.11 medium and whatever medium is used by the istribution system. Once again, the distribution system medium will almost always be an 802.3 Ethernet network as pictured in Figure 7.3.

FIGURE 7.3   Distribution system medium

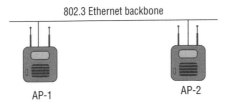

Although rare, 802.5 token ring access points do exist, and the distribution system medium would be the 802.5 token ring infrastructure. In the case of a wireless mesh network, the handoff is through a series of wireless devices with the final destination being an 802.3 network.

Wireless Distribution System (WDS)

Although the DS normally uses a wired Ethernet backbone, it is possible to use a wireless connection instead. A *wireless distribution system (WDS)* can connect access points together using what is referred to as a wireless backhaul.

A WDS may operate using access points with a single 802.11 radio or dual 802.11 radios. Figure 7.4 depicts two 802.11b/g access points, each with a single radio. The radios in the APs provide access to the client stations and communicate with each other directly as a WDS. A disadvantage to this solution is that throughput can be adversely affected due to the half-duplex nature of the medium, particularly in a single radio scenario where an access point cannot be communicating with a client station and another access point at the same time. The end result is a degradation of throughput.

FIGURE 7.4   Wireless distribution system, single radio

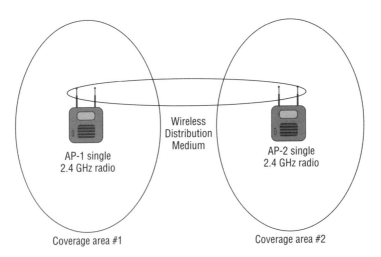

Which Distribution System Is Most Desirable?

Whenever possible, an 802.3 network will always be the best option for the distribution system. Since most enterprise deployments already have a wired 802.3 infrastructure in place, integrating a wireless network into a switched Ethernet network is the most logical solution. A wired distribution system medium does not encounter many of the problems that may affect a WDS, such as multipath and radio frequency interference. If the occasion does arise when a wired network cannot connect access points together, a WDS might be a viable alternative. The more desirable WDS solution utilizes different frequencies and radios for client access and distribution.

In Figure 7.5, two dual radio access points are shown, each with radios operating at different frequencies. The 2.4GHz 802.11b/g radios provide access for the client stations, and the 5GHz 802.11a radios serve as the WDS link between the two access points. Throughput is not adversely affected because the 2.4GHz radio cards can communicate at the same time as the 5GHz cards.

FIGURE 7.5   Wireless distribution system, dual radios

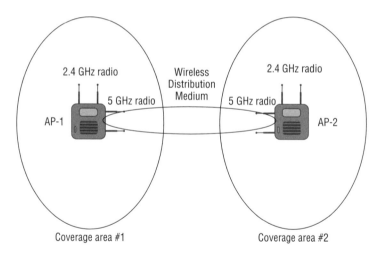

Service Set Identifier (SSID)

The *service set identifier (SSID)* is a network name used to identify an 802.11 wireless network. The SSID wireless network name is comparable to a Windows workgroup name. The three 802.11 topologies utilize the SSID so that radio cards may identify each other in a process known as active scanning or passive scanning. The SSID is a configurable setting on all radio cards, including access points and client stations. The SSID can be made up of as many as 32 characters and is case sensitive. Figure 7.6 shows an SSID configuration of an access point.

FIGURE 7.6   Service set identifier

SSID Configuration		
1. SSID	Sybex CWNA	☑ Broadcast SSID in Beacon

Most access points have the ability to cloak an SSID and keep the network name hidden from non-legitimate end users. Hiding the SSID is a very weak attempt at security that is not defined by the 802.11 standard; however, it is an option many administrators still choose to implement.

Active and passive scanning are discussed in detail in Chapter 8, "802.11 Medium Access." SSID cloaking is discussed in Chapter 13, "802.11 Network Security Architecture."

Basic Service Set (BSS)

The *basic service set (BSS)* is the cornerstone topology of an 802.11 network. The communicating devices that make up a BSS are solely one access point (AP) with one or more client stations. Client stations join the AP's wireless domain and begin communicating through the AP. Stations that are members of a BSS are termed as "associated." Figure 7.7 depicts a standard basic service set.

FIGURE 7.7   Basic service set

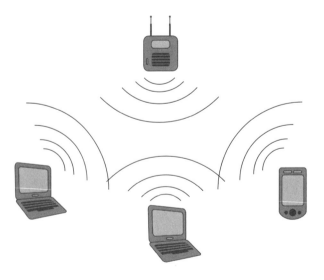

Typically the AP is connected to a distribution system medium (DSM), but that is not a requirement of a basic service set. If an AP is serving as a portal to the distribution system, client stations may communicate, via the AP, with network resources that reside on the distribution system medium. It should also be noted that if client stations wish to communicate with each other, they must relay their data through the access point. Stations cannot communicate directly with each other unless they go through the access point.

Basic Service Set Identifier (BSSID)

The 48-bit (6-octet) MAC address of an access point's radio card is known as the *basic service set identifier (BSSID)*. The BSSID address is simply the MAC address of a BSS access point. Do not confuse the BSSID address with the SSID address. The service set identifier (SSID) is a network name that is user configurable, while the basic service set identifier (BSSID) is the layer 2 MAC address of an AP provided by the hardware manufacturer.

As shown in Figure 7.8, the BSSID address is found in the header of most 802.11 wireless frames and is used for identification purposes. The BSSID address also plays a role in directing 802.11 traffic within the basic service set. The BSSID address is also used as a unique identifier of the basic service set. Furthermore, the BSSID address is also needed during the roaming process.

FIGURE 7.8   Basic service set identifier

```
⊟ 802.11 MAC header
    ⊞ frame control
      duration : 0 usec
      dest addr : FF:FF:FF:FF:FF:FF
      src  addr : 40:08:79:4D:57:25
      bssid : 2F:B2:CF:D5:30:A9
      frag number : 14
      seq number : 1412
```

Basic Service Area (BSA)

The physical area of coverage provided by an access point in a BSS is known as the *basic service area (BSA)*. Figure 7.9 shows a typical BSA. Client stations may move throughout the coverage area and maintain communications with the AP as long the received signal between the radios remains above RSSI thresholds. Client stations may also shift between concentric zones of variable data rates that exist within the BSA. The process of moving between data rates is known as dynamic rate switching and is discussed in Chapter 12, "WLAN Troubleshooting."

The size and shape of a BSA depend upon many variables, including AP transmit power, antenna gain, and physical surroundings. Because environmental and physical surroundings often change, the BSA can often be fluid.

FIGURE 7.9 Basic service area

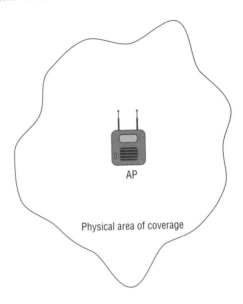

AP

Physical area of coverage

Extended Service Set (ESS)

While a BSS might be considered the cornerstone 802.11 topology, an *extended service set (ESS)* 802.11 topology would be analogous to an entire stone building. An extended service set is two or more basic service sets connected by a distribution system. An extended service set is a collection of multiple access points and their associated client stations, all united by a single DS. The most common example of an ESS has access points with partially overlapping coverage cells, as shown in Figure 7.10. The purpose behind an ESS with partially overlapping coverage cells is to provide seamless roaming to the client stations. Most vendors recommend cell overlap of 15 to 20 percent to achieve successful seamless roaming.

Although seamless roaming is usually a key aspect of WLAN design, there is no requirement for ESS to guarantee uninterrupted communications. For example, an ESS can utilize multiple access points with nonoverlapping coverage cells as pictured in Figure 7.11. In this scenario, a client station that leaves the basic service area (BSA) of the first access point will lose connectivity. The client station will later reestablish connectivity as it moves into the coverage cell of the second access point. This method of station mobility between disjointed cells is sometimes referred to as nomadic roaming.

One final example of an ESS deploys multiple access points with totally overlapping coverage areas, as pictured in Figure 7.12. This 802.11 ESS topology is called co-location, and the intended goal is increased client capacity. Co-location is discussed in more detail in Chapter 11, "Network Design, Implementation, and Management."

FIGURE 7.10   Extended service set, seamless roaming

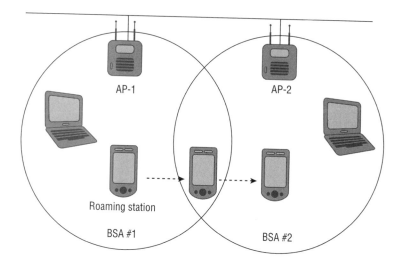

FIGURE 7.11   Extended service set, nomadic roaming

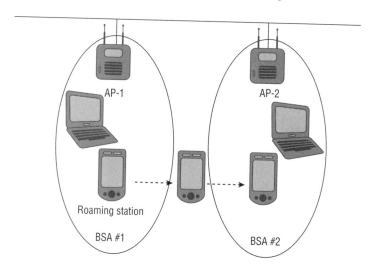

It should be noted that all three of the previously mentioned extended service sets share a distribution system. As stated earlier in this chapter, the distribution system medium is usually an 802.3 Ethernet network; however, the DS may use another type of medium. In the majority of extended service sets, the access points all share the same service set identifier

(SSID) network name. The network name of an ESS is often called an ESSID (extended service set identifier). Although an ESSID is essentially synonymous with an SSID, there is no requirement for all the access points in an ESS to share the exact same network name. Access points that share a DSM may have different SSIDs and still be classified as an extended service set.

FIGURE 7.12   Extended service set, co-location

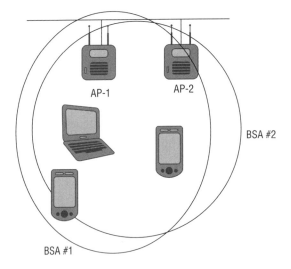

Independent Basic Service Set (IBSS)

The final service set topology defined by the 802.11 standard is an *independent basic service set (IBSS)*. The radio cards that make up an IBBS network consist solely of client stations, and no access point is deployed. An IBSS network that consists of just two stations (STAs) is analogous to a wired crossover cable. An IBSS can, however, have multiple client stations in one physical area communicating in an ad-hoc fashion. Figure 7.13 depicts four client stations communicating with each other in a peer-to-peer fashion.

All of the stations transmit frames to each other directly and do not route their frames from one client to another. All client station frame exchanges in an IBSS are peer-to-peer. All stations in an IBSS must contend for the half-duplex medium, and at any given time only one STA can be transmitting.

The independent basic service set has two other names. Wi-Fi vendors often refer to an IBSS as either a *peer-to-peer* network or an *ad-hoc* network.

In order for IBSS communications to succeed, all stations must all be transmitting on the same frequency channel. Furthermore, this entire set of stand-alone wireless stations connected together as a group must share the same SSID network name. Another caveat of an IBSS is that there is a BSSID address that is created. Earlier in this chapter, we defined a BSSID as the MAC address of the radio card in an access point. So how can an independent basic service set have a BSSID if no access point is used in the IBSS topology? The first station that starts up in an IBSS randomly generates a BSSID in the MAC address format. This randomly generated BSSID is a virtual MAC address and is used for identification purposes in the IBSS.

FIGURE 7.13   Independent basic service set

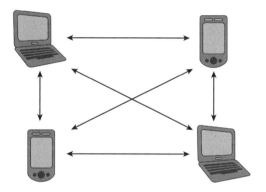

Nonstandard 802.11 Topologies

As you have just learned, the three service sets defined by the 802.11 standard are basic service set (BSS), extended service set (ESS), and independent basic service set (IBSS). Wi-Fi vendors also utilize 802.11 radio cards in nonstandard topologies while still remaining compliant with the 802.11 standard. The most common example is wireless bridging. 802.11 radios can be used to connect two wired networks together using a wireless bridged link.

Another very common nonstandard 802.11 topology is the workgroup bridge (WGB). A workgroup bridge acts as a gateway for a small wired workgroup, yet the workgroup bridge is a client station associated with an access point. A repeater is a special access point that forwards the data of client stations to a root access point. The net effect of a repeater is that the root access point's coverage cell is extended. Wireless mesh routers are essentially a combination of multiple repeaters using proprietary layer 2 routing protocols.

More detailed information about all the devices discussed in this paragraph can be found in Chapter 10, "Wireless Devices."

⊕ **Real World Scenario**

Vendor Considerations When Using 802.11 Equipment in Nonstandard Topologies

Nowhere in the 802.11 standard are there any guidelines or characterizations for bridges, workgroup bridges, repeaters, or mesh routers. The 802.11s draft amendment details mesh networking, but it has not yet been ratified. Whenever equipment that uses 802.11 radios is deployed in nonstandard topologies, the recommended practice is to purchase the equipment from one vendor. A bridge from Vendor A is not likely to work with a bridge from Vendor B. Because none of these topologies are standardized, the likelihood of vendor interoperability is low.

802.11 Configuration Modes

While the 802.11 standard clearly defines two major ways in which a radio card can operate, an access point (AP) radio and a client station radio can be configured in a number of ways. The default configuration of an AP is to allow it to operate inside a basic service set (BSS); however, an AP can be configured to function in a nonstandard topology. Client stations can be configured to participate in either a BBS or IBSS 802.11 service set. We will look at these two methods in the following sections.

Access Point Modes

The only configuration mode of an access point that is compliant with the 802.11 standard is known as root mode. The main purpose of an AP is to serve as a portal to a distribution system. The normal default setting of an access point is root mode, which allows the AP to transfer data back and forth between the DS and the 802.11 wireless medium.

The default root configuration of an AP allows it to operate as part of a basic service set (BSS). There are, however, other nonstandard modes in which an AP may be configured.

- **Bridge mode** The AP is converted into a wireless bridge.

- **Workgroup Bridge mode** The AP is transformed into a workgroup bridge.

- **Repeater mode** The AP performs as a repeater access point.

- **Scanner mode** The access point radio is converted into a sensor radio allowing the access point to integrate into a wireless intrusion detection system (WIDS) architecture.

Because these configurations are all considered nonstandard, not all vendors support these modes. Figure 7.14 shows a screen capture of an access point's various configurable modes.

FIGURE 7.14   Access point configuration modes

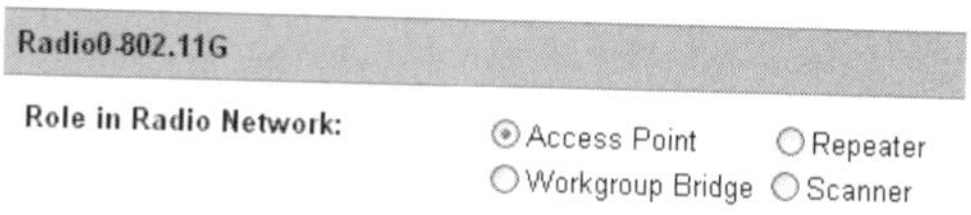

Radio0-802.11G

Role in Radio Network: ⊙ Access Point   ○ Repeater
○ Workgroup Bridge ○ Scanner

Client Station Modes

A client station may operate in one of two settings, as shown in the screen capture in Figure 7.15. The default mode for a client radio card is typically Infrastructure mode. When running in Infrastructure mode, the client station will allow communication via an access point. Infrastructure mode allows for a client station to participate in a basic service set or an extended service set. Clients that are configured in this mode may communicate, via the AP, with other wireless client stations within a BSS.

Clients may also communicate through the AP with other networking devices that exist on the distribution system, such as servers or wired desktops.

The second client station mode is called Ad-Hoc mode. Other vendors may refer to this mode as Peer-to-Peer mode. Client cards set to Ad-Hoc mode participate in an independent basic service set (IBSS) topology and do not communicate via an access point. All station transmissions and frame exchanges are peer-to-peer.

FIGURE 7.15   Client station configuration modes

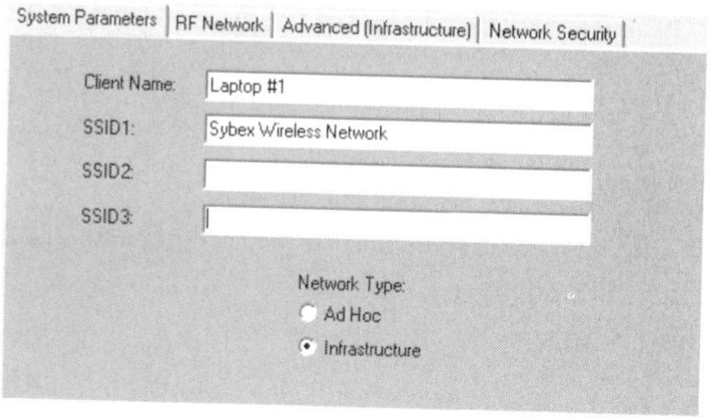

System Parameters | RF Network | Advanced (Infrastructure) | Network Security |

Client Name: Laptop #1
SSID1:   Sybex Wireless Network
SSID2:
SSID3:

Network Type:
○ Ad Hoc
⊙ Infrastructure

Summary

This chapter covered the major types of generic wireless topologies as well as the topologies specific to 802.11 wireless networking:

- The four wireless architectures that can be used by many different wireless technologies

- The three service sets as defined by the 802.11 standard, and the various aspects and purposes defined for each service set

- Standard and nonstandard configuration modes of both access points and client stations

As a wireless network administrator, it is important to have a full understanding of the defined 802.11 service sets and how they operate. An administrator will typically oversee the design and management of an 802.11 ESS, but there is a good chance that they will also deploy 802.11 radios using a nonstandard topology.

Exam Essentials

Know the four major types of wireless topologies.   Understand the differences between a WWAN, WLAN, WPAN, and WMAN.

Explain the three 802.11 service sets.   Be able to fully expound on all the components, purposes, and differences of a basic service set, an extended service set, and an independent basic service set. Understand how the radio cards interact with each other in each service set.

Identify the various ways in which an 802.11 radio can be used.   Understand that the 802.11 standard expects a radio card to be used either as a client station or inside an access point. Also understand that an 802.11 radio card can be used for other purposes, such as bridging, repeaters, and so on.

Explain the purpose of the distribution system.   Know that the DS consists of two pieces: distribution system services (DSS) and distribution system medium (DSM). Understand that the medium used by the DS can be any type of medium. Explain the functions of a wireless distribution system (WDS).

Define SSID, BSSID, and ESSID.   Be able to explain the differences or similarities of all three of these addresses and the function of each.

Describe the various ways in which an ESS can be implemented and the purpose behind each design.   Explain the three ways in which the coverage cells of the ESS access points can be designed and the purpose behind each design.

Demonstrate an understanding of the various nonstandard 802.11 topologies.   Understand that alternative 802.11 topologies such as bridging and mesh networks exist. Further discussion of these nonstandard topologies can be found throughout this book.

Explain access point and client station configuration modes.   Remember all the standard and nonstandard configuration modes of both an AP and a client station.

Key Terms

Before you take the exam, be certain you are familiar with the following terms:

access point (AP)

ad-hoc

basic service area (BSA)

basic service set (BSS)

basic service set identifier (BSSID)

client station

distribution system (DS)

distribution system medium (DSM)

extended service set (ESS)

independent basic service set (IBSS)

peer-to-peer

service set identifier (SSID)

station (STA)

topology

wireless distribution system (WDS)

Wireless Local Area Network (WLAN)

Wireless Metropolitan Area Network (WMAN)

Wireless Personal Area Network (WPAN)

Wireless Wide Are Network (WWAN)

Review Questions

1. An 802.11 wireless network name is which type of address? (Choose all that apply.)
   A. BSSID
   B. MAC address
   C. IP address
   D. SSID
   E. Extended service set identifier

2. Which two 802.11 topologies require the use of an access point? (Choose two.)
   A. WPAN
   B. IBSS
   C. Basic service set
   D. Ad-hoc
   E. ESS

3. The 802.11 standard defines which medium to be used in a distribution system (DS)?
   A. 802.3 Ethernet
   B. 802.15
   C. 802.5 token ring
   D. Star-bus topology
   E. None of the above

4. Which option is a wireless computer topology used for communication of computer devices within close proximity of a person?
   A. WLAN
   B. Bluetooth
   C. ZigBee
   D. WPAN
   E. WMAN

5. Support for roaming is required under the 802.11 standard. Which 802.11 service set may allow for roaming?
   A. ESS
   B. Basicservice set
   C. Co-located APs
   D. IBSS
   E. Spread spectrum service set

6. What factors might affect the size of a BSA coverage area of an access point?

 A. Antenna gain

 B. CSMA/CA

 C. Transmission power

 D. Indoor/outdoor surroundings

 E. distribution system

7. What is the default configuration mode that allows an AP radio to operate in a basic service set?

 A. Scanner

 B. Repeater

 C. Root

 D. Access

 E. Non-root

8. Which terms describe an 802.11 topology involving STAs but no access points? (Choose all that apply.)

 A. BSS

 B. Ad-hoc

 C. DSSS

 D. Infrastructure

 E. IBSS

 F. Peer-to-Peer

9. STAs operating in Infrastructure mode may communicate in which of the following scenarios? (Choose all that apply.)

 A. 802.11 frame exchanges with other STAs via an AP

 B. 802.11 frame exchanges with an AP in scanner mode

 C. 802.11 frame peer-to-peer exchanges directly with other STAs

 D. Upper-layer frame exchanges with network devices on the DSM

 E. All of the above

10. What are the only three topologies defined by the 802.11 standard? (Choose all that apply.)

 A. Bridge mode

 B. Extended service set

 C. BSS

 D. IBSS

 E. FHSS

11. Which wireless topology provides citywide wireless coverage?

    A. WMAN

    B. WLAN

    C. WPAN

    D. WAN

    E. WWAN

12. At which layer of the OSI model will a BSSID address be used?

    A. Physical

    B. Network

    C. Session

    D. Data-Link

    E. Application

13. The basic service set identifier address can be found in which topologies? (Choose all that apply.)

    A. FHSS

    B. IBSS

    C. ESS

    D. DSSS

    E. BSS

14. 802.11 wireless networking will not scale with which wireless topology?

    A. WLAN

    B. WPAN

    C. WMAN

    D. WWAN

    E. VLAN

15. Which wired network hardware devices do access points most resemble? (Choose all that apply.)

    A. Switch

    B. Node

    C. Hub

    D. Router

    E. Server

16. What are some nonstandard modes in which an AP radio may be configured? (Choose all that apply.)

    A. Scanner

    B. Root

    C. Bridge

    D. Non-root

    E. Repeater

17. A network consisting of clients and two or more access points connected by an 802.3 Ethernet backbone is one example of which 802.11 topology? (Choose all that apply.)

   A. ESS

   B. Basic service set

   C. Extended service set

   D. IBSS

   E. Ethernet service set

18. What term best describes two access points communicating with each other wirelessly while also allowing clients to communicate through the access point?

   A. WDS

   B. DS

   C. DSS

   D. DSSS

   E. DSM

19. What components make up a distribution system? (Choose all that apply.)

   A. DSSS

   B. Distribution system services

   C. DSM

   D. DSSS

   E. Intrusion Detection System

20. What type of wireless topology is defined by the 802.11 standard?

   A. WAN

   B. WLAN

   C. WWAN

   D. WMAN

   E. WPAN

Answers to Review Questions

1. D, E. The service set identifier (SSID) is a 32-character address used to identify a wireless network. An extended service set identifier (ESSID) is the SSID network name used in an extended service set. ESSID is often synonymous with SSID.

2. C, E. The 802.11 standard defines three service sets, or topologies. A basic service set (BSS) is defined as one AP and associated clients. An extended service set is defined as two or more APs connected by a distribution system medium. An independent basic service set (IBSS) does not use an AP and consists solely of client stations (STAs).

3. E. By design, the 802.11 standard does not specify a medium to be used in the distribution system. The distribution system medium (DSM) may be an 802.3 Ethernet backbone, an 802.5 token ring network, a wireless medium, or any other medium.

4. D. A Wireless Personal Area Network (WPAN) is a short distance wireless topology. Bluetooth and ZigBee are technologies that are often used in WPANs.

5. A. The most common implementation of an extended service set (ESS) has access points with partially overlapping coverage cells. The purpose behind an ESS with partially overlapping coverage cells is seamless roaming.

6. A, C, D. The size and shape of a basic service area can depend on many variables, including AP transmit power, antenna gain, and physical surroundings.

7. C. The normal default setting of an access point is root mode, which allows the AP to transfer data back and forth between the DS and the 802.11 wireless medium. The default root configuration of an AP allows it to operate inside a basic service set (BSS).

8. B, E, F. The 802.11 standard defines an independent basic service set (IBSS) as a service set using client peer-to-peer communications without the use of an AP. Other names for an IBSS include Ad-Hoc and Peer-to-Peer.

9. A, D. Clients that are configured in Infrastructure mode may communicate via the AP with other wireless client stations within a BSS. Clients may also communicate through the AP with other networking devices that exist on the distribution system medium, such as a server or a wired desktop.

10. B, C, D. The three topologies, or service sets, defined by the 802.11 standard are basic service set (BSS), extendedservice set (ESS), and independent basic service set (IBSS).

11. A. A Wireless Metropolitan Area Network (WMAN) provides coverage to a metropolitan area such as a city and the surrounding suburbs.

12. D. The basic service set identifier (BSSID) is a 48-bit (6-octet) MAC address. MAC addresses exist at the MAC sublayer of the Data-Link layer of the OSI model.

13. B, C, E. The 48-bit (6-octet) MAC address of an access point's radio card is known as the basic service set identifier (BSSID). Both BSS and ESS topologies utilize access points, thus the existence of a BSSID. In an IBSS network, the first station that powers up randomly generates a virtual BSSID in the MAC address format.

14. D. A Wireless Wide Area Network (WWAN) covers a vast geographical area. 802.11 solutions cannot scale to that magnitude.

15. A, C. An access point (AP) is a hybrid device that is half-duplex much like a hub yet possesses some switchlike intelligence.

16. A, C, E. The default standard mode for an access point is root mode. Examples of nonstandard modes include bridge, Workgroup Bridge, scanner, and repeater.

17. A, C. An extended service set (ESS) is two or more basic service sets connected by a distribution system. An extended service set is a collection of multiple access points and their associated client stations, all united by a single distribution system medium.

18. A. A wireless distribution system (WDS) can connect access points together using a wireless backhaul while allowing clients to also associate to the radio cards in the access point.

19. B, C. The distribution system consists of two main components. The distribution system medium (DSM) is a logical physical medium used to connect access points. distribution system services (DSS) consists of services built inside an access point, usually in the form of software.

20. B. The 802.11 Standard is considered a Wireless Local Area Networking (WLAN) standard. 802.11 hardware can, however, be utilized in other wireless topologies.

Chapter 8

802.11 Medium Access

IN THIS CHAPTER, YOU WILL LEARN ABOUT THE FOLLOWING:

- ✓ **CSMA/CA vs. CSMA/CD**
- ✓ **Distributed Coordination Function (DCF)**
  - ▪ Interframe Space (IFS)
  - ▪ Collision Detection
  - ▪ Duration/ID Field
  - ▪ Carrier Sense
  - ▪ Random Backoff Time
  - ▪ Distributed Coordination Function (DCF) Flowchart
- ✓ **Point Coordination Function (PCF)**
- ✓ **802.11 Frame Format vs. 802.3 Frame Format**
- ✓ **Three Frame Types**
  - ▪ Management Frames
  - ▪ Control Frames
  - ▪ Data Frames
- ✓ **Layer-3 Integration with 802.11 Frames**
- ✓ **Beacon Management Frames (Beacons)**
- ✓ **Passive Scanning**
- ✓ **Active Scanning**
- ✓ **Authentication**
  - ▪ Open System Authentication
  - ▪ Shared Key Authentication

- ✓ **Association**
- ✓ **Authentication and Association States**
- ✓ **Roaming**
- ✓ **Reassociation**
- ✓ **Disassociation**
- ✓ **Deauthentication**

One of the difficulties we had when writing this chapter was that in order for the reader to understand how a wireless station gains access to the media, it is necessary to teach more than what is needed for the CWNA exam. The details are needed to understand the concepts; however, it is the concepts that you will be tested on. If you like the details of this chapter, then you should look into the Certified Wireless Analysis Professional (CWAP) certification, which gets into the nitty-gritty details of 802.11 communications. At that time you will need to understand details far beyond what we have included in this chapter. However, at this time, take the details for what they are, and that is a foundation for helping you understand the overall process.

CSMA/CA vs. CSMA/CD

Network communication requires a set of rules to provide controlled and efficient access to the network medium. *Media access control (MAC)* is the generic term used when discussing the different methods of access. There are many ways of providing media access. The early mainframes used polling, which sequentially checked each terminal to see if there was data to be processed. Later, token-passing and contention methods were used to provide access to the media. Two forms of contention that are heavily used in today's networks are *Carrier Sense Multiple Access with Collision Detection (CSMA/CD)* and *Carrier Sense Multiple Access with Collision Avoidance (CSMA/CA)*.

CSMA/CD is well known and is used by Ethernet networks. CSMA/CA is not as well known and is used by 802.11 networks. Stations using either access method must first listen to see if any other device is transmitting. If another device is transmitting, then the station must wait until the medium is available. The difference between CSMA/CD and CSMA/CA exists when a client wants to transmit and no other clients are presently transmitting. A CSMA/CD node can immediately begin transmitting. If a collision occurs while a CSMA/CD node is transmitting, the collision will be detected and the node will temporarily stop transmitting. 802.11 wireless stations are not capable of transmitting and receiving at the same time, so therefore they are not capable of detecting a collision during their transmission. For this reason, 802.11 wireless networking uses CSMA/CA instead of CSMA/CD to try to avoid collisions.

When a CSMA/CA station has determined that no other stations are transmitting, the 802.11 radio will choose a random backoff value. The station will then wait an additional period of time, based on the backoff value, before transmitting. During this time, the station continues to monitor to make sure that no other stations begin transmitting. Because of the half-duplex nature of the RF medium, it is necessary to ensure that at any given time only one radio card has control of the medium. CSMA/CA is a process used to ensure that only one radio card is transmitting at a time. Is this process perfect? Absolutely not! Collisions still do occur when two or more radios transmit at the same time. However, CSMA/CA is a medium access method that utilizes multiple checks and balances to try to minimize collisions. These checks and balances can also be thought of as several lines of defense. The various lines of defense are put in place to once again hopefully ensure that only one radio is transmitting while all other radios are listening. CSMA/CA minimizes the risk of collisions without excessive overhead.

This entire process will be covered in more detail in the next section of this chapter.

CSMA/CA Overview

Carrier Sense determines if the medium is busy. *Multiple Access* assures that every radio gets a fair shot at the medium (but only one at a time). *Collision Avoidance* means only one radio gets on the medium at any given time, hopefully avoiding collisions.

Distributed Coordination Function (DCF)

Distributed Coordination Function (DCF) is the fundamental access method of 802.11. DCF is the mandatory access method of the 802.11 standard. The 802.11 standard also has an optional access method known as *Point Coordination Function (PCF)*, which will be covered later in this chapter. In the next few sections, you will learn about some of the components that are part of the CSMA/CA process. After you learn about these components, we will show you a flowchart and walk you through how DCF works.

Interframe Space (IFS)

Interframe space (IFS) is a period of time that exists between transmissions of wireless frames. There are four types of interframe spaces, which are listed here in order of shortest to longest:

- Short interframe space (SIFS), highest priority
- PCF interframe space (PIFS), middle priority
- DCF interframe space (DIFS), lowest priority
- Extended interframe space (EIFS), used with retransmissions

   The actual length of time of each of the interframe spaces varies depending upon the transmission speed of the network. Interframe spaces are one line of defense used by CSMA/CA to ensure that only certain types of wireless frames are transmitted following certain interframe spaces. For example, only ACK frames and CTS frames may follow a SIFS. The ACK frame is the highest-priority frame, and the use of a SIFS ensures that it will be transmitted first before some other type of wireless frame. Interframe spaces are all about what type of 802.11 traffic is allowed next. The main thing that you need to understand at this time is that there are four interframe spaces of different durations of time and the order is SIFS < PIFS < DIFS < EIFS.

   As you read further in this chapter, you will learn that timing is an important aspect of successful wireless communications. Interframe spaces are just one component of this tightly linked environment.

> The current version of the CWNA test does not cover interframe spacing. This, however, may change in the future. The Certified Wireless Analysis Professional (CWAP) certification tests very heavily on interframe spacing.

Collision Detection

Earlier in this chapter we mentioned that 802.11 radios were not able to transmit and receive at the same time so therefore they cannot detect collisions. So if they cannot detect a collision, how do they know if one occurred or not? The answer is simple. Every time an 802.11 radio transmits a unicast frame, if the frame is received properly, the 802.11 radio that received the frame will reply with an *acknowledgement (ACK)* frame. If the ACK is received, then the original station knows that the frame transfer was successful. If the ACK is not received, then the original radio will need to retransmit the frame. So for every unicast frame there should be an ACK frame. This does not specifically determine if a collision occurs; in other words, there is no collision detection. However, if an ACK frame is not received by the original radio, there is collision assumption. Think of the ACK frame as a method of delivery verification. If no proof of delivery is provided, then the original radio card assumes there was a delivery failure and retransmits the frame.

Duration/ID Field

One of the fields in the MAC header of an 802.11 frame is the Duration/ID field. When a client transmits a unicast frame, the Duration/ID field contains a value from 0 to 32,767. In this scenario, the Duration/ID value represents the time, in microseconds, that is required to transmit the ACK plus one SIFS interval, as illustrated in Figure 8.1. The client that is transmitting the data frame calculates how long it will take to receive an ACK frame and includes that length of time in the Duration/ID field in the MAC header of the transmitted unicast data frame. The value of the Duration/ID field in the MAC header of the ACK frame that follows is 0 (zero). To summarize, the value of the Duration/ID field indicates how long the RF medium will be busy before another station can contend for the medium.

FIGURE 8.1   Data and ACK frame exchange

Carrier Sense

The first step that an 802.11 CSMA/CA device needs to do to begin transmitting is to perform a carrier sense. This is a check to see if the medium is busy. Think of it like listening for a busy signal when you call someone on the phone. There are two ways that a carrier sense is performed: virtual carrier-sense and physical carrier-sense.

Virtual Carrier-Sense

Virtual carrier-sense uses a timer mechanism known as the *network allocation vector (NAV)*. The NAV timer maintains a prediction of future traffic on the medium based on duration value information seen in a previous frame transmission. When an 802.11 radio is not transmitting, it is listening. When the listening radio hears a frame transmission from another station, it looks at the header of the frame and determines if the Duration/ID field contains a Duration value or an ID value. If the field contains a Duration value, the listening station will set its NAV timer to this value. The listening station will now use the NAV as a countdown timer, knowing that the RF medium should be busy until the countdown reaches 0.

This process essentially allows the transmitting 802.11 radio to notify the other stations that the medium will be busy for a period of time (Duration/ID value). The stations that are not transmitting listen and hear the Duration/ID, set a countdown timer (NAV), and wait until the timer hits 0 before they can contend for the medium and eventually transmit on the medium. A station cannot contend for the medium until its NAV timer is 0, nor can a station transmit on the medium if the NAV timer is set to a nonzero value. As stated earlier, there are several lines of defense used by CSMA/CA to prevent collisions and the NAV timer is often considered the first line of defense.

Physical Carrier-Sense

The virtual carrier-sense is one method of keeping other stations from transmitting while another radio has control of the RF medium. However, it is possible that a station did not hear the other radio transmitting so was unable to read the Duration/ID field and set its NAV timer. There could be numerous reasons why, but that's irrelevant at the moment. CSMA/CA utilizes another line of defense to ensure that a station does not transmit while another is already transmitting. The 802.11 standard defines a *physical carrier-sense*. Physical carrier-sensing is performed constantly by all stations that are not transmitting or receiving. There are two purposes for physical carrier-sense. The first purpose is to determine if a frame transmission is inbound for a station to receive. If the medium is busy, the radio will attempt to synchronize with the transmission. The second purpose is to determine if the medium is busy before transmitting. This is known as the *clear channel assessment (CCA)*. The CCA involves listening for 802.11 RF transmissions at the Physical layer. The medium must be clear before a station can transmit.

It is important to understand that both virtual carrier-sense and physical carrier-sense are always happening at the same time. Virtual carrier-sense is a layer 2 line of defense, while physical carrier-sense is a layer 1 line of defense. If one line of defense fails, hopefully the other will prevent collisions from occurring.

Random Backoff Time

After a station has waited while performing both virtual and physical carrier-senses, it may contend for the medium during a window of time known as the *contention window*. At this point in the CSMA/CA process, the station selects a random backoff value. The random value is chosen from a range from 0 to the initial contention window value, as shown in Figure 8.2. The backoff value is then multiplied by the *slot time*, which is a period of time that differs between the different spread spectrum technologies. This starts a random backoff timer. The station's backoff timer begins to count down ticks of a clock known as slots. When the backoff time is equal to 0, the client can begin transmitting.

The random backoff timer is another line of defense and helps minimize the likelihood of two stations trying to communicate at the same time, although it does not fully prevent this from occurring. If a station does not receive an ACK, it starts the carrier-sense process over again.

FIGURE 8.2   Contention window length

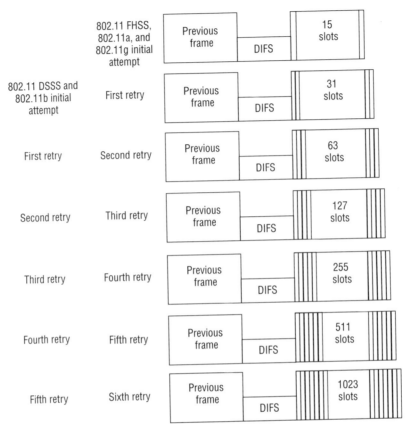

Distributed Coordination Function (DCF) Flowchart

Now that you have read about all of the different pieces and how they work, let's look at a flowchart of the DCF process, shown in Figure 8.3.

1. At the top of the figure is where the process begins. From the Start, proceed down to where the process splits toward two decision points.

2. These are the physical carrier-sense and virtual carrier-sense tests. Both tests are performed simultaneously.

3. In the right decision point, if the NAV is greater than 0 (yes), this means that another station is transmitting and the station has to wait.

4. The NAV is then decremented, and the flowchart loops back toward the beginning, back to the two decision points.

FIGURE 8.3   DCF flowchart

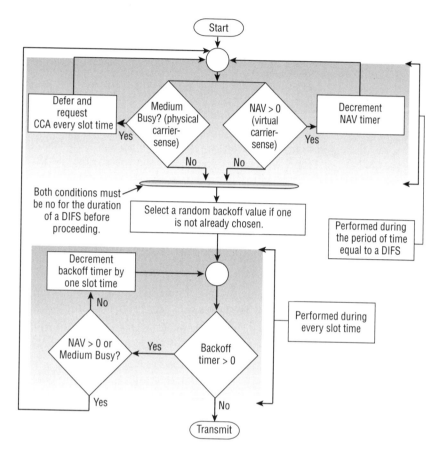

5. In the left decision point, if the clear channel assessment (CCA) indicates that the medium is busy (yes), this also means that another station is transmitting and the station has to wait.

6. The station must wait a slot time and loop back toward the beginning to perform another CCA.

7. When both of these decision points do not detect any wireless traffic for a period of a DIFS (both no), the process then continues.

8. The station now selects a random backoff value.

9. The backoff timer decision point is then tested to see if the backoff value is greater than 0. If it is not (no), the station can begin transmitting. However, it if is greater than 0 (yes), the station needs to perform another physical carrier-sense and a virtual carrier-sense to determine if any other stations have begun transmitting.

10. If the tests indicate that the medium is still idle (no), the station will decrement the backoff timer, and then go back to the backoff timer decision point to see if the timer has reached 0 yet. When it reaches 0 (no), the station can begin transmitting.

11. If the backoff timer is not 0 and another station begins to transmit (NAV > 0 or Medium Busy = yes), the station retains the current value of the backoff timer but goes back to the beginning of the process and starts over.

12. When the station eventually makes it past the DIFS period, the station does not select a random backoff value but rather retains its backoff timer and continues counting down from where it left off.

We realize that there were many steps in the flowchart and much more detail than is necessary for passing the CWNA test. Hopefully it helped you to better understand the CSMA/CA process and why transmission speed and data throughput vary so drastically. Now looking at the flowchart, let's walk through it and summarize it with less detail.

1. Again, we will start at the top.

2. This first group is the initial carrier-sense. After a DIFS of listening and hearing no traffic, the station can continue on. The station is almost ready to transmit.

3. The next thing the station needs to do is to select a random backoff value.

4. Once the station has chosen the backoff value, the station starts decrementing the backoff timer until it reaches 0, which is when the station can then transmit.

5. While the station is decrementing the backoff timer, the station continues to listen to see if any other stations have begun to transmit (another radio might have chosen a smaller backoff value).

6. If another radio has begun transmitting, the station keeps the current backoff value and goes back to the beginning of the process.

7. Ultimately the station will make it through the flowchart and the backoff will reach 0, then the station will transmit providing the medium is clear.

Point Coordination Function (PCF)

In addition to DCF, the IEEE 802.11 standard defines an additional, optional medium access method known as Point Coordination Function (PCF). This access method is a form of polling. The access point performs the function of the *point coordinator*. Since an access point is taking the role of the point coordinator, the PCF medium access method will only work in a basic service set (BSS). PCF cannot be utilized in an ad-hoc network because no access point exists in an independent basic service set (IBSS). Since polling is performed from a central device, PCF provides managed access to the medium.

In order for PCF to be used, both the access point and the station must support it. If PCF is enabled, DCF will still function. The access point will alternate between PCF mode and DCF mode. When the access point is functioning in PCF mode, this is known as the Contention-Free

Period (CFP). During the Contention-Free Period, the access point polls only clients in PCF mode about their intention to send data. This is a method of prioritizing clients. When the access point is functioning in DCF mode, this is known as the Contention Period (CP).

If you would like to learn more about PCF, we suggest that you read the 802.11 standard document. As was stated earlier, PCF is an optional access method, and as this book is being written, the authors do not know of any vendor that has implemented it. In Chapter 9, we will discuss medium access methods defined by the 802.11e amendment. The 802.11e amendment defines new medium access methods that can be used for prioritizing clients and prioritizing traffic.

802.11 Frame Format vs. 802.3 Frame Format

All of the IEEE 802 frame formats share similar characteristics, and the 802.11 frame is no exception. Since the frames are similar, it makes it easier to translate the frames as they move from the 802.11 wireless network to the 802.3 wired network and vice versa.

One of the differences between 802.3 Ethernet and 802.11 wireless frames is the frame size. Unlike 802.3, which will typically transport frames of up to 1,518 bytes, 802.11 is capable of transporting frames of up to 2,304 bytes of "upper layer" data. This means that as the data moves between the wireless and the wired network, the access point may receive a data frame that is too large for the wired network. This is rarely a problem thanks to TCP/IP. Since most networks use TCP/IP, and since TCP/IP typically has an IP maximum transmission unit (MTU) size of 1,500 bytes, these IP packets can be handled by both 802.11 and 802.3 frames.

Another difference between 802.3 and 802.11 frames is the MAC addressing fields. 802.3 frames have two MAC address fields, whereas 802.11 frames have four address fields. These four address fields will contain either three or four MAC addresses. The contents of these four fields can include the following MAC addresses: receiver address (RA), transmitter address (TA), basic service set identifier (BSSID), destination address (DA), and source address (SA). Even though the number of address fields is different, both 802.3 and 802.11 use the same MAC address format. The first three octets are known as the Organizationally Unique Identifier (OUI) and the last three octets are known as the extension identifier.

Three Frame Types

Unlike many wired network standards such as IEEE 802.3, which uses a single data frame type, the IEEE 802.11 standard defines three different frame types: management, control, and data. These frame types are further subdivided into multiple subtypes. Earlier in this chapter you learned about the optional media access method of Point Coordination Function (PCF). Some of the frame subtypes are defined to perform functions associated with PCF. Since PCF is optional and to date there are no known access points that support this technology, we will note any subtypes that are solely used for PCF by placing *PCF-Only* next to the subtype but will not address or define them.

Management Frames

Management frames make up a majority of the frames types in an 802.11 network. Management frames are used by wireless stations to join and leave the network. They are not necessary on wired networks since physically connecting or disconnecting the network cable performs this function. However, because wireless networking is a unbounded medium, it is necessary for the wireless station to first find a compatible wireless network, then authenticate to the network (assuming they are allowed to connect), and then associate with the network (typically with an access point) to gain access to the wired network (the distribution system). No upper-layer information is carried in the body of a management frame.

Following is a list of all 11 of the management frame subtypes as defined by the 802.11 standard:

- Association request
- Association response
- Reassociation request
- Reassociation response
- Probe request
- Probe response
- Beacon
- Announcement traffic indication message (ATIM)
- Disassociation
- Authentication
- Deauthentication

Control Frames

Control frames help to assist with the delivery of the data frames. Control frames must be able to be heard by all stations; therefore, they must be transmitted at one of the basic rates. Control frames are also used to clear the channel, acquire the channel, and provide unicast frame acknowledgements. They contain only header information.

Following is a list of all six of the control frame subtypes as defined by the 802.11 standard:

- Power Save (PS)-Poll
- Request to send (RTS)
- Clear to send (CTS)
- Acknowledgment (ACK)

- Contention-Free (CF)-End (PCF-Only)
- CF-End + CF-ACK (PCF-Only)

Data Frames

Data frames carry the actual data that is passed down from the higher-layer protocols. Null frames are used by power save mode to inform the access point of changes in power save status.

Following is a list of all eight of the data frame subtypes as defined by the 802.11 standard. Of the eight data frame subtypes, only the first two are used by DCF. The first subtype, the Data frame, is also known as the "simple data frame." It contains the Layer 3 to 7 information in the body of the frame.

- Data
- Null Function (no data)
- Data + CF-ACK (PCF-Only)
- Data + CF-Poll (PCF-Only)
- Data + CF-ACK + CF-Poll (PCF-Only)
- CF-ACK (no data) (PCF-Only)
- CF-Poll (no data) (PCF-Only)
- CF-ACK + CF-Poll (no data) (PCF-Only)

Layer 3 Integration with 802.11 Frames

802.11 integrates very well with layer 3 protocols, as do all of the IEEE 802 standards. Unlike stations configured with most of the other 802 standards, 802.11 stations are mobile and can move throughout the wireless infrastructure. This means that the person who designs and installs the network needs to take this into consideration; otherwise, connectivity problems can arise. Let's assume that the RF network plan has been properly implemented and that a user can roam anywhere within the building and maintain wireless connectivity. Since 802.11 cooperates well with upper-layer protocols, the user will not see any layer 3 communication problems. Roaming, which is an integral part of 802.11, will allow the user to disconnect and reconnect (roam) across the network while maintaining upper-layer connections such as email and web browsing.

A problem can arise if the user roams between access points that are connected to two different layer 3 networks, such as two TCP/IP networks. As the user roams between these access points, the DHCP client will request a new TCP/IP address. When the client is assigned a new address, connection-oriented upper-layer applications will lose their connections. A standard named Mobile IP as well as proprietary layer 3 roaming solutions exist that can allow a client station to roam to new access points while maintaining the current TCP/IP address. The details of these solutions are beyond the scope of the CWNA exam.

Beacon Management Frame (Beacon)

One of the most important frame types is the beacon management frame, commonly referred to as the beacon. Beacons are essentially the heartbeat of the wireless network. They are only sent by the access point of a basic service set. Client stations only transmit beacons when participating in an IBSS, also known as Ad-Hoc mode. Each beacon contains a time stamp, which client stations use to keep their clocks synchronized with the access point. Since so much of successful wireless communications is based on timing, it is imperative that all stations are in sync with each other. The following information is inside the body of a beacon frame:

- **Time stamp**—Synchronization information
- **Channel information**—Channel used by the AP or IBSS
- **Data rates**—Basic and supported rates
- **Service set capabilities**—Extra BBS or IBSS parameters
- **SSID**—Network name
- **Traffic indication map (TIM)**—A field used during the power save process
- **Vendor proprietary information**—Vendor-unique or vendor-specific information

The beacon frame contains all the necessary information for a client station to learn about the parameters of the AP before joining the basic service set. Beacons are transmitted about 10 times per second. This interval can be configured on some APs but it cannot be disabled.

Passive Scanning

In order for a station to be able to connect to an access point, it needs to first discover an access point. The way a station discovers an access point is by either active or passive scanning. Stations may either listen for access points (passive scanning) or search for access points (active scanning). *Passive scanning* involves the client station listening for the beacon frames that are continuously being sent by the access points, as seen in Figure 8.4.

The client station will listen for the beacons that contain the same SSID that has been pre-configured in the client station's software utility. When the station hears one, it can then connect to that network. If the client station hears beacons from multiple access points with the same SSID, it will determine which access point has the best signal, and it will attempt to connect to that AP.

It is important to understand that both active and passive scanning can be performed by different client stations at the same time. Also, when an independent basic service set is deployed, all of the stations in Ad-Hoc mode take turns transmitting the beacons since there is no access point. Passive scanning occurs in an ad-hoc environment just as it does in a basic service set.

FIGURE 8.4   Passive scanning

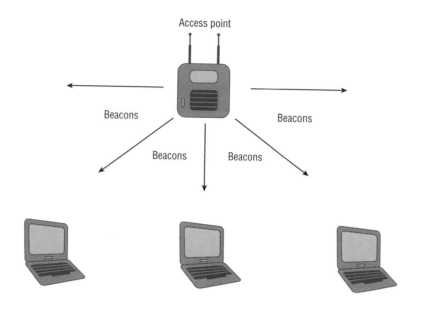

Active Scanning

In addition to passively scanning for access points, client stations can actively scan for them. *Active scanning* involves the client station transmitting management frames known as *probe requests*. These probe requests can either contain the SSID of the specific wireless network that the client station is looking for or look for any SSID. A client station that is looking for any SSID sends a probe request with the SSID field set to null.

If the SSID was specified in the probe request, all access points that support that SSID, and hear the request, should reply by sending a *probe response*. The information that is contained inside the body of a probe response frame is the exact same information that can be found in a beacon frame with the exception of the traffic indication map (TIM). Just like the beacon frame, the probe response frame contains all of the necessary information for a client station to learn about the parameters of the AP before joining the basic service set.

If the probe request is looking for any SSID, then all access points that hear the request should reply by sending a probe response, as seen in Figure 8.5. For security reasons, many vendors allow the access points to be configured to ignore probe requests looking for any SSID. Although this is not defined in the 802.11 standard, it is not uncommon for companies to take the approach "If you don't specifically know the SSID of the network, we won't let you connect to it." This helps prevent people who do not belong on your network from connecting to it accidentally. However, this should not be viewed as a form of security. This is simply a means to reduce accidental or unwanted connections to the AP.

If a client station receives probe responses from multiple access points, signal strength and quality characteristics are typically used by the client station to determine which access point has the best signal and thus which access point to connect to. The client station will sequentially send probe requests on each of the supported channels. In fact, it is common for a client station that is already associated to an access point and transmitting data to continue to send probe requests every few seconds across other channels. By continuing to actively scan, a client station can maintain a list of access points, and if the client station needs to roam, it can typically do so faster and more efficiently.

FIGURE 8.5   Active scanning

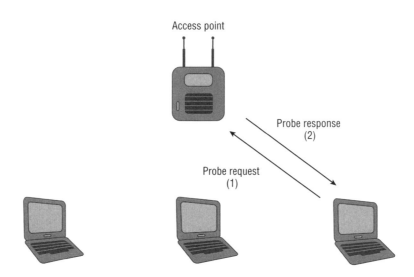

Authentication

Authentication is the first of two steps required to connect to the 802.11 network. Both authentication and association must occur, in that order, before an 802.11 client can pass traffic through the access point to another device on the network.

Authentication is a process that is often misunderstood. When many people think of authentication, they think of what is commonly referred to as network authentication, entering a username and password in order to get access to the network. In this chapter we are referring to 802.11 authentication. When an 802.3 device needs to communicate with other devices, the first step is to plug the Ethernet cable into the wall jack. When this cable is plugged in, the client creates a physical link to the wired switch and is now able to start transmitting frames. When an 802.11 device needs to communicate, it must first authenticate with the access point or with the other stations if it is configured for Ad-Hoc mode. This authentication is not much more of a task than plugging the Ethernet cable into the wall jack. The 802.11 authentication merely establishes an initial connection between the client and the access point.

The 802.11 standard specifies two different methods of authentication: Open System authentication and Shared Key authentication. The following two sections will describe these two authentication methods.

Open System Authentication

Open System authentication is the simpler of the two authentication methods. It provides authentication without performing any type of client verification. It is essentially an exchange of hellos between the client and the access point. It is considered a null authentication since there is no exchange or verification of identity between the devices. Open System authentication occurs with an exchange of four frames between the client and the access point, as described in the following list and seen in Figure 8.6. Figure 8.6 shows a packet capture of the four frames that are exchanged between the client and the access point:

1. In the first step, the client station sends an authentication frame to the access point. (frame 24)

2. The access point then replies to the client station with an ACK. (frame 25)

3. The access point then sends an authentication frame to the client station, confirming the authentication. (frame 26)

4. The client station then replies to the access point with an ACK. (frame 27)

Wired Equivalent Privacy (WEP) security can be used with Open System authentication; however, WEP is used only to encrypt the upper-layer information of data frames and only after the client station is authenticated and associated. Because of its simplicity, Open System authentication is used when more advanced network authentication methods such as 802.11i, 802.1X/EAP, and WPA are also implemented.

FIGURE 8.6   Open System authentication

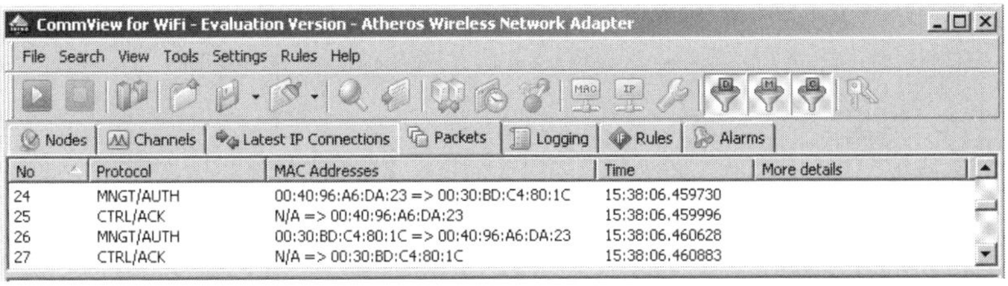

Shared Key Authentication

Shared Key authentication uses WEP to authenticate client stations and requires that a static WEP key be configured on both the station and the access point. In addition to WEP being mandatory, authentication will not work if the static WEP keys do not match. The authentication process is similar to Open System authentication but includes a challenge and response between the AP and client station. Shared Key authentication occurs with an exchange of eight frames between the station and the access point, as described in the following list and seen in Figure 8.7. Figure 8.7 shows a packet capture of the eight frames that are exchanged between the client and the access point:

1. In the first step, the client station sends an authentication frame to the access point. The frame indicates that Shared Key authentication is being used. (frame 245)

2. The access point then replies to the station with an ACK. (frame 246)

3. Inside the body of a second authentication frame, the access point now sends a challenge of 128 octets of cleartext to the client station. (frame 247)

4. The station then replies to the access point with an ACK. (frame 248)

5. The client station encrypts the challenge text using the station's static WEP key and sends it back to the access point inside the body of a third authentication frame (frame 249)

6. The access point then replies to the station with an ACK. (frame 250)

7. The access point decrypts the station's response and compares it to the challenge text. If they match, the access point will respond by sending a fourth and final authentication frame to the station confirming the success. If they don't match, the access point will respond negatively. (frame 251)

8. The client then replies to the access point with an ACK. (frame 252)

FIGURE 8.7   Shared Key authentication

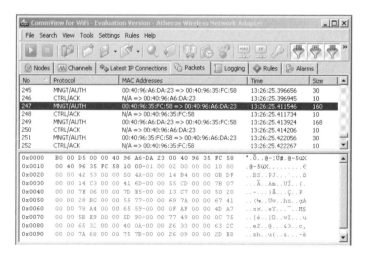

Shared Key authentication is actually less secure than Open System authentication. With Shared Key authentication, WEP is required, and after the authentication process is completed, any simple data frames that are transmitted are encrypted using the static WEP key. With Open System authentication, WEP is not used for the authentication process, but WEP can be used to encrypt any data frames that are transmitted. So when using either method, the data is able to be encrypted and transmitted using the same process. The security problem is in the Shared Key authentication process. During Shared Key authentication, the access point sends 128 octets of cleartext to the client. The client station then encrypts this cleartext and sends it back to the access point. Anyone who is eavesdropping or analyzing the packets can capture this information and now not only knows the encrypted data, but also the text version of what was encrypted. Once the challenge and response are captured, it may be easier to figure out the static encryption key. If the static WEP key is compromised, then all the data frames can be decrypted by a potential attacker. While Shared Key authentication may be a slightly stronger authentication method than Open System authentication, the potential of exposing the WEP key is a greater security risk with Shared Key authentication. Neither legacy authentication method is considered strong enough for enterprise security. More secure 802.1X/EAP authentication methods will be discussed in future security chapters.

Association

After the station has authenticated with the access point, the next step is for it to associate with the access point. When a client station associates, it becomes a member of a basic service set (BSS). *Association* means that the client station can send data through the access point and on to the distribution system medium. Association occurs after the station and the access point have exchanged four frames, as described in the following list and seen in Figure 8.8. Figure 8.8 shows a packet capture of the four frames that are exchanged between the client and the access point:

1. In the first step, the station sends an association request frame to the access point. (frame 33)
2. The access point then replies to the client station with an ACK. (frame 34)
3. The access point now sends an association response frame to the station. (frame 35)
4. The client station then replies to the access point with an ACK. (frame 36)

FIGURE 8.8 Association

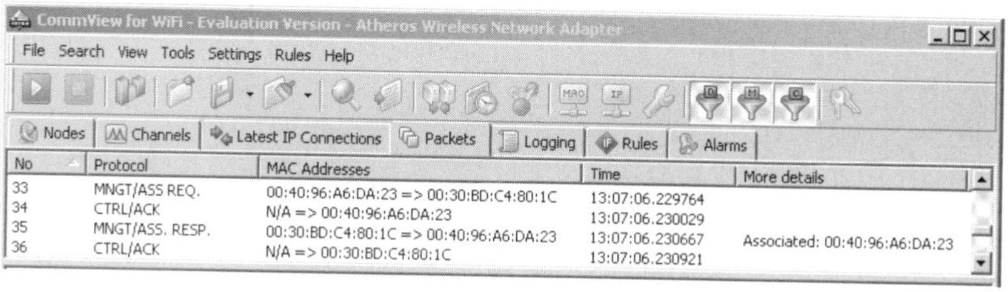

If the station has successfully authenticated, then barring a compatibility problem such as supported data rates that do not match or an incorrect WEP key, the station will also associate successfully.

Authentication and Association States

The 802.11 station keeps two variables for tracking the authentication state and the association state. The states that are tracked are as follows:

- Authentication state, unauthenticated or authenticated
- Association state, unassociated or associated

Together, these two variables create three possible states for the stations as listed here and shown in Figure 8.9:

- State 1, Initial start state; unauthenticated and unassociated
- State 2, authenticated and unassociated
- State 3, authenticated and associated

FIGURE 8.9   Authentication and association states

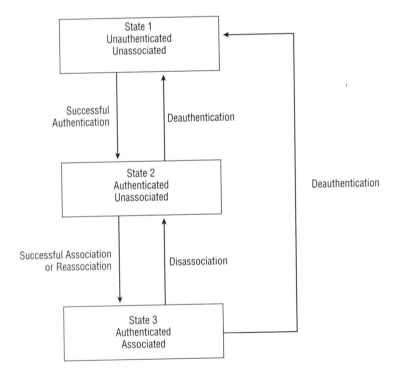

Since a station must authenticate before it can associate, it is never possible for it to be Unauthenticated and Associated.

> To remember the authentication and association states, you need to remember that authentication occurs first. Next think of authentication and association as two doors in a row. You start outside both doors (unauthenticated and unassociated). You then walk through the first door (authenticated and unassociated). You can then walk through the second door (authenticated and associated). It is impossible to walk through the second door without walking through the first door (unauthenticated and associated).

EXERCISE 8.1

Frame Analysis

The following directions should assist you with the installation and use of CommView so that you can explore some of the topics that were covered in this chapter. To determine if your wireless card is supported, or if you have difficulty installing or using the product, you can find support at www.tamos.com.

1. On the CD included with this book, locate the CommView directory. The installation must be performed from the command prompt in order to enable the fully functional 30-day trial.

2. At the command prompt, run the following command

   SETUP SYBEX

3. As the program installs, accept the default settings, and when the installation is completed, click on Finish.

4. When the installation completes, a Driver Installation Guide document will appear. Follow the directions for installing your wireless card.

5. After the driver is installed, you will need to restart CommView.

6. Begin by choosing Start Capture from the File menu.

7. Next, click on the Start Scanning button. The program will scan the 802.11 frequencies supported by your wireless card and will list the channels where it has found access points.

8. Select the band and channel that has an access point and click Capture. The program will now begin capturing wireless packets. As long as there is an AP nearby, you will at least be capturing the beacon management frames. After a minute or two of capturing packets, choose Stop Capture from the File menu.

9. Click the Packets button in the upper-middle portion of the program window. This will display the list of packets that you have captured. The Protocol column shows what type of packet each one is. By clicking on any packet, you will be able to see detailed information near the bottom of the program window.

The CWNA test does not cover any detailed packet information. If you want to learn about 802.11 packets, the Certified Wireless Analysis Professional (CWAP) course and test covers this topic extensively. For now, spend some time using CommView to look at some of the different types of frames that you were introduced to in this chapter. A good packet analyzer is a great tool for exploring what occurs during 802.11 communications.

Roaming

As wireless LANs grew to multiple access points, the 802.11 standard provided the ability for the client stations to transition from one access point to another while maintaining network connectivity for the upper-layer applications. This ability is known as *roaming*, although the 802.11 standard does not define what roaming is.

The decision to roam is currently made by the client station. What actually causes the client station to roam is a set of proprietary rules determined by the manufacturer of the wireless card, usually determined by the signal strength, noise level, and bit-error rate. As the client station communicates on the network, it continues to look for other access points and will authenticate to those that are within range. Remember, a station can be authenticated to multiple access points but only associated to one. As the client station moves away from the access point that it is associated with and the signal drops below a predetermined threshold, it will attempt to connect to another access point and roam from its current BSS to a new BSS. As the station roams, the old access point and the new access point should communicate with each other across the distribution system medium and help provide a clean transition between the two. Many manufacturers provide this handoff, but it is not officially part of the 802.11 standard, so each vendor does it using its own method. IAPP and 802.11F attempted to set standards, but these recommendations were never consistently followed. Since each vendor uses its own method of handoff, if a client station roams between access points manufactured by different vendors, the roam may not be smooth and there may be a delay of a few to many seconds.

Reassociation

When a client station decides to roam to a new access point, it will send a *reassociation* request frame to the new access point. It is called a reassociation not because you are reassociating to the access point but because you are reassociating to the SSID of the wireless network.

Reassociation occurs after the client and the access point have exchanged six frames, as described in the following list:

1. In the first step, the client station sends a reassociation request frame to the new access point. The reassociation frame includes the BSSID (MAC address) of the access point it is currently connected to (we will refer to this as the old access point).

2. The new access point then replies to the station with an ACK.

3. The new access point attempts to connect to the old access point using the distribution system medium and attempts to notify it that the station is trying to associate to the new access point. Remember that there is no standard for this communication, so it may or may not be successful.

4. If this communication is successful, using the distribution system medium, the old access point will communicate with the new access point and acknowledge that the client is attempting to roam.

5. The new access point will then send a reassociation response frame to the client via the wireless network.

6. The client will send an ACK to the new access point. The client does not need to send a disassociation frame to the old access point since it assumes that the two access points have communicated with each other across the distribution system medium.

If the reassociation is not successful, the client will retain its connection to the old access point and either continue to communicate with it or attempt to roam to another access point.

Disassociation

Disassociation is a notification, not a request. If a station wants to disassociate from an AP or an AP wants to disassociate from stations, either device can send a disassociation frame. This is a polite way of terminating the association. A client will do so when you shut down the operating system. An AP will do so if it is being disconnected from the network for maintenance. Disassociation cannot be refused by either party. If the disassociation frame is not heard by the other party, MAC management is designed to accommodate loss of communications.

Deauthentication

Like disassociation, a *deauthentication* frame is also a notification and not a request. If a station wants to deauthenticate from an AP or an AP wants to deauthenticate from stations, either device can send a deauthentication frame. Since authentication is a prerequisite for association, a deauthentication frame will automatically cause a disassociation to occur. Deauthentication cannot be refused by either party.

Summary

This chapter focused on 802.11 medium access. Every station has the right to communicate, and the management of access to the wireless medium is controlled through media access control. Distributed Coordination Function, also known as CSMA/CA, was reviewed along with some of its key components. This chapter also focused on the three key frame types: management, control, and data. Some of the important subtypes were looked at individually. These were primarily the management subtypes that are used during the process of media access.

Exam Essentials

Know the media access control process and all of the frames that are used during this process. Understand the function of each of the following: active scanning, passive scanning, beacon, probe request, probe response, authentication, association, reassociation, disassociation, deauthentication.

Know the three major 802.11 frame types.   Make sure you know the function of the management, control, and data frames. Be familiar with what they are used for.

Understand the similarities and differences of CSMA/CA and CSMA/CD.   Both access methods have similarities and differences. Know what makes them similar and know what makes them different.

Define virtual and physical carrier-senses.   Understand the purpose and basic mechanisms of the two carrier-senses.

Explain DCF and PCF.   Define the basic operations of both Distributed Coordination Function and Point Coordination Function.

Understand the similarities and differences of 802.11 frames and 802.3 frames.   The IEEE created both of these frame types. 802.11 and 802.3 frames share similar and different properties. Know how they compare to each other.

Key Terms

Before you take the exam, be certain you are familiar with the following terms:

acknowledgement (ACK)

active scanning

association

authentication

beacon management frame

Carrier Sense Multiple Access with Collision Avoidance (CSMA/CA)

Carrier Sense Multiple Access with Collision Detection (CSMA/CD)

clear channel assessment (CCA)

contention window

control frames

data frames

deauthentication

disassociation

Distributed Coordination Function (DCF)

management frames

network allocation vector (NAV)

Open System authentication

passive scanning

physical carrier-sense

Point Coordination Function (PCF)

point coordinator

probe requests

probe response

reassociation

roaming

Shared Key authentication

slot time

virtual carrier-sense

NOTE Included on the CD that you received with this book is a fully functional 30-day trail of CommView for WiFi v 5.2 by TamoSoft. CommView is a powerful network monitor and analyzer that runs on Windows-based computers and requires a supported 802.11 wireless card.

Review Questions

1. DCF is also known as what? (Choose all that apply.)
   A. Carrier Sense Multiple Access with Collision Detection (CSMA/CD)
   B. Carrier Sense Multiple Access with Collision Avoidance (CSMA/CA)
   C. Data Control Function
   D. Distributed Coordination Function

2. 802.11 collision detection is handled using which technology?
   A. Network allocation vector (NAV)
   B. Clear channel assessment (CCA)
   C. Duration/ID value
   D. Receiving an ACK from the destination station
   E. Positive collision detection cannot be determined

3. ACK and CTS frames can follow which interframe space?
   A. EIFS
   B. DIFS
   C. PIFS
   D. SIFS
   E. LIFS

4. The *Carrier Sense* portion of CSMA/CA is performed using which of the following methods? (Choose all that apply.)
   A. Virtual carrier-sense
   B. Physical carrier-sense
   C. Channel sense window
   D. Clear channel assessment

5. After the station has performed the carrier sense and determined that no other devices are transmitting, the next step is for the station to do what?
   A. Wait the necessary number of slot times before transmitting.
   B. Begin transmitting.
   C. Select a random backoff value.
   D. Begin the random backoff timer.

6. If PCF is implemented, it can function in which of the following network environments? (Choose all that apply.)

   A. Ad-Hoc mode

   B. BSS

   C. IBSS

   D. Infrastructure mode

   E. BSA

7. Which of the following differ in 802.11 and 802.3 frames? (Choose all that apply.)

   A. Frame size

   B. MAC addressing scheme

   C. Number of MAC addresses

   D. There are no differences. The frames are similar.

8. Which of the following statements are true about 802.11 frame types? (Choose all that apply.)

   A. There are three 802.11 frame types.

   B. There are 10 management frame subtypes.

   C. All of the frame types are capable of transporting upper-layer data.

   D. Some frame subtypes are only used by PCF.

   E. A beacon frame is a subtype of the management frame.

9. Which of the following are true about beacon management frames? (Choose all that apply.)

   A. Beacons can be disabled to hide the network from intruders.

   B. Time-stamp information is used by the clients to synchronize their clocks.

   C. In a BSS, clients share the responsibility of transmitting the beacons.

   D. Beacons can contain vendor-proprietary information.

10. Which of the following are true about scanning? (Choose all that apply.)

   A. There are two types of scanning, passive and active.

   B. Stations must transmit probe requests in order to learn about local access points.

   C. The 802.11 standard allows access points to ignore probe requests for security reasons.

   D. It is common for stations to continue to send probe requests after being associated to an access point.

11. Which of the following information is included in a probe response frame? (Choose all that apply.)

   A. Time stamp

   B. Supported data rates

   C. Service set capabilities

   D. SSID

   E. Traffic indication map

12. When a client station is first powered on, what is the order of frames generated by the client station and access point?

    A. Probe request, probe response, association request/response, authentication request/response

    B. Probe request, probe response, authentication request/response, association request/response

    C. Association request/response, authentication request/response, probe request, probe response

    D. Authentication request/response, association request/response, probe request, probe response

13. Which of the following are authentication methods? (Choose all that apply.)

    A. Shared Key authentication

    B. Secured Key authentication

    C. Open Source authentication

    D. Open System authentication

14. Select the valid association and authentication states? (Choose all that apply.)

    A. Unassociated and unauthenticated

    B. Associated and unauthenticated

    C. Associated and authenticated

    D. Unassociated and authenticated

15. Roaming is controlled by the client and occurs based upon a set of proprietary rules determined by the manufacturer of the wireless card. Which of the following parameters are often used when making the decision to roam? (Choose all that apply.)

    A. Signal strength

    B. Distance

    C. Noise level

    D. Bit-error rate

16. Which of the following frames cannot be refused? (Choose all that apply.)

    A. Authentication

    B. Association

    C. Reassociation

    D. Disassociation

    E. Deauthentication

17. When a client station is authenticated and associated to an access point, which of the following tasks can the client station still perform? (Choose all that apply.)

    A. Active scanning

    B. Passive scanning

    C. Associate to other access points

    D. Authenticate to other access points

18. Which of the following terms are affiliated with the carrier sense mechanism? (Choose all that apply.)

    A. Contention window

    B. Network allocation vector

    C. Random backoff time

    D. Duration/ID field

19. Which of the following statements about PCF are true? (Choose all that apply.)

    A. PCF will only work in a BSS.

    B. PCF can be used in an IBSS.

    C. Both the station and access point must support PCF for it to be used.

    D. The access point will alternate between PCF and DCF mode.

    E. PCF is a form a contention.

20. Layer 3 roaming can be provided by which of the following? (Choose all that apply.)

    A. Wireless Routing Protocol (WRP)

    B. Routing Mobility Protocol (RMP)

    C. Proprietary layer 3 solutions

    D. Mobile IP

Answers to Review Questions

1. B, D. DCF is an abbreviation for Distributed Coordination Function. DCF is a CSMA/CA media access control method. CSMA/CD is used by 802.3, not 802.11. There is no such thing as Data Control Function.

2. E. 802.11 can be used to determine that the frame was not received by the destination station, but it cannot positively determine the cause. It may be due to collision or to other reasons such as high noise level. All of the other options are used to help prevent collisions.

3. D. Only ACK frames and CTS frames may follow a SIFS. LIFS do not exist. The other three interframe spaces are not covered on the CWNA test.

4. A, B, D. The NAV timer maintains a prediction of future traffic on the medium based on duration value information seen in a previous frame transmission. The virtual carrier-sense uses the NAV to determine medium availability. Physical carrier-sense checks the RF medium for carrier availability. Clear channel assessment is another name for physical carrier-sense. Channel sense window does not exist.

5. C. The first step is to select a random backoff timer. After the value is selected, it is multiplied by the slot time. The random backoff timer then begins counting down the number of slot times. When the number reaches 0, the station can begin transmitting.

6. B, D. PCF requires an access point. Ad-Hoc mode and IBSS (independent basic service set) are the same and do not use an access point. BSS (basic service set) and Infrastructure mode are the same and use an access point. BSA is basic service area, the area of coverage of a basic service set

7. A, C. An 802.3 frame is typically up to 1,518 bytes, while 802.11 can transport frames of up to 2,304 bytes of "upper layer" data. 802.3 frames have two MAC address fields, while 802.11 frames have four address fields. Both frame types use the same MAC addressing scheme.

8. A, D, E. The three frame types are management, control, and data. There are 11 management frame subtypes. Only data frames can carry upper-layer data, and not all of the data subtypes can. Some frame subtypes are used for PCF only, some for DCF only, and some for both. A beacon is a subtype of the management frame, and is often referred to as a beacon management frame.

9. B, D. Beacons cannot be disabled. Clients use the time-stamp information from the beacon to synchronize with the other stations on the wireless network. Only access points send beacons in a BSS; clients participate sending beacons in an IBSS. Beacons can contain proprietary information.

10. A, D. There are two type of scanning: passive, which is when a station listens to the beacons to discover wireless networks, and active, which is when a station sends probe requests looking for wireless networks. Stations send probe requests only if they are performing an active scan. Some vendors will ignore probe requests for security reasons, but this is not defined in the 802.11 standard. After a station is associated, it is common for the station to continue to learn about nearby access points. This information is used to speed up roaming if a station decides to roam.

11. A, B, C, D. The probe response contains the same information as the beacon frame with the exception of the traffic indication map.

12. B. When the client first attempts to connect to an access point, it will first send a probe request and listen for a probe response. After it receives a probe response, it will attempt to authenticate to the access point and then associate to the network.

13. A, D. Shared Key authentication and Open System authentication are the two types of 802.11 authentication.

14. A, C, D. A station can be unassociated and unauthenticated, associated and authenticated, and unassociated and authenticated. This question was written to be tricky. Since authentication must occur before association, most texts will list authentication before association. The station can never be associated with first being authenticated.

15. A, C, D. Distance has nothing to do with the clients decision to roam to a new access point. Also, there is no way of determining the distanced between the client and the access point.

16. D, E. Both the disassociation and deauthentication frames are notifications and not requests. Therefore, they cannot be refused.

17. A, B, D. The client station can still look for other access points using active scanning and/or passive scanning. The client station can also authenticate to other access points, but a client station can be associated to only one access point at a time.

18. B, D. The Duration/ID field is used to set the network allocation vector, which is a part of the virtual carrier-sense process. The contention window and random backoff time are part of the backoff process that is performed after the carrier sense process.

19. A, C, D. PCF will only work in a BSS since an access point is required, which also means that it cannot be used in an IBSS. Both the station and access point must support PCF if it is going to be used. The access point will alternate between PCF mode (Contention-Free period) and DCF mode (Contention Period). PCF is a form of polling, not contention.

20. C, D. Roaming can be provided by either proprietary solutions or by the standards-based Mobile IP solution. WRP and RMP do not exist.

Chapter 9

802.11 MAC Architecture

IN THIS CHAPTER, YOU WILL LEARN ABOUT THE FOLLOWING:

- ✓ ACK Frame
- ✓ Fragmentation
- ✓ 802.11g Protection Mechanism
- ✓ RTS/CTS
- ✓ CTS-to-Self
- ✓ Power Management
  - ▪ Active Mode
  - ▪ Power Save Mode
- ✓ Traffic Indication Map (TIM)
- ✓ Delivery Traffic Indication Message (DTIM)
- ✓ Announcement Traffic Indication Message (ATIM)
- ✓ Wireless Multimedia (WMM) certification

This chapter will look at more of the different components of the 802.11 MAC architecture. After the function of the ACK frame is described, you will learn about frame fragmentation and how it is a part of the 802.11 architecture. An often misunderstood feature of 802.11 is the 802.11g protection mechanism. We will describe exactly how 802.11b and 802.11g stations can coexist in the same BSS using either the RTS/CTS or CTS-to-Self protection mechanism. The next section of the chapter will discuss 802.11 power management and the different pieces that are a part of power management. Finally, the chapter will culminate with an overview of wireless multimedia (WMM).

ACK Frame

The *ACK frame* is one of the six control frames and one of the key components of the 802.11 CSMA/CA media access control method. Since 802.11 is a wireless medium that cannot guarantee successful data transmission, the only way for a station to know that a frame it transmitted was properly received is for the receiving station to notify the transmitting station. This notification is performed using an ACK.

The ACK frame is a very simple frame consisting of 14 octets of information (Figure 9.1). When a station receives data, it waits a short period of time known as a *short interframe space (SIFS)*. The receiving station copies the MAC address of the transmitting station from the data frame and places it in the Receiver Address (RA) field of the ACK frame. The receiving station then replies by transmitting the ACK. If all goes well, the station that sent the data frame receives the ACK with its MAC address in the RA field and now knows that the frame was received and was not corrupted. The ACK frame is the highest-priority frame due to the half-duplex nature of the medium. The delivery of every unicast frame must be verified or a retransmission must take place. The ACK frame is used for delivery verification.

Every unicast frame must be followed by an ACK frame. If a unicast frame is not followed by an ACK, it will be retransmitted.

FIGURE 9.1 ACK control frame

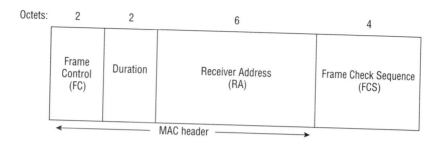

Fragmentation

Fragmentation is a common function of computer networking. TCP/IP typically has an IP maximum transmission unit (MTU) of 1,500 bytes, meaning that TCP/IP will take the data that is being sent and break it into groups of no greater than 1,500 bytes. When IP passes this packet to the Data-Link layer to be transmitted by 802.11, the size of this 1,500 byte packet is not a problem for the 802.11 network since it is capable of transporting data payloads of up to 2,304 bytes. Every 802.11 data frame consists of not only the data payload, but also extra MAC layer information known as the header. In order for a network to provide the best throughput, it is designed to transmit large enough frames to minimize the amount of overhead added by the header while making sure that the frames are not too big to limit shared access to the medium by other stations.

In an ideal environment when everything is functioning properly, the 802.11 network will work well transmitting the data frames. Unfortunately, since 802.11 uses RF transmissions, there is a risk of interference and a risk of the data not being received. Whenever the transmitting station does not receive an ACK, the transmission is assumed to be unsuccessful and the station will have to transmit the frame again.

802.11 fragmentation breaks the data into smaller pieces known as fragments, adds header information to each fragment, and transmits each fragment individually. Although the same amount of actual data is being transmitted, each fragment requires its own header, and the transmission of each fragment is followed by a SIFS and an ACK. In a properly functioning 802.11 network, smaller fragments will actually decrease data throughput due to the overhead of the additional header, SIFS, and ACK of each fragment. On the other hand, if the network is experiencing a large amount of data corruption, lowering the 802.11 fragmentation setting may improve data throughput.

Fragmentation always introduces more overhead to the network. If fragmentation reduces the number of retransmitted frames, then it is likely that network throughput will increase. Otherwise, the additional overhead caused by the fragmentation will cause the network throughput to decrease.

If an 802.11 frame is corrupted and needs to be retransmitted, the entire frame must be resent. When the 802.11 frame is broken into multiple fragments, each fragment is smaller and transmits for a shorter period of time. If interference occurs, instead of an entire large frame, it is likely that only one of the small fragments will become corrupted and need to be retransmitted. Retransmitting the small fragment will take much less time than retransmitting the larger frame.

Figure 9.2 illustrates how smaller fragments can actually improve throughput. (Please note that this is a representation and not drawn to scale. Additionally, to simplify the illustration, ACKs were not included.) This illustration shows the transmission and retransmission of a large 1,500 byte frame above and the transmission and retransmission of smaller 500 byte fragments below. If there was no RF interference, only the solid-lined rectangles would need to be transmitted. Due to the additional headers (H) and the time between the fragments for each SIFS and ACK, the smaller fragments would take longer to transmit. However, if RF interference occurred, it would take less time to retransmit the smaller fragment than it would to retransmit the larger frame, thus improving data throughput.

The transmission of a fragment is treated the same way as the transmission of a frame. Therefore, every fragment must be followed by an ACK. If a fragment is not followed by an ACK, it will be retransmitted.

FIGURE 9.2 Frame fragmentation

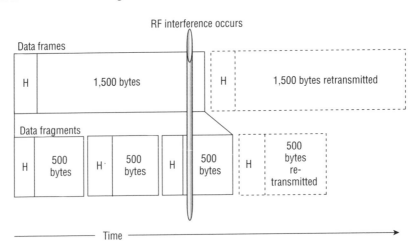

Not all wireless LAN adapters allow you to adjust the fragmentation settings. If you do set your wireless LAN adapter to use a smaller fragment size, you must realize that as you roam between access points and as you move between networks, all of your 802.11 frames will be fragmented using the setting you have configured. This means that if you roam to a location where there is no interference, your station will still be using the smaller frame fragments and will actually perform worse than if you had left the fragmentation value at its largest setting.

Changing the fragmentation value is useful to help identify that there is a problem. If a station is retransmitting many frames, and lowering the fragmentation value increases the data throughput, you have identified that an RF interference problem exists. You may need to try multiple fragmentation values before you find the one that provides you with the best data throughput. The best solution to the problem is to locate and remove the cause of the RF interference, not to continue to use your station with a smaller fragmentation value. This RF interference could be caused by a near/far issue, a neighboring transmitter, a microwave, multipath, or a collision with another client device trying to transmit. The behavior shown here simply tells you that there is an issue with your ability to transmit unharmed.

802.11g Protection Mechanism (EXAM)

When an 802.11g (ERP-OFDM) client station needs to communicate in a basic service set (BSS) that consists of an 802.11b (HR-DSSS) access point and 802.11b (HR-DSSS) client stations, the 802.11g station simply uses 802.11b protocols. The 802.11g standard amendment mandates support for both HR-DSSS and ERP-OFDM. Therefore, when 802.11b client stations need to communicate in a basic service set with an 802.11g access point and 802.11g client stations, the 802.11g devices need to provide compatibility for the slower 802.11b devices. This environment is often referred to as *mixed-mode*. Contrary to what some people believe, the 802.11g devices do not simply switch to 802.11b mode and communicate using 802.11b methods. For both standards to coexist, the 802.11g devices enable what is referred to as 802.11g protection mechanism, also known as 802.11g protected mode. As stated earlier, the 802.11g standard amendment mandates support for both HR-DSSS and ERP-OFDM. In Chapter 5 you learned that vendors offer three configuration modes for an 802.11g access point:

802.11b only mode   When an 802.11g AP is running in this operational mode, support for DSSS technology is solely enabled. Effectively, the access point has been configured to be an 802.11b access point and only clients running in 802.11b mode will be able to communicate with the AP. Aggregate throughput will be the same as achieved in an 80211b network.

802.11g only mode   APs configured as "G only" will only communicate with 802.11g client stations using OFDM technology. Support for DSSS is disabled, therefore 802.11b clients will not be able to associate with the access point. Aggregate throughput will be equivalent to what can be achieved in an 802.11a network. For example, the aggregate throughput of an AP with a data rate of 54 Mbps might be about 19 to 20 Mbps. A "G only" wireless LAN is sometimes referred to as a "Pure G" network.

802.11b/g mode This is the default operational mode of most 802.11g access points and is often called mixed-mode. Support for both DSSS and OFDM is enabled; therefore, both 802.11b and 802.11g clients can communicate with the access point.

You need to understand that these vendor configurations are not part of the 802.11g amendment. Although most vendors do indeed support these configurations, the 802.11g amendment mandates support for both 802.11b clause 18 devices and 802.11g clause 19 devices.

In Chapter 8 you learned that one of the ways of preventing collisions is for the stations to set a countdown timer known as the network allocation vector (NAV). When a station wants to transmit data, it tells the other stations how long it needs to reserve the medium. This notification is known as NAV distribution. Typically, NAV distribution is done through the Duration/ID field that is part of the data frame. When a data frame is transmitted, the Duration/ID field is used by the other stations to set their NAV. Unfortunately, this is not inherently possible in a mixed-mode environment. If an 802.11g device were to transmit a data frame, 802.11b devices would not be able to interpret the data frame or the Duration/ID value because the 802.11b DSSS devices are not capable of understanding 802.11g OFDM transmissions. The 802.11b devices would not set their NAV and could incorrectly believe that the medium is available. To prevent this from happening, the 802.11g devices switch into what is known as protected mode.

In a mixed-mode environment, when an 802.11g device wants to transmit data, it will first perform a NAV distribution by transmitting a request to send/clear to send (RTS/CTS) or a CTS-to-Self using a speed and modulation method that the 802.11b DSSS devices can understand. The RTS/CTS or CTS-to-Self will be heard and understood by all of the 802.11b and 802.11g devices. The RTS/CTS or CTS-to-Self will contain a Duration/ID value that will be used by all of the stations to set their NAV. To put it simply, using a slow transmission that all stations can understand, the 802.11g device notifies all the stations to reset their NAV value. Once the RTS/CTS or CTS-to-Self has been used to reserve the medium, the 802.11g station can transmit a data frame using OFDM modulation without worrying about collisions with DSSS stations.

 Real World Scenario

How can you make sure that 802.11g networks are transmitting at 802.11g speeds?

Even if all of the wireless devices in your company support 802.11g, if your network sees even one 802.11b device, it will enable 802.11g protection mechanism. This 802.11b device could be a visitor to your company, someone driving past your building with an 802.11b wireless adapter enabled in their laptop, or a nearby business or home that also has a wireless network. If you want your network to always use 802.11g, then you must configure the access points to support 802.11g only. Remember that if you do this, any 802.11b only devices will not be able to connect to your network.

> ### 🌐 Real World Scenario
>
> #### How Does 802.11b Affect 802.11g Throughput?
>
> When an 802.11b station causes an 802.11g BSS to enable protection mechanism, a large amount of overhead is added to every 802.11g data transmission. This overhead will reduce the 802.11g aggregate data throughput to below 13 Mbps, and possibly as low as 9 Mbps.

RTS/CTS

In order for a client station to participate in a basic service set, it must be able to communicate with the access point. This is straightforward and logical; however, it is possible for the client station to be able to communicate with the access point but not be able to hear or be heard by any of the other client stations. This can be a problem because, if you recall, a station performs collision avoidance by setting its NAV when it hears another station transmitting (virtual carrier sense) and by listening for RF (physical carrier sense). If a station cannot hear the other stations, or cannot be heard by the other stations, there is a greater likelihood that a collision can occur. *Request to send/clear to send (RTS/CTS)* is a mechanism that performs a NAV distribution and helps to prevent collisions from occurring. This NAV distribution reserves the medium prior to the transmission of the data frame.

The RTS/CTS is a simple process. Essentially, the transmitting station announces, "Everybody wait until I'm done transmitting my data," and then the receiving station announces, "Everybody wait until he is done transmitting his data." Since the access point participates in all transmissions in a basic service set, one of the devices that made an announcement had to be the access point, which almost guarantees that all devices in the basic service set heard one of these messages. Now while everyone is waiting, the transmitting station will send its data.

Now, let's look at the RTS/CTS from a slightly more technical perspective. This will be a basic explanation since an in-depth explanation is beyond the scope of the exam. When RTS/CTS is enabled on a station, every time the station wants to transmit a frame, it must perform an RTS/CTS exchange prior to the normal data transmissions. When the transmitting station goes to transmit data, it first sends an RTS frame. This RTS is used for NAV distribution, notifying all other stations that they must wait until the CTS, Data, and ACK have been transmitted. The receiving station then sends a CTS, which is also used for NAV distribution.

Figure 9.3 shows the order of the RTS/CTS, Data, and ACK frames. The station that is transmitting the data sends the RTS and Data frames. The station that is receiving the data sends the CTS and the ACK frames. If any station did not hear the RTS, it should hear the CTS. When a station hears either the RTS or the CTS, it will set its NAV to the value provided. At this point, all stations in the basic service set should have their NAV set and the station should wait until the data exchange is complete.

FIGURE 9.3 RTS/CTS communication

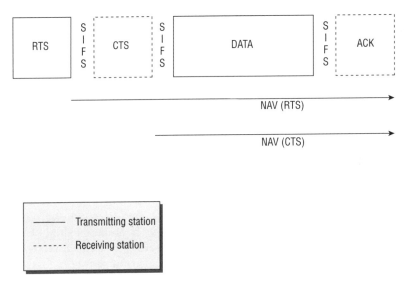

Figure 9.4 shows the communication between wireless station 1 and wired desktop 1. Station 1 uses RTS/CTS to communicate with the access point. It is important to remember that the figure is showing the logical flow of data to and from station 1 and the access point and then a wired physical and logical exchange between the access point and desktop 1. You must remember that during the wireless exchange, all wireless stations within range will hear the exchange and update their NAV accordingly. Station 2 will update its NAV when it hears either RTS (1) or CTS (2). Depending upon how far apart station 2 is from station 1, station 2 may not hear RTS (1) from station 1. However, since station 2 is a member of the basic service set, it should hear CTS (2). Station 2 will then wait until ACK (4) is sent before it will consider transmitting any data.

Figure 9.5 shows the communication between two wireless stations in a basic service set. Since this is a basic service set, the access point must participate in all communications. In this situation, this is actually two separate exchanges of data. The first exchange is between station 1 and the access point. Then the second exchange occurs between the access point and station 2. So all we are really doing here is showing you two separate RTS/CTS communications. During the first exchange, station 2 will update its NAV when it hears either RTS (1) or CTS (2). Again, depending upon how far apart station 2 is from station 1, station 2 may not hear RTS (1) from station 1. And since station 2 is a member of the basic service set, it should hear CTS (2). Station 2 will then wait until ACK (4) is sent before it will consider transmitting any data. Once ACK (4) has been sent, all stations will perform a CSMA/CA and all stations now have the right to transmit data. In this instance, we will assume that the access point is the next station to gain access to the medium. So now the second RTS/CTS exchange will begin (steps 5 through 8). Station 1 should hear RTS (5) from the access point. Station 1 will then wait until ACK (8) is sent before it will consider transmitting any data. Once ACK (8) has been sent, all stations will again have the right to transmit data.

RTS/CTS is a method of reserving the medium. The transmitting node announces its intent to transmit data by sending an RTS. The receiving station repeats the transmitting stations announcement by sending a CTS. Then the data frame is sent and hopefully an ACK reply is returned.

FIGURE 9.4   Data transfer between a wireless PC using RTS/CTS and a wired PC

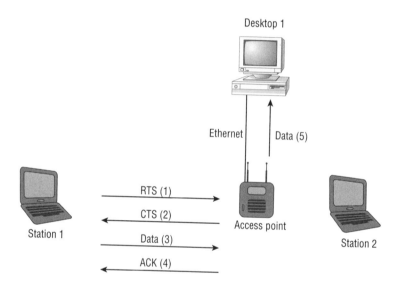

FIGURE 9.5   Data transfer between two wireless PCs in a BSS using RTS/CTS

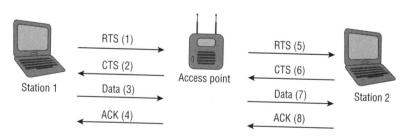

RTS/CTS is used primarily in two situations. It can be used when a hidden node exists (this will be covered in Chapter 12), or it can be used as a protection mechanism for a mixed-mode environment. If it is used in a mixed-mode environment, the RTS and the CTS will be transmitted using a slow transmission method that all stations can understand. Then the Data and the ACK will be transmitted at a faster 802.11g speed.

CTS-to-Self

CTS-to-Self is used strictly as a protection mechanism for mixed-mode environments. One of the benefits of using CTS-to-Self over RTS/CTS as a protection mechanism is that the throughput will be higher since there are fewer frames being sent.

When a station using CTS-to-Self wants to transmit data, it performs a NAV distribution by sending a CTS frame. This CTS notifies all other stations that they must wait until the Data and ACK have been transmitted. Any station that hears the CTS will set their NAV to the value provided.

Since the CTS-to-Self is used as a protection mechanism for mixed-mode environments, the 802.11g station will transmit the CTS using a slow 802.11b transmission method that all stations can understand. Then the Data and the ACK will be transmitted at a faster 802.11g speed using Orthogonal Frequency Division Multiplexing (OFDM).

CTS-to-Self is better suited for use by an access point. It is important to make sure that all stations hear the CTS to reserve the medium, and this is most likely to occur if it is being sent by an access point. If a client station were to use CTS-to-Self, there is a chance that another client station on the opposite side of the BSS might be too far away from the CTS-to-Self and would not realize that the medium is busy.

Power Management

One of the key uses of wireless networking is to provide mobility for the client station. Client mobility goes hand in hand with battery-operated client stations. When battery-operated devices are used, one of the biggest concerns is how long the battery will last until it needs to be recharged. To increase the battery time, a bigger, longer-lasting battery can be used or power consumption can be decreased. The 802.11 standard includes a power management feature that can be enabled to help increase battery life. The two power management modes supported by the 802.11 standard are active mode and power save mode.

Active Mode

Active mode is the default power management mode for most 802.11 stations. When a station is set for active mode, the wireless station is always ready to transmit or receive data. Active mode is sometimes referred to as "continuous aware mode," and it provides no battery conservation. In the MAC header of an 802.11 frame, the Power Management field is 1 bit in length and is used to indicate the power management mode of the station. A value of 0 indicates that the station is in active mode. Stations running in active mode will achieve higher throughput than stations running in power save mode, but the battery life will typically be much shorter.

Stations that are always connected to a power source should be configured to use active mode.

Power Save Mode

Power save mode is an optional mode for 802.11 stations. When a wireless station is set for power save mode, it will shut down some of the transceiver components for a period of time to conserve power. The wireless card basically takes a short nap. The station indicates that it is using power save mode by changing the value of the Power Management field to 1. Power save mode functions differently when the station is part of an infrastructure network or an ad-hoc network, which will be covered later in this chapter.

Traffic Indication Map (TIM)

If a station is part of a basic service set (BSS), it will notify the access point that it is enabling power save mode by changing the Power Management field to 1. When the access point receives a frame from a station with this bit set to 1, the access point knows that the station is in power save mode. Once the access point knows that a station is in power save mode, if the access point receives any data that is destined for the station, it will store the information in a buffer. Any time a station associates to an access point, the station receives an *association identifier (AID)*. The access point uses this AID to keep track of the stations that are associated and the members of the BSS. If the access point is buffering data for a station in power save mode, when the access point transmits its next beacon, the AID of the station will be transmitted as part of the frame known as the *traffic indication map (TIM)*. This TIM is a list of all stations that have undelivered data buffered on the access point waiting to be delivered. Every beacon will include the AID of the station until the data is delivered.

After the station notifies the access point that it is in power save mode, the station shuts down part of its transceiver to conserve energy. A station can be in one of two states, its normal state of awake or its power save state of asleep. Since beacons are transmitted at a consistent predetermined interval known as the target beacon transmission time (TBTT), all stations know when beacons will occur. The station will remain asleep for a short period of time and awaken in time to hear a beacon frame. The station does not have to awaken for every beacon. To conserve more power, the station can sleep for a longer period of time and then awaken in time to hear an upcoming beacon.

When the station receives the beacon, it checks to see if its AID is set in the TIM, indicating that a buffered unicast frame waits. If so, the station will remain awake and will send a PS-Poll frame to the access point. When the access point receives the PS-Poll frame, it will send the buffered frames to the station. The station will stay awake while the access point transmits the buffered frames. When the access point sends the data to the station, the station needs to know when all of the buffered data has been received so that it can go back to sleep. Each data frame contains a one bit field called the More Data field. When the station receives a buffered frame with the More Data field set to 1, the station knows that it cannot go back to sleep yet because there is some more buffered data that it has not yet received. When the More Data field is set to 1, the station knows that it needs to send another PS-Poll frame and wait to receive the next buffered data frame.

After all of the buffered frames have been sent, the More Data field in the last buffered frame will be set to 0, indicating that there is currently no more buffered data, and the station will go back to sleep. The access point will remove the station's AID from the TIM, and when the next TBTT arrives, the access point will send a beacon. The station will remain asleep for a short period of time and again awaken in time to hear a beacon frame. When the station receives the beacon, it will again check to see if its AID is set in the TIM. Assuming that there are no buffered frames awaiting this station, the stations AID will not be set in the TIM, and the station can simply go back to sleep until it is time to wake up and check again.

Delivery Traffic Indication Message (DTIM)

In addition to unicast traffic, network traffic includes multicast and broadcast traffic. Since multicast and broadcast traffic is directed to all stations, the BSS needs to provide a way to make sure that all stations are awake to receive these frames. *Delivery traffic indication message (DTIM)* is used to assure that all stations are awake when multicast or broadcast traffic is sent. DTIM is a special type of TIM. A TIM is transmitted as part of every beacon. A configurable setting on the access point called the DTIM interval results in how often a DTIM is transmitted as part of the beacon. A DTIM interval of 3 means that every third beacon is a DTIM, whereas a DTIM interval of 1 would mean that every beacon is a DTIM. Every beacon contains DTIM information that informs the stations when the next DTIM will occur. All stations will wake up in time to receive the beacon with the DTIM. If the access point has multicast or broadcast traffic to be sent, it will transmit the beacon with the DTIM and then immediately send the multicast or broadcast data.

After the multicast or broadcast data is transmitted, if a station's AID was in the DTIM, the station will remain awake and will send a PS-Poll frame and proceed with retrieving its buffered data from the access point. If a station did not see its AID in the DTIM, then the station can go back to sleep.

Announcement Traffic Indication Message (ATIM)

If a station is part of an independent basic service set (IBSS), there is no central access point to buffer data while the stations are in power save mode. A station will notify the other stations that it is enabling power save mode by changing the Power Management field to 1. When the station transmits a frame with this field set to 1, the other stations know to buffer any data that they may have for this station since this station is now in power save mode.

Periodically, all stations must wake up and notify each other if any station has buffered data that needs to be delivered to another station. This recurring period of time when all devices must be awake to exchange this information is known as the *announcement traffic indication message (ATIM) window*. During the ATIM window, if a station has buffered data for another station, it will send a unicast frame known as an ATIM frame to the other station. This unicast frame informs the station that it must stay awake until the next ATIM window so that it can receive the buffered data. Any station that either has buffered data for another station or has received an ATIM will stay awake so that the buffered data can be exchanged. All of the other stations can go to sleep and wait until the next ATIM window to go through this process again.

When the ATIM window expires, the nodes that have stayed awake go through the usual CSMA/CA process to exchange the unsent data. If a station is unable to transmit the data during this time, it will simply send another ATIM frame during the next ATIM window and then attempt to send the data during the following CSMA/CA period.

Wireless Multimedia (WMM)

The newly approved IEEE Std. 802.11e-2005 amendment defines the layer 2 MAC methods needed to meet the QoS requirements for time-sensitive applications over IEEE 802.11 wireless LANs. The 802.11e amendment defines a *Quality of Service Basic Service Set (QBSS)*. The original 802.11 standard defined two methods in which an 802.11 radio card may gain control of the half-duplex medium. The default method, *Distributed Coordination Function*

(DCF), is a completely random method for deciding who gets to transmit on the wireless medium next. The original standard also defined another medium access control method, called *Point Coordination Function (PCF)*, where the access point briefly takes control of the medium and polls the clients.

The 802.11e amendment defines enhanced medium access methods to support QoS requirements. *Hybrid Coordination Function (HCF)* is an additional coordination function that is applied in an 802.11e QoS wireless network. HCF has two access mechanisms to provide QoS: Enhanced Distributed Channel Access (EDCA) and HHCF (Hybrid Coordination Function) Controlled Channel Access (HCCA).

Enhanced Distributed Channel Access (EDCA) is an extension to DCF. The EDCA medium access method will provide for the "prioritization of traffic" via the use of 802.1d priority tags.

HFC Controlled Channel Access (HCCA) is similar to PCF. HCF gives the access point the ability to provide for "prioritization of stations" via a polling mechanism. In other words, certain client stations will be given a chance to transmit before others.

The Wi-Fi Alliance has introduced the *Wi-Fi Multimedia (WMM)* certification as a partial mirror of 802.11e amendment. Currently, WMM is based on EDCA and provides for traffic prioritization via four access categories, as shown in Table 9.1.

T A B L E 9 . 1   Wi-Fi Multimedia access categories

Access Category	Description	802.1d Tags
WMM Voice Priority	This is the highest priority. It allows multiple and concurrent VoIP calls with low latency and toll voice quality.	7, 6
WMM Video Priority	This supports prioritized video traffic before other data traffic. A single 802.11g or 802.11a channel can support three to four SDTV video streams or one HDTV video stream.	5, 4
WMM Best Effort Priority	This is traffic from applications or devices that are not capable of providing QoS capabilities, such as legacy devices. This traffic is not as sensitive to latency but affected by long delays, such as Internet browsing.	0, 3
WMM Background Priority	This is low-priority traffic that does not have strict throughput or latency requirements. This traffic includes file transfers and print jobs.	2, 1

The Wi-Fi Alliance also defined *WMM – PS (Power Save)*, which uses 802.11e mechanisms to increase the battery life via advanced power saving mechanisms. Also proposed is *WMM – SA (Scheduled Access)*, which is Contention Free access, based on HCCA. WMM and HCF as defined by 802.11e is an extremely complicated medium access method and entire books and classes will probably be created on the subject. Currently, most QoS mechanisms used in Wi-Fi deployments remain proprietary, but that may change in the future as acceptance of WMM and 802.11e grows in popularity.

The Wi-Fi Alliance has two white papers we recommend you read, located at www.wi-fi.org/white_papers/whitepaper-090104-wmm/ and www.wi-fi.org/white_papers/whitepaper-120505-wmmpowersave/.

Summary

This chapter covered five key areas of the MAC architecture:

- ACK frames
- Fragmentation
- 802.11g protection mechanism
- Power management
- Wi-Fi Multimedia (WMM) certification

It is important to understand the need for an 802.11g protection mechanism. Without one, mixed-mode networks would not be able to function. Both RTS/CTS and CTS-to-Self provide 802.11g protection mechanisms.

To help manage battery life, power management can be configured on a wireless station. Active mode provides no battery conservation of any kind, while power save mode can be invaluable for increasing the battery life of laptop and handheld computing devices. We discussed the following power management pieces in this chapter:

- Traffic indication map (TIM)
- Delivery traffic indication message (DTIM)
- Announcement traffic indication message (ATIM)

The last topic covered was the Wi-Fi Multimedia (WMM) certification, which was introduced by the Wi-Fi Alliance as a partial mirror of 802.11e amendment. WMM is designed to meet the QoS requirements for time-sensitive applications such as audio, video, and voice over IEEE 802.11.

Exam Essentials

Know the importance of the ACK frame for determining that a unicast frame was received and uncorrupted.   Understand that after a unicast frame is transmitted, there is a short interframe space (SIFS) and then the receiving station replies by transmitting an ACK. If this process is completed successfully, the transmitting station knows the frame was received and was not corrupted.

Know the benefits and detriments of fragmentation.   By default, fragmentation adds overhead and fragmented frames are inherently slower than unfragmented frames. If RF interference exists, fragmentation can reduce the amount of retransmitted data, thus actually increasing the data throughput. If fragmentation does increase bandwidth, this is a clear indication of a transmission problem. Remember that the cause could be RF interference, multipath, collisions, or a near-far issue.

Understand the importance of 802.11g protection mechanisms and how they function.   Protected mode allows 802.11g and 802.11b devices to coexist on the same BSS. Protected mode can be provided by RTS/CTS or CTS-to-Self. CTS-to-Self is strictly a protection mechanism, but RTS/CTS can be used to identify or prevent hidden nodes.

Understand all of the technologies that make up power management.   Power management can be enabled to decrease power usage and increase battery life. In order to achieve this, TIMs, DTIMs, and ATIMs are used to notify wireless devices when to stay awake to receive buffered data.

Understand Wi-Fi Multimedia (WMM) certification and its importance now and in the future.   WMM is designed to provide Quality of Service capabilities to 802.11 wireless networks. WMM is a partial mirror of the 802.11e amendment. WMM currently provides for traffic prioritorization via four access categories.

Key Terms

Before you take the exam, be certain you are familiar with the following terms:

802.11g protected mode

802.11g protection mechanism

ACK frame

active mode

announcement traffic indication message (ATIM) window

association identifier (AID)

CTS-to-Self

delivery traffic indication message (DTIM)

Distributed Coordination Function (DCF)

Enhanced Distributed Channel Access (EDCA)

Hybrid Coordination Function (HCF)

Hybrid Coordination Function Controlled Access (HCCA)

Mixed-Mode

Point Coordination Function (PCF)

power save mode

Quality of Service Basic Service Set (QBSS)

request to send/clear to send (RTS/CTS)

short interframe space (SIFS)

traffic indication map (TIM)

Wi-Fi Multimedia (WMM)

WMM – PS (Power Save)

WMM – SA (Scheduled Access)

Review Questions

1. What type of frame is an ACK?

   A. Management

   B. Control

   C. Data

   D. Reply

2. In an ideal environment, fragmentation will do which of the following? (Choose all that apply.)

   A. Increase data throughput.

   B. Decrease data throughput.

   C. Increase the amount of overall bits transmitted.

   D. Decrease the amount of overall bits transmitted.

3. Which of the following are protection mechanisms? (Choose all that apply.)

   A. NAV backoff

   B. RTS/CTS

   C. RTS-to-Self

   D. CTS-to-Self

   E. WEP encryption

4. Which of the following is the function of the RTS/CTS and CTS-to-Self?

   A. Physical clear channel assessment

   B. Virtual clear channel assessment

   C. Mixed-mode modulation

   D. NAV distribution

5. An access point keeps track of the power mode of the wireless stations connected to it using which of the following?

   A. IP address

   B. MAC address

   C. Association ID

   D. TIM

6. Which of the following is used to notify all stations that there is a multicast or broadcast frame waiting to be transmitted?

   A. TIM

   B. ATIM

   C. DTIM

   D. BTIM

7. After a station sees its AID in the TIM, what typically is the next frame that the station transmits?

   A. Data

   B. PS-Poll

   C. ATIM

   D. ACK

8. When CTS-to-Self is used, which station always transmits the CTS?

   A. The receiving station

   B. The transmitting station

   C. The source station

   D. The destination station

   E. The access point

9. How does a client station indicate that it is using power save mode?

   A. It transmits a frame to the access point with the Sleep field set to 1.

   B. It transmits a frame to the access point with the Power Management field set to 1.

   C. Using DTIM, the access point determines when the client station uses power save mode.

   D. It doesn't need to since power save mode is the default.

10. Currently, WMM is based on EDCA and provides for traffic prioritization via which of the following access categories? (Choose all that apply.)

    A. WMM Voice Priority

    B. WMM Video Priority

    C. WMM Audio Priority

    D. WMM Best Effort Priority

    E. WMM Background Priority

11. After a station transmits a data frame and waits a SIFS, if the station does not receive an ACK, which of the following is true? (Choose all that apply.)

    A. The receiving station did not receive the data.

    B. The receiving station may have received the data.

    C. The transmitting station will wait an additional SIFS to receive the ACK.

    D. The transmitting station will attempt to retransmit the data frame.

    E. The transmitting station will send a retransmit notification.

12. When transmitting fragmented frames in an environment where frame retransmission is common, which of the following is true? (Choose all that apply.)

    A. The overall number of bits transmitted will always be greater than if fragmentation was disabled.

    B. The overall number of bits transmitted will always be less than if fragmentation was disabled.

    C. Data throughput may decrease.

    D. Data throughput may increase.

13. When 802.11g protected mode is enabled, which of the following will provide the best throughput with the least likelihood of retransmissions? (Choose all that apply.)

    A. AP uses RTS/CTS, stations use RTS/CTS.

    B. AP uses RTS/CTS, stations use CTS-to-Self.

    C. AP uses CTS-to-Self, stations use CTS-to-Self.

    D. AP uses CTS-to-Self, stations use RTS/CTS.

14. If RTS/CTS is enabled on all devices in a BSS, how many frames are transmitted when a client station sends data to another client station?

    A. 2

    B. 4

    C. 6

    D. 8

15. If a station is in power save mode, how does it know that the AP has cached data waiting for it?

    A. By examining the PS-Poll frame

    B. By examining the TIM field

    C. When it receives an ATIM

    D. When the Power Management bit is set to 1

    E. When it receives a DTIM

16. If a BSS station is in power save mode, which of the following will cause the station to stay awake and wait to receive data? (Choose all that apply.)

    A. An ATIM sent to the station

    B. A broadcast that contains a DTIM

    C. Receiving a frame with the More Data field set to 1

    D. A TIM that contains the stations AID

17. WMM is a partial mirror of which 802.11 amendment?

   A. 802.11c

   B. 802.11e

   C. 802.11k

   D. 802.11q

18. The 802.11e amendment defines which of the following medium access methods to support QoS requirements? (Choose all that apply.)

   A. Distributed Coordination Function (DCF)

   B. Enhanced Distributed Channel Access (EDCA)

   C. Hybrid Coordination Function (HCF)

   D. Point Coordination Function (PCF)

   E. Hybrid Coordination Function Controlled Access (HCCA)

19. When a station sends an RTS, the Duration/ID field notifies the other stations that they must set their NAV to which of the following values?

   A. 213 microseconds

   B. The time necessary to transmit the Data and ACK frames

   C. The time necessary to transmit the CTS frame

   D. The time necessary to transmit the CTS, Data, and ACK frames

20. Which of the following is true regarding an ATIM? (Choose all that apply.)

   A. ATIMs are only used in an IBSS.

   B. It is a part of the beacon frame.

   C. It is a unicast frame.

   D. ATIMs are used in both BSS and IBSS networks.

Answers to Review Questions

1. B. Management, control, and data are the three type of frames. An ACK is a control frame.

2. B, C. When a frame is fragmented, the data is spread across multiple fragments. Each fragment requires a header, meaning that there are more bits being transmitted. Additionally, each fragment will receive an ACK when it is received. The additional bits along with the ACKs and additional SIFS mean that the data throughput will decrease.

3. B, D. RTS/CTS and CTS-to-Self provide 802.11g protection mechanisms, sometimes referred to as mixed-mode support. NAV backoff and RTS-to-Self do not exist. WEP encryption provides data security.

4. D. RTS/CTS and CTS-to-Self are used to perform NAV distribution. These frames are used by other stations to set their NAV. The other stations then use the NAV as part of their virtual clear channel assessment.

5. C. The access point tracks the wireless station using the association identifier (AID). TIM is used to notify a wireless station that there is some buffered data waiting for it, not for tracking it.

6. C. The DTIM (delivery traffic indication message) is used to notify stations of pending broadcast traffic. TIM is used to notify individual stations of pending unicast traffic. ATIM is used to notify individual stations of pending traffic in an ad-hoc network BTIM does not exist.

7. B. If a station finds its AID in the TIM, then there is data on the access point that the station needs to stay awake for and request to have downloaded. This request is performed by a PS-Poll frame.

8. B. The transmitting station send the CTS, waits a SIFS, and then sends the data frame.

9. B. When the client station transmits a frame with the Power Management field set to 1, it is enabling power save mode. The DTIM does not enable power save mode; it only notifies clients to stay awake in preparation for a multicast or broadcast.

10. A, B, D, E. WMM Audio Priority does not exist. The other four are the access categories.

11. B, D. The receiving station may have received the data, but the transmitting station may not have received the ACK. The transmitting station will then attempt to retransmit the data frame.

12. C, D. In a noisy environment, even though fragmented frames contain more bits than unfragmented frames, if frames need to be retransmitted, it is possible that the overall number of bits transmitted is actually less than if the frames had not been fragmented. It is possible that throughput may increase or decrease, depending upon how many frames are retransmitted.

13. D. Since all stations in a BSS are able to hear the AP, CTS-to-Self is the most efficient method for the AP to perform NAV distribution. Since it is possible for two stations to be hidden from each other while both are part of the same BSS, RTS/CTS is the best method for performing NAV distribution.

14. D. When a client station sends a frame to another client station in a BSS, the source station must first send the frame to the AP and then the AP will send the frame to the destination client. Since each RTS/CTS transmission consists of four frames (RTS, CTS, Data, ACK), the total number of frames transmitted is eight.

15. B. The PS-Poll frame is used by the station to request cached data. The ATIM is used to notify stations in an IBSS of cached data. The Power Management bit is used by the station to notify the AP that the station is going into power save mode. The DTIM is used to notify stations that there is cached multicast or broadcast data.

16. B, C, D. An ATIM will cause a station to stay awake, but the ATIM is used in an IBSS only. A DTIM notifies the station that it must stay awake and wait for a multicast or broadcast frame. If a station receives a frame with the More Data field set to 1, the AP has additional data for the station and the station is not allowed to go to sleep. If the TIM contains the station's AID, the station must stay awake so that it can receive the data that the AP has cached for it.

17. B. Wi-Fi Multimedia is a partial mirror of the 802.11e amendment, which defines the layer 2 MAC methods needed to meet the QoS requirements for time-sensitive applications over IEEE 802.11 wireless LANs.

18. B, C, E. DCF and PCF were defined in the original 802.11 standard. The other three access methods were defined as part of the 802.11e amendment.

19. D. When the RTS is sent, the value of the Duration/ID field is equal to the time necessary for the CTS, Data, and ACK frames to be transmitted.

20. A, C. An ATIM is used to notify an IBSS station to stay awake so that the other station can send it cached data. The ATIM is a unicast frame sent directly from the station with the cached data to the station for which the data is cached.

Chapter 10

Wireless Devices

IN THIS CHAPTER, YOU WILL LEARN ABOUT THE FOLLOWING:

✓ **Wireless LAN Client Devices**

- Radio Card Formats
- Radio Card Chipsets
- Client Utilities

✓ **Progression of WLAN Architecture**

- Access Point–Intelligent Edge Architecture
- Wireless Network Management System (WNMS)
- Centralized WLAN Architecture
- WLAN Switch/Controller
- Remote Office WLAN Switch
- Distributed WLAN Architecture
- Unified WLAN Architecture

✓ **Specialty WLAN Infrastructure Devices**

- Wireless Workgroup Bridge
- Wireless LAN Bridges
- Enterprise Wireless Gateway
- Residential Wireless Gateway
- VPN Wireless Router
- Wireless LAN Mesh Routers
- Enterprise Encryption Gateway
- Virtual AP System

✓ **Power over Ethernet (PoE)**

- PoE Devices
- Endspan
- Midspan

In Chapter 7, "Wireless LAN Topologies," we discussed the various 802.11 WLAN topologies. You learned that both client and access point stations can be arranged in service sets to provide some sort of access to another medium. In this chapter, we will discuss the multiple devices that can be used in both standard and nonstandard 802.11 topologies. Many choices exist for client station radio cards that can be used in desktops, laptops, PDAs, and so on. We will also discuss the progression of WLAN infrastructure devices over the years. We will cover the purpose of many WLAN specialty devices that exist in today's Wi-Fi marketplace. Finally, we will discuss how many of these WLAN devices are powered using standardized Power over Ethernet technology.

Wireless LAN Client Devices

The main hardware in a WLAN client adapter is a half-duplex radio transceiver, which can exist in many different hardware formats and chipsets. All client adapters require a special driver to interface with the operating system and software utilities to interface with the end user. Many cards can work with Windows, Linux, and Macintosh, requiring a different driver and client software for each operating system. The drivers for many manufacturers' cards may already be included in the operating system, but often newer cards require or can benefit from an updated driver installation. Most vendors will provide a CD disk with an automated driver installation wizard; however, some may require that the driver be installed manually in the operating system.

With a software interface, the end user can configure a card to participate in a WLAN using configuration settings that pertain to identification, security, and performance. These client utilities may be the manufacturer's own software utility or an internal software interface built into the operating system.

In the following sections, we will discuss the various radio card formats, the chipsets that are used, and software client utilities.

Radio Card Formats

Radio cards are used in both client adapters and access points. This section focuses mainly on how radio cards can be used as client devices.

For many years, the only option you had when purchasing an 802.11 client adapter was a standard *PCMCIA* type adapter. A PCMCIA adapter is also known as a *PC Card* and is pictured in Figure 10.1. The PCMCIA radio card can be used in any laptop or handheld device that has a PC Card slot. Most PCMCIA cards have integrated antennas. Some cards only have internal integrated antennas, while other have both integrated antennas and external connectors.

The radio format that is becoming the most widely used is the *Mini PCI*. The Mini PCI is a variation of the Peripheral Component Interconnect (PCI) bus technology and was designed for use mainly in laptops. A Mini PCI radio is often used inside access points and is also the main type of radio used by manufacturers as the internal 802.11 wireless adapter inside laptops. It is almost impossible to buy a brand-new laptop today that does not have an internal 802.11 Mini PCI radio card, pictured in Figure 10.2. The Mini PCI card typically is installed from the bottom of the laptop and is connected to small diversity antennas that are mounted along the edges of the laptop's monitor.

Secure Digital (SD) and *Compact Flash (CF)* are two radio card formats that are often used with handheld PDAs. These cards typically require very low power and are smaller than the size of a matchbook. Compact Flash radio cards can sometimes be used in the PC slot of a laptop with the aid of a CF-to-PCMCIA adapter.

So far we have discussed client adapters that are used with laptops or handheld devices. 802.11 client adapters also exist for desktops in the form of 802.11 PCI adapters or USB client adapters. Many 802.11 PCI adapters are simply a PCI peripheral card with a PCMIA card attached or soldered onto the PCI card. Most desktop users place their computers underneath a desk. Therefore, the integrated antenna of an 802.11 PCI adapter is surrounded by the desk, resulting in poor communications. Newer 802.11 PCI adapters have an integrated radio card with a jack for an external antenna so that the user may place the antenna on the top of the desk for better transmission and reception. Both examples of 802.11 PCI adapters are shown in Figure 10.3.

FIGURE 10.1   PCMCIA adapter/PC card. *Courtesy of Cisco Systems, Inc. Unauthorized use not permitted.*

FIGURE 10.2   Mini PCI radio

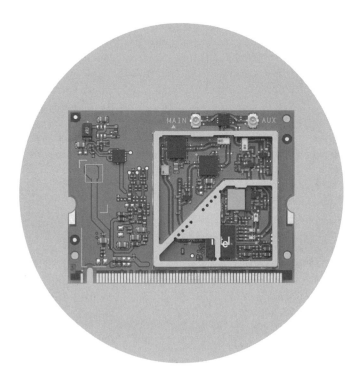

FIGURE 10.3   Desktop 802.11 PCI adapters. *Photos provided by D-Link.*

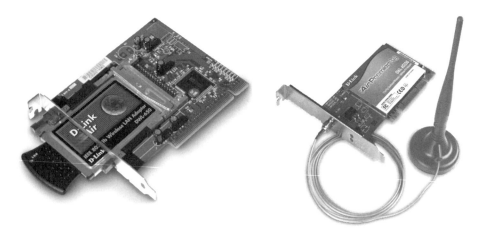

The USB 802.11 radio adapter is a very popular choice because almost all computers have USB ports. USB technology provides simplicity of setup as well as no need for an external power source. 802.11 USB radio adapters exist either in the form of a small dongle device (see Figure 10.4) or as an external wired USB device with a separate USB cable connector. The dongle devices are compact and portable for use with a laptop computer, while with the external devices can be connected to a desktop computer with a USB extension cable and placed on top of a desk for better reception.

FIGURE 10.4   802.11 USB adapters. *Photo provided by D-Link.*

We have discussed the various types of 802.11 radio card formats that are used with laptops, PDAs, and desktops. 802.11 radio cards are also used in many other types of handheld devices, such as the bar code scanner and Wi-Fi VoIP phones pictured in Figure 10.5.

It should be noted that 802.11 radio cards used as client devices have begun to show up in all sorts of machines and solutions. Radio cards already exist in gaming devices, stereo systems, and video cameras. Appliance manufacturers are experimenting with putting Wi-Fi cards in washing machines and refrigerators. Because of the low cost of 802.11 radio cards, in the not-too-distant future your entire house might be networked wirelessly and able to be controlled from remote locations.

 Real World Scenario

Can I Use the Same Radio in Different Laptops?

The answer to this question depends entirely on what type of radio card you are using. PCMCIA cards can be used in any laptop as long as the laptop has a PC Card slot. USB client adapters can be used by any laptop that has a USB port. Any laptop manufactured today will have both a USB port and a PC Card slot. Using the same Mini PCI radio card in different laptops might be a different story. Since Mini PCI radio cards are typically installed in a laptop computer, they should not be inserted and removed too many times. Another potential problem is that laptop manufacturers may support only a specific Mini PCI radio chipset, which will limit your choice of laptops in which the card can be installed. Check with your laptop vendor before switching Mini PCI radios.

FIGURE 10.5   SpectraLink Wi-Fi VoIP Phone

Another future technology also being talked about lately is the *software defined radio (SDR)*. SDRs will be able to dynamically switch across a wide range of frequency bands, transmission techniques, and modulation schemes so that a single radio could replace multiple hardware designs. At the time of this writing, one vendor has already received permission from the FCC to use SDR 802.11a radios to transmit in new unlicensed bands in the 5 GHz frequency range. Software defined radios may even have the capability to switch between different wireless technologies such as Wi-Fi and WiMAX.

Radio Card Chipsets

A group of integrated circuits designed to work together is often marketed as a *chipset*. Many 802.11 chipset manufacturers exist and sell their chipset technology to the various radio card manufacturers. Legacy chipsets will obviously not support all of the same features as newer chipset technologies. For example, a legacy chipset may support only DSSS while newer chipsets will support both DSSS and ERP-OFDM.

Some chipsets may only support the ability to transmit on the 2.4 GHz ISM band, while other chipsets can transmit on either the 2.4 GHz or 5 GHz unlicensed frequencies and are used in 802.11a/b/g client cards. The chipset manufacturers incorporate newer 802.11 technologies as they develop. Many proprietary technologies turn up in the individual chipsets, and some of these technologies become part of the standard in future 802.11amendments.

Although there are many chipset manufacturers, detailed information about some of the most widely used chipsets may be found at the following URLs: www.atheros.com, www.broadcom.com, and www.intel.com/products/centrino/index.htm.

Client Utilities

An end user must have the ability to configure a wireless client card. Therefore, a software interface is needed in the form of *client utilities*. The software interface will usually have the ability to create multiple connection profiles. One profile may be used to connect to the wireless network at work, another for connecting at home, and a third for connecting at a hotspot.

Configuration settings for a client utility typically include the service set identifier (SSID), transmit power, security settings, 802.11e/QoS capabilities, and power management settings. As mentioned in Chapter 7, any client card can also be configured for either Infrastructure or Ad-Hoc mode. Most good client utilities will typically have some sort of statistical information display along with some sort of received signal strength measurement indicator tool.

Four major types or categories of client utilities exist:

- Small office, home office (SOHO) client utilities

- Enterprise-class client utilities

- Integrated operating system client utilities

- Third-party client utilities

SOHO client utilities are usually very simplistic in nature and are designed for ease of use for the average home user. Surprisingly, though, many of the SOHO utilities support some rather advanced features as 802.11 technologies progress. Enterprise-class client utilities provide the software interface for the more expensive enterprise-grade vendor cards. Typically, the enterprise-class utilities support more configuration features and have better statistical tools. Figure 10.6 depicts the Intel ProSet wireless client interface.

The most widely used client utility is an integrated operating system client utility, more specifically known as the *Wireless Zero Configuration (WZC) service*, that is enabled by default in Windows XP. The WZC is pictured in Figure 10.7. The main advantage of the WZC is that as an administrator, you only have to support one client utility even though your end users may have different radio cards.

It should be noted that the WZC has many published security risks, and therefore many government agencies and corporations ban the use of the integrated operating system utilities. Other disadvantages of the WZC is that it supports only a limited number of EAP-type protocols and does not have a built -in received signal measurement tool.

An added advantage of the WZC is that it utilizes a proprietary roaming method called opportunistic PMK caching that is supported by many of the wireless switching vendors. It is beyond the scope of this book to discuss this roaming method; however, on the CD of this book is a white paper titled "802.11i RSN Fast Secure Roaming" by Devin Akin that explains opportunistic PMK caching.

The last type of software interface for an 802.11 radio card is a third-party client utility, such as Juniper Networks Odyssey Access Client pictured in Figure 10.8. Much like the WZC, a third-party utility will work with radio cards from different vendors, making administrative support much easier. Third-party client utilities often bring the advantage of supporting many different EAP types, giving a WLAN administrator a wider range of security choices. The main disadvantage of third-party client utilities is that they cost extra money.

FIGURE 10.6   Enterprise class client utility

 Real World Scenario

Which Wi-Fi Client Utility Should You Deploy in an Enterprise Environment?

This is a question that almost no one can agree on. Because of the ease of administration and the extended roaming capabilities, many of the wireless switching vendors recommend using the WZC that is built into Windows XP. Other administrators prefer to use a specific vendor's enterprise client utility that was designed to work with that vendor's card. This scenario, though, is only feasible in work environments where the administrator can mandate what type radio cards are to be deployed. Because of some known security risks of the WZC, it is currently the recommendation of the authors of this book to use a third-party client utility in an enterprise environment or use only one vendor's solution. On this book's CD is a 30-day evaluation copy of Juniper Networks Odyssey Access Client, which is a popular third-party client utility.

FIGURE 10.7 Wireless Zero Configuration service

FIGURE 10.8 Third-party client utility

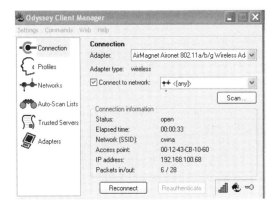

Progression of WLAN Architecture

While the acceptance of 802.11 technologies in the enterprise continues to grow, the evolution of WLAN architecture has kept an equivalent pace. In most cases, the main purpose of 802.11 technologies is to provide a wireless portal into a wired infrastructure network. The method of how an 802.11 wireless portal is integrated into a typical 802.3 Ethernet infrastructure continues to change drastically.

Figure 10.9 depicts the progression of WLAN architecture that will be discussed in the following sections.

FIGURE 10.9 WLAN architecture progression

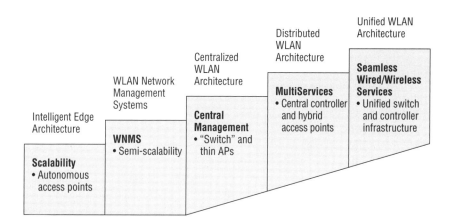

Access Point–Intelligent Edge Architecture

For many years the conventional access point has been thought of as a portal device where all the "brains" and horsepower exists inside the access point (AP) on the edge of the network architecture. Since all the intelligence exists inside each individual access point, they are often referred to as "fat APs" or "intelligent edge APs."

Another recently coined term for the traditional access point is the *autonomous AP*. An autonomous access point contains at least two physical interfaces: usually a radio frequency (RF) radio card and a 10/100BaseT port. The majority of the time these physical interfaces are bridged together by a virtual interface known as a *Bridged Virtual Interface (BVI)*. The BVI is assigned an IP address that is shared by the two physical interfaces.

An intelligent edge access point will typically encompass both the 802.11 protocol stack and the 802.3 protocol stack. These APs might have some of the following features:

- Multiple management interfaces, such as command line, web GUI, and SNMP
- Security features, such as 802.1X/EAP (WPA/WPA2)
- Fixed or detachable antennas
- Filtering options, such as MAC and protocol
- Connectivity modes, such as root, repeater, bridge, and scanner
- Removable radio cards
- Multiple radio card capability: 2.4 GHz and 5 GHz
- Adjustable transmit power, which is used mostly for cell sizing
- VLAN support (VLANs are created on a managed wired switch.)

- IEEE standards support
- 802.3af Power over Ethernet (PoE) support

The autonomous AP that utilizes edge intelligence was the foundation that WLAN architects deployed for many years and still remains a reliable and popular choice.

Wireless Network Management System (WNMS)

One of the challenges for a WLAN administrator using a large WLAN intelligent edge architecture is management. As an administrator, would you want to configure 300 fat APs individually? One major disadvantage of using the traditional autonomous access point is that there is no central point of management. Any intelligent edge WLAN architecture with 25 or more access points is going to require some sort of *wireless network management system (WNMS)*.

A WNMS provides a central point of management to configure and maintain as many as 5,000 fat access points. A WNMS can be either a hardware appliance or a software solution. The most widely known WNMS is the vendor-specific Cisco Wireless LAN Solution Engine (WLSE), shown in Figure 10.10. Vendor-neutral WNMS also exist, such as the AirWave software solution shown in Figure 10.11.

Since the main purpose of a WNMS is to provide a central point of management, both configuration settings and firmware upgrades can be pushed down to all the autonomous access points. Although centralized management is the main goal, a WNMS has other capabilities as well, such as including RF spectrum planning and management. A WNMS can also be used to monitor intelligent edge WLAN architecture with alarms and notifications, centralized and integrated into a management console. Other capabilities include network reporting, trending, capacity planning, and policy enforcement. A WNMS might also be able to perform some rogue AP detection, but by no means should a WNMS be considered a wireless intrusion detection system (WIDS). One of the main disadvantages of a WNMS is that it will not assist in the roaming capabilities between access points, whereas the wireless switching architecture has that ability.

FIGURE 10.10   Example of a vendor-specific WNMS: Cisco's WLSE. *Courtesy of Cisco Systems, Inc. Unauthorized use not permitted.*

FIGURE 10.11 Example of a vendor-neutral WNMS, AirWave's Management Platform software

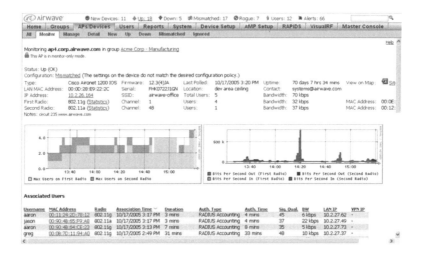

Currently WNMSs are completely separate from any wired network management systems. A WNMS may also not recognize certain hardware, and the most current firmware updates from a vendor are not always immediately usable in a WNMS.

Centralized WLAN Architecture

The next progression in the development of WLAN integration is the centralized WLAN architecture. This model uses a central WLAN switch or controller that resides in the core of the network. In the centralized WLAN architecture, autonomous APs have been replaced with "thin APs." A thin AP has minimal intelligence and is functionally just a radio card and an antenna. All the intelligence resides in the centralized WLAN switch and all of the configuration options are distributed to the thin APs from the WLAN switch. The encryption/decryption capabilities might reside in the centralized WLAN switch or may still be handled by the thin APs, depending on the vendor.

Many of the solutions initially started out as edge WLAN switch solutions; however, most have moved to a centralized architecture that exists at the core of the network. Thin APs may be connected directly to the core WLAN switch, but they are usually connected to a third-party wired switch on the edge of the network in a distributed fashion. Communications between the thin access points and the WLAN switch are often transported on the wired side using a *Generic Routing Encapsulation (GRE)* tunnel. The 802.11 frames are encapsulated in a GRE packet from the end point of the thin AP to the other end point, which is the WLAN switch.

The majority of WLAN switching vendors are startup companies such as Aruba Networks and Trapeze Networks, although more established companies such as Symbol and

Cisco both have centralized WLAN architecture solutions. The WLAN switch/thin AP model has gained huge acceptance in the enterprise and was used in over 50 percent of new deployments in 2004.

WLAN Switch/Controller

At the heart of the centralized WLAN architecture model is the *WLAN switch* (see Figure 10.12), also known as a *WLAN controller*.

FIGURE 10.12   WLAN Switch

A WLAN controller may have some of these many features:

AP management   Allows centralized management and configuration of thin access points.

VLANs   Created on the WLAN switch as opposed to a fat AP solution, where they are created on a managed wired switch. The ability to create VLANs is one of the main benefits of a WLAN switch because they can provide for segmentation and security. A more detailed discussion of wireless VLANs can be found in Chapter 13, "802.11 Network Security Architecture."

User management   The ability to control who, when, and where with role-based access control (RBAC). A more detailed discussion on RBAC can be found in Chapter 13, "802.11 Network Security Architecture."

Layer 2 security support   Support for 802.1X/EAP (WPA /WPA2) security solutions.

Layer 3 and 7 VPN concentrators   The WLAN switch acts as a VPN end point.

Captive portal   Used for web page authentication, usually for guest users.

Automatic failover and load balancing   Provides support for Virtual Router Redundancy Protocol (VRRP)

Internal Wireless Intrusion Detection Systems   Most WLAN switches have internal WIDS capabilities for security monitoring.

Site survey and RF spectrum management   Some Wi-Fi switches have automatic channel management and cell sizing capabilities.

Bandwidth management   Bandwidth pipes can be restricted upstream or downstream.

Firewall capabilities   Stateful packet inspection is available with an internal firewall.

Layer 3 roaming support   Capabilities to allow seamless roaming across layer 3 routed boundaries.

802.3af Power over Ethernet (PoE) support   Wireless switches can provide direct power to thin access points via PoE or thin access points can be powered by third-party edge switches.

The most obvious advantages of the centralized architecture of a WLAN controller include AP management, user management, RF spectrum planning and management, and VLAN segmentation. Another major advantage of the WLAN switch model is that most of the switches support some form of fast secure roaming, which can assist is resolving latency issues often associated with roaming.

One possible disadvantage of using a WLAN switch is that the WLAN switch might become a bottleneck because all data must be sent to and redirected from the WLAN switch. Most switch vendors are able to prevent this from occurring by providing a scalable hierarchical environment. Quality of Service (QoS) policies are also enforced at the WLAN switch, which may cause latency issues. WLAN switches and the thin access points might be separated by several hops, which can also introduce network latency. Some of the WLAN controllers have so many features and configuration settings that the user interface can be very confusing for novice administrators.

Remote Office WLAN Switch

Although WLAN switches typically reside on the core of the network, wireless edge switches exist usually in the form of a remote office WLAN switch.

A remote office WLAN switch will typically not be equipped with as many features as a core WLAN switch, and it will also be less expensive. The purpose of a remote office WLAN switch is so that remote and branch offices can be managed from a single location. These devices will allow for only a limited number of thin APs. Features typically include Power over Ethernet, internal firewalling, and an integrated router using NAT and DHCP for segmentation.

Distributed WLAN Architecture

A few vendors have recently implemented a distributed WLAN architecture that uses a WLAN switch that manages hybrid fat/thin access points. The centralized switch still acts as a central point of management for all the hybrid access points. However, QoS policies and all of the 802.11 MAC data forwarding is handled at the edge of the network at the access points instead of back on the WLAN switch.

The thinking behind these hybrid fat/thin solutions is that you maintain the centralized management but you eliminate the potential data bottlenecks and hopefully improve latency.

Unified WLAN Architecture

WLAN switching could very well take another direction by fully integrating wireless switching capabilities into wired network infrastructure devices. Wired switches at both the core and the edge would also have wireless switching capabilities, thereby allowing for the combined management of the wireless and wired network. This unified architecture has already begun to be deployed by some vendors and will likely grow in acceptance as WLAN deployments become more commonplace and the need for fuller integration continues to rise.

Specialty WLAN Infrastructure Devices

In the previous sections, we discussed the progression of WLAN network infrastructure devices that are used to integrate an 802.11 wireless network into a wired network architecture. The Wi-Fi marketplace has also produced many specialty WLAN devices in addition to autonomous APs and WLAN switches. Many of these devices, such as bridges and mesh routers, have become extremely popular, although they operate outside of the defined 802.11 standards. We will look at these devices in the following sections.

Wireless Workgroup Bridge

A wireless *workgroup bridge (WGB)* is a wireless device that provides wireless connectivity for wired infrastructure devices that do not have radio cards. The radio card inside the WGB associates with an access point and joins the basic service set (BSS) as a client station. As depicted in Figure 10.13, multiple Ethernet devices are connected behind the wired side of the WGB. This provides fast and quick wireless connectivity for wired devices through the association the WGB has with the access point. Because the WGB is an associated client of the access point, the WGB does not provide connectivity for other wireless clients. It is also important to understand that only the radio card inside the WGB can contend for the 802.11 wireless medium and the wired cards behind the WGB cannot contend for the half-duplex RF medium.

Most wireless workgroup bridges can provide connectivity for as many as eight wired devices, but it depends upon the vendor. Some WGBs only provide connectivity for one wired device and are sometimes referred to as a "universal client." The workgroup bridge can be very useful in providing wireless connectivity for small desktop workgroups, cash registers, network printers, and any other devices with Ethernet ports.

FIGURE 10.13 Wireless workgroup bridge

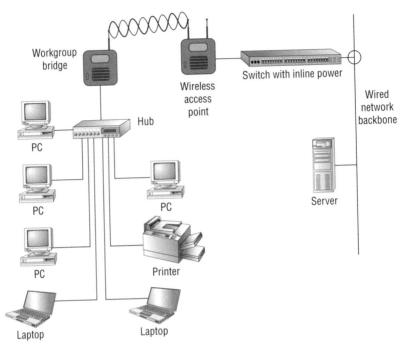

Wireless LAN Bridges

A very common nonstandard deployment of 802.11 technology is the *Wireless LAN bridge*. The purpose of bridging is to provide wireless connectivity between two or more wired networks. A bridge generally supports all the same features that a fat access point possesses, but the purpose is to connect wired networks and not to provide wireless connectivity to client stations. Although bridge links are sometimes used indoors, generally they are used outdoors to connect the wired networks inside two buildings. An outdoor bridge link is often used as a redundant backup to T1 or fiber connections between buildings. Outdoor wireless bridge links are even more commonly used as replacements to T1 or fiber connections between buildings due to their substantial cost savings.

Much like a switched network, an 802.11 wireless bridge utilizes Spanning Tree Protocol (STP) to prevent endless bridge loops. As a result, wireless bridges support two major configuration settings: *root* and *non-root*. Bridges work in a parent/child-type relationship, so think of the root bridge as the parent and the non-root bridge as the child.

A bridge link that connects only two wired networks is known as a *point-to-point (PtP)* bridge. Figure 10.14 shows a PtP connection between two wired networks using two 802.11 bridges and directional antennas. Note that one of the bridges must be configured as the parent root bridge while the other bridge in configured as the child non-root bridge.

A *point-to-multipoint (PtMP)* bridge link connects multiple wired networks. The root bridge is the central bridge with multiple non-root bridges connecting back to the parent root bridge. Figure 10.15 shows a PtMP bridge link between four buildings. Please note that the root bridge is using a high-gain omni-directional antenna while the non-root bridges are all using unidirectional antennas pointing back to the antenna of the root bridge. Also notice that there is only one root bridge in a PtMP connection. There can never be more than one root bridge.

FIGURE 10.14   Point-to-point WLAN bridging

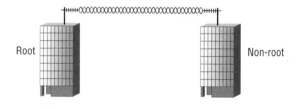

FIGURE 10.15   Point-to-multipoint WLAN bridging

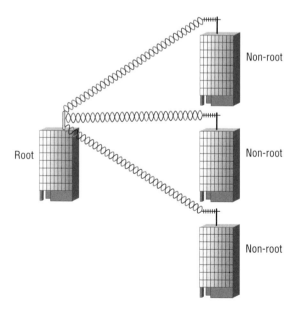

Besides the root and non-root modes, bridges have other vendor configuration modes:

AP mode   Converts a bridge into an access point

WGB mode   Converts a bridge into a workgroup bridge.

Repeater mode   Repeats the cell of a root bridge to a non-root bridge

Root with clients   Root bridge that also allows clients to associate

Non-root with clients   Non-root bridge that also allows clients to associate

The last two configuration settings that allow clients to associate are highly discouraged because of the security risks and the effect on the throughput of the bridge link because they allow clients to contend for the half-duplex medium. Also, due to performance issues, the repeater mode is not a recommended mode for wireless bridging. If at all possible, a better bridge deployment practice is to use two separate bridge links as opposed to repeating the link of a root bridge to a non-root bridge.

Considerations when deploying outdoor bridge links are numerous, including the Fresnel zone, earth bulge, free space path loss, link budget, and fade margin. There may be other considerations as well, including the IR and EIRP power regulations as defined by the regulatory body of your country.

Point-to-point links in the 2.4 GHz band can be as long as 24 miles. A problem that might occur over a very long distance link is an ACK time-out. Because of the half-duplex nature of the medium, every unicast frame must be acknowledged. Therefore, a unicast frame sent across a 24-mile link by one bridge must immediately receive an ACK frame from the opposite bridge, sent back across the same long-distance link. Even though RF travels at the speed of light, the ACK may not be received quickly enough. The original bridge will time-out after not receiving the ACK frame after a certain period of microseconds and assume that a collision has occurred. The original bridge will then retransmit the unicast frame even though the ACK frame is on the way. Retransmitting unicast traffic that does not need to be resent can cause throughput degradation of as much as 50 percent. To resolve this problem, most bridges have an ACK time-out setting that can be adjusted to allow a longer period of time for a bridge to receive the ACK frame across the long-distance link.

A common problem with point-to-multipoint bridging is mounting the high gain omni-directional antenna of the root bridge too high, as pictured in Figure 10.16. The result is that the vertical line of sight with the directional antennas of the non-root bridges is not adequate. The solution for this problem is to use a high-gain omni-directional antenna that provides a certain amount of downtilt or to use directional sector antennas aligned to provide omni-directional coverage.

Enterprise Wireless Gateway

An *enterprise wireless gateway (EWG)* is a middleware device used to segment autonomous access points from the protected wired network infrastructure, as pictured in Figure 10.17. An EWG can segment the unprotected wireless network from the protected wired network by acting as a router, a VPN end point, and/or a firewall.

FIGURE 10.16   Common bridging challenge

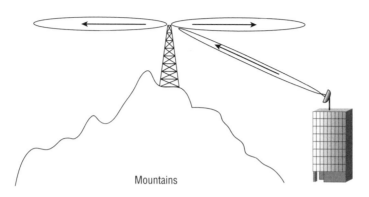

FIGURE 10.17   Enterprise wireless gateway

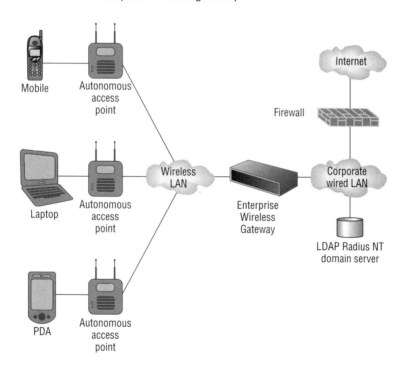

The EWG can provide many of the same capabilities that a WLAN switch provides, with some key differences. Because an EWG segments fat access points and not thin access points, there is no AP management available within a EWG. The need still exists for a third-party WNMS to provide management of the fat APs from another central location. Also, unlike most WLAN switches, an enterprise wireless gateway does not have an internal Wireless Intrusion Detection System (WIDS), and the need for an overlay WIDS remains. An EWG also does not provide any RF spectrum management or control.

There are some similarities between an EWG and a WLAN switch, including layer 3 roaming capabilities, user management, role based access control (RBAC), bandwidth throttling, redundancy support, layer 2 security support, and a captive portal. An EWG can also support VLANs that are created on a managed wired switch. Although enterprise wireless gateway devices still exist, they are a dying breed that have been slowly replaced by the various WLAN switch solutions. At least one of the EWG vendors has begun to add thin APs and RF management to their product line so that they can compete with the switch vendors. Effectively, they are transforming themselves into a switch vendor.

Residential Wireless Gateway

Residential wireless gateway(RWG) is a very fancy term for a home wireless router. The main function of a residential wireless gateway is to provide shared wireless access to a SOHO Internet connection while providing a level of security on the Internet. These SOHO Wi-Fi routers are generally inexpensive, yet they're surprisingly full featured.

The following features are supported by a residential wireless gateway:

- Configurable 802.11 radio card
- Support for simple routing protocols such as RIP
- Network Address Translation (NAT)
- Port Address Translation (PAT)
- Port forwarding
- Firewall
- L2 security support (WEP or WPA1 Personal or WPA2 Personal)
- DHCP server
- Multiport Ethernet switch for connecting wired clients

Keep in mind that any type of wireless router is a very different device than an access point. Unlike access points, which use a Bridged Virtual Interface (BVI), wireless routers have separate routed interfaces. The radio card exists on one subnet while the WAN Ethernet port exists on a different subnet.

Most CWNA candidates are already familiar with residential wireless gateways because more than likely they have one installed at home.

VPN Wireless Router

Much like the residential wireless gateway, enterprise-class wireless routers exist that can also act as an end point for a VPN tunnel. These enterprise *VPN wireless routers* have all of the same features that can be found in a SOHO wireless router, and they provide secure tunneling functionality in addition to 802.11 layer 2–defined security capabilities. Supported VPN protocols may include PPTP, L2TP, IPSec, and SSH2. VPN wireless routers are typically used as edge router solutions in remote or branch offices.

A short discussion of using VPN security with wireless networking can be found in Chapter 14.

Wireless LAN Mesh Routers

Another specialty WLAN device gaining in popularity is the *WLAN mesh router*. Wireless mesh routers communicate with each other using proprietary layer 2 routing protocols, creating a self-forming and self-healing wireless infrastructure (a mesh) over which edge devices can communicate, as shown in Figure 10.18.

A self-forming WLAN mesh network automatically connects access points upon installation and dynamically updates routes as more clients are added. Because interference may occur, a self-healing WLAN mesh network will automatically reroute data traffic in a Wi-Fi mesh cell. Proprietary layer 2 intelligent routing protocols determine the dynamic routes based upon measurement of traffic, signal strength, hops, and other parameters. Although a WLAN mesh network usually comprises a mesh of repeater-like access points that all operate on one frequency, dual-band mesh routers also exist. With dual-band WLAN mesh routers, typically the 802.11a radios are used for the mesh infrastructure and to provide backhaul while the 802.11b/g radios are used to provide access to the client stations.

Although the 802.11s Task Group is currently working on standardizing WLAN mesh networking, all current vendor solutions are proprietary.

Enterprise Encryption Gateway

An *enterprise wncryption gateway (EEG)* is an 802.11 middleware device that provides for segmentation and encryption. The EEG typically sits behind several fat access points and segments the wireless network from the protected wired network infrastructure. Proprietary encryption technology using the AES algorithm at layer 2 is provided by the enterprise encryption gateway. Figure 10.19 shows a picture of an EEG.

FIGURE 10.18   Wireless LAN mesh routers

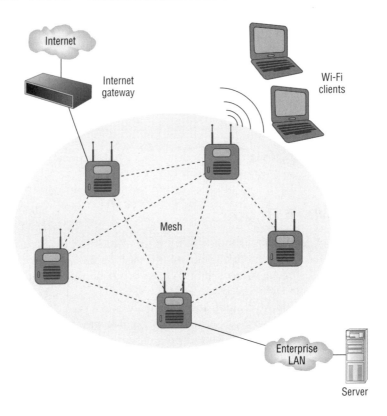

FIGURE 10.19   Enterprise encryption gateway

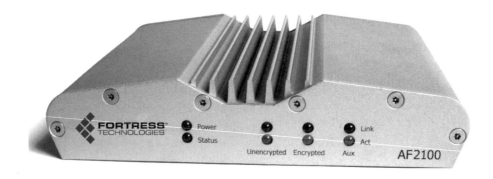

All the access points are managed from the unencrypted side of each gateway and special client software is required for the end user client stations. EEGs can also offer data compression and are typically certified to meet government security regulations such as FIPS 140-2. A central management server is also used so that user and device authentication methods are also provided.

Virtual AP System

One major wireless switching provider has a system know as a *virtual AP*. A virtual access point solution uses multiple access points that all share a single basic service set identifier (BSSID) MAC address. Because the multiple access points advertise only one single virtual MAC address (BSSID), client stations believe they are connected to only a single access point, although they may be actually roaming across multiple APs. The main advantage is that clients experience a "zero handoff" time and many of the latency issues associated with roaming are resolved. All the handoff and management is handled by a central WLAN switch. It should be understood that a virtual AP solution is extremely proprietary and operates way outside of the defined 802.11 standard.

Power over Ethernet (PoE)

Where is it that access points are usually mounted? The answer of course is usually on the ceiling or high up on a wall. Are there power outlets in the ceiling or on the wall that can be used to provide power for the access points? Probably not. Besides being mounted in the ceiling, APs are often installed in some unusual and hard-to-reach places, and the majority of the time there is not a nearby electrical outlet. *Power over Ethernet (PoE)* is a solution that can be used to power remote network devices over the same Ethernet cabling that carries data to the remote device. Using PoE to provide power to your 802.11 access points is often a simpler and more cost-effective solution than hiring an electrician to install new electrical drops and outlets for every AP.

PoE Devices

The standards for PoE are defined under the 802.3af amendment, which was ratified in 2003. The PoE standard calls for voltage of +48 volts of direct current (VDC). Be aware that some Wi-Fi vendors use proprietary PoE devices that uses nonstandard pin assignments and nonstandard voltages. There are two main components in any PoE solution: the *Power Sourcing Equipment (PSE)* and the *Powered Device (PD)*. Power is sent from the PSE to the PD over Ethernet cable. The Power Sourcing Equipment (PSE) might be housed inside an inline switch or an injector. The responsibilities of the Power Sourcing Equipment (PSE) are as follows:

- Searches for PDs with DC detection signal
- Withholds power until PoE compliance is determined

- Classifies the PD (optional)
- Provides power for the connected device
- Continuously checks that the powered device is present
- Monitors for conditions such as short circuits
- Scales power back when it's no longer required

An example of a PD would be an access point. The PD requires power from the PSE. For a PD to be 802.3af compliant, it must be able to meet these requirements:

- Must be able to accept power through either the data pairs or the unused pairs
- Must reply with a "Detection Signature" (25 Ohm)
- May reply with "Classification Signature" (optional)

Endspan

Two solutions are defined under the PoE standard. The first is known as an *Endspan* or Endpoint solution. An Endspan solution is a switch with integrated power-supplying equipment, or more specifically, a switch with a PSE. The switch can supply the power via its physical ports using either the data pairs or the unused conductors. An Endspan solution is compatible with 10BaseT, 100BaseTX, and 1000BaseT cabling and is the only option that will work with Gigabit Ethernet.

Midspan

A *Midspan* solution is a pass-through device with integrated power-supplying equipment (single-port or multiport). Examples of Midspan equipment include mutiport and single-port power injectors. With a Midspan solution the PSE device resides inside an injector that is located between the non-PSE switch and the Powered Device (PD). The Midspan device does not regenerate the Ethernet signal and must not disrupt the Ethernet signal. Midspan devices can send power only over the unused twisted pairs on the Ethernet cable. A Midspan solution will work with 10BaseT and 100BaseTX but not Gigabit Ethernet.

Summary

In this chapter, we discussed the different type of radio card formats, their chipsets, and the software interfaces needed for client station configuration. We also showed you the logical progression that WLAN devices have made, starting from autonomous access points, moving to WLAN switching, and then moving along a path toward fully integrating wireless switching capabilities into wired network infrastructure devices. In addition, we covered specialty WLAN infrastructure devices that often meet needs that may not be met by more traditional WLAN architecture. Finally, we discussed Power over Ethernet and how it used to power remote WLAN devices.

It is the recommendation of the authors of this book that before you take the CWNA exam, you get some hands-on experience with some WLAN infrastructure devices. We understand that most individuals cannot afford a $10,000 core WLAN switch; however, we do recommend that you purchase at least one 802.11a/b/g client adapter and either a fat autonomous access point or a SOHO wireless router. Hands-on experience will solidify much of what you have learned in this chapter as well as many of the other chapters in this book.

Exam Essentials

Know the major radio card formats.   The 802.11 standard does not mandate what type format can be used by an 802.11 radio. 802.11 radios exist in multiple formats.

Understand the need for client adapters to have an operating system interface and a user interface.   A client adapter requires a special driver to communicate with the operating system and a software client utility for user configuration.

Identify the four major types of client utilities.   The four types of client utilities are SOHO, enterprise, integrated, and third party.

Explain the progression of WLAN architecture.   Be able to explain the differences and similarities of autonomous AP solutions and WLAN switching solutions.

Identity the capabilities of all WLAN network infrastructure devices.   Understand the feature sets of both specialty and traditional WLAN equipment.

Explain the role and configuration of WLAN bridges and workgroup bridges   The CWNA test covers bridging quite extensively. Know all of the different types of bridges and the difference between root and non-root bridges. Be able to explain the difference between point-to-point and point-to-multipoint bridging. Understand bridging problems such as ACK time-out and study other bridging considerations that are covered in other chapters, such as the Fresnel zone and system operating margin.

Define WLAN mesh networking.   Be able to explain that WLAN mesh routers use self-healing and self-forming methods and proprietary layer 2 routing protocols. Understand the difference between single-band and dual-band mesh networks.

Explain the basic Power over Ethernet standards.   Know the difference between an Endspan and Midspan PoE solution.

Key Terms

Before you take the exam, be certain you are familiar with the following terms:

autonomous AP

Bridged Virtual Interface (BVI)

chipset

client utilities

Compact Flash (CF)

Endspan

enterprise encryption gateway (EEG)

enterprise wireless gateway (EWG)

Generic Routing Encapsulation (GRE)

Midspan

Mini PCI

non-root

PC Card

PCMCIA

point-to-multipoint (PtMP)

point-to-point (PtP)

Power over Ethernet (PoE)

Power Sourcing Equipment (PSE)

Powered Device (PD)

residential wireless gateway (RWG)

root

Secure Digital (SD)

software defined radio (SDR)

Virtual AP

VPN wireless routers

Wireless LAN bridge

wireless network management system (WNMS)

Wireless Zero Configuration (WZC)

WLAN controller

WLAN mesh router

WLAN switch

workgroup bridge (WGB)

Review Questions

1. What WLAN device is most often used to share Internet access?

   A. VPN WLAN Router

   B. Virtual AP

   C. Residential wireless gateway

   D. Enterprise wireless gateway

   E. Autonomous access point

2. How many root bridges exist in a point-to-multipoint bridge link?

   A. None

   B. One

   C. Two

   D. Multiple

   E. All of the above

3. Which radio formats can be used by 802.11 technology? (Choose all that apply.)

   A. CF

   B. Secure Digital

   C. PCMCIA

   D. Mini PCI

   E. USB dongle

   F. Proprietary

   G. All of the above

4. What security solutions are supported in a WLAN VPN router?

   A. 802.1X/EAP

   B. SSH2

   C. IPSec

   D. PPTP

   E. TKIP

   F. All of the above

5. What features can be found on both a WLAN switch and an enterprise wireless gateway? (Choose all that apply.)

  A. VRRP

  B. Captive portal

  C. HSRP

  D. RBAC

  E. Wireless Intrusion Detection System

6. What interfaces must be installed for a WLAN client device to work properly? (Choose all that apply.)

  A. Operating system interface

  B. User interface

  C. Command-line interface

  D. Driver

  E. Client utility

  F. All of the above

7. What devices can be used to manage multiple autonomous access points from a centralized location? (Choose all that apply.)

  A. WLAN controller

  B. WNMS

  C. WLAN switch

  D. Enterprise wireless gateway

  E. Wireless IDS

8. What features can be found on both a WLAN switch and an enterprise wireless gateway? (Choose all that apply.)

  A. RF spectrum management

  B. AP management

  C. Layer 3 roaming support

  D. Bandwidth throttling

  E. Firewall

9. Which option best describes a layer 3 device used to secure a Internet connection for a small number of wireless users?

  A. VPN router

  B. Wireless workgroup bridge

  C. Wireless mesh router

  D. Residential wireless gateway

  E. Wireless hub

10. Which option best describes a device used to provide wireless connectivity for a small number of wired clients?

   A. VPN router

   B. Wireless workgroup bridge

   C. Wireless mesh router

   D. Wireless Ethernet repeater

   E. Wireless bridge

11. Which terms best describe components of a centralized WLAN architecture in which all the intelligence resides in a core device and pushes the configuration settings down to the access points? (Choose all that apply.)

   A. WLAN controller

   B. Wireless Network Management System

   C. Enterprise wireless gateway

   D. WLAN switch

   E. Thin AP

12. A _____ uses a proprietary layer 2 roaming protocol, and a _____ utilizes a proprietary layer 2 encryption. (Choose all that apply.)

   A. Wireless mesh router

   B. Enterprise wireless gateway

   C. Enterprise encryption gateway

   D. WLAN switch

   E. Virtual AP

13. A network administrator is having a hard time getting two WLAN bridges to associate with one another in a PtP link. The bridge in Building One is on the 172.16.1.0/24 network, while the bridge in Building Two resides on the 172.16.2.0/24 network. What is the most likely cause?

   A. The bridges are on different subnets.

   B. The bridges are both configured as non-root.

   C. The gateway address is incorrect.

   D. The ACK time-out setting is short.

   E. There is impedance overflow.

14. Billy must connect Building A via a WLAN bridge link to Building C, which is 30 miles away. He cannot make a direct connection of that distance due to regulatory power restrictions in his country. Building B sits between the two remote buildings. What is the best way for Billy to link the two buildings together using WLAN bridges?

   A. Place a root bridge on Building A with a highly-directional antenna, a non-root bridge on Building B with an omni-directional antenna, and a root bridge on Building C with a highly-directional antenna.

   B. Place a root bridge on Building A with a highly-directional antenna, a repeater bridge on Building B with an omni-directional antenna, and a root bridge on Building C with a highly-directional antenna.

   C. Place a non- root bridge on Building A with a highly-directional antenna, a root bridge on Building B with an omni-directional antenna, and a non-root bridge on Building C with a highly-directional antenna.

   D. Place a root bridge on Building A with a highly-directional antenna and a non-root bridge on Building B with a highly-directional antenna. Set up another root bridge on Building B with a highly-directional antenna and a non-root bridge on Building C with a highly-directional antenna. Connect the two bridges on Building B via a switch or router.

   E. None of the above

15. On which device can you configure VLANs? (Choose all that apply.)

   A. FAT AP

   B. Thin AP

   C. Ethernet switch

   D. Enterprise wireless gateway

   E. All of the above

16. Which 802.11af solutions must use only the unused twisted pairs of 10BaseT cabling to power remote devices? (Choose all that apply.)

   A. Midspan solution

   B. Endspan solution

   C. Single port injector

   D. Mutiport injector

   E. Switch with inline power

17. What options best describe components of a WLAN intelligent edge architecture? (Choose all that apply.)

   A. Thin access point

   B. Autonomous AP

   C. WLAN switch

   D. VPN router

   E. WNMS

18. Which WLAN architecture best describes a hybrid fat/thin model?

A. Distributed WLAN architecture

B. Unified WLAN architecture

C. Intelligent Edge WLAN architecture

D. Centralized WLAN architecture

E. None of the above

19. What are the two main components of a PoE solution?

A. PD

B. Midspan

C. Endspan

D. PSE

E. MDI

20. Gigabit Ethernet can be used with which of these PoE solutions? (Choose all that apply.)

A. Switch with inline power

B. Multiport injector

C. Midspan

D. Endspan

E. Powered patch panel

Answers to Review Questions

1. C. The main function of a residential wireless gateway is to provide shared wireless access to a SOHO Internet connection. SOHO Wi-Fi routers are generally inexpensive yet surprisingly full featured.

2. B. All bridge links can have only one root bridge. A PtP link will have only one root bridge and a PtMP link will also have only one root bridge.

3. G. The 802.11 standard does not mandate what type form factor must used by an 802.11 radio. Although PCMCIA and Mini PCI client adapters are the most common, 802.11 radios exist in many other formats, such as Compact Flash cards, Secure Digital cards, USB dongles, and other proprietary formats.

4. F. The main function of a WLAN VPN router is to provide for a secure VPN tunneling solution such as SSH2, IPSec, or PPTP. However, a WLAN VPN router also supports the 802.11i-defined layer 2 security solutions such as 802.1X/EAP and TKIP encryption.

5. A, B, D. Wireless switches and enterprise wireless gateways (EWGs) share many of the same features with some notable differences. Both support the VRRP redundancy protocol. HSRP is a proprietary redundancy protocol. Both devices have a captive portal option and both support user management via role-based access control. WLAN switches typically have an internal IDS system, whereas an EWG does not.

6. A, B, D, E. All 802.11 client adapters require a driver to interface with the operating system. A user interface is also needed for configuration using software client utilities.

7. B. One major disadvantage of using the traditional autonomous access point is that there is no central point of management. Any intelligent edge WLAN architecture with 50 or more access points is going to require some sort of wireless network management system (WNMS).

8. C, D, E. Wireless switches and enterprise wireless gateways share many of the same features, with some notable differences. Both support layer 3 roaming capabilities, bandwidth policies, and stateful packet inspection. RF spectrum management and AP management is only supported on a WLAN switch.

9. D. The main function of a residential wireless gateway is to provide shared wireless access to a SOHO Internet connection.

10. B. A wireless workgroup bridge (WGB) is a wireless device that provides wireless connectivity for wired infrastructure devices that do not have radio cards.

11. A, D, E. In the centralized WLAN architecture, autonomous APs have been replaced with thin APs. All the intelligence resides on the centralized WLAN switch also know as a WLAN controller.

12. A, C. Wireless mesh routers use proprietary layer 2 roaming protocols. Proprietary encryption technology using the AES algorithm at layer 2 is provided by an enterprise encryption gateway.

13. B. In a point-to-point bridge link, one bridge must be the root bridge while the other must be a non-root bridge.

14. D. Due to performance issues, repeater mode is not a recommended mode for wireless bridging. If at all possible, a better bridge deployment practice is to use two separate bridge links as opposed to repeating the link of a root bridge to a non-root bridge.

15. C. All of these devices support VLANs, but VLANs must be configured on either a managed Ethernet switch or a WLAN switch.

16. A, C, D. An Endspan solution can carry the voltage on either the data transmissions pairs or the unused twisted pairs. A Midspan solution must use only the unused twisted pairs. Multiport and single-port injectors are Midspan solutions.

17. B, D. VPN routers and autonomous APs are both devices with intelligence that reside on the edge of network architecture.

18. A. Distributed WLAN architecture uses a WLAN switch that manages hybrid fat/thin access points.

19. A, D. There are two main components in any PoE solution, the Power Sourcing Equipment (PSE) and the Powered Device (PD).

20. A, D. An Endspan solution is compatible with 10BaseT, 100BaseTX, and 1000BaseT cabling and is the only option that will work with Gigabit Ethernet. A switch with inline power is considered an Endspan solution.

Chapter

11

Network Design, Implementation, and Management

IN THIS CHAPTER, YOU WILL LEARN ABOUT THE FOLLOWING:

- ✓ Core, Distribution, and Access
- ✓ Capacity versus Coverage
- ✓ Corporate Data Access and End-User Mobility
- ✓ Network Extension to Remote Areas
- ✓ Bridging—Building-to-Building Connectivity
- ✓ Wireless ISP (WISP)—Last-Mile Data Delivery
- ✓ Small Office/Home Office (SOHO)
- ✓ Mobile Office Networking
- ✓ Educational/Classroom Use
- ✓ Industrial—Warehousing and Manufacturing
- ✓ Healthcare—Hospitals and Offices
- ✓ Hotspots—Public Network Access

This chapter will look at the typical wired network architecture and how it relates to the architecture and components of a wireless network. Wireless network design is different than wired network design, so we will look at the issues of capacity and coverage when designing a wireless network. We will then learn about some of the different environments where wireless networks are commonly deployed. At times some of the pros and cons of wireless in the different environments will be looked at along with some of the areas of concern.

Core, Distribution, and Access

If you have ever taken a networking class or read a book about network design, then you have probably heard the terms *core*, *distribution*, and *access* when referring to networking architecture. Proper network design is imperative no matter what type of network topology is used. The core of the network is the high-speed backbone or the superhighway of the network. The goal of the core is to carry large amounts of information between key data centers or distribution areas, just as superhighways connect cities and metropolitan areas.

The core layer does not route traffic nor manipulate packets but rather performs high-speed switching. Redundant solutions are usually designed at the core layer to ensure the fast and reliable delivery of packets. The distribution layer of the network routes or directs traffic toward the smaller clusters of nodes or neighborhoods of the network.

The distribution layer routes traffic between VLANs and subnets. The distribution layer is akin to the state and county roads which provide medium travel speeds and distributes the traffic within the city or metropolitan area.

The access layer of the network is responsible for slower delivery of the traffic directly to the end user or end node. The access layer mimics the local roads and neighborhood streets that are used to reach your final address. The access layer ensures the final delivery of packets to the end user. Remember that speed is a relative concept.

Due to traffic load and throughput demands, as data moves from the access layer to the core layer, the speed and throughput capabilities will increase. The additional speed and throughput tends to also mean higher cost.

Just as it is not practical to build a superhighway so that traffic can travel between your neighborhood and the local school, it would not be practical or efficient to build a two-lane road as the main thoroughfare to connect two large cities such as New York and Boston. These same principles apply to network design. Each of the network layers—core, distribution, and access—are designed to provide a specific function and capability to the network. It is important to understand how wireless networking fits into this network design model.

As you know from previous chapters, wireless networking can be implemented as either point-to-point or point-to-multipoint solutions. Most wireless networking is used to provide network access to the individual client stations and are designed as point-to-multipoint networks. This type of implementation is designed and installed on the access layer, providing connectivity to the end user. 802.11 wireless networking is most often implemented at the access layer.

Wireless bridge links are typically used to provide connectivity between buildings in the same way that county or state roads provide distribution of traffic between neighborhoods. The purpose of wireless bridging is to connect two separate wired networks wirelessly. Routing data traffic between networks is usually associated with the distribution layer. Wireless bridge links cannot typically meet the speed or distance requirements of the core layer, but they can be very effective at the distribution layer. An 802.11 bridge link is an example of wireless technology being implemented at the distribution layer.

Although wireless is not typically associated with the core layer, you must remember that speed and distance requirements vary greatly between large and small companies and that one person's distribution layer could be another person's core layer. Very small companies may even implement wireless for all networking, forgoing any wired devices. Higher-bandwidth proprietary wireless bridges and some 802.11 mesh network deployments could be considered an implementation of wireless at the core layer.

Capacity vs. Coverage

When a wireless network is designed, two concepts that typically compete with each other are *capacity* and *coverage*. In the early days of wireless networks, it was very common to install an access point with the power set to the maximum level to provide the largest coverage area possible. This was typically acceptable because there were very few wireless devices. Since the access points were also very expensive, companies tried to provide the most coverage while using the fewest access points. Figure 11.1 shows the outline of a building along with the coverage area that is provided by three APs. If there are few wireless stations, this type of wireless design is quite acceptable.

FIGURE 11.1   RF coverage of a building using three APs with few wireless stations

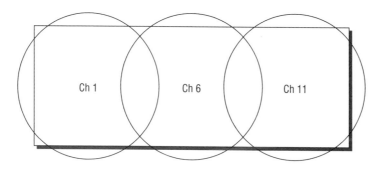

With the proliferation of wireless devices, network design has changed drastically from the early days. Proper network design now entails providing necessary coverage while trying to limit the number of devices connected to any single access point at the same time. This is what is meant by capacity versus coverage. As you know, all of the client stations that connect to a single access point share the throughput capabilities of that access point. Therefore it is important to design the network to try to limit the number of stations that are simultaneously connected to a single access point. This is performed by first determining the maximum number of stations that you want connected to an access point at the same time (this will vary from company to company depending upon network usage). Then you need to determine how big the cell size needs to be to provide this capacity, and then you need to adjust the power level of the access point in order to create a cell of the desired size. Figure 11.2 shows the outline of the same building, but since there are many more wireless stations, the cell sizes have been decreased while the number of cells has been increased.

Another way of providing wireless support for a large capacity of users is by access point *co-location*. Co-location refers to placing multiple access points near each other, where the RF signal from one AP could potentially affect the signal from another AP. 802.11b and 802.11g APs are only capable of having three access points in the same area without causing interference. The three APs would need at least a five-channel separation to prevent RF interference. By co-locating three APs, theoretically the potential cumulative speed is three times the speed of a single AP (assuming the three APs are equal). For example, three co-located 802.11g APs would provide a cumulative maximum speed of 162 Mbps (remember that actual throughput will be significantly less). Access point co-location is recommended only when the concentration of users is so dense that even when the cell size is at its smallest, there are still more stations per cell than desired. It is important to note that while the channels may be separate, it is crucial that the antennas have enough separation so they will not drown out the other signals. This often will occur in large meeting halls or university lecture halls. When co-located, end users can be load-balanced and segmented by MAC filters or by separate SSIDs. Co-location is a method of meeting capacity needs; however, cell-sizing is almost always the preferable method. Currently there are no standards for load balancing, so any load balancing technologies that exist are proprietary.

FIGURE 11.2   RF coverage of a building using 12 APs with dense deployment of wireless stations

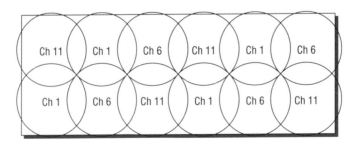

Corporate Data Access and End User Mobility

As corporations decide whether to install wireless networking, they typically look toward the wireless network to provide two capabilities to their existing network. The first is the ability to easily add network access in areas where installation of wired connections is difficult or expensive. The second is to provide easy mobility for the wireless user within the corporate building or campus environment.

The installation of wired network jacks is very expensive, often costing as much as or even more than $200 (in U.S. dollars) per jack. As companies reorganize workers and departments, network infrastructure typically needs to be changed as well. Other areas such as warehouses, conference rooms, manufacturing lines, research labs, and cafeterias are often difficult places to effectively install wired network connections. In these and other environments, the installation of wireless networks can save the company money and provide consistent network access to all users.

Another key reason for companies to install wireless networking is to provide continuous access and availability throughout the facility. With computer access and data becoming critical components of many people's jobs, it is important for them to be continuously available and to be able to get up-to-the moment information. By installing a wireless network throughout the building or campus, the company makes it easier for employees to meet and discuss or brainstorm while maintaining access to corporate data, email, and the Internet from their laptops, no matter where they are in the building or on the campus.

Whatever the reason for installing wireless networking, companies must remember its benefits and its flaws. Wireless networking is typically slower than wired networking and therefore cannot always provide a direct replacement to wired networking. Wireless provides mobility, accessibility, and convenience, but can lack in performance and throughput. Wireless is an access technology, providing connectivity to end user stations. Wireless should rarely be considered for distribution or core roles, except for building-to-building bridging. Even in these scenarios, make sure that the wireless bridge will be capable of handling the traffic load and throughput needs.

Network Extension to Remote Areas

If you think about it carefully, network extension to remote areas was one of the driving forces of home wireless networking, which also helped to drive the demands for wireless in the corporate environment. As households connected to the Internet and as more households purchased additional computers, there was a need to connect all of the computers in the house to the Internet. Although many people installed Ethernet cabling to connect the computers, this was typically too costly, impractical due to accessibility, or beyond the capabilities of the average homeowner. Around this time 802.11b wireless devices were becoming more affordable. The same reasons for installing wireless networking in a home are also valid reasons for installing wireless in offices, warehouses, and just about any other environment. The cost of installing network cabling for each computer is expensive, and in many environments running cable or fiber is difficult due to building design or aesthetic restrictions. When wireless networking equipment is installed, far fewer cables are required, and equipment placement can often be performed without affecting the aesthetics of a building.

Bridging — Building-to-Building Connectivity

To provide network connectivity between two buildings, you can install an underground cable or fiber between the two buildings, you can pay for a high-speed leased telephone connection, or you can use a building-to-building wireless bridge. All three are very capable solutions, each with its benefits and downfalls.

Although a copper or fiber connection between two buildings will provide you with the highest throughput, installing copper or fiber between two buildings can be very expensive. If the buildings are separated by a long distance or by someone else's property, this may not even be an option. Once its installed, there are no monthly service fees since you own the cable.

Leasing a high-speed telephone connection can provide flexibility and convenience, but since you do not own the connection, you will pay monthly service fees. Depending upon the type of service that you are paying for, you may or may not be able to easily increase the speed of the link.

A wireless building-to-building bridge requires that the two buildings have a clear RF line of sight between them. Once this has been determined or created, a point-to-point or point-to-multipoint transceiver and antenna can be installed. The installation is typically easy to perform by trained professionals, and once it's installed, there are no monthly service fees since you own the equipment. In addition to connecting two buildings using a point-to-point bridge, three or more buildings can be networked together using a point-to-multipoint solution. In a point-to-multipoint installation, the building that is most centrally located will be the central communication point, with the other devices communicating directly to the central building. This is known as a "hub and spoke" or star configuration. A potential problem with the point-to-multipoint solution is that the central communication point becomes a single point of failure for all of the buildings. To prevent a single point of failure and to provide higher data throughput, it is not uncommon to install multiple point-to-point bridges.

Wireless ISP (WISP)

The term *last-mile* is often used by the telephone and cable companies to refer to the last segment of their service that connects the home subscriber to their network. The last-mile of service can often be the most difficult and costly to run since at this point, a cable must be run individually to every subscriber. This is particularly true in rural areas where there are very few subscribers and they are separated by large distances. In many instances, even if a subscriber is connected, since services such as xDSL have a maximum distance limitation of 18,000 feet (5.7 km) from the central office, the subscriber may not be able to receive some services such as high-speed Internet.

Wireless Internet service providers (WISPs) deliver Internet services via wireless networking. Instead of directly cabling each subscriber, a WISP can provide services via RF communications from central transmitters. WISPs often use wireless technology other than 802.11, allowing them to provide wireless coverage to much greater areas. Service from WISPs is not without its own problems. As with any RF technology, the signal can be degraded or corrupted by obstacles such as roofs, mountains, trees, and other buildings. Proper designs and professional installations can ensure a properly working system.

Small Office, Home Office (SOHO)

One common theme of a small or home office is that your job description includes everything from janitor to IT staff and everything in between. Small business owners and home office employees are typically required to be very self-sufficient since there are usually few if any other people around to help them. Wireless networking has helped to make it easier for a small or home office employee to connect the office computers and peripheral devices together and also to the Internet. The main purpose of a SOHO 802.11 network is typically to provide wireless access to an Internet gateway.

Most *small office, home office (SOHO)* wireless routers provide fairly easy-to-follow installation instructions and offer performance and security near what their corporate counterparts provide. They are generally not as flexible or feature rich as comparable corporate products, but most SOHO environments do not need all of the additional capabilities. What the small or home office person gets is a capable device at a quarter of the price their corporate counterparts pay. Dozens of devices are available to provide the SOHO worker with the ability to install and configure their own secure Internet-connected network without spending a fortune.

Mobile Office Networking

Mobile home offices are used for many different purposes: as construction site offices, as temporary offices during construction or after a disaster, or as temporary classrooms to accommodate unplanned changes in student population. Mobile offices are simply an extension of the office environment. These structures are usually buildings on wheels that can be easily deployed for short- or long-term use on an as-needed basis. Since these structures are not permanent, it is usually easier to extend the corporate or school network to these offices by using wireless networking.

A wireless bridge can be used to distribute wireless networking to the mobile office. If needed, an AP can then be used to provide wireless network access to multiple occupants of the office. By providing networking via wireless communications, you can alleviate the cost of running wired cables and installing jacks. Additional users can connect and disconnect from the network without having to make any changes to the networking infrastructure. When the mobile office is no longer needed, the wireless equipment can simply be unplugged and removed.

Moveable wireless networks are used in many environments, including military maneuvers, disaster relief, concerts, flea markets, and construction sites. Due to the ease of installation and removal, mobile wireless networking can be an ideal networking solution.

Educational/Classroom Use

Wireless networking can be used to provide a safe and easy way of connecting students to the school network. Since the layout of most classrooms is flexible (with no permanently installed furniture), it is not possible to install a wired network jack for each student. Because students would be constantly connecting and disconnecting to the network at the beginning and end of class, the jacks would not last long even if they were installed. Prior to wireless networking, in classrooms that were wired with Ethernet, usually all of the computers were placed on tables along the classroom walls, with the students typically facing away from the instructor. Wireless networking allows any classroom seating arrangement to be used, without the safety risk of networking cables being strung across the floor. A wireless network also allows students to connect to the network and work on schoolwork anywhere in the building without having to worry whether a wired network jack is nearby or whether someone else is already using it. The use of wireless bridging is also very prevalent in campus environments. Many universities and colleges use many types of wireless bridge links, including 802.11, to connect buildings campuswide.

Industrial — Warehousing and Manufacturing

Warehouses and manufacturing facilities are two environments in which wireless networking has been used for years, even before the 802.11 standard was created. Due to the vast space and the mobile nature of the employees in these environments, companies saw the need to provide mobile network access to their employees so they could more effectively perform their jobs. Warehouse and manufacturing environments often deploy wireless handheld devices such as bar code scanners, which are often used for inventory control. Most 802.11 networks deployed in either a warehouse or manufacturing environment are designed for coverage rather than capacity. Handheld devices typically do not require much bandwidth, but large coverage areas are needed to provide true mobility. Most early deployments of 802.11 frequency hopping technology was in manufacturing and warehouse environments. Some legacy 802.11 FHSS deployments still exist today. Wireless networks are able to provide the coverage and mobility required in a warehouse environment and provide it cost effectively.

Healthcare—Hospitals and Offices

Although healthcare facilities such as hospitals, clinics, and doctors offices may seem very different than other businesses, they essentially have the same networking needs as other companies: corporate data access and end-user mobility. Healthcare providers need quick, secure, and accurate access to their data so they can react and make decisions. Wireless networks can provide mobility, giving healthcare providers faster access to important data by delivering the data directly to a handheld device that the doctor or nurse carries with them. Hospitals rely upon many forms of proprietary and industry-standard wireless communications that may have the potential of causing RF interference with 802.11 wireless networks. Medical carts used to monitor patient information often have wireless connections back to the nursing station. VoWiFi is another common use of 802.11 technology in a medical environment. Many hospitals have designated a person or department to keep track of the frequencies and bio-medical equipment that are used within the hospital to help avoid conflicts.

 Advanced security is often required for hospitals to meet government regulations on privacy.

Public Network Access

The term *hotspot* typically refers to a free or pay-for-use wireless network that is provided as a service by a business. When people think of hotspots, they typically associate them with cafes, bookstores, or a hospitality-type business such as a hotel or convention center. Hotspots can be used effectively by businesses to attract customers. Business travelers often frequent restaurants or cafes that are known to provide free Internet access. Many of these establishments benefit from the increased business generated by offering a hotspot. Free hotspots have drawn much attention for the 802.11 wireless industry, helping to make more people aware of the benefits of the technology.

Other hotspot providers have had difficulty convincing people to pay upwards of $40 per month for a subscription. Many airports and hotel chains have installed pay-for-use hotspots; however, there are many different providers, each one offering a separate subscription from the other, which is often not practical for the consumer.

Most hotspot providers perform network authentication using a special type of web page known as a captive portal. When a user connects to the hotspot, the user must open up a web browser. No matter what web page the user attempts to go to, a logon web page will be displayed instead. This is the captive portal page. If the hotspot provider is a paid service, then the user must enter either their subscription information, if they are a subscriber to the service, or credit card information, if they are paying for hourly or daily usage. Many free hotspots also use captive portals as a method for requiring users to agree to a usage policy before they are allowed access to the Internet. If the user agrees to the terms of the policy, they are required to either enter some basic information or click a button, validating their agreement with the usage policy. Many corporations also use captive portals to authenticate guest users onto their corporate networks.

 Real World Scenario

Do Hotspots Provide Data Security?

It is important to remember that hotspot providers (free or pay-for-use) do not care about the security of your data. The free provider typically is offering you Internet access as a way of encouraging you to visit their location, such as a café, and buy some of whatever it is they sell. The pay-for-use hotspot provider performs authentication to make sure you are a paid subscriber, and once you have proven that, they will provide you with access to the Internet. Except for rare occasions, neither of these hotspot providers perform any data encryption. Because of this, business users often use VPN client software to provide a secure encrypted tunnel back to their corporate network whenever they are using a hotspot. Many companies make the use of a VPN a requirement whenever an employee connects to a public hotspot.

Summary

This chapter covered some of the design, implementation, and management environments in which wireless networking is used. Although many of these environments are similar, each has unique characteristics. It is important to understand these similarities and differences and how wireless networking is commonly deployed.

Exam Essentials

Know the components that make up the networking architecture. Understand the core, distribution, and access layers. In addition, know their roles and how they relate to each other.

Understand the relationship between capacity and coverage. Know how capacity and coverage compete with each other. Be familiar with co-location and how it can be used in large-capacity environments.

Know the different wireless environments. Wireless networking can be used in many environments, with each environment having a different primary reason or focus for installing the wireless network. Know these environments and their main reasons for installing wireless networking.

Key Terms

Before you take the exam, be certain you are familiar with the following terms:

access	distribution
capacity	hotspot
co-location	last-mile
core	small office, home office (SOHO)
coverage	Wireless Internet service provider (WISP)

Review Questions

1. 802.11 wireless networking is typically installed at which network architecture layer?

    A. Core

    B. Distribution

    C. Access

    D. Physical

2. 802.11 wireless bridge links are typically associated with which network architecture layer?

    A. Core

    B. Distribution

    C. Access

    D. Network

3. Which of the following is sometimes used as a core technology?

    A. BSS

    B. IBSS

    C. Mesh

    D. ESS

4. What are two network design concepts that often compete with each other?

    A. Speed

    B. Capacity

    C. Frequency

    D. Coverage

5. In most countries, what is the maximum cumulative speed for co-located 802.11g APs without subjecting the APs to channel overlap?

    A. 11 Mbps

    B. 33 Mbps

    C. 54 Mbps

    D. 162 Mbps

6. When co-located, end users can be load-balanced and segmented by what methods? (Choose all the apply.)

    A. IEEE 802.11F

    B. MAC filtering

    C. Separate channels

    D. Separate SSIDs

7. Corporations typically install wireless networks to provide which of the following capabilities? (Choose all that apply.)

    A. Easy mobility for the wireless user within the corporate building or campus environment

    B. High-speed network access comparable to wired networking

    C. Secure access for employees from their home or on the road

    D. The ability to easily add network access in areas where installation of wired connections is difficult or expensive

8. Last-mile Internet service is provided by which of the following? (Choose all that apply.)

    A. Telephone company

    B. Long-distance carrier

    C. Cable provider

    D. WISPs

9. Which of the following is the main purpose of a SOHO 802.11 network?

    A. Shared networking

    B. Internet gateway

    C. Network security

    D. Print sharing

10. Which of the following are examples of mobile office networking? (Choose all that apply.)

    A. Construction site offices

    B. Temporary disaster assistance office

    C. Remote sales office

    D. Temporary classrooms

11. Warehousing and manufacturing environments typically have which of the following requirements? (Choose all that apply.)

    A. Mobility

    B. High speed access

    C. High capacity

    D. High coverage

12. Which of the following is least likely to be offered by a hotspot provider?

    A. Free access

    B. Paid access

    C. Network authentication

    D. Data encryption

13. Providing necessary coverage while limiting the number of devices connected to any single access point at the same time is known as what?

A. Load balancing

B. Coverage planning

C. Capacity planning

D. Throughput optimization

14. Which of the following terms refer to the same network design? (Choose all that apply.)

A. PTP

B. PTMP

C. Hub and spoke

D. Star

15. Most early deployments of 802.11 FHSS were used in which type of environment?

A. Mobile office networking

B. Educational/classroom use

C. Industrial (warehousing and manufacturing)

D. Healthcare (hospitals and offices)

16. When using a hotspot, in order to ensure security back to your corporate network, you should do which of the following?

A. Enable WEP

B. Enable 802.1X/EAP

C. Use an IPSec VPN

D. Security cannot be provided since you do not control the access point

17. Load balancing is implemented using which of the following methods?

A. IEEE 802.11k

B. IEEE 802.11e

C. IEEE 802.1X

D. There is no standard. Currently, load balancing techniques are proprietary.

18. Multiple point-to-point bridges between the same locations are often installed for which of the following reasons? (Choose all that apply.)

A. To provide higher throughput

B. To prevent channel overlap

C. To prevent single point of failure

D. To enable support for VLANs

19. What are some of the key concerns of healthcare providers when installing a wireless network? (Choose all that apply.)

A. RF interference

B. Faster access

C. Secure and accurate access

D. Faster speed

20. What type of 802.11 devices typically operate at the access layer? (Choose all that apply.)

A. 802.11a bridges

B. 802.11g bridges

C. 802.11a client stations

D. 802.11b client stations

E. 802.11g access points

Answers to Review Questions

1. C. 802.11 wireless networking is typically used to connect client stations to the network, which occurs at the access layer, not the core or distribution layer. The Physical layer is a layer of the OSI model, not a network architecture layer.

2. B. 802.11 wireless bridge links are typically used to perform distribution layer services. Core layer devices are usually much faster than 802.11 wireless devices, and bridges are not used to provide access layer services. The Network layer is a layer of the OSI model, not a network architecture layer.

3. C. Both basic service set (BSS) and extended service set (ESS) are used to provide access to client stations. An independent basic service set (IBSS) is an ad-hoc network. Depending upon their deployment, a mesh network can be used to provide access, distribution, or core networking.

4. B, D. Capacity and coverage are natural offsets of each other. The objective of designing a network for coverage is to provide the greatest amount of coverage with the fewest number of access points. A network designed for capacity is concerned with maintaining a maximum number of clients per access point and using this client per access point count to determine the number of access points required.

5. D. 802.11g supports three non-overlapping channels, each with a maximum speed (not throughput) of 54 Mbps, providing a cumulative maximum speed of 162 Mbps.

6. B, D. Since there is no load balancing standard, implementing MAC filtering and multiple SSIDs across the co-located access points can help to distribute the users across the access points, providing a minimum level of load balancing. Separate channels are desired to prevent co-channel interference, but they do not provide load balancing capabilities.

7. A, D. Corporations typically install wireless to provide easy mobility and/or access to areas that are difficult or extremely expensive to connect via wired networks. Although providing connectivity to the Internet is a service that the corporate wireless network offers, it is not the driving reason for installing the wireless network.

8. A, C, D. The telephone company, cable providers, and WISPs are all examples of companies that provide last-mile services to users and businesses.

9. B. The main purpose of SOHO networks is to provide a gateway to the Internet.

10. A, B, D. Mobile office networking solutions are temporary solutions that include all of the options listed except for the remote sales office, which would more likely be classified as a SOHO installation.

11. A, D. Warehousing and manufacturing environments typically have a need for mobility, but their data transfers are typically very small. Therefore, their networks are often designed for high coverage rather than high capacity.

12. D. Hotspot providers are not likely to provide data encryption. It is more difficult to deploy and there is no benefit or business reason for them to provide it.

13. C. Capacity planning involves designing the wireless network so that only an ideal maximum number of client stations connect to an access point at a time, providing an ideal amount of data throughput.

14. B, C, D. Point-to-multipoint, hub and spoke, and star all describe the same communication technology, which connects multiple devices using a central device. Point-to-point communications connects two devices.

15. C. Most of the 802.11 implementations used FHSS, with industrial (warehousing and manufacturing) companies being some of the biggest implementers. Their requirements of mobility with low data transfer speeds was ideal for using the technology.

16. C. To make wireless access easy for the subscriber, hotspot vendors typically deploy authentication methods that are easy to use but that do not provide data encryption. Therefore, to ensure security back to your corporate network, the use of an IPSec VPN is necessary.

17. D. Currently all load balancing techniques are proprietary. 802.1X is the port-based access control standard. 802.11e is the wireless QoS standard. 802.11k is the proposed standard for radio resource management.

18. A, C. The installation of multiple point-to-point bridges is either to provide higher throughput or to prevent a single point of failure. Care must be taken in arranging channel and antenna installations to prevent self-inflicted interference.

19. A, B, C. Healthcare providers often have many other devices that use RF communications, and therefore, RF interference is a concern. Fast access along with secure and accurate access is critical in healthcare environments. Faster access can be performed without faster speed. The mobility of the technology will satisfy the faster access that is typically needed.

20. C, D, E. Wireless bridge links are typically used to perform distribution layer services. Client stations and access points typically are used at the access layer. Whether the client radios and access point radios are 802.11b, 802.11g, or 802.11a compliant is irrelevant.

Chapter 12

WLAN Troubleshooting

IN THIS CHAPTER, YOU WILL LEARN ABOUT THE FOLLOWING:

- ✓ **802.11 Coverage Considerations**
  - ▪ Dynamic Rate Switching
  - ▪ Roaming
  - ▪ Layer 3 Roaming
  - ▪ Co-Channel Interference
  - ▪ Channel Reuse
  - ▪ Hidden Node
  - ▪ Near/Far
- ✓ **Interference**
- ✓ **Performance**
- ✓ **Weather**

Diagnostic methods that are used to troubleshoot wired 802.3 networks should also be applied when troubleshooting a wireless local area network (WLAN). A bottoms-up approach to analyzing the OSI reference model layers also applies with wireless networking. A wireless networking administrator should always try to first determine if problems exist at layer 1 and layer 2. As with most networking technologies, most problems usually exist at the Physical layer. Simple layer 1 problems such as non-powered access points or client card driver problems are often the root cause of connectivity or performance issues. Because WLANs use radio frequencies to deliver data, troubleshooting a WLAN offers many unique layer 1 challenges not found in a typical wired environment. The bulk of this chapter will discuss the numerous potential problems that can occur at layer 1 and what solutions might be implemented to prevent or rectify the layer 1 problems. A spectrum analyzer is often a useful tool when diagnosing layer 1 issues.

After eliminating layer 1 as a source of possible troubles, a WLAN administrator should try to determine if the problem exists at the Data-Link layer. Authentication and association problems often occur due to improperly configured security and administrative settings on access points, wireless switches, and client utility software. A WLAN protocol analyzer is often an invaluable tool for troubleshooting layer 2 problems.

In this chapter, we will discuss many coverage considerations and troubleshooting issues that may develop when deploying an 802.11 wireless network. RF propagation behaviors and RF interference will affect both the performance and coverage of your WLAN. Because mobility is usually required in a WLAN environment, many roaming problems often occur and must be addressed. The half-duplex nature of the medium also brings unique challenges typically not seen in a full-duplex environment. Different considerations also need to be given to outdoor 802.11 deployments due to weather conditions. In this chapter we will discuss how to identify, troubleshoot, prevent and fix instances of potential WLAN problems.

802.11 Coverage Considerations

Providing for both coverage and capacity in a WLAN design solves many problems. Roaming problems and interference issues will often be mitigated in advance if proper WLAN design techniques are implemented as well as a thorough site survey. In the following sections, we will discuss many considerations that should be addressed to provide proper coverage, capacity, and performance within an 802.11 coverage zone.

Dynamic Rate Switching

As client station radios move away from an access point, they will shift down to lower bandwidth capabilities using a process known as *dynamic rate switching (DRS)*. Access points can support multiple data rates depending on the spread spectrum technology used by the AP's radio card. For example, an 802.11b radio supports data rates of 11, 5.5, 2, and 1 Mbps. Data rate transmissions between the access point and the client stations will shift down or up depending on the quality of the signal between the two radio cards, as pictured in Figure 12.1. There is a correlation between signal quality and distance from the AP. As a result, transmissions between two 802.11b radio cards may be at 11 Mbps at 30 feet but 2 Mbps at 150 feet.

Dynamic rate switching (DRS) is also referred to as dynamic rate shifting, adaptive rate selection, and automatic rate selection. All these terms refer to a method of speed fallback on a wireless LAN client as signal quality from the access point decreases. The objective of DRS is upshifting and downshifting for rate optimization and improved performance. Effectively, the lower date rates will have larger concentric zones of coverage than the higher data rates, as pictured in Figure 12.2.

FIGURE 12.1   Dynamic rate switching

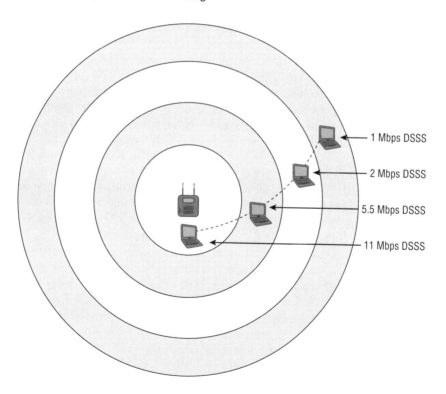

1 Mbps DSSS

2 Mbps DSSS

5.5 Mbps DSSS

11 Mbps DSSS

FIGURE 12.2   Data rate coverage zones

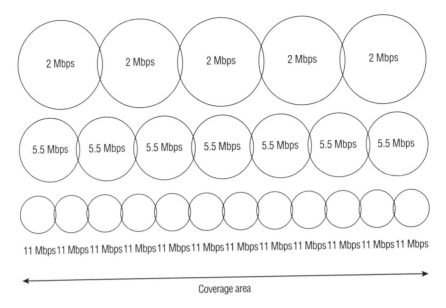

Coverage area

The algorithms used for dynamic rate switching are proprietary and are defined by radio card manufacturers. Most vendors base DRS on receive signal strength indicator (RSSI) thresholds, packet error rate, and retransmissions. RSSI metrics are usually based on signal strength and signal quality. In other words, a station might shift up or down between data rates based on both received signal strength in dBm and possibly on a signal-to-noise ratio (SNR) value. Because vendors implement DRS differently, you may have two different vendor client cards at the same location while one is communicating at 5.5 Mbps and the other is communicating at 1 Mbps. For example, one vendor might shift down from data rate 11 Mbps to 5 Mbps at −70 dBm while another vendor might shift between the same two rates at −75 dBm. Keep in mind that DRS works with all 802.11 PHYs. For example, the same shifting of rates will also occur with ERP-OFDM radios shifting between 54, 48, 36, 24, 18, 12, 9, and 6 Mbps data rates. As a result, there is a correlation between signal quality and distance from the AP.

It is often a recommend practice to turn off the two lowest data rates of 1 and 2 Mbps when designing an 802.11b/g network. The two reasons that a WLAN network administrator might want to consider disabling the two lowest rates on an 802.11b/g access point are medium contention and the hidden node problem. In Figure 12.3, you will see that there are multiple client stations in the 1 Mbps zone and only one lone client in the 11 Mbps zone. Remember that wireless is a half-duplex medium and only one radio card can transmit on the medium at a time. By forcing the higher data rates, it is easier to force more distributed capacity over the access points. This is not typically necessary when planning solely for coverage.

FIGURE 12.3   Frame transmission time

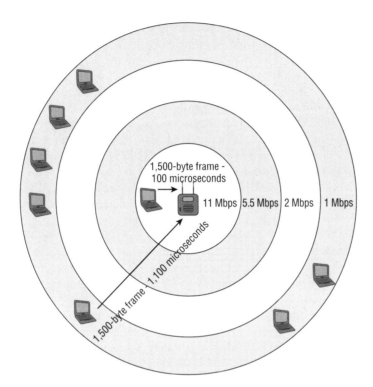

All radio cards access the medium in a pseudo-random fashion as defined by CSMA/CA. A radio transmitting a 1,500-byte data frame at 11 Mbps might occupy the medium for 100 microseconds. Another radio transmitting at 1 Mbps per second will take 1,100 microseconds to deliver that same 1,500 bytes. Radio cards transmitting at slower data rates will occupy the medium much longer, while faster radios have to wait. If multiple radio cards get on the outer cell edges and transmit at slower rates consistently, the perceived throughput for the cards transmitting at higher rates is much slower due to waiting for slower transmissions to finish. For this reason, too many radios on outer 1 and 2 Mbps cells can adversely affect throughput. Another reason to consider turning off the lower data rates is the hidden node problem, which will be explained later in this chapter.

Roaming

As you have learned throughout this book, *roaming* is the method where client stations move between RF coverage cells in a seamless manner. Client stations switch communications through different access points. Seamless communications for stations moving between the coverage zones within an Extended Service Set (ESS) is vital for uninterrupted mobility. One of the most common issues you'll need troubleshoot is problems with roaming. Roaming problems are usually caused by poor network design. Due to the proprietary nature of roaming, problems can also occur when radio cards from multiple vendors are deployed. Changes in the WLAN environment can also cause roaming hiccups.

Client stations and not the access point make the decision on whether or not to roam between access points. Some vendors may involve the access point or wireless switch in the roaming decision, but ultimately, the client station initiates the roaming process with a reassociation request frame. The method in which client stations decide how to roam is entirely proprietary. All vendor client stations use roaming algorithms that can be based on multiple variables. The variable of most importance will always be received signal strength. As the received signal from the original AP grows weaker and a station hears a stronger signal from another known access point, the station will initiate the roaming process. However, other variables such as SNR, error rates, and retransmissions may also have a part in the roaming decision. Because roaming is proprietary, a specific vendor client station may roam sooner than a second vendor client station as they move through various coverage cells. Some vendors like to encourage roaming while others use algorithms that roam at lower received signal thresholds. In an environment where a WLAN administrator must support multiple vendor radios, different roaming behaviors will most assuredly be seen. For the time being, a WLAN administrator will always face unique challenges because of the proprietary nature of roaming. In the future, the 802.11k draft and much anticipated 802.11r roaming draft will hopefully standardize many aspects of roaming.

The best way to assure that seamless roaming will commence is proper design and a thorough site survey. When designing an 802.11 WLAN, most vendors recommend 15 to 20 percent overlap in coverage cells at the lowest desired signal level. The only way to determine if proper cell overlap is in place is by conducting a coverage analysis site survey. Proper site survey procedures are discussed in detail in Chapter 16. Roaming problems will occur if there is not enough overlap in cell coverage. Too little overlap will effectively create a roaming dead zone, and connectivity may even temporarily be lost. On the flip side, too much cell overlap will also cause roaming problems. For example, if two cells have 60 percent overlap, a station may stay associated with its original AP and not connect to a second access point even though the station is directly underneath the second access point. This can also create a situation in which the client device is constantly switching back and forth between the two or more APs. This often presents itself when a client device is directly under an AP and there are constant dropped frames.

Another design issue of great importance is latency. The 802.11i amendment defines an 802.1X/EAP security solution in the enterprise. The average time involved during the authentication process can be 700 milliseconds or longer. Every time a client station roams to a new access point, reauthentication is required when an 802.1X/EAP security solution has been deployed. The time delay that is a result of the authentication process can cause serious interruptions with time-sensitive applications. VoWiFi requires a handoff of 50 milliseconds or less when roaming. A *fast secure roaming (FSR)* solution is needed if 802.1X/EAP security and time-sensitive applications are used together in a wireless network. Currently, FSR solutions are proprietary, although the 802.11i amendment defines optional FSR and the 802.11r draft will hopefully standardize fast secure roaming.

Changes in the WLAN environment can also cause roaming headaches. RF interference will always affect the performance of a wireless network and can make roaming problematic as well. Very often new construction in a building will affect the coverage of a WLAN. If the physical environment where the WLAN is deployed changes, the coverage design may have to change as well. It is always a good idea to periodically conduct a coverage survey to monitor changes in coverage patterns.

Layer 3 Roaming

One major consideration when designing a WLAN is what happens when client stations roam across layer 3 boundaries. As pictured in Figure 12.4, the client station is roaming between two access points. The roam is seamless at layer 2, but a router sits between the two access points and each access point resides in a separate subnet. In other words, the client station will lose layer 3 connectivity and must acquire a new IP address. Any connection oriented applications that are running when the client reestablishes layer 3 connectivity will have to be restarted. For example, a VoIP phone conversation would disconnect in this scenario and the call would have to be reestablished.

FIGURE 12.4   Layer 3 roaming boundaries

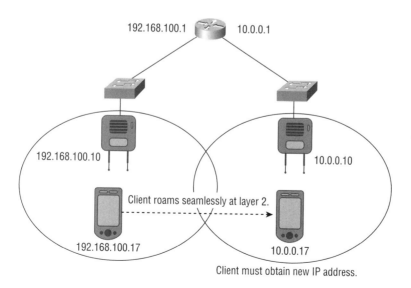

The preferred method when designing a WLAN is to only have overlapping Wi-Fi cells that exist in the same layer 3 domains through the use of VLANs. However, because 802.11 wireless networks are usually integrated into preexisting wired topologies, crossing layer 3 boundaries is often a necessity, especially in large deployments. The only way to maintain upper-layer communications when crossing layer 3 subnets is to provide either a *Mobile IP* solution or a proprietary *layer 3 roaming* solution. Mobile IP is an Internet Engineering Task Force (IETF) standard protocol that allows mobile device users to move from one layer 3 network to another while maintaining their original IP address. Mobile IP is defined in IETF request for comment (RFC) 3344. Mobile IP and proprietary solutions both use some type of tunneling method and IP header encapsulation to allow packets to traverse between separate layer 3 domains with the goal of maintaining upper-layer communications. It is beyond the scope of this book to explain either the standards-based Mobile IP or proprietary layer 3 roaming solutions; however, most wireless switches and controllers now support some type of layer 3 roaming solution. While maintaining upper-layer connectivity is possible with these layer 3 roaming solutions, increased latency is often an issue. Additionally, it may not be a requirement for your network. Even if there are layer 3 boundaries, your users may not need to seamlessly roam between subnets. Before you go to all the hassle of building a roaming solution, be sure to properly define your requirements.

Co-Channel Interference

As you learned in Chapter 6, the 802.11b and 802.11g amendments require 25 MHz of separation between the center frequencies of HR-DSSS channels to be considered non-overlapping. The 802.11g amendment also requires 20 MHz of separation between the center frequencies of ERP-OFDM channels. As pictured in Figure 12.5, only channels 1, 6, and 11 can meet these IEEE requirements in the 2.4 GHz ISM band in the United States if 3 channels are needed. Channels 2 and 7 are non-overlapping, as well as 3 and 8, 4 and 9, and 5 and 10. The important thing to remember is that there must be 5 channels of separation in adjacent coverage cells. Some countries use all 14 channels in the 2.4 GHz ISM band, but due to positioning of the center frequencies, no more than 3 channels can be used while still avoiding frequency overlap. Even if all 14 channels are available, most countries still choose to use channels 1, 6, and 11.

When designing a wireless LAN, you need overlapping coverage cells in order to provide for roaming. However, the overlapping cells should not have overlapping frequencies, and only channels 1, 6, and 11 should be used in the 2.4 GHz ISM band in the United States to get the most available, non-overlapping channels. Overlapping coverage cells with overlapping frequencies causes what is known as *co-channel interference (CCI)*, which causes a severe degradation in performance and throughput. If overlapping coverage cells also have frequency overlap, frames will become corrupted, retransmissions will increase, and throughput will suffer significantly. In the next section, we will discuss channel reuse patterns that are used to mitigate co-channel interference.

FIGURE 12.5   2.4 GHz non-overlapping channels

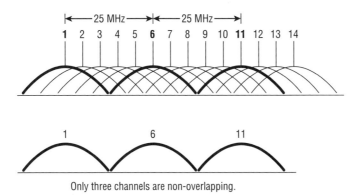

Only three channels are non-overlapping.

As defined by the IEEE, there are currently 12 channels available in the 5 GHz UNII bands. These 12 channels are technically considered non-overlapping channels because there is 20 MHz of separation between the center frequencies. However, in reality there will also be some frequency overlap of the sidebands of each ERP-OFDM channel. The good news is that you are not limited to 3 channels and all 12 channels can be used in a channel reuse pattern, which is discussed in the next section. As pictured in Figure 12.6, the United States and other countries have designated more license-free frequency space in the 5 GHz range and 11 more channels have been approved for use. In some countries, 802.11a radio cards will soon have the ability to transmit on a total of 23 channels.

FIGURE 12.6   5 GHz non-overlapping channels

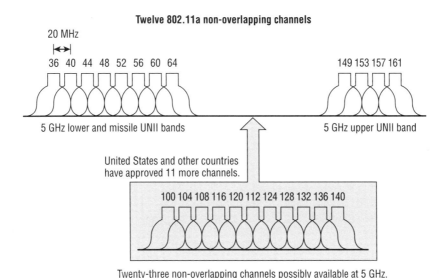

Twenty-three non-overlapping channels possibly available at 5 GHz.

Channel Reuse

One of the most common mistakes many businesses make when first deploying a WLAN is to configure multiple access points all on the same channel. This will of course cause co-channel interference and degrade performance significantly. To avoid co-channel interference, a channel reuse design is necessary. Once again, overlapping RF coverage cells are needed for roaming but overlap frequencies must be avoided. The only three channels that meet these criteria in the 2.4 GHz ISM band are channels 1, 6, and 11 in the United States. Overlapping coverage cells therefore should be placed in a *channel reuse* pattern similar to the one pictured in Figure 12.7.

Channel reuse patterns should also be used in the 5 GHz UNII bands. All 12 802.11a channels can be used, as pictured in Figure 12.8. Due to the frequency overlap of channel sidebands, there should always be at least 2 cells between access points on the same channel. It is also a recommend practice that any adjacent cells use a frequency that is at least 2 channels apart and not use an adjacent frequency.

It is necessary to always think three-dimensional when designing a channel reuse pattern. If access points are deployed on multiple floors in the same building, a reuse pattern will be necessary, such as the one pictured in Figure 12.9. A common mistake is to deploy a cookie-cutter design by performing a site survey on only one floor and then placing the access points on the same channels and same locations on each floor. A site survey must be performed on all floors, and the access points often need to be staggered to allow for a three-dimensional reuse pattern. Also, the coverage cells of each access point should not extend beyond more than one floor above and below the floor on which the access point is mounted. It is inappropriate to always assume that the coverage bleed over to other floors will provide sufficient signal strength and quality. In some cases, the floors are concrete or steel and allow very little, if any, signal coverage through. As a result, a survey is absolutely required.

Many enterprise access points currently have dual radio card capabilities, allowing for both 2.4 GHz and 5 GHz wireless networks to be deployed at the same. The 802.11a radio in an access point transmits at 5 GHz, and the signal will attenuate faster than the signal that is being transmitted at 2.4 GHz from the 802.11b/g radio card. Therefore, when performing a site survey for deploying dual frequency WLANs, it is a recommended practice to perform the 5 GHz site survey first and determine the placement of the access points. Once those locations are identified, channel reuse patterns will have to be used for each respective frequency. In some cases, only the 802.11a radio will be active.

FIGURE 12.7   802.11 b/g channel reuse

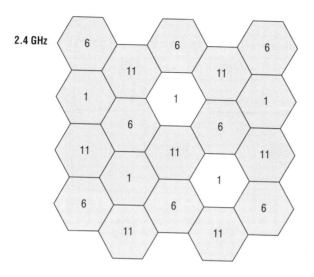

2.4 GHz

FIGURE 12.8   802.11a channel reuse

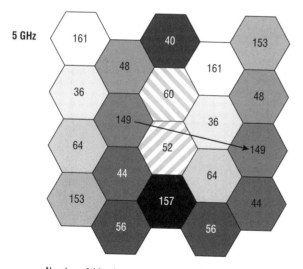

5 GHz

Number of 11a channels available = 12
Distance to cell with same channel is at least 2 cells.

FIGURE 12.9   Three-dimensional channel reuse

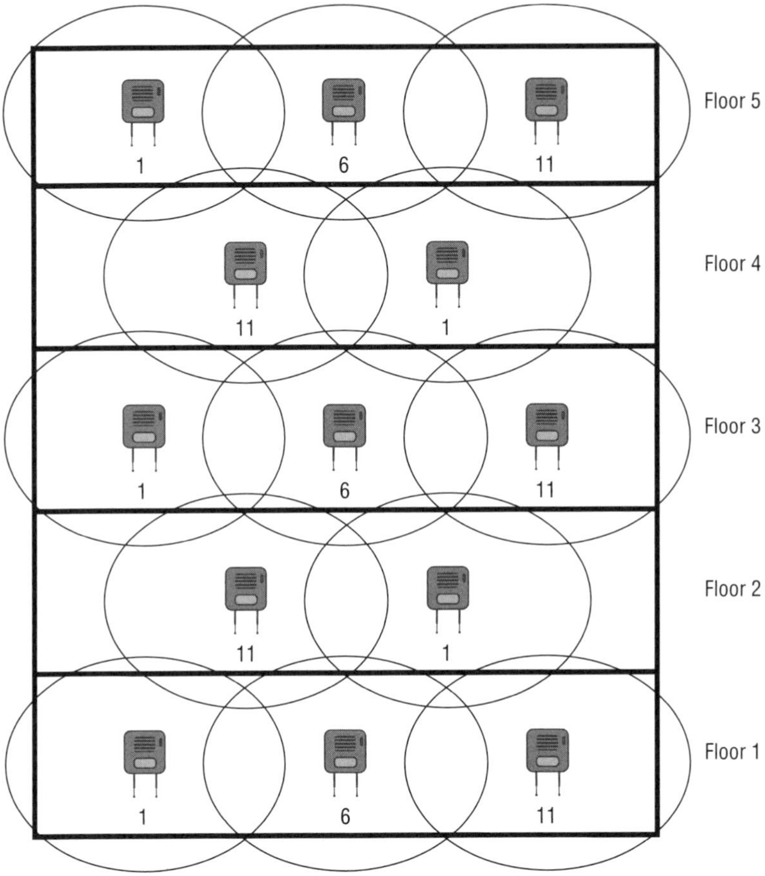

Hidden Node

In Chapter 8 you learned about physical carrier-sense and the clear channel assessment (CCA). The CCA involves listening for 802.11 RF transmissions at the Physical layer, and the medium must be clear before a station can transmit. The problem with physical carrier-sense is that all stations may not be able to hear each other. Remember that the medium is half-duplex and, at any given time, only one radio card can be transmitting. What would happen, however, if one client station that was about to transmit performed a CCA but did not hear another station that was already transmitting? If the station that was about to transmit did not detect any RF energy during the CCA, it will also transmit. The problem is that you now have two stations transmitting at the same time. The end result is a collision, and the frames will become corrupted. The frames will have to be retransmitted. The *hidden node* problem occurs when one client station's transmissions are unheard by any or all the other client stations in the basic service set (BSS).

In Figure 12.10 you see the coverage area of an access point. Note that a thick block wall resides between one client station and all of the other client stations that are associated to the access point. The RF transmissions of the lone station on the other side of the wall cannot be heard by all of the other 802.11 client stations even though all the stations can hear the AP. That unheard station is the hidden node. What keeps occurring is that every time the hidden node transmits, another station is also transmitting and a collision occurs. The hidden node continues to have collisions with the transmissions from all the other stations that cannot hear it during the clear channel assessment. The collisions continue on a regular basis and so do retransmissions, with the final result being a decrease in throughput. A hidden node can drive retransmission rates above 15 to 20 percent or even higher. Retransmissions, of course, will affect throughput.

FIGURE 12.10   Hidden node—obstruction

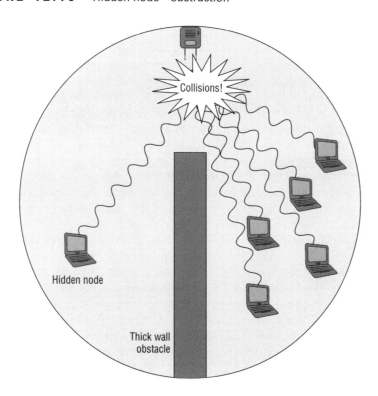

The hidden node problem may exist because of several reasons. Poor WLAN design often leads to a hidden node problem. Obstacles such as a newly constructed wall or newly installed bookcase can cause a hidden node problem. A user moving behind some sort of obstacle can cause a hidden node problem. Users with wireless desktops often place their radio card underneath a metal desk and effectively transform that radio card into an unheard hidden node. The hidden node problem can also occur when two client stations are at opposite ends of an RF coverage cell and they cannot hear each other, as seen in Figure 12.11. This often happens when coverage cells are too large as a result of the access point's radio transmitting at too much power. As mentioned earlier in this chapter, it is a recommended practice to disable the data rates of 1 and 2 Mbps on an 802.11b/g access point if you are planning for capacity. Another reason for disabling those data rates is that a 1 and 2 Mbps coverage cell at 2.4 GHz can be quite large and often results in hidden nodes. If hidden node problems occur in a network planned for coverage, then RTS/CTS may be needed. This will be discussed in detail later.

Another cause of the hidden node problem is distributed antenna systems. Some manufacturers design distributed systems, which are basically made up of a long coaxial cable with multiple antenna elements. Each antenna in the distributed system has its own coverage area. Many companies purchase distributed antenna systems for cost-saving purposes, but a hidden node problem as pictured in Figure 12.12 will almost always occur. Distributed antenna systems and leaky cable systems should always be avoided.

So how do you troubleshoot a hidden node problem? If your end users complain of a degradation of throughput, one possible cause is a hidden node. A protocol analyzer is a useful tool in determining hidden node issues. If the protocol analyzer indicates a high retransmission rate for the MAC address of one station, chances are a hidden node has been found. Some protocol analyzers even have hidden node alarms based on retransmission thresholds. Another way is to use request to send/clear to send (RTS/CTS) to diagnose the problem. Try lowering the RTS/CTS threshold on a suspected hidden node to about 500 bytes. This level may need to be adjusted depending on what type of traffic is being used. For instance, let's say you have deployed a terminal emulation application in a warehouse environment and a hidden node problem exists. In this case, the RTS/CTS threshold should be set for a much lower size, such as 30 bytes. Use a protocol analyzer to determine the appropriate size. As you learned in Chapter 9, RTS/CTS is a method in which client stations can reserve the medium. In Figure 12.13 you see a hidden node initiating an RTS/CTS exchange.

The stations on the other side of the obstacle may not hear the RTS frame, but they will hear the CTS frame sent by the access point. The stations that hear the CTS frame will reset their NAV for the period of time necessary for the hidden node to transmit the data frame and receive its ACK frame. Implementing RTS/CTS on a hidden node will reserve the medium and force all other stations to pause, thus the collisions and retransmissions will stop. Collisions and retransmissions as a result of a hidden node will cause throughput to decrease. RTS/CTS normally decreases throughput as well. However, if RTS/CTS is implemented on a suspected hidden node, throughput will probably increase due to the stoppage of the collisions and retransmissions. If you implement RTS/CTS on a suspected hidden node and throughput increases, you have confirmed the existence of a hidden node. RTS/CTS should normally not be viewed as a mechanism to fix the hidden node problem. RTS/CTS can be a temporary fix for the hidden node problem but should normally just be used for diagnostic purposes. One exception to that rule is Point-to-MultiPoint(PtMP) bridging. The non-root bridges in a PtMP scenario will not be able to hear each other because they are miles apart. RTS/CTS should be implemented on non-root PtMP bridges to eliminate collisions caused by hidden node bridges that cannot hear each other. If non-802.11 bridges are used, this may be an inherent feature.

FIGURE 12.11   Hidden node—large coverage cell

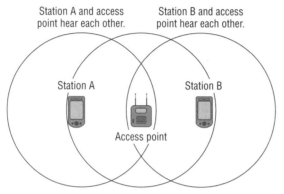

FIGURE 12.12   Hidden node—distributed antenna system

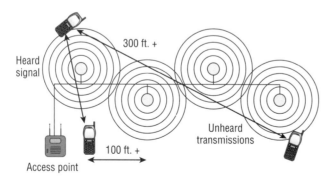

FIGURE 12.13 Hidden node and RTS/CTS

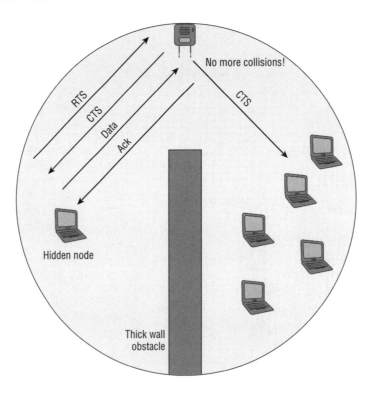

The following methods can be used to fix a hidden node problem:

Use RTS/CTS to diagnose. Use either a protocol analyzer or RTS/CTS to diagnose the hidden node problem.

Increase power to all stations. Most client stations have a fixed transmission power output. However, if power output is adjustable on the client side, increasing the transmission power of client stations will increase the transmission range of each station. If the transmission range of all stations is increased, the likelihood of the stations hearing each other also increases.

Remove the obstacles. If it is determined that some sort of obstacle is preventing client stations from hearing each other, simply removing the obstacle will solve the problem. Obviously, you cannot remove a wall, but if a metal desk or file cabinet is the obstacle, then it can be moved to resolve the problem.

Move the hidden node station. If one or two stations are in an area where they become unheard, simply moving them within transmission range of the other stations will solve the problem.

Add another access point. If moving the hidden nodes is not an option, adding another access point in the hidden area to provide coverage will also rectify the problem.

Near/Far

As stated earlier, most client stations have a fixed power output. However, the transmission power can be configured on some vendors' client radios. A low-powered client station that is a great distance from the access point could potentially become an unheard client if other high-powered stations are very close to the access point. The transmissions of the high-powered stations could raise the noise floor to a higher level that would prevent the lower-powered station from being heard, as seen in Figure 12.14. This scenario is referred to as the *near/far* problem.

FIGURE 12.14   The near/far problem

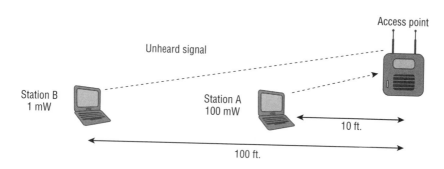

The half-duplex nature of the medium usually prevents most near/far occurrences, but you can troubleshoot near/far with a protocol analyzer by looking at the frame transmissions of the suspected far station. A near/far problem exists if the frame transmissions of the far station are corrupted when listened to with the protocol analyzer near the access point but are not corrupted when listened to with the protocol analyzer near the far station. If a near/far situation does exist, the following solutions can be used to correct the problem:

- Decrease power to the near stations.

- Increase power to the remote station.

- Move the remote station closer to the access point.

- Add another access point near the far node.

Please understand that the medium access methods employed by Carrier Sense Multiple Access with Collision Avoidance (CSMA/CA) usually averts the near/far problem and that it is not as common a problem of, say, hidden node or roaming issues.

Interference

Various types of interference can greatly affect the performance of an 802.11 WLAN. Interfering devices may actually prevent an 802.11 radio from transmitting. If another RF source is transmitting with strong amplitude, an 802.11 radio can sense the energy during the clear channel assessment (CCA) and defer transmission entirely. The other typical result of interference is that 802.11 frame transmissions become corrupted. If frames are corrupted due to interference, there will be excessive retransmissions and therefore throughput will be reduced significantly. There are several different types of interference:

Physical interference Although physical interference is not technically a source of RF interference, physical obstructions can indeed disrupt and corrupt an 802.11 signal. An example of this would be the scattering effect caused by a chain-link fence or safety glass with wire mesh. The signal is scattered and rendered useless. The only way to eliminate physical interference is to remove the obstruction or add more APs.

Narrowband interference A narrowband RF signal occupies a smaller and finite frequency space and will not cause a denial of service (DoS) for an entire band such as the 2.4 GHz ISM band. A narrowband signal is usually very high amplitude and will absolutely disrupt communications in the frequency space in which it is being transmitted. Narrowband signals can disrupt one or several 802.11 channels. The only way to eliminate narrowband interference is to locate the source of the interfering device with a spectrum analyzer. To work around interference, use a spectrum analyzer to determine the affected channels and then design the channel reuse plan around the interfering narrowband signal.

Wideband interference A source of interference is normally considered wideband if the transmitting signal has the capabilities of disrupting the communications of an entire frequency band. Wideband jammers exist that can create a complete DoS for the 2.4 GHz ISM band. The only way to eliminate wideband interference is to locate the source of the interfering device with a spectrum analyzer and remove the interfering device.

All-band interference The term *all-band interference* is normally associated with frequency hopping spread spectrum (FHSS) communications that disrupt HR-DSSS and/or ERP-OFDM channel communications. As you learned in earlier chapters, FHSS constantly hops across an entire band intermittingly transmitting on very small subcarriers of frequency space. A legacy 802.11 FHSS radio, for example, transmits on 1 MHz hops. While hopping and dwelling, an FHSS device will transmit in sections of the frequency space occupied by an HR-DSSS or ERP-OFDM channel. Although a FHSS device will not cause a denial of service, the frame transmissions from the HR-DSSS and ERP-OFDM devices can be corrupted from the all-band transmissions of the FHSS interfering radio. Corruption results in retransmissions, which of course results in decreased throughput. *Bluetooth (BT)* is a short distance RF technology defined by the 802.15 standard. Bluetooth uses FHSS and hops across the 2.4 GHz ISM band at 1,600 hops per second. Older Bluetooth devices were known to cause all-band interference. Newer Bluetooth devices utilize adaptive mechanisms to avoid interfering with 802.11 WLANs. A now-defunct WLAN technology known as HomeRF also used FHSS; therefore HomeRF devices can potentially cause all-band interference. Some other all-band interferers are FHSS cordless phones and FHSS cordless headsets. The only way to eliminate narrowband interference is to locate the source of the interfering device with a spectrum analyzer and remove the interfering device.

Inter-symbol interference As discussed in Chapter 2, *multipath* can cause *inter-symbol interference (ISI)*, which causes data corruption. Because of the difference in time between the primary signal and the reflected signals known as the *delay spread*, along with the fact that there may be multiple reflected signals, the receiver can have problems demodulating the RF signal's information. The delay spread time differential results in corrupted data. Many of the negative effects of multipath, including inter-symbol interference, can be compensated for with the use of antenna diversity, which is covered in Chapter 4. Using unidirectional antennas in areas such as hallways, long corridors, and where metal racks are present can cut down on reflections and hopefully reduce mutipath. ERP-OFDM technology is also more resistant to multipath than DSSS.

 Real World Scenario

What Devices Cause RF Interference?

Numerous devices, including cordless phones, microwave ovens, and fluorescent bulbs, can cause RF interference and degrade the performance of an 802.11 WLAN. The 2.4 GHz ISM band is extremely crowded, with many known interfering devices. Interfering devices also transmit in the 5 GHz UNII bands, but the 2.4 GHz frequency space is much more crowded. Often the biggest source of interference is signals from nearby WLANs. The tool that is necessary to locate sources of interference is a spectrum analyzer. In Chapter 16, we will discuss proper mandatory spectrum analysis that should be part of every wireless site survey. Chapter 16 also lists the many interfering devices that can cause problems in both the 2.4 GHz and 5 GHz frequency ranges.

Performance

When designing and deploying a WLAN, you will always be concerned about both coverage and capacity. Various factors can affect the coverage range of a wireless cell, and just as many factors can affect the aggregate throughput in an 802.11 WLAN. The following variables can affect the *range* of a WLAN:

Transmission power rates   The original transmission amplitude (power) will have an impact on the range of an RF cell. An access point transmitting at 30 mW will have a larger coverage zone than an access point transmitting a 1 mW assuming that the same antenna is used.

Antenna gain   Antennas are passive gain devices that focus the original signal. An access point transmitting at 30 mW with a 6 dBi antenna will have greater range than it would if it used only a 3 dBi antenna.

Antenna type   Antennas have different coverage patterns. Using the right antenna will give the greatest coverage and reduce multipath and nearby interference.

Wavelength   Higher frequency signals have a smaller wavelength property and will attenuate faster than a lower frequency signal with a larger wavelength. 2.4 GHz access points have greater range than 5 GHz access points.

Free space path loss   In any RF environment, free space path loss (FSPL) attenuates the signal as a function of distance and frequency.

Physical environment   Walls and other obstacles will attenuate an RF signal due to absorption and other RF propagation behaviors. A building with concrete walls will require more access points than a building with drywall because concrete is denser and attenuates the signal faster than drywall.

As you have learned in earlier chapters, proper WLAN design must take into account both coverage and capacity. The above-mentioned variables all affect range so therefore also affect coverage. Capacity performance considerations are equally as important as range considerations. Please remember that 802.11 data rates are considered bandwidth and not throughput. The following are among the many variables that can affect the *throughput* of a WLAN:

Carrier Sense Multiple Access/Collision Avoidance (CSMA/CA)   The medium access method that uses interframe spacing, physical carrier sense, virtual carrier sense and the random backoff timer creates overhead and consumes bandwidth. The overhead due to medium contention usually is 50 percent or greater.

Encryption   Extra overhead is added to the body of an 802.11 data frame whenever encryption is implemented. WEP/RC4 encryption adds an extra 8 bytes of overhead per frame, TKIP/RC4 encryption adds an extra 20 bytes of overhead per frame, and CCMP/AES encryption adds an extra 16 bytes of overhead per frame. Layer 3 VPNs often use DES or 3DES encryption, both of which consume significant bandwidth.

Application use   Different types of applications will have variant affects in bandwidth consumption. VoWiFi and data collection scanning typically do not require a lot of bandwidth. Other applications that require file transfers or database access often are more bandwidth intensive.

Number of clients   Remember that the WLAN is a shared medium. All throughput is aggregate and all available bandwidth is shared.

Interference   All types of interference can cause frames to become corrupted. If frames are corrupted, they will need to be retransmitted and throughput will be affected.

Weather

When deploying a wireless mesh network outdoors or perhaps an outdoor bridge link, a WLAN administrator must take into account the adverse affect of weather conditions. The following three weather conditions must be considered:

Lightning   Direct and indirect lightning strikes can damage WLAN equipment. Lightning arrestors should be used for protection against transient currents. Solutions such as lightning rods or copper/fiber transceivers may offer protection against lightning strikes.

Wind   Due to the long distances and narrow beamwidths, highly directional antennas are susceptible to movement or shifting caused by wind. Even slight movement of a highly directional antenna can cause the RF beam to be aimed away from the receiving antenna, interrupting the communications. In high-wind environments, a grid antenna will typically remain more stabile than a parabolic dish. Other mounting options may be necessary to stabilize the antennas from movement.

Water   Conditions such as rain, snow, and fog present two unique challenges. First, all outdoor equipment must be protected from damage from exposure to water. Water damage is often a serious problem with cabling and connectors. Connectors should be protected with drip loops and coax seal to prevent water damage. Cables and connectors should be checked on a regular basis for damage. A radome should be used to protect antennas from water damage. Outdoor bridges, access points, and mesh routers should be protected from the weather elements using appropriate National Electrical Manufacturers Association (NEMA) enclosure units. Precipitation can also cause an RF signal to attenuate. A torrential downpour can attenuate a signal as much as .08 dB per mile (.05 dB per kilometer) in both the 2.4 GHz and 5 GHz frequency ranges. Over long-distance bridge links, a system operating margin (SOM) of 20 dB is usually recommended to compensate for attenuation due to rain or fog or snow.

Air stratification   A change in air temperature at high altitudes is known as air stratification (layering). Changes in air temperature can cause refraction. Bending of RF signals over long-distance point-to-point links can cause misalignment and performance issues. K-factor calculations may be necessary to compensate for refraction over long-distance links.

UV/sun   UV rays and ambient heat from rooftops can damage cables over time unless proper cable types are used.

Summary

In this chapter, we discussed numerous 802.11 coverage considerations. Quite often troubleshooting coverage, capacity, and performance problems can be avoided with proper network design and comprehensive site surveys. However, because wireless should always be considered an ever-changing environment, problems such as roaming, hidden nodes, and interference are bound to surface. Tools such as protocol analyzers and spectrum analyzers are invaluable when troubleshooting both layer 2 and layer 1 problems. We also discussed the many performance variables that can affect both range and throughput. Finally, we discussed weather conditions that can impact outdoor RF communications and what steps might be necessary for protection against Mother Nature.

Exam Essentials

Define dynamic rate switching.   Understand that process of stations shifting between data rates. Know that dynamic rate switching is also referred to as dynamic rate shifting, adaptive rate selection, and automatic rate selection. Explain why disabling the two lower 802.11b/g data rates is often recommended.

Explain the various aspects of roaming.   Understand that roaming is proprietary in nature. Know the variables that client stations may use when imitating the roaming process. Understand the importance of proper coverage cell overlap. Describe latency issues that can occur with roaming. Understand why crossing layer 3 boundaries can cause problems and what solutions might exist.

Define co-channel interference.   Understand the negative effects of co-channel interference and explain why channel reuse patterns minimize the problem. Know what to consider when designing channel reuse patterns at both 2.4 GHz and 5 GHz.

Identify the various types of interference.   Know the differences between all-band, narrowband, wideband, physical, and inter-symbol interference. Understand that a spectrum analyzer is your best interference troubleshooting tool.

Explain the hidden node problem.   Identify all the potential causes of the hidden node problem. Explain how to troubleshoot hidden node as well as how to fix the hidden node problem.

Define the near/far problem.   Explain what causes near/far and how the problem can be rectified.

Identify performance variables.   Explain all the variables that affect both the range of RF coverage and the throughput that can result within a basic service set.

Understand the consequences of weather conditions.   Explain the problems that might arise due to water conditions, wind, lightning, and air stratification. Explain how these problems might be solved.

Key Terms

Before you take the exam, be certain you are familiar with the following terms:

all-band interference	layer 3 roaming
Bluetooth (BT)	Mobile IP
channel reuse	multipath
co-channel interference (CCI)	near/far
dynamic rate switching (DRS)	range
fast secure roaming (FSR)	roaming
hidden node	throughput
inter-symbol interference (ISI)	

Review Questions

1. What type of solution must be deployed to provide continuous connectivity when a client station roams across layer 3 boundaries? (Choose all that apply.)

    A. Nomadic roaming solution

    B. Proprietary layer 3 roaming solution

    C. Seamless roaming solution

    D. Mobile IP solution

    E. Fast secure roaming solution

2. Mr. Harkin, the WLAN administrator at the ACME Company, discovers that water has damaged some coaxial cables to one of the company's outdoor wireless bridges. He replaces the cabling but soon discovers that the equivalent isotropically radiated power (EIRP) leaving the bridge antenna now exceeds the power output limit of his nation's regulatory body. What might have happened? (Choose all that apply.)

    A. Water also damaged the wireless bridge

    B. He installed a shorter cable

    C. He installed higher-grade cabling

    D. He installed lower-grade cabling

    E. The old cable was 50 ohms and the new cable is 75 ohms

3. What variables might affect range in an 802.11 WLAN? (Choose all that apply.)

    A. Transmission power

    B. CSMA/CA

    C. Encryption

    D. Antenna gain

    E. Physical environment

4. What can be done to fix the hidden node problem? (Choose all that apply.)

    A. Increase the power on the access point.

    B. Move the hidden node station

    C. Increase power on all client stations

    D. Remove the obstacle

    E. Decrease power on the hidden node station

5. Have much cell overlap is typically needed for seamless roaming?

    A. 25 to 50 percent

    B. 15 to 20 percent

    C. 50 percent

    D. 15 to 30 percent

    E. 5 to 10 percent

6. What scenarios might result in a hidden node problem? (Choose all that apply.)

   A. Distributed antenna system

   B. Too large coverage cell

   C. Too small coverage cell

   D. Physical obstacle

   E. Co-channel interference

7. Which of these devices are potential sources of all-band interference? (Choose all that apply.)

   A. Bluetooth

   B. Microwave oven

   C. 2.4 GHz DSSS cordless phone

   D. 802.11 FHSS access point

   E. HomeRF access point

8. What variables might affect throughput in an 802.11 WLAN? (Choose all that apply.)

   A. Wavelength

   B. CSMA/CA

   C. Free space path loss

   D. Application use

   E. Number of clients

9. How many channels are considered non-overlapping in the 5 GHz UNII bands?

   A. 3

   B. 12

   C. 11

   D. 23

   E. 6

10. What type of interference is caused by overlapping frequencies within overlapping coverage cells?

    A. Inter-symbol interference

    B. Physical interference

    C. All-band interference

    D. Narrowband interference

    E. Co-channel interference

11. Concentric zones of variable rate bandwidth coverage exists around an access point due to the upshifting and downshifting of client radio cards between data rates. What is the name of this process? (Choose all that apply.)

    A. Dynamic rate shifting

    B. Dynamic rate switching

    C. Automatic rate selection

    D. Adaptive rate selection

    E. All of the above

12. Which of these weather conditions is a concern when deploying a long-distance point-to-point bridge link? (Choose all that apply.)

    A. Wind

    B. Rain

    C. Fog

    D. Changes in air temperature.

    E. All of the above

13. What variables might affect range in an 802.11 WLAN? (Choose all that apply.)

    A. Wavelength

    B. Free space path loss

    C. Brick walls

    D. Trees

    E. All of the above

14. What actions might be taken to diagnose a hidden node problem? (Choose all that apply.)

    A. Use RTS/CTS

    B. Use a spectrum analyzer

    C. Use a protocol analyzer

    D. Use CSMA/CA

    E. Use fragmentation

15. Which of the following can cause roaming problems? (Choose all that apply.)

    A. Too little cell coverage overlap

    B. Too much cell coverage overlap

    C. Free space path loss

    D. CSMA/CA

    E. Hidden node

16. What methods can be used to mitigate the near/far problem? (Choose all that apply.)

    A. Increase power to the near stations

    B. Decrease power to the remote station

    C. Increase power to the remote station

    D. Decrease power to the near stations

    E. Increase power to all stations

17. Why would a WLAN network administrator consider disabling the two lowest rates on an 802.11b/g access point? (Choose all that apply.)

    A. Medium contention

    B. CSMA/CA

    C. Hidden node

    D. Co-channel interference

    E. All of the above

18. Which type of interference is cause by multipath?

    A. Inter-symbol interference

    B. All-band interference

    C. Narrowband interference

    D. Wideband interference

    E. Physical interference

19. What is the greatest number of non-overlapping channels that can be deployed in the 2.4 GHz ISM band?

    A. 3

    B. 12

    C. 11

    D. 14

    E. 4

20. What methods can be used to mitigate the near/far problem? (Choose all that apply.)

    A. Move the near stations farther away from the access point.

    B. Add another access point near the far node.

    C. Move the remote station near the access point.

    D. Add another access point by the near stations.

    E. None of the above

Answers to Review Questions

1. B, D. The only way to maintain upper-layer communications when crossing layer 3 subnets is to provide either a Mobile IP solution or a proprietary layer 3 roaming solution.

2. B, C. The shorter cable will result in less power loss and could exceed power output regulations. Cabling is rated for dB loss per 100 feet. If he installed a higher-grade cable that is rated for less loss per 100 feet, this could also exceed power output regulations.

3. A, D, E. The original transmission amplitude will have an impact on the range of an RF cell. Antennas amplify signal strength and can increase range. Walls and other obstacles will attenuate an RF signal and affect range. CSMA/CA and encryption do not affect range but do affect throughput.

4. B, C, D. The hidden node problem arises when client stations cannot hear the RF transmissions of another client station. Increasing the transmission power of client stations will increase the transmission range of each station, resulting in increased likelihood of all the stations hearing each other. Moving the hidden node station within transmission range of the other stations also results in stations hearing each other. Removing an obstacle that prevents stations from hearing each other also fixes the problem.

5. B. Most manufacturers have their own recommendations on what is needed for coverage cell overlap in regard to roaming, but 15 to 20 percent cell overlap is usually recommended.

6. A, B, D. The hidden node problem arises when client stations cannot hear the RF transmissions of another client station. Distributed antenna systems with multiple antenna elements are notorious for causing the hidden node problem. When coverage cells are too large as a result of the access point's radio transmitting at too much power, client stations at opposite ends of an RF coverage cell often cannot hear each other. Obstacles such as a newly constructed wall can also result in stations not hearing each other.

7. A, D, E. All the devices listed are known sources of RF interference in the 2.4 GHz ISM band. All-band interference is caused by frequency hopping radio transmissions. FHSS is used by Bluetooth, legacy 802.11 FHSS access points, and HomeRF equipment.

8. B, D, E. Carrier Sense Multiple Access/Collision Avoidance (CSMA/CA) is the medium contention method than can create 50 percent or greater overhead, affecting throughput. Certain applications are bandwidth intensive and can affect throughput. A WLAN is a shared medium and all throughput is aggregate. All available bandwidth is shared by all associated client stations. The wavelength property of an RF signal and free space path loss affect range.

9. B. The 802.11a amendment requires 20 MHz of separation between the center frequencies of ERP-OFDM channels in the 5 GHz UNII bands to be considered non-overlapping. There are 4 channels each of the three UNII bands, each with 20 MHz of separation for a total of 12 non-overlapping channels. In the future, 11 more channels may be used by 802.11a radios.

10. E. Overlapping coverage cells with overlapping frequencies causes co-channel interference (CCI), which causes a severe degradation in performance and throughput. If overlapping coverage cells also have frequency overlap, frames will become corrupt, retransmissions will increase, and throughput will suffer significantly.

11. E. As client station radios move away from an access point, they will shift down to lower bandwidth capabilities using a process known as dynamic rate switching (DRS). The objective of DRS is upshifting and downshifting for rate optimization and improved performance. Although dynamic rate switching is the proper name for this process, all these terms refer to the method of speed fallback a wireless LAN client uses as distance increases from the access point.

12. E. Highly directional antennas are susceptible to what is known as "antenna wind loading," which is antenna movement or shifting caused by wind. Grid antennas may be needed to alleviate the problem. Rain and fog can attenuate an RF signal; therefore, a system operating margin (also known as fade margin) of 20 dB is necessary. A change in air temperature is also known as air stratification, which causes refraction. K-factor calculations may also be necessary to compensate for refraction.

13. E. Higher-frequency signals have a smaller wavelength property and will attenuate faster than a lower-frequency signal with a larger wavelength. Higher-frequency signals therefore will have shorter range. In any RF environment, free space path loss (FSL) attenuates the signal as a function of distance. Loss in signal strength affects range. Brick walls exist in an indoor physical environment, while trees exist in an outdoor physical environment. Both will attenuate an RF signal, thereby affecting range.

14. A, C. If the protocol analyzer indicates a high retransmission rate for one MAC address of one station, chances are a hidden node has been found. Some protocol analyzers even have hidden node alarms based on retransmission thresholds. If RTS/CTS if implemented on a suspected hidden node, throughput will probably increase due to the stoppage of the collisions and retransmissions. RTS/CTS can be used to confirm the existence of a hidden node.

15. A, B. Roaming problems will occur if there is not enough overlap in cell coverage. Too little overlap will effectively create a roaming dead zone and connectivity may even temporarily be lost. If two RF cells have too much overlap, a station may stay associated with its original AP and not connect to a second access point even though the station is directly underneath the second access point.

16. C, D. A low-powered client station that is a great distance from the access point could potentially become an unheard client if other high-powered stations are very close to the access point. The transmissions of the high-powered stations could raise the noise floor to a higher level where the lower-powered station cannot be heard. Increasing the power of the remote station and/or decreasing the power of the near stations will result in the remote station's transmissions once again being heard.

17. A, B, C. Medium contention, also known as CSMA/CA, requires that all radios access the medium in a pseudo-random fashion. Radio cards transmitting at slower data rates will occupy the medium much longer, while faster radio have to wait. Dates rates of 1 and 2 Mbps can create very large coverage cells, which may prevent a hidden node station at one edge of the cell from being heard by other client stations at the opposite side of the coverage cell.

18. A. Multipath can cause inter-symbol interference (ISI), which causes data corruption. Because of the difference in time between the primary signal and the reflected signals, known as the delay spread, the receiver can have problems demodulating the RF signal's information. The delay spread time differential results in corrupted data.

19. A. The 802.11b and 802.11g amendments require 25 MHz of separation between the center frequencies of HR-DSSS channels to be considered non-overlapping. The 802.11g amendment also requires 20 MHz of separation between the center frequencies of ERP-OFDM channels. The three channels 1, 6, and 11 meet these requirements.

20. B, C. A low-powered client station that is a great distance from the access point could potentially become an unheard client if other high-powered stations are very close to the access point. The transmissions of the high-powered stations could raise the noise floor to a higher level where the lower powered station cannot be heard. Moving the remote station closer to the access point will result in the remote station's transmissions once again being heard. Adding another access point in the area of the remote stations will provide a new coverage zone.

Chapter 13

802.11 Network Security Architecture

IN THIS CHAPTER, YOU WILL LEARN ABOUT THE FOLLOWING

- ✓ **802.11 Security Basics**
  - Encryption
  - AAA
  - Segmentation
- ✓ **Legacy 802.11 Security**
  - Legacy Authentication
  - Static WEP Encryption
  - MAC Filters
  - SSID Cloaking
- ✓ **Authentication and Authorization**
  - 802.1X/EAP Framework
  - EAP Types
  - Dynamic Encryption Key Generation
- ✓ **WPA/802.11i**
  - Robust Security Network (RSN)
  - 4-Way Handshake
  - WPA/WPA2 Personal
  - TKIP
  - CCMP

✓ **Segmentation**
  - VLANs
  - RBAC

✓ **Infrastructure Security**
  - Physical Security
  - Interface Security

✓ **VPN Wireless Security**
  - Layer 3 VPNs

In the next two chapters you will learn about what is probably the most often discussed topic in terms of 802.11 wireless networks… security. In this chapter, we will discuss legacy 802.11 security solutions as well as more robust solutions that are now defined by the 802.11i security amendment. Although there is no such thing as 100 percent security, solutions do exist that can help fortify and protect your wireless network. Numerous wireless security risks exist, and in Chapter 14, "Wireless Attacks, Intrusion Monitoring, and Policy," you will learn about many of the potential attacks that can be attempted against an 802.11 wireless network and how these attacks can be monitored.

Many of the attacks against an 802.11 network can be defended against with proper implementation of the security architectures that are discussed in this chapter. However, many attacks cannot be mitigated and can merely be monitored and hopefully responded to. While 16 percent of the CWNA exam covers 802.11 security, the CWNP program also offers another certification titled Certified Wireless Security Professional (CWSP), which focuses just on the topic of wireless security. The CWSP certification exam requires a more in-depth understanding of 802.11 security; however, the next two chapters will give you a foundation of wireless security that should help you pass the security portions of the CWNA exam as well as a head start in the knowledge you will need to implement proper wireless security.

802.11 Security Basics

When you're securing a wireless 802.11 network, three major components are normally required:

- Strong encryption
- Mutual authentication
- Segmentation

Because data is transmitted freely and openly in the air, proper protection is needed to ensure data privacy, so strong encryption is needed. The function of most wireless networks is to provide a portal into some other network infrastructure, such as an 802.3 Ethernet backbone. The wireless portal must be protected and therefore an authentication solution is needed to ensure that only authorized users may pass through the portal via a wireless access point. The wireless network should always be treated as untrusted and should also be segmented in some fashion from the wired infrastructure.

Encryption

802.11 wireless networks operate in license-free frequency bands and all data transmissions travel in the open air. Protecting data privacy in a wired network is much easier because physical access to the wired medium is more restricted. However, physical access to wireless transmissions is available to anyone in listening range. Therefore, using cipher encryption technologies to obscure information is mandatory. A cipher is an algorithm used to perform encryption.

The two most common algorithms used to protect data are the *RC4* algorithm (RC stands for Ron's Code or Rivest's Cipher) and the Advanced Encryption Standard (AES) algorithm. Some ciphers encrypt data in a continuous stream while others encrypt data in blocks. The RC4 algorithm is a streaming cipher used in technologies that are often used to protect Internet traffic, such as Secure Sockets Layer (SSL). The RC4 algorithm is used to protect 802.11 wireless data and is incorporated into two encryption methods known as WEP and TKIP, both of which will be discussed later in this chapter. The AES algorithm, originally named the Rijndael algorithm, is a block cipher that offers much stronger protection than the RC4 streaming cipher. AES is used to encrypt 802.11 wireless data using an encryption method known as Counter mode with Cipher Block Chaining–Message Authentication Code (CCMP), which will also be discussed later in this chapter. The AES algorithm encrypts data in fixed data blocks with choices in encryption key strength of 128, 192, or 256 bits. The AES cipher is the mandated algorithm of the United States government for protecting both sensitive and classified information.

In Chapter 8, you learned about the three major types of 802.11 wireless frames. The bodies of management frames contain layer 2 information necessary for the operation of the 802.11 network and therefore are not encrypted. Control frames have no body and also are not encrypted. The information that needs to be protected is the upper-layer information inside the body of 802.11 data frames. Most of the encryption methods discussed in this chapter use layer 2 encryption, which is used to protect the layer 3 through 7 information found inside the body of an 802.11 data frame.

AAA

AAA is a computer security concept that refers to authentication, authorization, and accounting. Authentication is the verification of user identity and credentials. Users must identify themselves and present credentials such as usernames and passwords or digital certificates. More-secure authentication systems exist that require multifactor authentication, where at least two sets of different credentials must be presented.

Authorization involves granting access to network resources and services. Before authorization to network resources can be granted, proper authentication must occur.

Accounting is tracking the use of network resources by users. It is an important aspect of network security, used to keep a paper trail of who used what resource and when and where. A record is kept of user identity, which resource was accessed, and at what time. Keeping an accounting trail is often a requirement of many industry regulations such as the Health Insurance Portability and Accountability Act of 1996 (HIPAA).

Remember that the usual purpose of an 802.11 access point is to act as a portal into an 802.3 wired network. It is therefore necessary to protect that portal with very strong authentication methods so that only legitimate users with the proper credentials will be authorized onto network resources.

Segmentation

While it is of the utmost importance to secure an enterprise wireless network utilizing both strong encryption and an AAA solution, an equally important aspect of wireless security is segmentation. Prior to the introduction of stronger authentication and encryption techniques, wireless was viewed as an untrusted network segment. Therefore, before the ratification of the 802.11i security amendment, the wireless segment of a network was always treated as the untrusted segment while the wired 802.3 network was considered the trusted segment. However, if the proper encryption and authentication solutions are deployed, the wireless network can be just as secure if not more so than the wired segments of a network. It is still important to segment users in proper groups, much like what is done on any traditional network. Once authorized onto network resources, users can be further restricted as to what resources may be accessed and where they can go. Segmentation can be achieved through a variety of means, including firewalls, routers, VPNs, and VLANs. The most common wireless segmentation strategy often used in 802.11 enterprise WLANs is layer 3 segmentation using Virtual LANs (VLANs). Segmentation is often intertwined with role-based access control (RBAC), which is discussed later in this chapter.

Legacy 802.11 Security

The original 802.11 standard defined very little in terms of security. The authentication methods first outlined in 1997 basically provided an open door into the network infrastructure. The encryption method defined in the original 802.11 standard has long been cracked and is considered inadequate for data privacy. In the following sections, you will learn about the legacy authentication and encryption methods that were the only defined standards for 802.11 wireless security from 1997 until 2004. Later in this chapter, you will learn about the more-robust security that has been defined in the *802.11i* security amendment.

Legacy Authentication

You have already learned about legacy authentication in Chapter 8. The original 802.11 standard specifies two different methods of authentication: Open System authentication and Shared Key authentication. Open System authentication provides authentication without performing any type of client verification. It is essentially a two-way exchange between the client and the access point. The client sends an authentication request and the access point then sends an authentication response. Because Open System authentication does not require the use of any credentials, every client gets authenticated and therefore authorized onto network resources once they have been associated. Static WEP encryption is optional with Open System authentication but may be used to encrypt the data frames after Open System authentication and association occur.

As you learned in Chapter 8, Shared Key authentication uses Wired Equivalent Privacy (WEP) to authenticate client stations and requires that a static WEP key be configured on both the station and the access point. In addition to WEP being mandatory, authentication will not work if the static WEP keys do not match. The authentication process is similar to Open System authentication but includes a challenge and response between the radio cards. Shared Key authentication is a four-way authentication frame handshake. The client station sends an authentication request to the access point and then the access point sends a cleartext challenge to the client station in an authentication response. The client station then encrypts the cleartext challenge and sends it back to the access point in the body of another authentication request frame. The access point decrypts the station's response and compares it to the challenge text. If they match, the access point will respond by sending a fourth and final authentication frame to the station confirming the success. If they do not match, the access point will respond negatively. If the access point cannot decrypt the challenge, it will also respond negatively. If Shared Key authentication is successful, the same static WEP key that was used during the Shared Key authentication process will also be used to encrypt the 802.11 data frames.

Although it might seem that Shared Key authentication is a more secure solution than Open System authentication, in reality Shared Key could be the bigger security risk. Anyone who captures the cleartext challenge phrase and then captures the encrypted challenge phrase in the response frame could potentially derive the static WEP key. If the static WEP key is compromised, then a whole new can of worms has been opened because now all the data frames can be decrypted. Neither of the legacy authentication methods is considered strong enough for enterprise security. More-secure 802.1X/EAP authentication methods will be discussed later in this chapter.

Static WEP Encryption

Wired Equivalent Privacy (WEP) is a layer 2 encryption method that uses the RC4 streaming cipher. The original 802.11 standard defined 64-bit WEP as the default encryption method. The three main intended goals of WEP encryption include confidentiality, access control, and data integrity. The primary goal of confidentiality was to provide data privacy by encrypting the data before transmission. WEP also provides access control, which is basically a crude form of authorization. Client stations that do not have the same matching static key as an access point are refused access to network resources. A data integrity checksum known as the Integrity Check Value (ICV) is computed on data before encryption and used to prevent data from being modified.

While 64-bit WEP is defined by the 802.11 standard, once the U.S. government loosened export restrictions on key size, radio card manufacturers began to produce equipment that used 128-bit WEP encryption. Because 128-bit WEP encryption is not defined by the standard, there is a small chance that equipment from different vendors using 128-bit WEP will not be compatible. As pictured in Figure 13.1, 64-bit WEP uses a secret 40-bit static key, which is combined with a 24-bit number that is selected by the card's device drivers. This 24-bit number, known as the *Initialization Vector (IV)*, is sent in cleartext and is different on every frame. Although the IV is said to be different on every frame, there are only 16,777,216 different IV combinations, therefore you are forced to reuse the IV values. The effective key strength of combining the IV with the 40-bit static key is 64 bit encryption. 128-bit WEP encryption uses a 104-bit secret static key that is also combined with a 24-bit Initialization Vector.

A static WEP key can be entered as hexadecimal (hex) characters (0–9 and A–F) or ASCII characters. The static key must match on both the access point and the client device. A 40-bit static key consists of 10 hex characters or 5 ASCII characters, while a 104-bit static key consists of 26 hex characters or 13 ASCII characters. Not all client stations or access points support both hex and ASCII. Most clients and access points support the use of up to four separate static WEP keys from which a user can choose as the default transmission key (Figure 13.2 shows an example). The transmission key is the static key that is used to encrypt data by the transmitting radio. A client or access point may use one key to encrypt outbound traffic and a different key to decrypt received traffic. However, all keys much match exactly on both sides of a link for encryption/decryption to work properly.

FIGURE 13.1   Static WEP encryption key and Initialization Vector

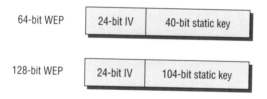

FIGURE 13.2   Transmission Key

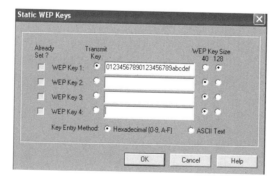

How does WEP work? WEP runs a cyclic redundancy check (CRC) on the plaintext data that is to be encrypted and then appends the Integrity Check Value (ICV) to the end of the plaintext data. A 24-bit cleartext Initialization Vector (IV) is then generated and combined with the static secret key. WEP then uses both the static key and the IV as seeding material through a pseudo-random algorithm that generates random bits of data known as a key-stream. These pseudo-random bits are equal in length to the plaintext data that is to be encrypted. The pseudo-random bits in the keystream are then combined with the plaintext data bits using a Boolean XOR process. The end result is the WEP ciphertext, which is the encrypted data. The encrypted data is then prefixed with the cleartext IV. Figure 13.3 illustrates this process.

Unfortunately, WEP has quite a few weaknesses, including the following four main attacks:

IV collisions attack   Because the 24-bit Initialization Vector is in cleartext and is different in every frame, in a busy WEP encrypted network, all 16 million IVs will eventually repeat themselves. Due to the limited size of the IV space, IV collisions occur, and an attacker can recover the secret key much easier when IV collisions occur in wireless networks.

Weak key attack   Due to the RC4 key-scheduling algorithm, weak IV keys are generated. An attacker can recover the secret key much easier by recovering the known weak IV keys.

FIGURE 13.3   WEP Encryption Process

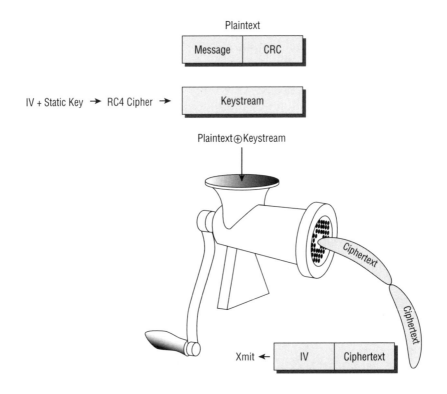

Re-injection attack   Hacker tools exist that implement a packet re-injection attack to accelerate the collection of weak IVs on a network with little traffic.

Bit-flipping attack   The ICV data integrity check is considered weak. WEP encrypted packets can be tampered with.

Current WEP cracking tools may use a combination of the first three mentioned attacks and can crack WEP in less than 5 minutes time. Once an attacker has compromised the static WEP key, any data frame can be decrypted with the newly discovered key. Later in this chapter we will discuss TKIP, which is an enhancement of WEP and currently has not been cracked. CCMP encryption uses the AES algorithm and is an even stronger encryption method. As defined by the original 802.11 standard, WEP encryption is considered optional and is not required. Although WEP encryption has indeed been cracked and is viewed as unacceptable in the enterprise, it is still better than using no encryption at all.

MAC Filters

Every network card has a physical address known as a MAC address. This address is a 12-digit hexadecimal number. 802.11 client stations each have unique MAC addresses, and as you have already learned, 802.11 access points use MAC addresses to direct frame traffic. Most vendors provide MAC filtering capabilities on their access points. MAC filters can be configured to either allow or deny traffic from specific MAC addresses.

Most MAC filters apply restrictions that will allow traffic only from specific client stations to pass through based on their unique MAC addresses. Any other client stations whose MAC addresses are not on the allowed list will not be able to pass traffic through the virtual port of the access point and onto the distribution system medium. It should be noted that MAC addresses can be "spoofed," or impersonated, and any amateur hacker can easily bypass any MAC filter by spoofing an allowed client station's address. Because of spoofing and because of all the administrative work that is involved with setting up MAC filters, MAC filtering is not considered a reliable means of security for wireless enterprise networks. The 802.11 standard does not define MAC filtering and any implementation of MAC filtering is vendor specific.

SSID Cloaking

Remember in *Star Trek* when the Klingons "cloaked" their spaceship but somehow Captain Kirk always found the ship anyway? Well there is a way to "cloak" your service set identifier (SSID). Access points typically have a setting called Closed Network or Broadcast SSID. By either enabling a closed network or disabling the broadcast SSID feature, you can hide, or cloak, your wireless network name. When you implement a closed network, the SSID field in the beacon frame is null (empty), and therefore passive scanning will not reveal the SSID to client stations that are listening to beacons.

Many wireless client software utilities transmit probe requests with null SSID fields when actively scanning for access points. Additionally, there is a very popular and freely available software program called NetStumbler that is used by individuals to discover wireless networks.

NetStumbler also sends out null probe requests actively scanning for access points. When you implement a closed network, the access point responds to null probe requests with null probe responses, and therefore the SSID is hidden to client stations that are using active scanning. Effectively, your wireless network is temporarily invisible, or cloaked. An access point in a closed network will respond to any configured client station that transmits probe requests with the properly configured SSID. This ensures that legitimate end users will be able to authenticate and associate to the AP. However, any stations that are not configured with the correct SSID will not be able to authenticate or associate. Although implementing a closed network will indeed hide your SSID from NetStumbler and other WLAN discovery tools, anyone with a layer 2 wireless protocol analyzer can capture the frames transmitted by any legitimate end user and discover the SSID, which is transmitted in cleartext. In other words, a hidden SSID can be found usually in seconds with the proper tools. Many wireless professionals will argue that hiding the SSID is a waste of time, while others view a closed network as just another layer of security.

While you can hide your SSID to cloak the identity of your wireless network from novice hackers (often referred to as script kiddies) and non-hackers, it should be clearly understood that SSID cloaking is by no means an end-all wireless security solution. The 802.11 standard does not define SSID cloaking, and therefore all implementations of a closed network are vendor specific. As a result, incompatibility can potentially cause connectivity problems with older legacy cards or when using cards from mixed vendors on your own network. Be sure to know the capabilities of your devices before implementing a closed network.

Authentication and Authorization

As you learned earlier in the chapter, authentication is the verification of user identity and credentials. Users must identify themselves and present credentials such as passwords or digital certificates. Authorization involves granting access to network resources and services. Before authorization to network resources can be granted, proper authentication must occur.

The following sections detail more advanced authentication and authorization defenses. You will also learn that dynamic encryption capabilities are also possible as a byproduct of these stronger authentication solutions.

802.1X/EAP Framework

The IEEE *802.1X* standard is not specifically a wireless standard and often is mistakenly referred to as 802.11x. The 802.1X standard is a *port-based access control* standard. 802.1X provides an authorization framework that allows or disallows traffic to pass through a port and thereby access network resources. An 802.1X framework may be implemented in either a wireless or wired environment. The 802.1X framework consists of three main components:

Supplicant   A host with software that is requesting authentication and access to network resources.

Authenticator   A device that blocks or allows traffic to pass through its port entity. Authentication traffic is normally allowed to pass through the authenticator while all other traffic is blocked until the identity of the supplicant has been verified. The authenticator maintains two virtual ports: an uncontrolled port and a controlled port. The uncontrolled port allows EAP authentication traffic to pass through, while the controlled port blocks all other traffic until the supplicant has been authenticated.

Authentication server (AS)   A server that validates the credentials of the supplicant that is requesting access and notifies the authenticator that the supplicant has been authorized. The authentication server will maintain a user database or may proxy with an external user database to authenticate user credentials.

Within an 802.3 Ethernet network, the supplicant would be a desktop host, the authenticator would be a managed switch, and the authentication server would normally be a Remote Authentication Dial-In User Service (RADIUS) server. In an 802.11 wireless environment, the supplicant would be a client station requesting access to network resources. An access point or wireless switch would be the authenticator, blocking access via virtual ports. The AS is typically a RADIUS server.

Although the *supplicant*, *authenticator*, and *authentication server* work together to provide the framework for 802.1X port-based access control, an authentication protocol is needed to actually perform the authentication process. *Extensible Authentication Protocol (EAP)* is used to provide user authentication. EAP is a flexible layer 2 authentication protocol that resides under Point-to-Point Protocol (PPP). The supplicant and the authentication server communicate with each other using the EAP protocol. The authenticator allows the EAP traffic to pass through its virtual uncontrolled port. Once the AS has verified the credentials of the supplicant, the server sends a message to the authenticator that the supplicant has been authenticated and the authenticator is now authorized to open the virtual controlled port, allowing all other traffic to pass through. Figure 13.4 depicts the generic 802.1X/EAP frame exchanges.

FIGURE 13.4   802.1X/EAP authentication

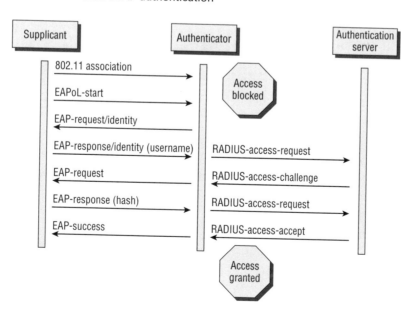

The 802.1X/EAP framework, when used with wireless networks, provides the necessary means of validating user identity as well as authorizing client stations onto the wired network infrastructure.

EAP Types

EAP stands for Extensible Authentication Protocol. The key word in EAP is *Extensible*. The protocol is very flexible, and many different flavors of EAP exist. Some, such as Cisco's Lightweight Extensible Authentication Protocol (LEAP), are proprietary, while others, such as Protected Extensible Authentication Protocol (PEAP), are considered standard-based. Some may provide for only one-way authentication, while others provide two-way authentication. Mutual authentication not only requires that the authentication server validate the client credentials, but the supplicant must also authenticate the validity of the authentication server. Most types of EAP that require mutual authentication use a server-side digital certificate to validate the authentication server. In Table 13.1 you will find a comparison chart of many of the various types of EAP. The CWNA exam will not test you on any individual types of EAP authentication.

TABLE 13.1   EAP Comparison Chart

	EAP-MD5	EAP-LEAP	EAP-TLS	TTLS (EAP-MSCHAPv2)	PEAP (EAP-MSCHAPv2)	PEAP (EAP-TLS)	PEAP (EAP-GTC)	EAP-FAST
Security Solution	RFC-2284	Cisco Proprietary	RFC-2716	IETF Draft	IETF Draft	IETF Draft	IETF Draft	IETF Draft
Digital Certificates - Client	No	No	Yes	No	No	Yes	No	No
Digital Certificates - Server	No	No	Yes	Yes	Yes	Yes	Yes	No
Client Password Authentication	No	Yes	N/A	Yes	Yes	No	Yes	Yes
PACs - Client	No	No	No	No	No	No	No	Yes
PACs - Server	No	No	No	No	No	No	No	Yes

TABLE 13.1   EAP Comparison Chart *(continued)*

	EAP-MD5	EAP-LEAP	EAP-TLS	TTLS (EAP-MSCHAPv2)	PEAP (EAP-MSCHAPv2)	PEAP (EAP-TLS)	PEAP (EAP-GTC)	EAP-FAST
Credential Security	Weak	Weak (depends on password strength)	Strong	Strong	Strong	Strong	Strong	Strong (if Phase 0 is secure)
Encryption Key Management	No	Yes	Yes	Yes	Yes	Yes	Yes	Yes
Mutual Authentication	No	Yes	Yes	Yes	Yes	Yes	Yes	Yes
Tunneled Authentication	No	No	Yes	Yes	Yes	Yes	Yes	Yes
Works with Wi-Fi Protected Access (WPA)	No	Yes	Yes	Yes	Yes	Yes	Yes	Yes
Man-in-the-Middle Protection	No	Yes	Yes	Yes	Yes	Yes	No	Yes
Dictionary Attack Resistance	No	No	Yes	Yes	Yes	N/A	Yes	N/A
Identity Exposed	N/A	Yes	Yes	No	Depends on implementation	No	No	No

Dynamic Encryption Key Generation

Although the 802.1X/EAP framework does not require encryption, it highly suggests the use of encryption. A side benefit of EAP protocols that utilize mutual authentication is the generation and distribution of dynamic encryption keys. Until now, you have learned about only static or preshared WEP keys. The use of static keys is typically an administrative nightmare, and when the same static key is shared between multiple users, the secret is easy to compromise via social engineering.

After an EAP frame exchange where mutual authentication is required, both the AS and the supplicant now know information about each other due to the exchange of credentials. This new-found information is used as seeding material or keying material to generate a matching dynamic encryption key for both the supplicant and the authentication server. These dynamic keys are generated *per session per user*, meaning that every time a client station authenticates, a new key is generated and every user has a unique and separate key. This dynamic session key is often referred to as the *unicast key* because it is the dynamically generated key that is used to encrypt and decrypt all unicast data frames. After the key is created, the AS delivers its copy of the unicast key to the access point. The access point and the client station now both have unique unicast keys that can be used. A second static key exists on the access point known as the *broadcast key*. The broadcast key is used to encrypt and decrypt all broadcast and multicast data frames. Each client station has a unique and separate unicast key, but every station must share the same broadcast key. The broadcast key is delivered from the access point in a unicast frame encrypted with each individual client station's unicast key.

Is Dynamic WEP Encryption Secure?

The generation and distribution of dynamic WEP keys as a byproduct of the EAP authentication process has many benefits and is preferable to the use of static WEP keys. Static keys are no longer used and do not have to be entered manually. Also, every user has a separate and independent key. If a user's dynamic unicast key was compromised, only that one user's traffic could be decrypted. However, a dynamic WEP key can still be cracked, and if compromised, it can indeed be used to decrypt data frames. Dynamic WEP still has risks. Please understand that dynamic WEP is not the same as 802.11i dynamic key management. The 802.11i security amendment defines the creation of stronger and safer dynamic TKIP/RC4 or CCMP/AES encryption keys that can also be generated as a byproduct of the EAP authentication process.

WPA/802.11i

In 2004, the 802.11i security amendment was ratified. The 802.11i amendment defines an enterprise authentication method as well as a method of authentication for home use. The 802.11i amendment requires the use of an 802.1X/EAP authentication method in the enterprise and the use of a preshared key or a passphrase in a SOHO environment. The 802.11i amendment also requires the use of stronger dynamic key management encryption methods. CCMP/AES encryption is the default encryption method, while TKIP/RC4 is the optional encryption method as defined by the 802.11i amendment.

Prior to the ratification of the 802.11i amendment, the Wi-Fi Alliance introduced the *Wi-Fi Protected Access (WPA)* certification as a snapshot of the not-yet-released 802.11i amendment, supporting only TKIP/RC4 dynamic encryption key management. 802.1X/EAP authentication was required in the enterprise and passphrase authentication in a SOHO environment.

After 802.11i was ratified, the Wi-Fi Alliance introduced the WPA2 certification. WPA2 is a more complete implementation of the 802.11i amendment and supports both CCMP/AES and TKIP/RC4 dynamic encryption key management. 802.1X/EAP authentication is required in the enterprise and passphrase authentication in a SOHO environment. Table 13.2 offers a valuable comparison of all the various security standards.

Robust Security Network (RSN)

The 802.11i amendment defines what is known as a *robust security network (RSN) and robust security network associations (RSNAs)*. Under 802.11i, two stations (STAs) must establish a procedure to authenticate and associate with each other as well as create dynamic encryption keys through a process known as the 4-way handshake. This association between two stations is referred to as an RSNA. A robust security network (RSN) is a network that only allows for the creation of robust security network associations (RSNAs). An RSN can be identified by a new field found in beacons, probe response frames, association request frames, and re-association request frames. This new field is known as the RSN Information Element (IE). This field may identify the cipher suite capabilities of each station. The 802.11.i amendment does allow for the creation of pre-robust security network associations (pre-RSNAs) as well as RSNAs. In other words, legacy security measures can be supported in the same basic service set (BSS) along with 802.11i security defined mechanisms. A *transition security network (TSN)* supports 802.11i defined security as well as legacy security such as WEP within the same BSS.

TABLE 13.2   Security Standards Comparison

Standard	Authentication Method	Encryption Method	Cipher
802.11 Legacy	Open System or Shared Key	WEP	RC4
WPA Personal	WPA Passphrase (Also known as WPA PSK and WPA Pre-Shared Key)	TKIP	RC4
WPA Enterprise	802.1X/EAP	TKIP	RC4
WPA2 Personal 802.11i	WPA2 Passphrase (Also known as WPA2 PSK and WPA2 Pre-Shared Key)	CCMP (default) TKIP (optional)	AES (default) RC4 (optional)
WPA2 Enterprise 802.11i	802.1X/EAP	CCMP (default) TKIP (optional)	AES (default) RC4 (optional)

4-Way Handshake

Dynamic encryption key management is much more complicated under the 802.11i amendment as opposed to the generation of dynamic WEP keys described earlier. Robust secure network associations (RSNAs) utilize a dynamic encryption key management method that actually involves the creation of five separate keys. It is beyond the scope of this book to fully explain this entire process, but a brief explanation is appropriate. Part of the RSNA process involves the creation of two master keys known as the Group Master Key (GMK) and the Pairwise Master Key (PMK). These keys are created as a result of 802.1X/EAP authentication. A PMK can also be created from a preshared key (WPA2 Passphrase) typically used in SOHO authentication. These master keys are the seeding material that is used to create the final dynamic keys that are actually used for encryption and decryption. The final encryption keys are known as the Pairwise Transient Key (PTK) and the Group Temporal Key (GTK). These final keys are created during a four-way EAP frame exchange that is known as the *4-way handshake*. The 4-way handshake will always be the final four frames exchanged during either 802.1X/EAP authentication or passphrase authentication. Whenever TKIP/RC4 or CCMP/AES dynamic keys are created, the 4-way handshake must occur.

The CWNA exam currently does not test on the dynamic encryption key creation process as defined by the 802.11i amendment. The process is heavily tested in the CWSP exam. Included on the CD of this book is a white paper titled "802.11i Authentication and Key Management (AKM)" authored by Devin Akin. This white paper is often referred to as the "chicken-and-egg" white paper and is highly recommended extra reading.

WPA/WPA2 Personal

Do you have a RADIUS server in your home or small business? The answer to that question will almost always be no. If you do not own a RADIUS server, 802.1X/EAP authentication will not be possible. WPA/WPA2 Enterprise solutions require 802.1X for mutual authentication using some form of EAP. Additionally, an authentication server will be needed. Because most of us do not have a RADIUS server in our basement, the 802.11i amendment offers a simpler method of authentication using a preshared key (PSK). This method involves manually typing matching passphrases on both the access point and all client stations that will need to be able to associate to the wireless network. An algorithm is run that converts the passphrase to a Pairwise Master Key (PMK) used with the 4-way handshake to create the final dynamic encryption keys.

This simple method of authentication and encryption key generation is known as WPA/WPA2 Personal. Other names include WPA/WPA2 Pre-Shared Key and WPA/WPA2 PSK. While this is certainly better than static WEP, it still requires significant administrative overhead and has potential social engineering issues in a corporate or enterprise environment. In Chapter 14, you will learn that WPA/WPA2 Personal is susceptible to offline dictionary attacks and should be avoided in an enterprise environment whenever possible. An 802.1X/EAP solution as defined by WPA/WPA2 Enterprise is the preferred method of security in a corporate and workplace environment.

TKIP

The optional encryption method defined by the 802.11i amendment is *Temporal Key Integrity Protocol (TKIP)*. This method uses the RC4 cipher just as WEP encryption does. As a matter of fact, TKIP is actually an enhancement of WEP encryption that addresses many of the known weaknesses of WEP. TKIP starts with a 128-bit temporal key that is combined with a 48-bit Initialization Vector (IV) and source and destination MAC addresses in a complicated process known as per-packet key mixing. This key mixing process mitigates the known IV collision and weak key attacks used against WEP. TKIP also uses a sequencing method to mitigate the re-injection attacks used against WEP. Additionally, TKIP uses a stronger data integrity check known as the *Message Integrity Check (MIC)* to mitigate known bit-flipping attacks against WEP. The MIC is sometimes referred to by the nickname Michael.

WEP encryption will add an extra 8 bytes of overhead to the body of an 802.11 data frame. When TKIP is implemented, because of the extra overhead from the extended IV and the MIC, a total of 20 bytes of overhead is added to the body of an 802.11 data frame. Because TKIP uses the RC4 algorithm and is simply WEP that has been enhanced, most vendors released a WPA firmware upgrade that gave legacy WEP-only cards the capability of using TKIP encryption.

CCMP

The default encryption method defined under the 802.11i amendment is known as *Counter mode with Cipher Block Chaining-Message Authentication Code (CCMP)*. This method uses the *Advanced Encryption Standard (AES)* algorithm (Rijndael algorithm). CCMP/AES uses a 128-bit encryption key size and encrypts in 128-bit fixed length blocks. An 8-byte Message Integrity Check is used that is considered much stronger than the one used in TKIP. Also, because of the strength of the AES cipher, per-packet key mixing is unnecessary.

CCMP/AES encryption will add an extra 16 bytes of overhead to the body of an 802.11 data frame. Because the AES cipher is processor intensive, older legacy radio cards will not have the processing power necessary to perform AES calculations. Older radio cards will not be firmware upgradeable and a hardware upgrade is often needed to support WPA2. Because of the requirement to upgrade the hardware to implement AES, the transition to WPA2 has been slow. For wireless security solutions, it is a recommended practice to choose hardware that handles the processing needs of CCMP/AES encryption. There are some vendors that still attempt to achieve this in software rather than through a hardware mechanism. Software solutions will always perform substantially slower. It is recommended that a device is selected with a CCMP/AES solution implemented on the card's chipset.

Segmentation

As discussed earlier in the chapter, segmentation is a key part of a network design. Once authorized onto network resources, users can be further restricted as to what resources may be accessed and where they can go. Segmentation can be achieved through a variety of means, including firewalls, routers, VPNs, and VLANs. The most common wireless segmentation strategy used in 802.11 enterprise WLANs is layer 3 segmentation using virtual LANs (VLANs). Segmentation is often intertwined with role-based access control (RBAC).

VLANs

Virtual local area networks (VLANs) are used to create separate broadcast domains in a layer 2 network and are often used to restrict access to network resources without regard to physical topology of the network. VLANs are used extensively in switched 802.3 networks for both security and segmentation purposes. In a WLAN environment, individual SSIDs can be mapped to individual VLANs and users can be segemented by the SSID/VLAN pair, all while communicating through a single access point. The connection between the switch and the access point is an IEEE 802.1Q trunk. Each SSID can also be configured with separate security settings. Most vendors can have as many as 16 wireless VLANs with the capability of actually segmenting the users into separate layer 3 domains. A common strategy is to create a guest, voice, and data VLAN as pictured in Figure 13.5. The SSID mapped to the guest VLAN will have no security and all users are restricted away from network resources and routed off to an Internet gateway. The voice VLAN SSID might be using a security solution such a WPA2 Passphrase and the VoWiFi client phones are routed to a VoIP server that provides proprietary QoS services through the VLAN. The data VLAN SSID uses a stronger security solution such as WPA2 Enterprise and the access control lists allow the data users to access full network resources once authenticated. In a wireless switching environment, all VLAN, SSID, and security configurations are performed on the Wi-Fi switch and then pushed or distributed to the thin access points. When using autonomous access points, the VLANs are created on a third-party managed switch and then the VLANs are mapped to SSID and security settings that are configured on the fat access points.

RBAC

Role-based access control (RBAC) is an approach to restricting system access to authorized users. The majority of Wi-Fi switching vendors have RBAC capabilities. The three main components of an RBAC approach are users, roles, and permissions. Separate roles can be created such as the sales role or the marketing role. Individuals or groups of users are assigned to one of these roles. Permissions can be defined as firewall permissions, layer 2 permissions, layer 3 permissions, and bandwidth permissions and can be time based. The permissions are then mapped to the roles. When wireless users authenticate via the WLAN, they inherit the permissions of whatever roles they have been assigned to. For example, users on a guest VLAN might authenticate via a captive portal and then inherit bandwidth permissions that restrict them to 100 kbps of bandwidth and allow them to use only ports

80 (HTTP), 25 (SMTP) and (110) POP. This scenario would restrict guest users who are accessing the Internet from hogging bandwidth and only allow them to view web pages and check email. When used in a WLAN environment, role-based access control can provide granular wireless user management.

FIGURE 13.5   Wireless VLANs

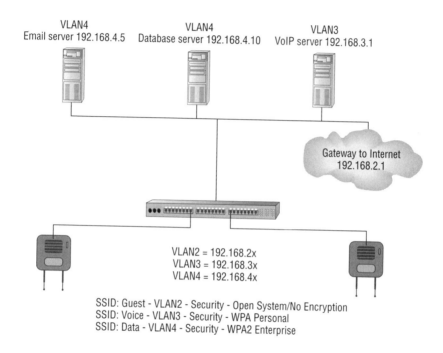

SSID: Guest - VLAN2 - Security - Open System/No Encryption
SSID: Voice - VLAN3 - Security - WPA Personal
SSID: Data - VLAN4 - Security - WPA2 Enterprise

Infrastructure Security

An often overlooked aspect of wireless security is protecting the infrastructure equipment. In addition to protecting Wi-Fi hardware from theft, you must also secure the management interfaces so that only authorized administrators have access. Protecting hardware and interfaces should never be ignored in an 802.11 enterprise.

Physical Security

Access points and other WLAN hardware can be quite expensive. Many enterprise access points can cost as much as $1,000 (in U.S. dollars). Although access points are usually mounted in or near the ceiling, theft can be a problem. Enclosure units with locks can be mounted in the ceiling or to the wall. Access points locked inside the enclosure units are safeguarded against theft. The enclosure units also prevent unwanted individuals from using a serial cable or console cable to try to gain access to the AP. Secure enclosure units may also meet aesthetic demands by keeping the access point out of plain sight.

Interface Security

All wireless infrastructure devices must be able to be accessed by administrators through a management interface. Enterprise equipment usually can be configured either through a command-line interface or a web interface or via Simple Network Management Protocol (SNMP). Any interface that is not used should be turned off. For example, if the administrator configures the access points only via a command-line interface, turn off the web interface capabilities on the access point. At a minimum, all the passwords for these configuration options should be changed from the factory defaults.

Most infrastructure devices should also support some type of encrypted management capabilities. Newer Wi-Fi hardware should support either secure command-shell, HTTPS, or SNMPv3. Older legacy equipment may not support encrypted login capabilities. It is also a highly recommended practice to only configure your infrastructure devices from the wired side and never configure them wirelessly. If devices are configured from the wireless side, an intruder might capture your wireless packets and be able to watch what you are doing. There is also a very good chance that you will accidentally lock yourself out of the device while configuring Wi-Fi hardware wirelessly.

VPN Wireless Security

Although the 802.11i security amendment clearly defines layer 2 security solutions, the use of upper-layer *virtual private network (VPN)* solutions can also be deployed with WLANs. VPNs are typically not recommended to provide wireless security due to the overhead and since there are faster, more-secure solutions now available. Although not usually a recommended practice, VPNs are often used for WLAN security because the VPN solution was already in place inside the wired infrastructure. VPNs do have their place in Wi-Fi security and should definitely be used for remote access. They are also often used in wireless bridging environments. The two major types of VPN topologies are router to router or client/server based.

Use of VPN technology is mandatory for remote access. Your end users will take their laptops off site and will most likely use public access Wi-Fi hot spots. Since there is no security at most hot spots, a VPN solution is needed. The VPN user will need to bring the security to the hot spot in order to provide a secure connection. It is imperative that users implement a VPN solution coupled with a personal firewall whenever accessing any public access Wi-Fi networks.

Layer 3 VPNs

VPNs have several major characteristics. They provide encryption, encapsulation, authentication, and data integrity. VPNs use secure tunneling, which is the process of encapsulating one IP packet within another IP packet. The first packet is encapsulated inside the second packet. The original destination and source IP address of the first packet is encrypted along with the data payload of the first packet. VPN tunneling therefore protects your original layer 3 addresses and also protects the data payload of the original packet. Layer 3 VPNs use layer 3 encryption; therefore, the payload that is being encrypted is the layer 4 to 7 information. The IP addresses of the second packet are seen in cleartext and are used for communications between the tunnel end points. The destination and source IP addresses of the second packet will point to the virtual IP address of the VPN server and VPN client software. Figure 13.6 depicts a layer 3 VPN in a wireless environment.

The two major types of layer 3 VPN technologies are *Point-to-Point Tunneling Protocol (PPTP)* and *Internet Protocol Security (IPSec)*. PPTP uses 128-bit *Microsoft Point-to-Point Encryption (MPPE)*, which uses the RC4 algorithm. PPTP encryption is considered adequate but not strong. PPTP uses MS-CHAP version 2 for user authentication. Unfortunately, the chosen authentication method can be compromised with offline dictionary attacks. VPNs using PPTP technology typically are used in smaller SOHO environments. IPSec VPNs use stronger encryption methods and more secure methods of authentication. IPSec supports multiple ciphers including DES, 3DES, and AES. Device authentication is achieved by using either a server side certificates or a pre-shared key. It is beyond the scope of this book for a full explanation of IPSec technology, but IPSec is normally the choice for VPN technology in the enterprise. VPN technologies do exist that operate at other layers of the OSI model, including layer 7 SSL tunneling and SSH2 VPNs.

FIGURE 13.6   VPN tunnel

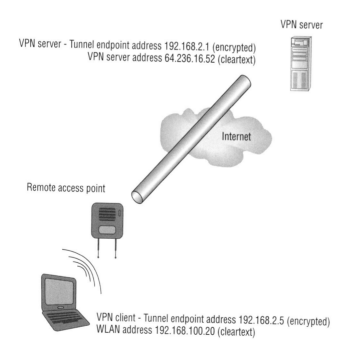

Unlike 802.1X/EAP solutions, an IP address is needed before a VPN tunnel can be established. A downside to using a VPN solution is that access points are potentially open to attack because a potential attacker can get both a layer 2 and layer 3 connection before the VPN tunnel is established. 802.1X/EAP requires that all security credentials and transactions are completed before any layer 3 connectivity is even possible.

Summary

In this chapter, you learned that three major facets are needed for wireless security. A strong encryption solution is needed to protect the data frames. A mutual authentication solution is needed to ensure that only legitimate users are authorized to use network resources. A segmentation solution is necessary to further restrict users as to what resources they may access and where they can go. We discussed legacy 802.11 authentication and encryption solutions and why they are weak. We covered the stronger 802.1X/EAP authentication solutions and the benefits of dynamic encryption key generation, as well as what is defined by the 802.11i security amendment and the related WPA/WPA2 certifications. 802.11i defines a layer 2 robust secure network using 802.1X/EAP for authentication and defines CCMP/AES or TKIP/RC4 for encryption. Finally, we covered proper infrastructure and interface security as well as VPN technology in a WLAN environment.

It is important to understand the capabilities and limitations of the devices that will be deployed within your 802.11 wireless networks. Ideally, devices will be segmented into separate VLANs using 802.1X/EAP authentication and CCMP/AES encryption. VoIP phones, mobile scanners, mobile printers, handheld devices, and so on are often not equipped with the ability to handle the advanced 802.11i security capabilities. Proper designs must take into account all of these components to ensure the most dynamic and secure network.

Exam Essentials

Define the concept of AAA.   Be able to explain the difference between authentication, authorization, and accounting and why each is needed for a WLAN network.

Explain why encryption and segmentation are needed.   Be able to discuss why data frames must be protected with encryption. Know the differences between the various encryption ciphers. Understand that the wireless segment of your network should always be treated as an untrusted segment while all or portions of the wired 802.3 network are considered trusted segment.

Understand legacy 802.11 security.   Identify and understand Open System authentication and Shared Key authentication. Understand how WEP encryption works and all of its weaknesses.

Explain the 802.1X/EAP framework.   Be able to explain all of the components of an 802.1X solution and the EAP authentication protocol. Understand that dynamic encryption key generation is one final result of mutual authentication.

Define the requirements of the 802.11i amendment.   Understand what the 802.11i security amendment specifically defines and be able to contrast the amendment to what is defined by both WPA and WPA2.

Understand TKIP/RC4 and CCMP/AES.   Be able to explain the basics of both dynamic encryption types and why they are the end result of an RSN 802.11i network solution.

Explain VLANs and VPNs.   Understand that VLANs are typically used for wireless segmentation solutions. Define the basics of VPN technology and when it might be used in a WLAN environment.

Key Terms

Before you take the exam, be certain you are familiar with the following terms:

4-way handshake

802.11i

802.1X

AAA

Advanced Encryption Standard (AES)

authentication server

authenticator

broadcast key

Counter mode with Cipher Block Chaining-Message Authentication Code (CCMP)

Extensible Authentication Protocol (EAP)

Initialization Vector (IV)

Internet Protocol Security (IPSec)

Message Integrity Check (MIC)

Microsoft Point-to-Point Encryption (MPPE)

per session per user

Point-to-Point Tunneling Protocol (PPTP)

port -based access control

RC4

robust security network (RSN)

robust security network associations (RSNAs)

role-based access control (RBAC)

supplicant

transition security network (TSN)

Temporal Key Integrity Protocol (TKIP)

unicast key

virtual local area networks (VLANs)

virtual private network (VPN)

Wi-Fi Protected Access (WPA)

Wired Equivalent Privacy (WEP)

Review Questions

1. MAC filtering is susceptible to which type of attack?

   A. Cracking

   B. MAC re-injection

   C. ARP poisoning

   D. Spoofing

   E. IV Collisions

2. Which wireless security standard defines the use of CCMP/AES encryption? (Choose all that apply.)

   A. WPA

   B. 802.11i

   C. 802.1X

   D. WPA2

   E. 802.11

3. 128-bit WEP encryption uses a static key of what size?

   A. 104 bytes

   B. 64 bits

   C. 124 bits

   D. 128 bits

   E. 104 bits

4. What three main components constituent an 802.1X framework?

   A. Supplicant

   B. Authorizer

   C. Authentication server

   D. Intentional radiator

   E. Authenticator

5. The 802.11 standard defines which wireless security solution?

   A. Dynamic WEP

   B. 802.1X/EAP

   C. 64-bit static WEP

   D. Temporal Key Integrity Protocol

   E. CCMP/AES

6. Jimmy has been hired as a consultant to secure the Donahue Corporation's WLAN infrastructure. He has been asked to choose a solution that will both protect the company's equipment from theft and hopefully protect the access point's configuration interfaces from outside attackers. What recommendations would be appropriate? (Choose all that apply.)

   A. Mounting all access points in lockable enclosure units

   B. IPSec VPN

   C. Configuring all access points via Telnet

   D. Configuring access points from the wired side using HTTPS or Secure Command Shell

   E. 802.1X/EAP

7. Which security solutions may be used to segment a wireless LAN? (Choose all that apply.)

   A. VLAN

   B. PPTP VPN

   C. Firewall

   D. CCMP/AES

   E. WEP

8. What wireless security solutions are defined by Wi-Fi Protected Access? (Choose all that apply.)

   A. Passphrase authentication

   B. LEAP

   C. TKIP/RC4

   D. Dynamic WEP

   E. CCMP/AES

9. Name the three main components of a role-based access control solution.

   A. EAP

   B. Roles

   C. Encryption

   D. Permissions

   E. Users

10. 64-bit WEP encryption uses a _____ IV and a _____ static key.

   A. 64 bit, 24 bit

   B. 24 bit, 64 bit

   C. 24 bit, 40 bit

   D. 20 bit, 44 bit

   E. 48 bit, 64 bit

11. Which technologies use the RC4 cipher? (Choose all that apply.)

    A. Static WEP

    B. Dynamic WEP

    C. CCMP

    D. TKIP

    E. MPPE

12. What must occur before dynamic TKIP/RC4 or CCMP/AES encryption keys are generated?

    A. Shared Key authentication

    B. 801.1x/EAP authentication

    C. 4-way handshake

    D. AAA

13. For an 802.1X/EAP solution to work properly, which two components must both support the same type of EAP protocol?

    A. Supplicant

    B. Authorizer

    C. Authenticator

    D. Authentication server

14. When using an 802.11 wireless switch solution, which device would be considered the authenticator?

    A. Access point

    B. Radius database

    C. LDAP

    D. Wi-Fi switch

    E. VLAN

15. Identify some aspects of the Temporal Key Integrity Protocol. (Choose all that apply.)

    A. 128-bit temporal key

    B. 24-bit Initialization Vector

    C. Message Integrity Check

    D. 48-bit IV

    E. Diffe-Hellman Exchange

16. WEP is susceptible to which types of attacks? (Choose all that apply.)

   A. Bit-flipping attacks

   B. IV collisions attacks

   C. Weak key attacks

   D. Re-injection attacks

   E. IV spoofing attacks

17. Which encryption key sizes does the AES cipher support? (Choose all that apply.)

   A. 192 bits

   B. 64 bits

   C. 256 bits

   D. 198 bits

18. Identify the security solutions that are defined by the 802.11i amendment. (Choose all that apply.)

   A. 802.1X/EAP authentication

   B. Dynamic WEP encryption

   C. Optional CCMP/AES encryption

   D. Passphrase authentication

   E. DES encryption

19. Identify examples of layer 2 encryption. (Choose all that apply.)

   A. WEP/AES

   B. MPPE/RC4

   C. IPSec/VPN

   D. TKIP/RC4

   E. CCMP/AES

20. Which protocol is used for authentication in an 802.1X framework?

   A. Extensible Authorization Protocol

   B. Extended Authentication Protocol

   C. Extensible Authentication Protocol

   D. CHAP/PPP

   E. Open System

Answers to Review Questions

1. D. The MAC address of a radio card can always be seen in cleartext in the layer 2 header of an 802.11 frame. MAC addresses can be "spoofed," allowing any amateur hacker to bypass any MAC filter by using an allowed client station's MAC address.

2. B, D. The 802.11i amendment defines CCMP/AES encryption as the default encryption method, while TKIP/RC4 is the optional encryption method. The Wi-Fi Alliance created the WPA2 security certification, which is a mirror of the 802.11i amendment. WPA2 supports both CCMP/AES and TKIP/RC4 dynamic encryption key management.

3. E. 128-bit WEP encryption uses a secret 104-bit static key that is combined with a 24-bit Initialization Vector for an effective key strength of 128 bits.

4. A, C, E. The supplicant, authenticator, and authentication server work together to provide the framework for an 802.1X port-based access control solution. The supplicant requests access to network resources. The authentication server authenticates the identity of the supplicant, and the authenticator allows or denies access to network resources via virtual ports.

5. C. The original 802.11 standard ratified in 1997 define the use of a 64-bit static encryption solution called Wired Equivalent Privacy (WEP). Dynamic WEP was never defined under any wireless security standard. The use of 802.1X/EAP, TKIP/RC4, and CCMP/AES are all defined by the 802.1i security amendment.

6. A, D, E. Access points may be mounted in lockable enclosure units to provide theft protection. All access points should be configured from the wired side and never wirelessly. Encrypted management interfaces such as HTTPS should be used instead of HTTP or Telnet. An 802.1X/EAP solution guarantees that only authorized users will receive an IP address. Attackers can get an IP address prior to setting up an IPSec VPN tunnel and potentially attack the access points.

7. A, B, C. Virtual LANs, VPN solutions, and firewalls can all be used to segment wireless users. The most common wireless segmentation strategy often used in 802.11 enterprise WLANs is segmentation using VLANS. CCMP/AES and WEP are encryption solutions.

8. A, C. Wi-Fi Protected Access (WPA) was a snapshot of the not-yet-released 802.11i amendment, supporting only the TKIP/RC4 dynamic encryption key management. 802.1X/EAP authentication was required in the enterprise and passphrase authentication in a SOHO environment. LEAP is Cisco proprietary and is not specifically define by WPA. Neither Dynamic WEP nor CCMP/AES is defined for encryption.

9. B, D, E. Role-based access control (RBAC) is an approach to restricting system access to authorized users. The three main components of an RBAC approach are users, roles, and permissions.

10. C. 64-bit WEP encryption uses a secret 40-bit static key that is combined with a 24-bit Initialization Vector for an effective key strength of 64 bits.

11. A, B, D, E. All forms of WEP encryption uses the Rivest's Cipher 4 (RC4) algorithm. TKIP is WEP that has been enhanced and also uses the RC4 cipher. PPTP uses 128-bit Microsoft Point-to-Point Encryption (MPPE), which uses the RC4 algorithm. CCMP uses the AES cipher.

12. Answer: C. Shared Key authentication is not defined by 802.11i. A robust secure network association requires a four-frame EAP exchange known as the 4-way handshake that is used to generate dynamic TKIP or CCMP keys. The handshake may occur either after an 802.1X/EAP exchange or as a result of WPA/WPA2 passphrase.

13. A, D. An 802.1X/EAP solution requires that both the authenticator and the supplicant support the same type of encryption. The authenticator must be configured for 802.1X/EAP authentication but does not care which EAP protocol type passes through.

14. D. 802.11 wireless switches use thin access points, which are dumb terminals with radio cards and an antenna. When an 802.1X/EAP solution is deployed in a wireless switching environment, the virtual controlled and uncontrolled ports exist on the wireless switch.

15. A, C, D. TKIP starts with a 128-bit temporal key that is combined with a 48-bit Initialization Vector (IV) and source and destination MAC addresses in a process known as per-packet key mixing. TKIP uses an additional data integrity check known as the Message Integrity Check (MIC).

16. A, B, C, D. Because of the limited size of the IV space, IV collisions occur, and an attacker can recover the secret key much easier when IV collisions occur in wireless networks. Due to the RC4 key-scheduling algorithm, weak IV keys are generated. Lack of sequencing allow for packet re-injection attacks to accelerate the collection of weak IVs on a network with little traffic. The ICV data integrity check is considered weak and WEP encrypted packets can be tampered with during bit-flipping attacks. IV spoofing attacks do not exist.

17. A, C. The AES algorithm encrypts data in fixed data blocks with choices in encryption key strength of 128, 192, or 256 bits.

18. A, D. The 802.11i amendment requires the use of an 802.1X/EAP authentication method in the enterprise and the use of a preshared key or a passphrase in a SOHO environment. The 802.11i amendment also requires the use of stronger dynamic key management encryption methods. CCMP/AES encryption is the default encryption method, and TKIP/RC4 is the optional encryption method.

19. D, E. Layer 2 encryption solutions include WEP/RC4. TKIP/RC4, and CCMP/AES. layer 2 solutions will encrypt the layer 3 to 7 payload of a data frame. MPPE/RC4 is used in PPTP VPNs and is considered layer 3 encryption. IPSec VPNs use layer 3 encryption. There is no such thing as WEP/AES.

20. C. The supplicant, authenticator, and authentication server work together to provide the framework for 802.1X port-based access control, and an authentication protocol is needed to assist in the authentication process. The Extensible Authentication Protocol (EAP) is used to provide user authentication.

Chapter

14

Wireless Attacks, Intrusion Monitoring, and Policy

IN THIS CHAPTER, YOU WILL LEARN ABOUT THE FOLLOWING:

✓ **Wireless Attacks**

- Rogue Access Point
- Peer-to-Peer Attacks
- Eavesdropping
- Encryption Cracking
- Authentication Attacks
- Mac Spoofing
- Management Interface Exploits
- Wireless Hijacking
- Denial of Service (DoS)

✓ **Intrusion Monitoring**

- Wireless Intrusion Detection System (WIDS)
- Wireless Intrusion Prevention System (WIPS)
- Mobile WIDS
- Spectrum Analyzer

✓ **Wireless Security Policy**

- General Security Policy
- Functional Security Policy
- Legislative Compliance
- 802.11 Wireless Policy Recommendations

In Chapter 13, we discussed legacy 802.11 security solutions as well as the more robust security that is defined by the 802.11i security amendment. In this chapter, we will cover the wide variety of attacks that can be launched against 802.11 wireless networks. Some of these attacks can be mitigated using the strong encryption and mutual authentication solutions that were discussed in Chapter 13. However, others cannot be prevented and can only be detected. Therefore, we will also discuss the wireless intrusion detection systems that can be implemented to expose both layer 1 and layer 2 attacks. The most important component for a secure wireless network is a properly planned and implemented corporate security policy.

This chapter will also discuss some of the fundamental components of a wireless security policy that are needed to cement a foundation of Wi-Fi security.

Wireless Attacks

As you have learned throughout this book, the main function of 802.11 access points is to provide a portal into a wired network infrastructure. The portal must be protected with strong authentication methods so that only legitimate users with the proper credentials will be authorized to have access to network resources. If the portal is not properly protected, unauthorized users can also gain access to these resources. The potential risks of exposing these resources are endless. An intruder could gain access to financial databases, corporate trade secrets, or personal health information. Network resources can also be damaged.

What would be the financial cost to an organization if an intruder used the wireless network as a portal to disrupt or shut down a SQL server or email server? If the Wi-Fi portal is not protected, any individual wishing to cause harm could upload data such as viruses, Trojan horse applications, keystroke loggers, or remote control applications. Spammers have already figured out that they can use open wireless gateways to the Internet to commence spamming activities. Other illegal activities, such as software theft and remote hacking, may also occur through an unsecured gateway.

While an intruder can use the wireless network to attack wired resources, equally at risk are all of the wireless network resources. Any information that passes through the air can be captured and possibly compromised. If not properly secured, the management interfaces of Wi-Fi equipment can be accessed. Many wireless users are fully exposed for peer-to-peer attacks. Finally, the possibility of denial of service attacks against a wireless network always exits.

With the proper tools, any individual with ill intent can temporarily disable a Wi-Fi network, thus denying legitimate users access to the network resources.

In the following sections you will learn about all the potential attacks that can be launched against 802.11 wireless networks.

Rogue Access Point

The big buzz phrase in Wi-Fi security has always been the *rogue access point*. In Chapter 13, you learned about 802.1X/EAP authentication solutions that can be put in place to prevent unauthorized access. However, what is there to prevent an individual from installing their own wireless portal onto the network backbone? A rogue access point is any Wi-Fi device that is connected to the wired infrastructure but is not under the management of the proper network administrators. Any $50 SOHO Wi-Fi access point or router can be plugged into a live data port. The rogue device will just as easily act as a portal into the wired network infrastructure. Because the rogue device has no authorization and authentication security in place, any intruder can now use this open portal to gain access to network resources.

It is not uncommon for a company to have a wireless network installed and not even know about its existence. The individuals most responsible for installing rogue access points are not hackers; they are employees not realizing the consequences of their actions. According to some statistics, well over 50 percent of home users have wireless access at home and have become accustomed to the convenience and mobility that Wi-Fi offers. As a result, employees often install their own wireless devices in the workplace because the company they work for has yet to deploy an enterprise wireless network. The problem is that, while these self-installed access points might provide the wireless access that the employees desire, they are rarely secured. Every rogue access point is a potential open and unsecured gateway straight into the wired infrastructure that the company wants to protect. Although only a single open portal is needed to expose network resources, many large companies have discovered literally dozens of rogue access points that have been installed by employees.

Ad-hoc networks also have the potential of providing rogue access into the corporate network. Very often an employee will have a laptop or desktop plugged into the wired network via an Ethernet network card. On that same computer, the employee has a Wi-Fi radio and has set up an ad-hoc Wi-Fi connection with another employee. Because the Ethernet connection and the Wi-Fi card can be bridged together, an intruder might also access the ad-hoc wireless network and then potentially route their way to the Ethernet connection and get onto the wired network. Many government agencies and corporations ban the use of ad-hoc networks for this very reason. The ability to configure an ad-hoc network can be disabled on most enterprise client devices.

As stated earlier, most rogue APs are installed by employees not realizing the consequences of their actions, but any malicious intruder can use these open portals to gain access. Furthermore, besides physical security, there is nothing to prevent an intruder from also connecting their own rogue access point via an Ethernet cable into any live data port provided in a wall plate. Later in this chapter we will discuss intrusion prevention systems that can both detect and disable rogue access points.

If an 802.1X solution is deployed for the wireless network, it can also be used to secure the network ports on the wired network. In that case, any new access points would need to authenticate to the network prior to being given access. This is a good way to not only utilize existing resources, but also to provide better security for your wired network by protecting against rogue APs.

Peer-to-Peer Attacks

As mentioned earlier, wireless resources may also be attacked. A commonly overlooked risk is the *peer-to-peer attack*. As you have learned in earlier chapters, an 802.11 client station can be configured in either Infrastructure mode or Ad-Hoc mode. When configured in Ad-Hoc mode, the wireless network is known as an independent basic service set (IBSS) and all communications are peer-to-peer without the need for an access point. Because an IBSS is by nature a peer-to-peer connection, any user who can connect wirelessly with another user can potentially gain access to any resource available on either laptop. A common use of ad-hoc networks is to share files on-the-fly. If shared access is provided, files and other assets can accidentally be exposed. A personal firewall is often used to mitigate peer-to peer attacks.

Users that are associated to the same access point are typically just as vulnerable to peer-to-peer attacks as IBSS users. Properly securing your wireless network often involves protecting authorized users from each other since hacking at companies is often performed internally by employees. Users associated to the same access point are members of the same basic service set (BSS). Because they reside in the same wireless domain, the users are exposed to peer-to-peer attacks. In most WLAN deployments, Wi-Fi clients communicate only with devices on the wired network such as email or web servers and peer-to-peer communications are not needed. Therefore, most vendors provide some proprietary method of preventing users from inadvertently sharing files with other users. If connections are required to other wireless peers, the traffic is routed through a layer 3 switch or other network device prior to passing to the desired destination station.

Public Secure Packet Forwarding (PSPF) is a feature that can be enabled on WLAN access points or switches to block wireless clients from communicating with other wireless clients on the same wireless segment. With PSPF enabled, client devices cannot communicate with other client devices on the wireless network, as pictured in Figure 14.1. Although, *PSPF* is a term most commonly used by Cisco, other vendors have similar capabilities under different names.

Eavesdropping

As you have learned throughout this book, 802.11 wireless networks operate in license-free frequency bands and all data transmissions travel in the open air. Access to wireless transmissions is available to anyone within listening range, and therefore strong encryption is mandatory. Wireless communications can be monitored via two eavesdropping methods: casual eavesdropping and malicious eavesdropping.

FIGURE 14.1   Public Secure Packet Forwarding

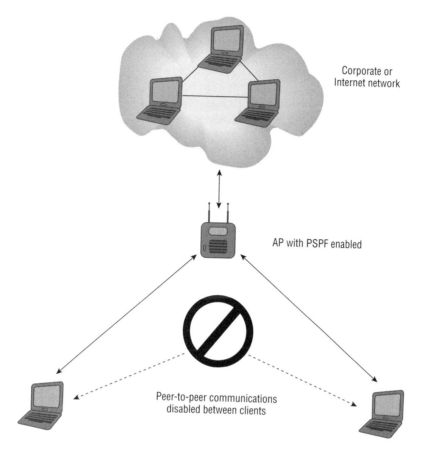

Corporate or
Internet network

AP with PSPF enabled

Peer-to-peer communications
disabled between clients

Casual eavesdropping is typically considered harmless and is also often referred to as *wardriving*. Software utilities known as WLAN discovery tools exist for the purpose of finding open WLAN networks. Wardriving is strictly the act of looking for wireless networks, usually while in a moving vehicle. The most common wardriving software tool is a freeware program called NetStumbler, pictured in Figure 14.2.

FIGURE 14.2   NetStumbler

Network Stumbler - [20060531200351]

File Edit View Device Window Help

MAC	SSID	Name	Chan	Speed	Vendor	Type	Enc...	SNR
000E38490580	AirSpy Networks		1	11 Mbps	Cisco	AP	WEP	66
000FB5ACC858	kentnet		6	54 Mbps		AP	WEP	15
0020A64D2070	SpectraLink Wi-Fi Phones		11	54 Mbps		AP	WEP	68
0020A64FD589	WonderPuppy Coffee Company		36	54 Mbps		AP		76

Channels
SSIDs
Filters

NetStumbler sends out null probe requests across all license-free 802.11 frequencies with the hope of receiving probe response frames containing wireless network information such as SSID, channel, encryption, and so on.

By technical design, the very nature of 802.11 passive and active scanning is to provide the identifying network information accessible to anyone with an 802.11 radio card. Because this is an inherent necessary function of 802.11, wardriving is not a crime. However, the goal of many wardrivers is to find open 802.11 wireless networks that can provide free gateway access to the Internet. While the legality of using an open wireless gateway to the Internet remains unclear in most countries, the majority of wardrivers are not hackers intending harm but rather simply wireless users wanting temporary free Internet access. The legality of using someone else's wireless network without permission is often unclear, but people have been arrested and prosecuted as a result of these actions.

We recommend that you connect only to wireless networks that you are authorized to access.

While casual eavesdropping is considered harmless, *malicious eavesdropping*, the unauthorized use of protocol analyzers to capture wireless communications, is typically considered illegal. Most countries have some type of wiretapping law that makes it a crime to listen in on someone else's phone conversation. Additionally, most countries have laws making it unlawful to listen in on any type of electromagnetic communications, including 802.11 wireless transmissions.

Many commercial and freeware 802.11 protocol analyzers exist that allow wireless network administrators to capture 802.11 traffic for the purpose of analyzing and troubleshooting their own wireless networks. Protocol analyzers are passive devices that work in an RF monitoring mode that captures any transmissions that are within range. The problem is that anyone with malicious intent can also capture 802.11 traffic from any wireless network and go undetected. For this reason, a strong dynamic encryption solution such as TKIP/RC4 or CCMP/AES is mandatory. Any cleartext communications such as email and Telnet passwords can be captured if no encryption is provided. Furthermore, any unencrypted 802.11 frame transmissions can be reassembled at the upper layers of the OSI model. Email messages can be reassembled and therefore read by an eavesdropper. Web pages and instant messages can also be reassembled. VoIP packets can be reassembled and saved as a WAV sound file. Malicious eavesdropping of this nature is highly illegal; therefore, because of the passive and undetectable nature of this attack, encryption must always be implemented to provide data privacy.

It should be noted that the most common target of malicious eavesdropping attacks is public access hotspots. Public hotspots rarely offer security and usually transfer data without encryption, making hotspot users prime targets. As a result, it is imperative that a VPN-type solution be implemented for all mobile users who connect outside of your company's network.

What Tools Are Needed for Wardriving?

To get started wardriving, you will need an 802.11 client card, a software WLAN discovery application, and an automobile! Numerous freeware-based discovery tools exist, including NetStumbler for Windows, MiniStumbler for Windows CE, MacStumbler for Macintosh, and Kismet for Linux. A copy of NetStumbler is included on the CD that accompanies this book and can also be downloaded at www.netstumbler.com. Another, optional tool is a high-gain external antenna that can be connected to your wireless card via a pigtail connector. Many wardrivers also use Global Positioning System (GPS) devices in conjunction with NetStumbler to pinpoint longitude and latitude coordinates of the signal from access points that they discover. Wardriving capture files with GPS coordinates can be uploaded to large dynamic mapping databases on the Internet. One such database, called the Wireless Geographic Logging Engine (WIGLE), maintains a searchable database of over 5 million access points. Go to www.wigle.net and type in your address to see if any wireless access points have already been discovered in your neighborhood.

Encryption Cracking

In Chapter 13, you learned that Wired Equivalent Privacy (WEP) encryption has been cracked. The current WEP cracking tools that are freely available on the Internet can crack WEP encryption in as little as 5 minutes. There are several methods used to crack WEP encryption. However, an attacker usually needs only to capture several hundred thousand encrypted packets with a protocol analyzer and then run the captured data through a WEP cracking software utility. The software utility will usually then be able to derive the secret 40-bit or 104-bit key in a matter of seconds. Once the secret key has been revealed, the attacker can decrypt any and all encrypted traffic. In other words, an attacker can now eavesdrop on the WEP-encrypted network. Because the attacker can decrypt the traffic, they can reassemble the data and read it as if there was no encryption whatsoever.

Authentication Attacks

As you have already learned, the 802.11i security amendment defines for authentication either an 802.1X/EAP authentication solution or the use of a pre-shared key for authentication. The 802.11i amendment does not define which type of EAP authentication method to use, and all flavors of EAP are not created equally. Some types of EAP authentication are more secure than others. As a matter of fact, Lightweight Extensible Authentication Protocol (LEAP), one of the most commonly deployed 802.1X/EAP solutions, is susceptible to offline dictionary attacks. The hashed password response during the LEAP authentication process is crackable.

An attacker merely has to capture a frame exchange when a LEAP user authenticates and then the capture file is run through an offline dictionary attack tool. The password can be derived in a matter of seconds. The user name is also seen in clear text during the LEAP authentication process. Once the attacker gets the user name and password, they are free to impersonate the user by authenticating onto the WLAN and then access any network resources that are available to that user. Stronger EAP authentication protocols exist that are not susceptible to offline dictionary attacks.

WPA/WPA2 Personal, using pre-shared keys, is also a weak authentication method that is vulnerable to offline dictionary attacks. Hacking utilities are available that can derive the WPA/WPA2 passphrase using an offline dictionary attack. Once the attacker has the passphrase, they can associate to the WPA/WPA2 access point. Even worse is that once the hacker has the passphrase, they can also begin to decrypt the dynamically generated TKIP/RC4 or CCMP/AES encryption key. In Chapter 13, you learned that an algorithm is run to convert the passphrase to a Pairwise Master Key (PMK), which is used with the 4-way handshake to create the final dynamic encryption keys. If a hacker has the passphrase and captures the 4-way handshake, they can re-create the dynamic encryption keys and decrypt traffic. WPA/WPA2 Personal is not considered a strong security solution for the enterprise because if the passphrase is compromised, the attacker can access network resources and decrypt traffic. A policy mandating very strong passphrases should always be in place whenever a WPA/WPA2 Personal solution must be used in situations where there is no AAA server or the client devices do not support 802.1X authentication.

MAC Spoofing

All 802.11 wireless network cards have a physical address known as a MAC address. This address is a 12-digit hexadecimal number that is seen in clear text in the layer 2 header of 802.11 frames. Wi-Fi vendors provide MAC filtering capabilities on their access points. Usually, MAC filters are configured to apply restrictions that will allow traffic only from specific client stations to pass through. These restrictions are based on their unique MAC addresses. All other client stations whose MAC addresses are not on the allowed list will not be able to pass traffic through the virtual port of the access point and onto the distribution system medium. Unfortunately, MAC addresses can be "spoofed," or impersonated, and any amateur hacker can easily bypass any MAC filter by spoofing an allowed client station's address.

MAC spoofing can often be achieved in the Windows operating system by simply editing the wireless card's MAC address in Device Manager or by performing a simple edit in the Registry. Third-party software utilities such as the one pictured in Figure 14.3 can also be used be assist in MAC spoofing.

Because of spoofing and because of all the administrative work that is involved with setting up MAC filters, MAC filtering is not considered a reliable means of security for wireless enterprise networks and should be implemented only as a last resort. In some cases, it is used as part of a tier security architecture to better secure client devices that are not capable of 802.1X or stronger encryption.

FIGURE 14.3   MAC spoofing software utility

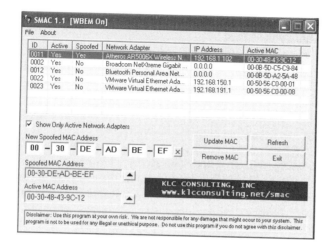

Management Interface Exploits

Wireless infrastructure hardware such as access points and wireless switches can be managed by administrators via a variety of interfaces, much like managing wired infrastructure hardware. Devices can be accessed via a web interface, a command-line interface, a serial port, a console connection and/or Simple Network Management Protocol (SNMP). As we discussed, it is imperative that these interfaces be protected. Interfaces that are not used should be disabled. Strong passwords should be used and encrypted login capabilities such as Hypertext Transfer Protocol Secure (HTTPS) should be utilized if available. Lists of all the default settings of every major manufacturer's access points exist on the Internet and are often used for security exploits by hackers. It is not uncommon for intruders to use security holes left in management interfaces to reconfigure access points. Legitimate users and administrators can find themselves locked out of their own wireless networking equipment.

After gaining access via a management interface, an attacker might even be able to initiate a firmware upgrade of the wireless hardware and, while the upgrade is being performed, power off the equipment. This attack could likely render the hardware useless, requiring it to be returned to the manufacturer for repair.

Wireless Hijacking

An attack that often generates a lot of press is *wireless hijacking*, also known as the *evil twin attack*. The attacker configures access point software on a laptop, effectively turning a Wi-Fi client card into an access point. The access point software is configured with the same SSID that is used by a public hotspot access point. The attacker then sends spoofed disassociation or deauthentication frames, forcing users associated with the hotspot access point to roam to the evil twin access point. At this point, the attacker has effectively hijacked wireless clients at layer 2 from the original access point.

The evil twin will typically be configured with a Dynamic Host Configuration Protocol (DHCP) server available to issue IP addresses to the clients. At this point, the attacker will have hijacked the users at layer 3 and now has a private wireless network and is free to perform peer-to-peer attacks on any of the hijacked clients.

The attacker may also be using a second wireless card with their laptop to execute what is known as a *man-in-the-middle attack,* as pictured in Figure 14.4. The second wireless card is associated to the hotspot access point as a client. In operating systems, networking cards can be bridged together to provide routing. The attacker has bridged together their second wireless card with the Wi-Fi card that is being used as the evil twin access point. Once the attacker hijacks the users from the original AP, the traffic is then routed from the evil twin access point through the second Wi-Fi card right back to the original access point from which they have just been hijacked. The result is that the users remain hijacked; however, they still have a route back through the gateway to their original network, so they never know they have been hijacked. The attacker can therefore sit in the middle and execute peer-to-peer attacks indefinitely while remaining completely unnoticed.

These attacks can also take another form in what is know as the *Wi-Fi phishing attack.* The attacker may also have web server software and captive portal software. Once the users have been hijacked to the evil twin access point, they will be redirected to a login web page that looks exactly like the hotspot's login page. Then the attacker's fake login page may request a credit card number from the hijacked user. Phishing attacks are very common on the Internet and are now appearing at your local hotspot. The only way to prevent a hijacking, man-in-the-middle, and/or Wi-Fi phishing attack is to use a mutual authentication solution. Mutual authentication solutions not only validate the user that is connecting to the network, they also validate the network to which the user is connecting. 802.1X/ EAP authentication solutions require that mutual authentication credentials be exchanged before a user can be authorized. A user cannot get an IP address unless authorized; therefore, they cannot be hijacked.

Denial of Service (DoS)

The attacks on wireless networks that seem to receive the least amount of attention are *denial of service (DoS)* attacks. With the proper tools, any individual with ill intent can temporarily disable a Wi-Fi network by preventing legitimate users from accessing network resources. The good news is that monitoring systems exist that can detect and identify DoS attacks immediately. The bad news is that there is absolutely nothing that can be done to prevent denial of service attacks other than locating and removing the source of the attack.

FIGURE 14.4   Man-in-the-middle attack

Valid client

Access
point

Before the attack

Hacker with access point software and DHCP software

Valid client

Access
point

Man-in-the-middle attack in progress

DoS attacks can occur at either layer 1 or layer 2 of the OSI model. Layer 1 attacks are known as RF jamming attacks. The two most common types of RF jamming attacks are intentional jamming and unintentional jamming. Intentional jamming attacks occur when an attacker uses some type of signal generator to cause interference in the unlicensed frequency space. Both narrowband and wideband jammers exist that will interfere with the 802.11 transmissions, either causing all data to become corrupted or causing the 802.11 radio cards to continuously defer when performing a Clear Channel Assessment (CCA).

While an intentional jamming attack is malicious, unintentional jamming is more common. Unintentional interference from microwave ovens, cordless phones, and other devices can also cause denial of service. Although unintentional jamming is not necessarily an attack, it can cause as much harm as an intentional jamming attack. The best tool to detect any type of layer 1 interference, whether intentional or unintentional, is a spectrum analyzer.

The more common type of denial of service attacks that originate from hackers are layer 2 DoS attacks. A wide variety of layer 2 DoS attacks exist that are a result of tampering with 802.11 frames. The most common involves spoofing disassociation or deauthentication frames. The attacker can edit the 802.11 header and spoof the MAC address of an access point or a client in either the destination address field or source address field. The attacker then retransmits the spoofed disassociation or deauthentication frame repeatedly. Because these types of management frames are notification frames that cannot be ignored, the stations will constantly be denied service. Many more types of layer 2 DoS attacks exist, including association floods, authentication floods, PS-Poll floods, and virtual carrier attacks. Luckily, any good wireless intrusion detection system will be able to alert an administrator immediately to a layer 2 DoS attack. The 802.11w draft amendment is the proposed "protected" management frame amendment with a goal of delivering management frames in a secure manner. The end result will hopefully prevent many of the layer 2 denial of service attacks that currently exist, but it is doubtful that all layer 2 DoS attacks will ever be circumvented.

A spectrum analyzer is your best tool to detect a layer 1 DoS attack and a protocol analyzer or wireless IDS is your best tool to detect a layer 2 DoS attack. The best way to prevent any type of denial of service attack is physical security. The authors of this book recommend guard dogs and barbed wire. If that is not an option, there are several solutions that provide intrusion detection at layers 1, 2, and 3.

Intrusion Monitoring

When most people think of wireless, they think only in terms of access and not in terms of attacks or intrusions. It has become increasingly necessary to constantly monitor for the many types of attacks mentioned in this chapter because of the potential damage they can cause. Businesses of all sizes have begun to deploy 802.11 wireless networks for mobility and access and at the same time are running a wireless intrusion detection system (WIDS) to monitor for attacks. Many companies are very concerned about the potential damage that would result from rogue access points. It is not unusual for a company to actually deploy a WIDS before the company deploys the wireless network that is meant to provide access. Wireless intrusion monitoring has evolved, and most current systems have methods to prevent and mitigate some of the known wireless attacks. While most systems are distributed for scalability across a large enterprise, single laptop versions of intrusion monitoring systems also exist. Most wireless intrusion monitoring exists at layer 2, but layer 1 intrusion monitoring systems are now also available to scan for potential attacks.

Wireless Intrusion Detection System (WIDS)

In today's world, a *wireless intrusion detection system (WIDS)* might be necessary even if there is not an 802.11 Wi-Fi network on site. Wireless can be an intrusive technology and if data ports at a business are not controlled, any individual including employees can install a rogue access point. Because of this risk, many companies like banks and other financial institutions as well as hospitals choose to install a WIDS prior to deploying a Wi-Fi network for employee access. Once an 802.11 network is installed for access, it has become almost mandatory in most situations to also have a WIDS because of the other numerous attacks against Wi-Fi, such as denial of service, hijacking, and so on. The typical wireless intrusion detection system is a client/server model that consists of three components:

WIDS server   A software or hardware server acts as a central point of management.

Management consoles   Software-based management consoles that connect back to a WIDS server as clients can be used for 24/7 monitoring of wireless networks.

Sensors   Hardware- or software-based sensors are placed strategically to listen to and capture all 802.11 communications.

Figure 14.5 depicts the client/server model used by most wireless ntrusion detection systems.

FIGURE 14.5   Wireless intrusion detection system (WIDS)

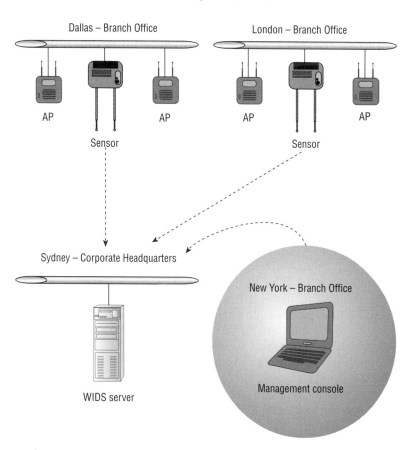

Sensors are basically radio cards that are in a constant listening mode as passive devices. The sensor devices are usually hardware based and resemble an access point. The sensors have some intelligence but also communicate with the centralized WIDS server. The centralized server can collect data from literally thousand of sensors from many remote locations, meeting the scalability needs of many large corporations. Management consoles can also be installed at remote locations, and while they talk back to the centralized server, they can also monitor all remote WLANs where sensors are installed. Figure 14.6 shows a WIDS management console and a hardware sensor.

FIGURE 14.6   WIDS management console and hardware sensor

WIDS are best at monitoring layer 2 attacks such as MAC spoofing, disassociation attacks, and deauthentication attacks. Most WIDS will usually have alarms for as many as 60 potential security risks. Part of deploying a WIDS is setting the policies and alarms. False positives are often a problem with intrusion detection systems, but they can be less of a problem if proper policies are defined. Policies can be created to define the severity of various alerts as well as provide for alarm notifications. For example, an alert for broadcasting the SSID might not be considered severe and might even be disabled. However, a policy might be configured that classifies a deauthentication spoofing attack as severe and an email message or pager notification might be sent automatically to the network administrator. Although most of the scrutiny that is performed by a WIDS is for security purposes, many WIDS also have performance monitoring capabilities. For example, performance alerts might be in the form of excessive bandwidth utilization or excessive reassociation and roaming of VoWiFi phones.

Currently, three different WIDS design models exist:

Overlay   The most common model is an overlay WIDS that is deployed on top of the existing wireless network. This model uses an independent vendor's WIDS and can be deployed to monitor any existing or planned WLAN. The overlay systems typically have more extensive features, but they are usually more expensive.

Integration enabled   Wi-Fi vendors are currently working to integrate their access points and management systems with the major WIDS vendors. The Wi-Fi vendor access points integrate software code that can be used to turn the APs into sensors that will communicate with the third-party WIDS server.

Integrated   Many wireless switching vendors have fully integrated WIDS capabilities. The wireless controller acts as the centralized server. The thin access points can be configured in a sensor-only mode or can act as sensors in a minor fashion when not transmitting as an access point. The integrated solution is a less-expensive solution but may not have all the capabilities that are offered in an overlay WIDS.

Wireless Intrusion Prevention System (WIPS)

Most WIDS vendors prefer to call themselves a *wireless intrusion prevention systems (WIPS)*. The reason that they refer to themselves as prevention systems is that they are all now capable of mitigating attacks from rogue access points. A WIPS characterizes access points and client radios in three classifications:

Infrastructure device   This classification refers to any client station or access point that is an authorized member of the company's wireless network. A network administrator can manually label each radio as an infrastructure device after detection from the WIPS or can import a list of all the company's radio card MAC addresses into the system.

Known device   This classification refers to any client station or access point that is detected by the WIPS but is not considered an interfering device or a rogue access point. The known device label is typically assigned to radio cards of neighboring businesses and is not considered a threat.

Rogue device   The rogue classification refers to any client station or access point that is considered an interfering device and a potential threat. Most WIPS define rogue access points as devices that are actually plugged into the network backbone. Most of the WIPS vendors use a variety of proprietary methods of determining if a rogue access point is actually plugged into the wired infrastructure.

Once a client station or access point has been classified as a rogue device, the WIPS can effectively mitigate the attack. Every WIPS vendor has several ways of accomplishing this, but the most common method is to use spoofed deauthentication frames. The WIPS will have the sensors go active and begin transmitting deauthentication frames that spoof the MAC addresses of the rogue access points and rogue clients. The WIPS is using a known layer 2 denial of service attack as a countermeasure. The effect is that all communications between the rogue access point and clients are rendered useless. This countermeasure can be used to disable rogue access points, individual client stations, and rogue ad-hoc networks. Another method of rogue containment uses the Simple Network Management Protocol (SNMP). Most WIPS can determine that the rogue access point is connected to the wired infrastructure and may be able to use SNMP to disable the managed switch port that is connected to the rogue access point. If the switch port is closed, the attacker cannot attack network resources that are behind the rogue AP.

The WIPS vendors have other proprietary methods of disabling rogue access points and client stations and often their methods are not published. Currently, the main purpose of a wireless intrusion prevention system is to contain and disable rogue devices. In the future, other wireless attacks might be mitigated as well.

 Real World Scenario

Will a WIPS Protect against All Known Rogue Devices?

The simple answer is no. Although the wireless intrusion prevention systems are outstanding products that can mitigate most rogue attacks, some rogue devices will go undetected. The radio cards inside the WIPS sensors typically monitor the 2.4 GHz ISM band and the 5 GHz UNII frequencies. Older legacy wireless networking equipment exists that transmits in the 900 MHz ISM band and these devices will not be detected. The radio cards inside the WIPS sensors also only use direct sequence spread spectrum (DSSS) and Orthogonal Frequency Division Multiplexing (OFDM) technologies. Wireless networking equipment exists that uses frequency hopping spread spectrum (FHSS) transmissions in the 2.4 GHz ISM and will go undetected. The only tool that will 100 percent detect either a 900 MHz or frequency hopping rogue access point is a spectrum analyzer capable of operating in those frequencies. The WIPS should also monitor all the available channels and not just the ones permitted in your resident country. A common strategy used by hackers is to place rogue devices transmitting on 2.4 GHz channels 12 through 14, which are not permitted in the United States.

Mobile WIDS

Several of the wireless intrusion detection/prevention vendors also sell laptop versions of their distributed products. The software program is a protocol analyzer capable of decoding frames with some layer 1 analysis capabilities as well. The mobile WIDS software uses a standard Wi-Fi client radio as the sensor. However, the main purpose of the software is to provide a stand-alone mobile security and performance analysis tool. The mobile WIDS will have all the same policy, alarm, and detection capabilities as the vendor's distributed solution. Think of a mobile WIDS as a single sensor, server, and console all built into one package. The mobile WIDS will be able to detect only attacks within its listening range, but the advantage is that the device is mobile. One useful feature of a mobile WIDS is that it can detect a rogue access point and client and then be used to track them down. The mobile WIDS locks onto the RF signal of the rogue device and then an administrator can locate the transmitting rogue with a directional antenna. Figure 14.7 pictures a location feature common in a mobile WIDS.

FIGURE 14.7   Mobile WIDS locater tool

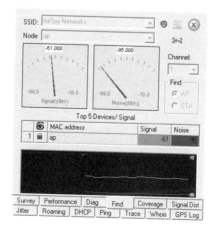

 We highly recommend that you test-drive a mobile WIDS solution to gain hands-on experience with the capabilities that this type of product offers. One such solution is AirDefense Mobile. Download a fully working 30-day trial copy of AirDefense Mobile at www.airdefense.net/products/admobile/trial.php.

Spectrum Analyzer

In Chapters 15 and 16, we will discuss the benefits of using a *spectrum analyzer* during a wireless site survey. WLAN administrators have begun to realize the benefit of using spectrum analyzers for security purposes. The WIDS vendors currently make claims that their products can detect layer 1 denial of service attacks, namely, RF jamming. The truth of the matter is that the WIDS vendors are excellent at detecting all of the numerous layer 2 attacks but have limited success with layer 1 detection because they are not spectrum analyzers. A spectrum analyzer is a frequency domain tool that can detect any RF signal in the frequency range that is being scanned. A spectrum analyzer that monitors the 2.4 GHz ISM band will be able to detect both intentional jamming and unintentional jamming. Some spectrum analyzers can look at the RF signature of the interfering signal and classify the device. For example, the spectrum analyzer might identify the signal as a microwave oven, a Bluetooth transmitter, or an 802.11 FHSS radio. A spectrum analyzer might also be used to locate rogue 900 MHz or frequency hopping access points.

Most spectrum analyzers are stand-alone solutions; however, one company, Cognio, manufactures a distributed solution that uses a centralized server and remote hardware spectrum analyzer sensors. The Cognio client/server spectrum analyzer is effectively a layer 1 wireless intrusion detection system. The layer 1 intrusion detection system also has the ability to categorize interference types based on frequency signatures. This can be useful to help classify and locate the interfering device.

Wireless Security Policy

In Chapter 13, you learned about the various authentication, encryption, and segmentation methods that can be used to secure an 802.11 wireless network. In this chapter, you have learned about wireless intrusion detection systems that can be used to monitor for possible threats. Securing a wireless network and monitoring for threats are absolute necessities, but both are worthless unless proper security policies are in place. What good is an 802.1X/EAP solution if the end users share their passwords? Why purchase an intrusion detection system if a policy has not been established on how to deal with rogue access points? More and more businesses have started to amend their network usage policies to include a wireless policy section. If you have not done so already, a WLAN section should absolutely be added to the corporate security policy. Two good resources for learning about best practices and computer security policies are the SANS Institute and the National Institute of Standards and Technologies (NIST).

Security policy templates from the SANS Institute can be downloaded from www.sans.org/resources/policies. The NIST special publication document 800-48 regarding wireless security can be downloaded from http://csrc.nist.gov/publications/nistpubs.

General Security Policy

When establishing a wireless security policy, you must first define a *general policy*. A general wireless security policy establishes why a wireless security policy is needed for an organization. Even if a company has no plans for deploying a wireless network, there should be at a minimum a policy for how to deal with rogue wireless devices. A general wireless security policy will define the following items:

Statement of authority   Defines who put the wireless policy in place and the executive management that backs the policy.

Applicable audience   Defines the audience to whom the policy applies, including employees, visitors, contractors, and so on.

Violation reporting procedures   Defines how the wireless security policy will be enforced, including what actions should be taken and who is in charge of enforcement.

Risk assessment and threat analysis   Defines the potential wireless security risks and threats and what the financial impact will be on the company if a successful attack occurs.

Security Auditing   Defines internal auditing procedures as well as the need for independent outside audits.

Functional Security Policy

A *functional policy* is also needed to define the technical aspects of wireless security. The functional security policy establishes how to secure the wireless network in terms of what solutions and actions are needed. A functional wireless security policy will define the following items:

Policy essentials   Defines basic security procedures such as password policies, training, and proper usage of the wireless network.

Baseline practices   Defines minimum wireless security practices such as configuration checklists, staging and testing procedures, and so on.

Design and implementation   Defines the actual authentication, encryption, and segmentation solutions that are to be put in place.

Monitoring and response   Defines all wireless intrusion detection procedures and the appropriate response to alarms.

Legislative Compliance

In most countries there are mandated regulations on how to protect and secure data communications within all government agencies. In the United States, the National Institute of Standards and Technologies (NIST) maintains the *Federal Information Processing Standards (FIPS)*. Of special interest to wireless security is the FIPS 140-2 standard, which defines security requirements for cryptography modules. The use of validated cryptographic modules is required by the United States government for all unclassified communications. Other countries also recognize the FIPS 140-2 standard or have similar regulations.

In the United States, other legislation exists for protecting information and communications in certain industries. Some of these include:

HIPAA   The Health Insurance Portability and Accountability Act (HIPAA) establishes national standards for electronic health care transactions and national standards for providers, health insurance plans, and employers. The goal is to protect patient information and maintain privacy.

Sarbanes-Oxley   The Sarbanes-Oxley Act of 2002 defines more stringent controls on corporate accounting and auditing procedures with a goal of corporate responsibility and enhanced financial disclosure.

GLBA   The Gramm-Leach-Bliley Act requires banks and financial institutions to notify customers of policies and practices of disclosing customer information. The goal is protect personal information such as credit card numbers, social security numbers, names, addresses, etc.

Information about the FIPS regulations can be found at http://csrc.nist.gov/publications/fips. More information about HIPAA can be found at www.hhs.gov/ocr/hipaa. General information about Sarbanes-Oxley can be found via the web at www.sarbanes-oxley.com. Further information about GLBA can be located at www.ftc.gov.

802.11 Wireless Policy Recommendations

Although a very detailed and thorough policy document should be created, we highly recommend these five wireless security policies:

Remote Access WLAN Policy   End users will be taking their laptops and handheld devices off site and away from company grounds. Most users will likely use wireless networks at home and at wireless "hotspots" to access the Internet. By design, many of these remote wireless networks have absolutely no security in place, and it is imperative that a remote access WLAN policy be strictly enforced. This policy should include the required use of an IPSec VPN solution to provide device authentication, user authentication, and strong encryption of all wireless data traffic. Hotspots are prime targets for malicious eavesdropping attacks. Personal firewalls should also be installed on all remote computers to prevent peer-to-peer attacks. Personal firewalls will not prevent hijacking attacks or peer-to-peer attacks but will prevent attackers from accessing most critical information. The remote access policy is mandatory because the most likely location for an attack to occur is at a public access hotspot.

Rogue AP Policy   No end users should ever be permitted to install their own wireless devices on the corporate network. This includes access points, wireless routers, wireless hardware USB clients, and wireless cards. Any users installing their own wireless equipment could potentially open unsecured portals into the main infrastructure network. This policy should be strictly enforced.

Ad-Hoc Policy   End users should not be permitted to set up ad-hoc or peer-to-peer networks. Peer-to-peer networks rarely use encryption, are susceptible to peer attacks, and can also serve as an unsecured portal to the infrastructure network if the computer's Ethernet port is also in use.

Wireless LAN Proper Use Policy   A thorough policy should outline the proper use and implementation of the main corporate wireless network. This policy should include proper installation procedures, proper security implementations, and allowed application use on the wireless LAN.

IDS Policy   Policies should be written defining how to properly respond to alerts generated by the wireless intrusion detection system. An example would be how to deal with the discovery of rogue access points and all the necessary actions that should take place.

These five policies are simplistic but are a good starting point in writing a wireless security policy document. The authors of this book also recommend that the built-in Microsoft

Windows XP Wi-Fi client utilities known as the Wireless Zero Configuration (WZC) service be disabled at all times due to numerous documented security risks. We recommend using one single vendor's software client or using third-party client utilities if multiple vendor cards must be supported.

Several vendors now offer policy enforcement software agents. These agents can protect mobile users at hotspots and other public Wi-Fi networks from wireless-specific risks that could expose private data and transactions. One example of a policy enforcement solution is AirDefense Personal. You can download a free copy of AirDefense Personal Lite at www.airdefense.net/products/adpersonal/index.php.

 Real World Scenario

What Type of Security Is Needed for Home Wireless Networks?

As you learned in Chapter 13, security for enterprise WLANs requires an 802.1X/EAP authentication solution, strong dynamic encryption such as TKIP/RC4 or CCMP/AES, and a segmentation solution such as wireless VLANs. Usually SOHO Wi-Fi security is not as strong or complex as enterprise security because of cost considerations and available resources. However, many security steps can still be taken to offer a reasonably secure solution for a home wireless network. Included with the CD of this book is a white paper from AirSpy Networks titled "The Top 10 Security Checklist for SOHO Wireless LANs," which makes 10 common-sense suggestions toward small office and home Wi-Fi security. While there is no such thing as perfect security, the implementation of these 10 suggestions will bring you well on your way toward being much more secure than the majority of your neighbors. Security in a SOHO environment is still dependent upon the value of what you're trying to be protect, and in some instances, enterprise-type security might be needed in a SOHO environment.

Summary

In this chapter we discussed all the potential wireless attacks and threats. The rogue access point has always been the biggest concern in terms of wireless threats. However, we discussed many other serious threats, such as peer-to-peer attacks and eavesdropping, that can have consequences that are just as serious. We also discussed denial of service attacks that cannot be mitigated and can only be monitored. We covered the various solutions that are available for intrusion monitoring. Most intrusion detection solutions use a distributed client/server model and some offer rogue prevention capabilities. Finally, we discussed the need for sound wireless security policies that will act as a foundation for the wireless security solutions that you implement.

Exam Essentials

Understand the risk of the rogue access point. Be able to explain why the rogue AP provides a portal into network resources. Understand that employees are often the source of a rogue AP.

Define peer-to-peer attacks. Understand that peer-to-peer attacks can happen via an access point or through an ad-hoc network. Explain how to defend against this type of attack.

Know the risks of eavesdropping. Explain the difference between casual and malicious eavesdropping. Explain why encryption is needed for protection.

Define authentication and hijacking attacks. Explain the risks behind these types attacks. Understand that a strong 802.1X/EAP solution is needed to mitigate them.

Explain wireless denial of service attacks. Know the difference between layer 1 and layer 2 DoS attacks. Explain why these attacks cannot be mitigated and can only be monitored.

Understand the types of wireless intrusion solutions. Explain the difference between a WIDS and a WIPS. Understand that most solutions are distributed client/server models. Know the various components of an intrusion monitoring solution as well as the various models. Understand which attacks can be monitored and which can be prevented.

Understand the need for wireless security policy. Explain the difference between general and functional policies.

Key Terms

Before you take the exam, be certain you are familiar with the following terms:

casual eavesdropping	Public Secure Packet Forwarding (PSPF)
denial of service (DoS)	rogue access point
evil twin attack	spectrum analyzer
Federal Information Processing Standards (FIPS)	wardriving
functional policy	Wi-Fi phishing attack
general policy	wireless hijacking
malicious eavesdropping	wireless intrusion detection system (WIDS)
man-in-the-middle attack	wireless intrusion prevention systems (WIPS)
peer-to-peer attack	

Review Questions

1. Which of these attacks are considered denial of service attacks? (Choose all that apply.)
   A. Man-in-the-middle
   B. Jamming
   C. Deauthenication spoofing
   D. MAC spoofing
   E. Peer-to-peer

2. Which of these attacks would be considered malicious eavesdropping? (Choose all that apply.)
   A. NetStumbler
   B. Peer-to-peer
   C. Protocol analyzer capture
   D. Packet reconstruction
   E. PS polling attack

3. Which of these attacks will not be detected by a wireless instruction detection system (WIDS)?
   A. Deauthentication spoofing
   B. MAC spoofing
   C. Rogue access point
   D. Protocol analyzer
   E. Association flood

4. Which of these attacks can be mitigated with a mutual authentication solution? (Choose all that apply.)
   A. Malicious eavesdropping
   B. Deauthentication
   C. Man-in-the-middle
   D. Wireless hijacking
   E. Authentication flood

5. Name two types of rogue devices that cannot be detected by current layer 2 wireless intrusion prevention systems (WIPS).
   A. 900 MHz radio
   B. 802.11h compliant device
   C. FHSS radio
   D. 802.11b routers
   E. 802.11g mixed mode device

6. When designing a wireless policy document, what two major areas of policy should be addressed?

   A. General policy

   B. Functional policy

   C. Rogue AP policy

   D. Authentication policy

   E. Physical security

7. What can happen when an intruder compromises the pre-shared key used during WPA/WPA2 Personal authentication? (Choose all that apply.)

   A. Decryption

   B. Hijacking

   C. Spoofing

   D. Encryption cracking

   E. Access to network resources

8. Which of these attacks are considered layer 2 denial of service attacks? (Choose all that apply.)

   A. Deauthentication spoofing

   B. Jamming

   C. Virtual carrier attacks

   D. PS-Poll floods

   E. Authentication floods

9. Which of these can cause unintentional RF jamming attacks against an 802.11 wireless network? (Choose all that apply.)

   A. Microwave oven

   B. Signal generator

   C. 2.4 GHz cordless phones

   D. 900 MHz cordless phones

   E. Deauthentication transmitter

10. Which of these tools will best detect frequency hopping rogue devices? (Choose all that apply.)

   A. Stand-alone spectrum analyzer

   B. Distributed spectrum analyzer

   C. Distributed layer 2 WIDS

   D. Mobile layer 2 WIDS

   E. Layer 2 WIPS

11. Name two solutions that can help to mitigate peer-to-peer attacks from other clients that are associated to the same 802.11 access point?

    A. Personal firewall

    B. PSPF

    C. OSPF

    D. MAC filter

    E. Access control lists

12. What type of solution can be used to perform countermeasures against a rogue access point?

    A. WIDS

    B. 802.1X/EAP

    C. WIPS

    D. TKIP/RC4

    E. WINS

13. Name the three labels that a WIPS uses to classify an 802.11 device.

    A. Infrastructure

    B. Known

    C. Enabled

    D. Disabled

    E. Rogue

14. Scott is an administrator at the Williams Lumber Company and his WIPS has detected a rogue access point. What actions should he take after discovering the rogue AP? (Choose the best two answers.)

    A. Enable the layer 2 rogue containment feature that his WIPS provides

    B. Unplug the rogue AP from the wall upon discovery

    C. Call the police

    D. Call his mother

    E. Unplug the rogue AP from the data port upon discovery

15. Which of these attacks are wireless users susceptible to at a public access hotspot? (Choose all that apply.)

    A. Wi-Fi phishing

    B. Happy AP attack

    C. Peer-to-peer attack

    D. Malicious eavesdropping

    E. 802.11 reverse ARP attack

    F. Man-in-the-middle

    G. Wireless hijacking

16. Name two components that should be mandatory in every remote access wireless security policy.

    A. IPSec VPN

    B. 802.1X/EAP

    C. Personal firewall

    D. Captive portal

    E. Wireless stun gun

17. MAC filters are typically considered useless in most cases because of what type of attack?

    A. Spamming

    B. Spoofing

    C. Phishing

    D. Cracking

    E. Eavesdropping

18. Wireless switches typically deploy which type of WIDS deployment model?

    A. Integrated

    B. Overlay

    C. Integration enabled

    D. Edge distribution

    E. Overlay enabled

19. Which of these encryption technologies have currently been cracked? (Choose all that apply.)

    A. 64-bit WEP

    B. TKIP/RC4

    C. CCMP/AES

    D. 128-bit WEP

    E. Wired Equivalent Privacy

20. What is another name for a wireless hijacking attack?

    A. Wi-Fi phishing

    B. Man-in-the-middle

    C. Fake AP

    D. Evil twin

    E. AirSpy

Answers to Review Questions

1. B, C. DoS attacks can occur at either layer 1 or layer 2 of the OSI model. Layer 1 attacks are known as RF jamming attacks. A wide variety of layer 2 DoS attacks exist that are a result of tampering with 802.11 frames, including the spoofing of deauthentication frames.

2. C, D. Malicious eavesdropping is achieved with the unauthorized use of protocol analyzers to capture wireless communications. Any unencrypted 802.11 frame transmission can be reassembled at the upper layers of the OSI model.

3. D. A protocol analyzer is a passive device that captures 802.11 traffic and can be used for malicious eavesdropping. A WIDS cannot detect a passive device. Strong encryption is the solution to prevent a malicious eavesdropping attack.

4. C, D. The only way to prevent a wireless hijacking, man-in-the-middle, and/or Wi-Fi phishing attack is to use a mutual authentication solution. 802.1X/EAP authentication solutions require that mutual authentication credentials be exchanged before a user can be authorized.

5. A, C. The radio cards inside the WIPS sensors monitor the 2.4 GHz ISM band and the 5 GHz UNII frequencies. Older legacy wireless networking equipment exists that transmits in the 900 MHz ISM band and these devices will not be detected. The radio cards inside the WIPS sensors also only use DSSS and OFDM technologies. Wireless networking equipment exists that uses frequency hopping spread spectrum (FHSS) transmissions in the 2.4 GHz ISM and will go undetected. The only tool that can detect either a 900 MHz or frequency hopping rogue access point is a spectrum analyzer.

6. A, B. The general wireless security policy establishes why a wireless security policy is needed for an organization. Even if a company has no plans for deploying a wireless network, there should be at a minimum a policy detailing how to deal with rogue wireless devices. The functional security policy establishes how to secure the wireless network in terms of what solutions and actions are needed.

7. A, E. Once the attacker has the passphrase, they can also associate to the WPA/WPA2 access point and therefore access network resources. The encryption technology is not cracked, but the key can be re-created. If a hacker has the passphrase and captures the 4-way handshake, they can re-create the dynamic encryption keys and therefore decrypt traffic. WPA/WPA2 Personal is not considered a strong security solution for the enterprise because if the passphrase is compromised, the attacker can access network resources and decrypt traffic.

8. A, C, D, E. Numerous types of layer 2 DoS attacks exist, including association floods, deauthentication spoofing, disassociation spoofing, authentication floods, PS-Poll floods, and virtual carrier attacks. RF jamming is a layer 1 DoS attack.

9. A, C. Microwave ovens operate in the 2.4 GHz ISM band and are often a source of unintentional interference. 2.4 GHz cordless phones can also cause unintentional jamming. A signal generator is typically going to be used as a jamming device, which would be considered intentional jamming. 900 MHz cordless phones will not interfere with 802.11 equipment that operates in the 2.4 GHz ISM band and the 5 GHz UNII bands. There is no such thing as a deauthentication transmitter.

10. A, B. The radio cards inside the WIPS/WIDS sensors currently use only DSSS and OFDM technologies. Wireless networking equipment exists that uses frequency hopping spread spectrum (FHSS) transmissions in the 2.4 GHz ISM and will go undetected by WIPS/WIDS devices. The only tool that can detect either a 900 MHz or a frequency hopping rogue access point is a spectrum analyzer.

11. A, B. Public Secure Packet Forwarding (PSPF) is a feature that can be enabled on WLAN access points or WLAN controllers to block wireless clients from communicating with other wireless clients on the same wireless segment. The use of a personal firewall can also be used to mitigate peer-to peer attacks.

12. C. A wireless intrusion prevention system (WIPS) is capable of mitigating attacks from rogue access points. A WIPS sensor can use layer 2 DoS attacks as a countermeasure against a rogue device. SNMP may also be used to shut down ports that a rogue AP has been connected to. WIPS vendors also use unpublished methods for mitigating rogue attacks.

13. A, B, E. The WIPS solution labels 802.11 radios into three classifications. An infrastructure device refers to any client station or access point that is an authorized member of the company's wireless network. A known device refers to any client station or access point that is detected by the WIPS but is not considered as an interfering device or as a rogue access point. A rogue device refers to any client station or access point that is considered an interfering device and a potential threat.

14. A, E. Every company should have a policy forbidding installation of wireless devices by employees. Every company should also have a policy on how to respond to all wireless attacks, including the discovery of a rogue access point. If a WIPS discovers a rogue AP, temporarily implementing layer 2 rogue containment abilities is advisable until the rogue device can be physically located. Once the device is found, immediately unplug it from the data port but not from the electrical outlet. It would be advisable to leave the rogue AP on so that the administrator can do some forensics and look at the association tables and log files to possibly determine who installed it.

15. A, C, D, F, G. Currently, there is no such thing as a Happy AP attack or an 802.11 reverse ARP attack. Wireless users are especially vulnerable to attacks at public use hotspots because there is no security. Because no encryption is used, the wireless users are vulnerable to malicious eavesdropping. Because no mutual authentication solution is in place, they are vulnerable to hijacking, man-in-the-middle, and phishing attacks. The hotspot access point might also be allowing peer-to-peer communications, making the users vulnerable to peer-to-peer attacks. Every company should have a remote access wireless security policy to protect their end users when they leave company grounds.

16. A, C. Public access hotspots have absolutely no security in place, and it is imperative that a remote access WLAN policy be strictly enforced. This policy should include the required use of an IPSec VPN solution to provide device authentication, user authentication, and strong encryption of all wireless data traffic. Hotspots are prime targets for malicious eavesdropping attacks. Personal firewalls should also be installed on all remote computers to prevent peer-to-peer attacks.

17. B. MAC filters are configured to apply restrictions that will only allow traffic from specific client stations to pass through based on their unique MAC addresses. MAC addresses can be "spoofed," or impersonated, and any amateur hacker can easily bypass any MAC filter by spoofing an allowed client station's address.

18. A. Many wireless switching vendors have fully integrated WIDS capabilities. The wireless controller acts as the centralized server. Because the IDS capabilities are fully integrated, there is no need for an overlay solution.

19. A, D, E. Wired Equivalent Privacy (WEP) encryption has been cracked, and currently available tools may be able to derive the secret key within a matter of minutes. The size of the key makes no difference, and both 64-bit WEP and 128-bit WEP can be cracked. Currently TKIP/RC4 and CCMP/AES encryption have not been cracked.

20. D. An attack that often generates a lot of press is wireless hijacking, also known as the evil twin attack. The attacker hijacks wireless clients at layer 2 and layer 3 using an evil twin access point and a DHCP server. The hacker may take the attack several steps further and initiate a man-in-the-middle attack and/or a Wi-Fi phishing attack.

Chapter

15

Radio Frequency Site Survey Fundamentals

IN THIS CHAPTER, YOU WILL LEARN ABOUT THE FOLLOWING:

- ✓ **WLAN Site Survey Interview**
  - Customer Briefing
  - Business Requirements
  - Capacity and Coverage Requirements
  - Existing Wireless Network
  - Infrastructure Connectivity
  - Security Expectations
- ✓ **Documentation and Reports**
  - Forms and Customer Documentation
  - Deliverables
  - Additional Reports
- ✓ **Vertical Market Considerations**
  - Outdoor Surveys
  - Aesthetics
  - Government
  - Education
  - Healthcare
  - Hotspots
  - Retail
  - Warehouses
  - Manufacturing
  - Multitenant Buildings

In Chapter 16, "Site Survey Systems and Devices," we will discuss wireless site surveys from a technical perspective. You will learn about all the procedures and tools required for proper coverage, spectrum, and application analysis. In this chapter, however, we will discuss the wireless site survey from an administrative perspective. Much preparation must take place before the actual WLAN site survey is conducted. The needs of the wireless LAN must be predetermined and the proper questions must be asked.

We will discuss all the necessary preparations for the site survey and the documentation that must be assembled prior to it. We will also discuss all the final reports that are delivered upon completion of the WLAN site survey. Finally, we will outline unique wireless site survey considerations that should be given to different vertical markets.

WLAN Site Survey Interview

Is a site survey even needed? The answer to that question is almost always a resounding yes. If an owner of a small retail flower shop desires a wireless network, the site survey that is conducted may be as simple as placing a residential wireless gateway in the middle of the shop, turning the transmit power to a lower setting, and making sure you have connectivity. Performing a site survey in a medium-size to large-size business entails much more physical work and time. Before the actual survey is conducted, a proper *site survey interview* should occur to both educate the customer and properly determine their needs.

Asking the correct questions during a site survey interview will not only ensure that the proper tools are used during the survey, it will also make the survey more productive. Most important, the end result of a thorough interview and thorough survey will be a WLAN that meets all the intended mobility, coverage, and capacity needs. In the following sections, we will discuss the questions that should be thoughtfully considered during the site survey interview.

Customer Briefing

Even though 802.11 technologies have been around since 1997, much misunderstanding and misinformation about wireless networking still exists. Many businesses and individuals are familiar with Ethernet networks, therefore a "just plug it in and turn it on" mentality is prevalent. If a wireless network is being planned for your company or for a prospective client, it is highly recommended that you sit management down and give them a quick overview of 802.11

wireless networking and talk with them about how and why site surveys are conducted. You do not need to explain the inner workings of Orthogonal Frequency Division Multiplexing or Distributed Coordination Function; however, a conversation about the advantages of Wi-Fi as well as the limitations of a WLAN is a good idea.

For example, a brief explanation about the advantages of mobility would be an excellent start. Chances are that a wireless network is already being considered because the company's end users have requested mobility or a specific application such as Voice over Wi-Fi (VoWiFi) is being contemplated.

Just as important is a discussion about the bandwidth and throughput limitations of current 802.11a/b/g technology. Enterprise users are accustomed to 100 Mbps full-duplex or better speeds on the wired network. Because of vendor hype, people often might believe that a Wi-Fi network will provide them with similar bandwidth and throughput. Management will need to be educated that because of overhead, the aggregate throughput is usually one half or less of the advertised data rate.

As you learned in earlier chapters, the aggregate throughput of a 54 Mbps data rate is 20 Mbps or less. It should also be explained that the medium is a half-duplex shared medium and not full-duplex. Chances are that an 802.11b/g network is being considered and it might be necessary to briefly explain the aeffect on throughput as a result of the 802.11g protection mechanism. In the future, 802.11n WLAN equipment will address greater throughput needs, thus making the bandwidth/throughput conversation less painful. However, with the demand for faster networks, in the future we are sure we will be explaining why 802.11n is so much slower than Gigabit Ethernet.

Another appropriate discussion is why a site survey is needed. A very brief explanation on how RF signals propagate and attenuate will provide management with a better understanding of why an RF site survey is needed to ensure the proper coverage and enhance performance. A discussion and comparison of a 2.4 GHz versus a 5 GHz WLAN might also be necessary. If management is properly briefed on the basics of Wi-Fi as well as the importance of a site survey, the forthcoming technical questions will be answered in a more suitable fashion.

Business Requirements

The first question that should be proposed is, What is the purpose of the WLAN? If you have a complete understanding of what is the intended use of a wireless network, the result will be a better-designed WLAN. For example, a VoWiFi has very different requirements than a heavily used data network. If the purpose of the WLAN is only to provide users a gateway to the Internet, security and segmentation recommendations will be different. A warehouse environment with 200 handheld scanners is very different than an office environment. A hospital's wireless network will have different business requirements than an airport's wireless network. Here are some of the business requirement questions that should be asked:

What applications will be used over the WLAN?   This question could have both capacity and Quality of Service (QoS) implications. A wireless network for graphic designers moving huge graphics files across a WLAN network would obviously need more bandwidth than a wireless network for nothing but wireless bar code scanners. If time-sensitive applications such as voice or video are required, proprietary QoS needs might have to be addressed. 802.11e/WMM will address these QoS needs in the future.

Who will be using the WLAN?   Different types of users have different capacity and performance needs. Groups of users might be segmented into VLANs or even segmented by different frequencies. This is also an important consideration for security roles.

What types of devices will be connecting to the WLAN?   Handheld devices may also be segmented into separate VLANs or by frequency. VoWiFi phones are always put in a separate VLAN than data users with laptops. Also, most handheld devices currently only operate in the 2.4 GHz ISM band. The capabilities of the devices may also force decisions in security, frequency, technology, and data rates.

We will discuss the varying business requirements of different vertical markets later in this chapter. Defining the purpose of the WLAN in advance will lead to a more productive site survey and is imperative to the eventual design of the WLAN.

Capacity and Coverage Requirements

Once the purpose of the WLAN has been clearly defined, the next step is to begin asking all the necessary questions for planning the site survey and designing the wireless network. While the final design of a WLAN is completed after the site survey is completed, some preliminary design based on the *capacity* and *coverage* needs of the customer is recommended. You will need to sit down with a copy of the building's floor plan and ask the customer where they want RF coverage. The answer will almost always be everywhere.

If a VoWiFi deployment is planned, that answer is probably legitimate because Wi-Fi VoIP phones will need mobility and connectivity throughout the building. If the WLAN is strictly a data network, the need for blanket coverage might not be necessary. Do laptop data users need access in a storage area? Do they need connectivity in the outdoor courtyard? Do handheld bar code scanners used in a warehouse area need access in the front office? The answer to these questions will often vary depending on the earlier questions that were asked about the purpose of the WLAN. However, if you can determine that certain areas of the facility do not require coverage, you will save the customer money and yourself time when conducting the physical survey. Depending on the layout and the materials used inside the building, some preplanning might need to be done as to what type of antennas to use in certain areas of the facility. A long hallway or corridor will most likely need an indoor semi-directional antenna for coverage as opposed to an omni-directional antenna. When the survey is performed, this will be confirmed or adjusted accordingly.

The most often neglected aspect prior to the site survey is determining capacity needs of the WLAN. As mentioned in Chapter 11, "Network Design, Implementation, and Management," you must not just consider coverage; you must also plan for capacity. Cell sizing and/or co-location might be necessary to properly address your capacity requirements. In order for the wireless end user to experience acceptable performance, a ratio of average amount of users per access point must be established. The answer to the capacity question depends on a host of variables, including answers from earlier questions about the purpose of the WLAN. Capacity will not be as big of a concern in a warehouse environment using mostly handheld data scanners. However, if the WLAN has average to heavy data requirements, capacity will absolutely be a concern. The following are among the many factors that need to be considered when planning for capacity:

Data applications   The applications that are used will have a direct impact on how many users should be communicating on average through an access point. So the next question is, What is a good average number of data users per access point? Once again, it depends entirely on the purpose of the WLAN and the applications in use. However, in an average 802.11b/g network, 12 to 15 data users per access point is an often-quoted figure.

User density   Three important questions need to be asked with regard to users. First, how many users currently will need wireless access? Second, how many users may need wireless access in the future? These first two questions will help you to begin adequately planning for a good ratio of users per access point while allowing for future growth. The third question of great significance is, Where are the users? Sit down with network management and indicate on the floor plan of the building any areas of high user density. For example, one company might have offices with only 1 or 2 people per room, while another company might have 30 or more people in a common area separated by cubicle walls. Other examples of areas with high user density are call centers, classrooms, and lecture halls. Also plan to conduct the physical survey when the users are present and not during off hours. A high concentration of human bodies can attenuate the RF signal due to absorption.

Peak on/off use   Be sure to ask what the peak times are, that is, when access to the WLAN is heaviest. For example, a conference room might be used only once a day or once a month. Also, certain applications might be heavily accessed through the WLAN at specified times. Another peak period could be when one shift leaves and another arrives.

Existing transmitters   This does not refer just to previously installed 802.11 networks. Rather, it is referring to interfering devices such as microwaves, cordless headsets, cordless phones, wireless machinery mechanisms, and so on. Often this is severely overlooked. If a large open area will house the help desk once the wireless is installed, you may be thinking of capacity. However, if you don't know that they are using 2.4 GHz cordless headsets or Bluetooth keyboard and mouse, then you may be designing a network destined for failure.

Mobile vs. mobility   There are two types of mobility. The first is related to being mobile and the other is true mobility. To help explain this, think of the marketing manager working on a presentation and saving it on a network share. He later wants to give that presentation in the boardroom. If he picks up his laptop, closes the lid, and walks to the conference room where he opens the laptop, connects to the wireless network, and gives his presentation, that is being mobile. He may have disconnected in between points and that is OK. However, having true mobility means that a user must remain connected 100 percent of the time while traveling through the facility. This would be indicative of VoWiFi or warehouse scanning applications. Determining which type is necessary can be key for not only troubleshooting an existing network but also designing a new one.

802.11g protection mechanism It should be understood in advance that if there is any requirement for backward compatibility with 802.11b HR-DSSS clients, the 802.11g protection mechanism will always adversely affect throughput. The majority of enterprise deployments will always require backward compatibility to provide access to handhelds, VoIP phones, or older 802.11b radio cards.

Carefully planning coverage and capacity needs prior to the site survey will assist you in determining some of the design scenarios you may possibly need, including AP power settings, type of antennas, cell sizes, and so on. The physical site survey will still have to be conducted to validate and further determine coverage and capacity requirements.

 Real World Scenario

How Many Simultaneous VoIP Telephone Calls Can an Access Point Support?

Several factors come into play, including cell bandwidth, average use, and vendor specifics. One of the leading VoWiFi telephone vendors, SpectraLink, recommends a maximum of 12 calls per 11 Mbps cell. Due to bandwidth limitations, that number drops to a recommended maximum of 7 calls per 2 Mbps cell. A typical call requires 4.5 percent of AP bandwidth at 11 Mbps and 12 percent of AP bandwidth at 2 Mbps. Different vendor-specific access point characteristics can also affect the number of concurrent calls, and extensive testing is recommended. Probability models also exist for predicting VoIP traffic. Not every Wi-Fi phone user will be making a call at the same time. Probabilistic traffic formulas use a telecommunications unit of measurement known as an *Erlang*. An Erlang is equal to one hour of telephone traffic in one hour of time. Some online VoIP Erlang traffic calculators can be found at www.erlang.com.

Existing Wireless Network

Quite often the reason you are conducting a WLAN site survey is that you have been called in as a consultant to fix an existing deployment. Professional site survey companies have reported that as much as 40 percent of their business is being hired to troubleshoot existing WLANs, which often requires conducting a second site survey or discovering that one was never conducted to begin with.

As more corporations and individuals become educated in 802.11 technologies, the percentage will obviously drop. Sadly, many untrained customers just install the access points wherever they can mount them and leave the default power and channel settings on every AP. Usually, site surveys must be conducted either because of performance problems or difficulty roaming. Performance problems are often caused by co-channel interference and multipath interference as well as other sources of interference. Roaming problems may also be interference related or caused by a lack of adequate coverage and/or by a lack of proper cell overlap. Here are some of the questions that should be asked prior to the reparative site survey:

What are the current problems with the existing WLAN?   Ask the customer to clarify the problems. Are they throughput related? Are there frequent disconnects? Is there any difficulty roaming? In what part of the building do the problems occur most often? How often do they occur and have there been any steps taken to duplicate the troubles?

Are there any known sources of RF interference?   More than likely the customer will have no idea, but it does not hurt to ask. Are there any microwave ovens? Do they use cordless phones or headsets? Does anyone use Bluetooth for keyboards or mouse? After asking these interference questions, you should always conduct a spectrum analysis. This is the *only* way to determine whether or not there is any RF interference in the area that may inhibit future transmissions. Something like a new Wireless Internet Service Provider (WISP) in the area may simply be interfering with one of your channels.

Are there any known coverage dead zones?   This is related to the roaming questions, and areas probably exist where proper coverage is not being provided. Remember, this could be too little or too much coverage. Both create roaming and connectivity problems.

Does prior site survey data exist?   Chances are that an original site survey was not even conducted. However, if old site survey documentation exists, it may be helpful when troubleshooting existing problems. It is important to note that unless quantifiable data was collected that shows dB strengths, the survey report should be taken with extreme caution.

What equipment is currently installed?   Ask what type of equipment is being used, such as 802.11a or 802.11b/g and which vendor has been used. Once again, chances are the customer has no idea and it will be your job to determine what has been installed and why it is not working properly. Also check the configurations of the devices, including SSIDs, WEP keys, channels, power levels, and firmware versions. Oftentimes issues can be as simple as all the access points are transmitting on the same channel or there is a buffer issue that is resolved with the latest firmware.

Depending upon the level of troubleshooting that is required on the existing wireless network, a second site survey consisting of coverage and spectrum analysis will usually be necessary. After the new site survey has been conducted, adjustments to the existing WLAN equipment should be adequate; however, the worst case scenario would involve a complete redesign of the WLAN. Keep in mind that whenever a second site survey is necessary, all the same questions that are asked as part of a survey for a new installation (Greenfield survey) should also be asked prior to the second site survey.

Infrastructure Connectivity

You have already learned that the usual purposes of a WLAN are to provide mobility and to provide access via an AP into another network infrastructure. Part of the interview process will be to ask the correct questions so that the WLAN will integrate properly into the existing wired architecture. Asking for a copy of the wired network topology map is highly recommended. For security reasons, the customer may not want to disclose the wired topology and a nondisclosure agreement might need to be signed. It is a good idea to request that an agreement be signed to protect you legally as the integrator. Understanding the existing topology will also be of help when planning WLAN segmentation and security proposals and recommendations. With or without a topology map, the following topics are important to ensure the desired infrastructure connectivity:

Roaming   Is roaming required? In most cases, the answer will always be yes because mobility is a key advantage of wireless networking. Any devices that run connection-oriented applications will need seamless roaming. Roaming is mandatory if handheld devices and/or VoWiFi phones are deployed. Surprisingly, many customers do not require roaming capabilities. In these cases, being mobile is sufficient, as mentioned previously. Coverage may be needed only in some areas of the building and roaming may not a requirement. Some network administrators may want to be able to restrict certain areas where a user or a group of users can roam. For example, the sales team is allowed to roam only between access points on floors one and two and not permitted to roam to APs on floors three and four. The marketing team, however, is allowed to roam between access points on all four floors. The role-based access control (RBAC) capabilities of a wireless switch or controller will deliver the granular control needed to segment and control roaming. This may also have to be segmented with different SSIDs and VLANs. Another important roaming consideration is whether users will need to roam across layer 3 boundaries. A Mobile IP solution or a proprietary layer 3 roaming solution will be needed if client stations need to roam across subnets. Special considerations will have to be given to roaming with VoWiFi devices due to the issues that can arise from network latency. With regard to the existing network, it is imperative that you determine whether or not the network infrastructure will support all the new wireless features. For instance, if you want to roll out five SSIDs with different VLANs but haven't checked to see if the customer's network switches can be configured with VLANs, you may have a serious problem.

Wiring closets   Where are the wiring closets located? Will the locations that are being considered for AP installation be within a 100-meter (328-foot) cable drop from the wiring closets?

Antenna structure   If an outdoor network or point-to-point bridging application is requested, then there may be some additional structure that will need to be built to mount the antennas.

Hubs/switches   Will the access points be connected by CAT5 cabling to hubs or managed switches? A managed switch will be needed if VLANs are required. Connecting access points to hubs is not a recommended practice because of security and performance reasons. All traffic is broadcast to every port on a hub, and any traffic that traverses through an access point connected to a hub port can be heard on any of the other ports. Are there enough switch ports? Who will be responsible for programming the VLANs?

PoE   How will the access points be powered? Because APs are often mounted in the ceiling, Power over Ethernet will be required to remotely power the access points. Very often the customer will not yet have a PoE solution in place and further investment will be needed. If the customer already does have a PoE solution installed, it must be determined if the PoE solution is 802.3af compliant or a proprietary PoE solution. Also, is the solution an Endspan or Midspan solution? Regardless of what they have, it is important to make sure that it is compatible with the system you are installing. If PoE injectors need to be installed, you will need to make sure there are sufficient power outlets. If not, who will be responsible for installing those?

Segmentation   How will the WLAN and/or users of the WLAN be segmented from the wired network? Will the entire wireless network be on a separate IP subnet? Will VLANs be used and is a guest VLAN necessary? Will firewalls or VPNs be used for segmentation? Or will the wireless be a natural extension to the wired network and follow the same wiring, numbering, and design schemes as the wired infrastructure? All these questions are also directly related to security expectations.

Naming convention   Does the customer already have a naming convention for cabling and network infrastructure equipment and will one need to be created for the WLAN?

User management   Considerations regarding role-based access control (RBAC), bandwidth throttling, and load balancing should be discussed.

Infrastructure management   How will the WLAN remote access points be managed? Is a central management solution a requirement? Will devices be managed using SSH2, SNMP, HTTP/HTTPS, and so on?

A detailed site interview that provides detailed feedback about infrastructure connectivity requirements will result in a more thorough site survey and a well-designed wireless network. Seventy-five percent of the work for a good wireless network is in the pre-engineering. It creates the road map for all the other pieces.

Security Expectations

Network management should absolutely be interviewed about security expectations. All segmentation and encryption needs should be discussed. All authorization, authentication, and accounting (AAA) requirements must also be documented. It should also be determined whether the customer has plans to implement a wireless intrusion detection system (WIDS) solution for protection against rogue APs and the many other types of wireless attacks. Some security solutions, such as layer 3 VPNs, may put extra overhead on the WLAN because of the type of encryption that is used. Overhead caused by encryption should be accounted for during the capacity planning stages. Special considerations will have to be given to VoWiFi devices due to the latency issues that might result from EAP authentication.

A comprehensive interview regarding security expectations will provide the necessary information to make competent security recommendations after the site survey has been conducted and prior to deployment. Industry-specific regulations such as HIPAA, Gramm-Leach-Bliley, and Sarbanes-Oxley may have to be taken into consideration when making security recommendations. U.S. government installations may have to abide by the strict FIPS 140-2 regulations and all security solutions may need to be FIPS compliant.

All of these answers should also assist in determining if the necessary hardware and software exists to perform these functions. If not, it will be your job to consider the requirements and recommendations that may be necessary.

Documents and Reports

During the site survey interview (and prior to the site survey), proper documentation about the facility and network must be obtained. Additionally, site survey checklists should be created and adhered to during the physical survey. After the physical survey is performed, you'll deliver to the customer a professional and comprehensive final report. Additional reports and customer recommendations may also be included with the final report.

Forms and Customer Documentation

Prior to the site survey interview, it will be necessary to obtain some critical documentation from the customer:

Blueprints   A floor plan layout will be necessary in order to discuss coverage and capacity needs with network administration personnel. As discussed earlier in this chapter, while reviewing floor plan layouts, keep in mind that capacity and coverage requirements will be preplanned. Photocopies of the floor plan will also need to be created and used to record the RF measurements that are taken during the physical site survey as well as to record the locations of hardware placement. What if the customer does not have a set of blueprints? Blueprints can be located via a variety of sources. The original architect of the building will probably still have a copy of the blueprints. Many public and private buildings floor plans might also be located at a public government resource such as city hall or the fire department. Businesses are usually required to post a fire escape plan. Many site surveys have been conducted using a simple fire escape plan that has been drawn to scale if blueprints cannot be located. In a worst case scenario, you may have to use some graph paper and map out the floor plan manually. In Chapter 16 we will discuss RF modeling software that can be used to create predictive capacity and coverage simulations. Predictive analysis tools require detailed information about building materials that may be found in blueprints. Blueprints may already be in a vector graphic format (with the extensions `.dwg` and `.dwf`) for importing into a predictive analysis application or they may have to be scanned.

Topography map   If an outdoor site survey is planned, a topographic map, also called a contour map, will be needed. These contour maps display terrain information such as elevations, forest cover, and locations of streams and other bodies of water. Figure 15.1 depicts a typical topographic map. A topography map will be a necessity when performing bridging calculations such as Fresnel zone.

Network topology map   Understanding the layout of the customer's current wired network infrastructure will speed up the site survey process and allow for better planning of the WLAN during the design phase. A computer network topology map will provide necessary information such as the location of the wiring closets and layer 3 boundaries. The WLAN topology will be integrated as seamlessly as possible into the wired infrastructure. VLANS will normally be used for segmentation and security for both the wired and wireless networks. Acquiring a network topology map from the customer is a highly recommended practice that will result in a well-designed and properly integrated WLAN. Some organizations may not wish to reveal their wired network topology due to security reasons. It may be necessary to obtain security clearance and/or sign nondisclosure agreements.

Security credentials   Proper security authorization may be necessary to access facilities when conducting the site survey. Hospitals, government facilities, and many businesses require badges, passes, and maybe even an escort for entrance into certain areas. A meeting with security personal and/or the facilities manager will be necessary in order to meet all physical security requirements in advance of the survey. You do not want to show up at the customer site and be asked to return at another time because somebody forgot to schedule a security escort. Regardless of the security requirements, it is always a good idea to have the network administrator alert everyone that you will be in the area.

FIGURE 15.1   Topographic map

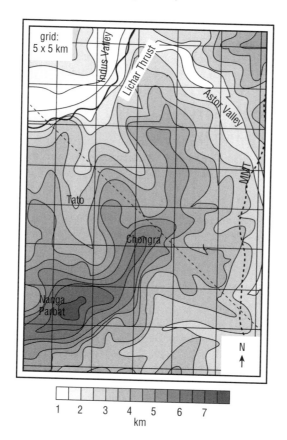

As a site survey professional, you will have created your own documentation or necessary checklists that will be used during the site survey interview as well as during the actual physical survey. There are several different types of survey checklists:

Interview checklist   A detailed checklist that contains all the questions asked during the site survey interview should be created in advance. The many detailed interview questions discussed earlier in this chapter will all be outlined in the interview checklist.

Installation checklist   Many site survey professionals prefer to record all installation details on the floor plan documents. An installation checklist detailing hardware placement and mounting for each individual access point is also an option. Information about AP location, antenna type, antenna orientation, mounting devices, and power sources may be logged.

Equipment checklist   For organizational purposes, a checklist of all the hardware and software tools used during the survey might also be a good idea. All the necessary tools needed for both indoor and outdoor site surveys will be covered in Chapter 16.

Deliverables

Once the interview process has been completed and the actual survey has been conducted, a final report must be delivered to the customer. Information gathered during the site survey will be organized and formatted into a professional technical report for the customer's review. Compiled information contained in the *deliverables* will include the following:

Spectrum analysis   Identifies potential sources of interference

RF coverage analysis   Defines RF cell boundaries

Hardware placement and configuration   Recommends AP placement, antenna orientation, channel reuse pattern, power settings, and so on

Application analysis   Includes results from application throughput testing, which is often an optional analysis report included with the final survey report

Chapter 16 covers in detail the methods and tools necessary to compile all the necessary analytical information that belongs in the final report. A detailed site survey report may be hundreds of pages depending upon the size of the facility. Site survey reports very often include pictures that were taken with a digital camera during the survey. Pictures can be used to record AP placement as well as identify problems such as interfering RF devices or potential installation problems like a solid ceiling. Professional site survey software applications exist that also generate professional quality reports using preformatted forms.

On the CD included with this book is a Microsoft Word file called sitesurvey.doc that is an example of a professional site survey report.

Additional Reports

Along with the site survey report, other recommendations will be made to the customer so that appropriate equipment and security are deployed. Normally the individuals and/or company that performed the site survey are also hired for the installation of the wireless network. The customer, however, might use the information from the site survey report to conduct their own deployment. Regardless of who handles the installation work, other recommendations and reports will be provided along with the site survey report:

Vendor recommendations   Many enterprise wireless vendors exist in the marketplace. It is a highly recommended practice to conduct the site survey using equipment from the same vendor who will supply the equipment that will later be deployed on site. Although the IEEE has set standards in place to ensure interoperability, every Wi-Fi vendor's equipment operates in some sort of proprietary fashion. You already have learned that many aspects of roaming are proprietary. The mere fact that every vendor's radio cards use proprietary RSSI thresholds is reason enough to stick with the same vendor during surveying and installation. Many site survey professionals have different vendor kits for the survey work. For example, a surveyor might own a kit that uses autonomous access points (fat APs) and might also own a wireless switching (thin APs) survey kit. It is not unheard of for a survey company to conduct two surveys with equipment from two different vendors and present the customer with two separate options. However, the interview process usually will determine in advance the vendor recommendations that will be made to the customer.

Implementation diagrams   Based upon information collected during the site survey, a final design diagram will be presented to the customer. The implementation diagram is basically a wireless topology map that illustrates where the access points will be installed and how the wireless network will be integrated into the existing wired infrastructure. AP placement, segmentation, and layer 3 boundaries will all be clearly defined.

Bill of materials   Along with the implementation diagrams will be a detailed bill of materials (BOM) that itemizes every hardware and software component necessary for the final installation of the wireless network. The model number and quantity of each piece of equipment will be necessary. This includes access points, bridges, wireless switches, antennas, cabling, connectors, and lightning arrestors.

Project schedule and costs   A detailed deployment schedule should be drafted that outlines all timelines, equipment costs, and labor costs.

Security solution recommendations   As mentioned earlier in this chapter, security expectations should be discussed during the site survey interview. Based upon these discussions, the surveying company will make comprehensive wireless security recommendations. All aspects of authentication, authorization, accounting, encryption, and segmentation should be included in the security recommendations documentation.

Wireless policy recommendations An extra addendum to the security recommendations might be corporate wireless policy recommendations. You might need to assist the customer in drafting a wireless network security policy if they do not already have one.

Training recommendations One of the most overlooked areas when deploying new solutions is proper training. It is highly recommended that wireless administration and security training sessions be scheduled with the customer's network personnel. Additionally, condensed training sessions should be scheduled with all end users.

Vertical Market Considerations

No two site surveys will ever be exactly alike. Every business has its own needs, issues, and considerations when conducting a survey. Some businesses may require an outdoor site survey instead of an indoor survey. A vertical market is a particular industry or group of businesses in which similar products or services are developed and marketed. The following sections outline the distinctive subjects that must be examined when a WLAN is being considered in specialized vertical markets.

Outdoor Surveys

Outdoor site surveys are occasionally performed for the purpose of providing outdoor wireless access for users. If outdoor access is required, ruggedized access points may need to be deployed or APs may need to be protected in weatherproof enclosures. As the popularity of wireless mesh networking continues to grow, outdoor wireless access will become more commonplace. Outdoor site survey kits using mesh wireless routers will be needed. Currently, most outdoor site surveys are for establishing bridge links. Calculations necessary for outdoor surveys are numerous, including the Fresnel zone, earth bulge, free space path loss, link budget, and fade margin. Weather conditions such as lightning, snow and ice, and wind must also be contemplated. Most important is the apparatus that the antennas will be mounted to. Unless the hardware is designed for outdoor use, the outdoor equipment must ultimately be protected from the weather elements using NEMA-rated enclosure units (NEMA stands for National Electrical Manufacturers Association). NEMA weatherproof enclosures are available with a wide range of options, including heating, cooling, and Power over Ethernet interfaces.

Safety is also a very big concern during outdoor site surveys. Consideration should be given to hiring professional installers. Certified tower climbing courses and tower safety and rescue training course are available.

Information about RF health and safety classes can be found at www.sitesafe .com. Also, tower climbing can be very dangerous work. Information about tower climbing and safety training can be found at www.comtrainusa.com.

All RF power regulations as defined by the regulatory body of your country will need to be considered. If towers are to be used, several government agencies may need to be contacted. Local and state municipalities may have construction regulations, and a permit is almost always required. In the United States, if any tower exceeds a height of 200 feet above ground level (AGL) or is within a certain proximity to an airport, both the FCC and FAA must be contacted. Other countries will have similar height restrictions, and the proper RF regulatory authority and aviation authority must be contacted to find out the details.

Aesthetics

A very important aspect of installation of wireless equipment is the "pretty factor." The majority of businesses prefer that all wireless hardware remain completely out of sight. Aesthetics is extremely important in retail environments and in the hospitality industry (restaurants and hotels). Any business that is dealing with the public will require that the Wi-Fi hardware be hidden. Many vendors are designing more aesthetic-looking access points and antennas. Some vendors have even camouflaged access points to resemble smoke detectors. Indoor enclosures can also be used to conceal access points from sight.

Government

The key concern during government wireless site surveys is security. When security expectations are addressed during the interview process, careful consideration should be given to all aspects of planned security. Many United States government agencies, including the military, require that all wireless solutions be FIPS-140-2 compliant. Other government agencies may require that the wireless network be completely shielded or shut off during certain times of the day. Be sure to check export restrictions before traveling to other countries with certain equipment. The United States forbids the export of AES encryption technology to some countries. Other countries will also have their own regulations and customs requirements.

Obtaining the proper security credentials will most likely be a requirement before conducting the government survey. An identification badge or pass often will be required. In some government facilities, it is likely that an escort will be needed in certain sensitive areas.

Education

As with government facilities, obtaining the proper security credentials in an education environment usually will be necessary. Properly securing access points in lockable enclosure units will also be necessary to prevent theft. Apple Macintosh computers are used quite extensively in the education arena, so it will be necessary to deploy client radio cards that support Macintosh drivers. Also, because of the high concentration of students, user density should be accounted for during capacity and coverage planning. In campus environments, wireless access will be required in most buildings, and very often bridging solutions will be needed between buildings across the campus. Some of the older educational facilities were constructed in such a manner to provide a disaster shelter. That means that propagation in these areas will be very limited.

Healthcare

One of the biggest concerns in a healthcare environment is sources of interference from the biomedical equipment that exists on site. Many biomedical devices operate in the ISM bands. For example, cauterizing devices in operating rooms have been known to cause problems with wireless networks. There is also a concern with 802.11 radios possibly interfering with the biomedical equipment. A meeting will be necessary with the biomedical department that maintains and services all biomedical equipment. Some hospitals have a person responsible for tracking and managing all RF devices in the facility. A thorough spectrum analysis survey using a spectrum analyzer will be extremely important. It is recommended that several sweeps of these areas be conducted and compared to ensure the greatest probability of capturing all of the possible interferers. Because of the many potential sources of interference in the 2.4 GHz ISM band, it is likely that 5 GHz 802.11a hardware will be deployed in many areas. Hospitals are usually large in scale and a site survey may take many weeks. Long hallways, multiple floors, fire safety doors, reflective materials, concrete construction, and wire mesh safety glass are some of the physical conditions that will be encountered during the survey.

The applications used in the medical environment should all be considered during the interview and the survey. Handheld PDAs are being used by doctors to transfer large files like X-ray graphics. Medical carts use radios to transfer patient data back to the nursing stations. Wi-Fi VoIP phone deployments are commonplace in hospitals because of the communication mobility that they provide to nurses. Because of the presence of medical patients, proper security credentials and/or an escort will often be necessary. Many applications are connection oriented and drops in connectivity can be detrimental to the operation of the applications.

Hotspots

Hotspots continue to grow in popularity and many businesses are looking to provide wireless Internet access for their customers. Rarely do hotspots deploy 802.11a hardware since most of the general public still uses 2.4 GHz radio cards. Many hotspots are very small in size, and care should be taken to limit the RF coverage area using a single access point at a lower power setting. However, some large facilities such as airports and convention centers have begun offering wireless access, and obviously multiple access points and wider coverage will be needed. Security solutions at hotspots are usually limited to a captive portal solution for user authentication to a customer database.

Retail

A retail environment often has many potential sources of 2.4 GHz interference. Store demonstration models of cordless phones, baby monitors, and other ISM band devices can cause problems. The inventory storage racks and bins and the inventory itself are all potential sources of multipath problems. Heavy user density should also be considered, and a retail site survey should be done in the height of the shopping season as opposed to late January when the malls are empty.

Wireless applications that are used in retail stores include handheld scanners used for data collection and inventory control. Point of sale devices such as cash registers may also have radio cards. Often this equipment is older frequency hopping equipment that may cause all-band interference with an 802.11b/g network. Steps may be necessary to upgrade the older equipment. Coverage is usually a greater concern than capacity because wireless data collection devices require very little bandwidth.

Warehouses

Some of the earliest deployments of 802.11 technology were in warehouses for the purpose of inventory control and data collection. A 2.4 GHz WLAN will be deployed because currently all handheld devices use 2.4 GHz radios. Coverage, not capacity, is the main objective when designing a wireless network in a warehouse. Warehouses are filled with metal racks and all sorts of inventory that can cause reflections and multipath. The use of directional antennas in a warehouse environment is almost a requirement. High ceilings often cause mounting problems as well as coverage issues. Indoor chain-link fences that are often used to secure certain areas will scatter and block a 2.4 GHz RF signal. Seamless roaming is also mandatory because the handheld devices will be mobile. Forklifts that can move swiftly through the warehouse may also have computing devices with radio cards. Many legacy deployments of 802.11 FHSS hardware and/or legacy 900 MHz radios still exist in many warehouse environments.

It is also important to keep stock levels in mind during the survey. Care should be taken to survey during peak times to create the worst case scenario for coverage. It is also important to note that warehouses are probably the most dynamic RF environment. When stocks are low, the entire RF environment is different. It is recommended that the environment be surveyed during low stocking levels to get a comparison. It is probable that RF power levels will need to be adjusted as stock comes in and out.

Manufacturing

A manufacturing environment is often similar to a warehouse environment in terms of multipath interference and coverage design. However, a manufacturing plant presents many unique site survey challenges, including safety and the presence of employee unions. Heavy machinery and robotics may present safety concerns to the surveyor, and special care should be taken so as not to mount access points where they may be damaged by other machines. Many manufacturing plants also work with hazardous chemicals and materials. Proper protection may need to worn and ruggedized access points may have to be installed. Technology manufacturing plants often have clean rooms, and the surveyor will have to wear a clean suit and follow clean room procedures if they are even allowed in the room.

Many manufacturing plants are union shops with union employees. A meeting with the plant's union representative is necessary to make sure that no union policies will be violated by the site surveyor team.

Multitenant Buildings

By far the biggest issue when conducting a survey in a multitenant building is the presence of other WLAN equipment used by nearby businesses. Office building environments are extremely cluttered with 802.11b/g wireless networks that operate at 2.4 GHz. Almost assuredly all of the other tenants' WLANs will be powered to full strength, and some equipment will be on nonstandard channels such as 2 and 8, which will likely interfere with your WLAN equipment. If at all possible, strong consideration should be given to deploying an 802.11a WLAN using the 5 GHz UNII indoor and middle bands.

Summary

In this chapter, you have learned about all the necessary preparations and questions that must be asked prior to conducting a wireless site survey. The site survey interview is an important process necessary to both educate the customer and determine the customer's wireless needs. Defining the business purpose of the wireless network will lead to a more productive survey. Capacity and coverage planning as well as planning for infrastructure connectivity is all part of the site survey interview. Prior to the site survey interview, it will be necessary to obtain some critical documentation such as blueprints or topography maps from the customer. Interview and installation checklists will be used during the site survey interview and during the actual physical survey. Different survey considerations will be necessary for different vertical markets. Once the site survey is completed, you will deliver to the customer a final site survey report as well as additional reports and recommendations.

Exam Essentials

Define the site survey interview.   Be able to explain the importance of the interview process prior to the wireless site survey. Understand that the interview is for educating the customer and clearly defining all their wireless needs.

Identify the questions necessary to determine capacity and coverage needs.   Understand the importance of proper capacity and coverage planning. Define all the numerous considerations when planning for RF cell coverage, bandwidth, and throughput.

Explain existing wireless network troubleshooting concerns.   Be able to explain the questions necessary to troubleshoot an existing WLAN installation prior to conducting a secondary site survey.

Define infrastructure connectivity issues.   Understand all the necessary questions that must be asked in order to guarantee proper integration of the WLAN into the existing wired infrastructure.

Identify site survey documentation and forms. Correctly identify all the documentation that will need to be assembled and created prior to the site survey.

Explain vertical market considerations. Understand the different business requirements of different vertical markets and how these requirements will alter the site survey and final deployment.

Key Terms

Before you take the exam, be certain you are familiar with the following terms:

capacity   Erlang

coverage   site survey interview

deliverables

Review Questions

1. You have been hired by the XYZ Company for a wireless site survey. Which statements best describe site survey best practices when choosing vendor equipment to be used during the survey? (Choose two answers.)

   A. When conducting a wireless site survey with a WLAN switch, you should use both autonomous and thin access points.

   B. When conducting a wireless site survey with fat access points, you should use different vendors' APs together.

   C. When conducting a wireless site survey with a WLAN controller, you should use a WLAN controller and thin access points from the same vendor.

   D. When conducting a wireless site survey with fat access points, you should use fat access points from the same vendor.

   E. When a wireless site survey is conducted, proprietary security solutions are often implemented.

2. Name a unique consideration when deploying a wireless network in a hotel or other hospitality business? (Choose the best answer.)

   A. Equipment theft

   B. Aesthetics

   C. Segmentation

   D. Roaming

   E. User management

3. Which of the following statements best describe security considerations during a wireless site survey? (Choose all that apply.)

   A. Questions will be asked to define the customer's security expectations.

   B. Wireless security recommendations will be made after the survey.

   C. Recommendations about wireless security policies may also be made.

   D. During the survey, both mutual authentication and encryption should be implemented.

4. The XYZ Company has hired you to design a wireless network that will have data clients, VoWiFi phones, and access for guest users. The company wants the strongest security solution possible for the data clients and phones. Which design best fits the customer's requirements?

   A. Create one wireless VLAN. Segment the data clients, VoIP phones, and guest users from the wired network. Use an 802.1X/EAP authentication and CCMP/AES encryption for a wireless security.

   B. Create three separate VLANS. Segment the data clients, VoIP phones, and guest users into three distinct VLANs. Use an 802.1X/EAP authentication and TKIP encryption for security in the data VLAN. Use WPA2-Personal in the voice VLAN. The guest VLAN will have no security other than possibly a captive portal.

C. Create three separate VLANS. Segment the data clients, VoIP phones and guest users into three distinct VLANs. Use an 802.1X/EAP authentication with CCMP/AES encryption for security in the data VLAN. Use WPA2-Personal in the voice VLAN. The guest VLAN will have no security other than possibly a captive portal.

D. Create two separate VLANS. The data and voice clients will share one VLAN while the guest users will reside in another. Use an 802.1X/EAP authentication and CCMP/AES encryption for security in the data/voice VLAN. The guest VLAN will have no security other than possibly a captive portal.

5. What are some additional recommendations that can be made along with the final site survey report? (Choose all that apply.)

A. Training recommendations

B. Security recommendations

C. Coverage recommendations

D. Capacity recommendations

E. Roaming recommendations

6. What documents might be needed prior to an indoor site survey?

A. Blueprints

B. Network topography map

C. Network topology map

D. Coverage map

E. Frequency map

7. What roaming issues should be discussed during an interview for a future VoWiFi network? (Choose all that apply.)

A. Layer 2 boundaries

B. Layer 3 boundaries

C. Layer 4 boundaries

D. Latency

E. Throughput

8. You have been hired by the ABC Corporation to conduct an indoor site survey. What information will be in the final site survey report that is delivered? (Choose all that apply.)

A. AP placement

B. Firewall settings

C. Router access control lists

D. Access point transmit power settings

E. Antenna orientation

9. The XYZ Corporation has hired you to troubleshoot an existing WLAN. The end users are reporting having difficulties when roaming. What are some of the possible causes?

   A. The RF coverage cells have only 20 percent overlap. Fifty percent cell overlap is normally needed for seamless roaming.

   B. The RF coverage cells have only 5 percent overlap. Fifteen to 20 percent cell overlap is normally needed for seamless roaming.

   C. The RF coverage cells are co-located.

   D. There is interference from the cellular network.

   E. There is interference from 2.4 GHz portable phones.

10. After conducting a simple site survey in the office building where your company is located on the fifth floor, you have discovered that other businesses are also operating access points on nearby floors on channels 2 and 8. What is the best recommendation you will make to management about deploying a new WLAN for your company?

   A. Install a 2.4 GHz access point on channel 6 and use the highest available transmit power setting to overpower the WLANs of the other businesses.

   B. Speak with the other businesses. Suggest that they use channels 1 and 6 at lower power settings. Install a 2.4 GHz access point using channel 9.

   C. Speak with the other businesses. Suggest that they use channels 1 and 11 at lower power settings. Install a 2.4 GHz access point using channel 6.

   D. Recommend installing an 802.11a access point.

   E. Install a Wireless Intrusion Prevention System (WIPS). Classify the other businesses access points as interfering and implement de-authentication countermeasures.

11. The ABC Company has hired you to make recommendations about a future wireless deployment that will require over 300 access points to meet all coverage requirements. What is the most cost-efficient and practical recommendation in regard to providing electrical power to the access points?

   A. Recommend that the customer replace older edge switches with new switches with inline PoE.

   B. Recommend that the customer replace the core switch with a new core switch with inline PoE.

   C. Recommend that the customer use single-port power injectors.

   D. Recommend that the customer hire an electrician to install new electrical outlets.

12. The XYZ Corporation has hired you to troubleshoot an existing WLAN. The end users are reporting having difficulties with throughput performance. What are some of the possible causes of the difficulties? (Choose all that apply.)

   A. Multipath interference

   B. Co-channel interference

   C. Co-location interference

   D. Inadequate capacity planning

   E. Low client cards transmit power

13. What factors need to be considered when planning for capacity in an 802.11a WLAN? (Choose all that apply.)

   A. Data applications

   B. User density

   C. Peak usage level

   D. 802.11g protection mechanism

   E. All of the above

14. During the interview process, which topics will be discussed so that the WLAN will integrate properly into the existing wired architecture? (Choose all that apply.)

   A. PoE

   B. Segmentation

   C. User management

   D. Infrastructure management

   E. All of the above

15. The Jackson County Regional Hospital has hired you for a wireless site survey. Prior to the site survey, employees from which departments at the hospital should be consulted? (Choose all that apply.)

   A. Network management

   B. Biomedical department

   C. Hospital security

   D. Custodial department

   E. Marketing department

16. Typically what are the biggest concerns when planning for a WLAN in a warehouse environment? (Choose all that apply.)

   A. Capacity

   B. Coverage

   C. Security

   D. Roaming

17. What type of hardware may be necessary when installing APs to be used for outdoor wireless coverage?

   A. NEMA enclosure

   B. Parabolic dish antennas

   C. Patch antennas

   D. Outdoor ruggedized core switch

18. What is a telecommunications unit of measurement of traffic equal to one hour of telephone traffic in one hour of time?

    A. Ohm

    B. dBm

    C. Erlang

    D. Call hour

    E. Voltage Standing Wave Ratio

19. What additional documentation is normally provided along with the final site survey deliverable? (Choose all that apply.)

    A. Bill of materials

    B. Implementation diagrams

    C. Network topology map

    D. Project schedule and costs

    E. Access point user manuals

20. The WonderPuppy Coffee Company has hired you to make recommendations about deploying wireless hotspots in 500 coffee shops across the country. What solutions might you recommend? (Choose all that apply.)

    A. 802.11a access point at 40 mW transmit power[

    B. 802.11b/g access point at 100 mW transmit power

    C. 802.11b/g access point at 1 to 5 mW transmit power

    D. 802.11a access point at 1 to 5 mW transmit power

    E. Captive portal authentication

    F. 802.1X/EAP authentication solution

Answers to Review Questions

1. C, D. It is a highly recommended practice to conduct the site survey using equipment from the same vendor who will supply the equipment that will later be deployed on site. Mixing vendors during the survey is not recommended. Mixing a fat AP solution with a thin AP solution is also not recommended. Security is not implemented during the survey.

2. B. While all the options are issues that may need addressing when deploying a WLAN in hospitality environment, aesthetics is usually a top priority in the hospitality industry. The majority of customer service businesses prefer that all wireless hardware remain completely out of sight.

3. A, B, C. While security in itself is not part of the WLAN site survey, network management should be interviewed about security expectations. The surveying company will make comprehensive wireless security recommendations. An extra addendum to the security recommendations might be corporate wireless policy recommendations. Authentication and encryption solutions are not usually implemented during the physical survey.

4. C . Segmentation, authentication, authorization, and encryption should all be considered during the site survey interview. In chapter 13 you learned about the necessary components of wireless security. Segmenting three different types of users into separate VLANs with separate security solutions is the best recommendation. The data users using 802.1X/EAP and CCMP/AES will have the strongest solution available. WPA-2 provides the voice users with CCMP/AES encryption as well but avoids using an 802.1X/EAP solution that will cause latency problems. The guest user VLAN requires minimal security for ease of use.

5. A, B. Training, security, and choice of vendor are extra recommendations that may also accompany the site survey report. The site survey report should already be addressing coverage, capacity, and roaming requirements.

6. A, C. Blueprints will be needed for the site survey interview to discuss coverage and capacity needs. A network topology map will be useful to assist in the design of integrating the wireless network into the current wired infrastructure.

7. B, D. Latency is an important consideration whenever any time-sensitive application such as voice or video is to be deployed. A Mobile IP solution or proprietary layer 3 roaming solution will be needed if layer 3 boundaries are crossed during roaming.

8. A, D, E. The final site survey report known as the deliverable will contain spectrum analysis information identifying potential sources of interference. Coverage analysis will also define RF cell boundaries. The final report also contains recommended access point placement, configuration settings, and antenna orientation. Application throughput testing is often an optional analysis report included in the final survey report. Firewall settings and router access control lists are not included in a site survey report.

9. B, E. Roaming problems may be interference related or caused by a lack of adequate coverage and/or cell overlap. In Chapter 12 you learned that 15 to 20 percent cell overlap is typically needed for roaming. 2.4 GHz portable phones may be a source of interference. Cellular phones operate in a frequency space that will not interfere with the existing WLAN.

10. D. While answer C is a possible solution, the best recommendation would be to deploy 802.11a hardware that operates at 5 GHz and interference from the neighboring businesses 2.4 GHz network will never be an issue.

11. A. The cheapest and most efficient solution will be to replace the older edge switches with newer switches with inline power that can provide PoE to the access points. A core switch will not be used to provide PoE because of cabling distance limitations. Deploying single-port injectors is not practical and hiring an electrician will be extremely expensive.

12. A, B, D. Multipath and co-channel interference are common causes of poor performance. Inadequate capacity planning can result in too many users per access point leading to throughput problems.

13. A, B, C . User density, data applications, peak usage levels, and the 802.11g protection mechanism are all considerations when capacity planning for an 802.11b/g network. When planning for an 802.11a WLAN, the protection mechanism is not an issue.

14. E. Multiple questions are related to infrastructure integration. How will the access points be powered? How will the WLAN and/or users of the WLAN be segmented from the wired network? How will the WLAN remote access points be managed? Considerations such as role-based access control (RBAC), bandwidth throttling, and load balancing should be discussed.

15. A, B, C. Network management will be consulted during most of the site survey and deployment process for proper integration of the WLAN. The biomedical department will be consulted about possible RF interference issues. Hospital security will be contacted in order to obtain proper security passes and possible escort.

16. B, C, D. Coverage, not capacity, is the main objective when designing a wireless network in a warehouse. Seamless roaming is also mandatory because handheld devices are normally deployed. Security is a major requirement for all WLAN enterprise installations.

17. A. Outdoor equipment must ultimately be protected from the weather elements using enclosure units rated by the National Electrical Manufacturers Association (NEMA). NEMA weatherproof enclosures are available with a wide range of options, including heating, cooling, and Power over Ethernet interfaces.

18. C. Probabilistic traffic formulas use a telecommunications unit of measurement known as an Erlang. An Erlang is equal to one hour of telephone traffic in one hour of time.

19. A, B, D. Based upon information collected during the site survey, a final design diagram will be presented to the customer. Along with the implementation diagrams will be a detailed bill of materials (BOM) that itemizes every hardware and software component necessary for the final installation of the wireless network. A detailed deployment schedule should be drafted that outlines all timelines, equipment costs, and labor costs.

20. C, E. Rarely do hotspots deploy 802.11a hardware since most of the general public still uses 2.4 GHz radio cards. Many hotspots are very small in size, and care should be taken to limit the RF coverage area using a single access point at a lower power setting. Security solutions at hotspots are usually limited to a captive portal solution for user authentication to a customer database.

Chapter 16

Site Survey Systems and Devices

IN THIS CHAPTER, YOU WILL LEARN ABOUT THE FOLLOWING:

✓ **Site Survey Defined**

- Mandatory Spectrum Analysis
- Mandatory Coverage Analysis
- AP Placement and Configuration
- Optional Application Analysis

✓ **Site Survey Tools**

- Indoor Site Surveys Tools
- Outdoor Site Survey Tools

✓ **Coverage Analysis**

- Manual
- Assisted
- Predictive
- Self-Organizing Wireless LANs

In Chapter 15, we discussed wireless site surveys from an administrative perspective. You learned what information to gather and what to plan for prior to the actual Wi-Fi site survey. In this chapter, we will discuss the wireless site survey from a technical perspective. A proper site survey should include spectrum analysis as well as coverage analysis so that optimum 802.11 communications are realized. Determining the proper placement and configuration of the 802.11 equipment during the site survey is essential to reaching your expected performance goals for the wireless network. RF signal propagation studies are needed to determine existing and new RF coverage patterns. Many variables—such as walls, floors, doors, plumbing, windows, elevators, buildings, trees, and mountains—can have a direct effect on the coverage of an access point or wireless bridge.

In this chapter, we will discuss how to perform a site survey, the different types of site surveys, and the different types of tools that can be used during a site survey. Site survey professionals often have their own unique technical approach for executing a site survey. We like to think of it as almost an art form, and in this chapter, we'll help you take the first steps in becoming a wireless site survey Picasso.

Site Survey Defined

When most individuals are asked to define a wireless site survey, the usual response is that a site survey is for determining RF coverage. While that definition is absolutely correct, the site survey encompasses so much more, including looking for potential sources of interference as well as the proper placement, installation, and configuration of 802.11 hardware. In the following sections, we will discuss the often overlooked, yet necessary, spectrum analysis requirement of the site survey and the often misunderstood coverage analysis requirement. During the coverage analysis process, a determination will be made for the proper placement of access points, the transmission power of the access point radio card, and the proper use of antennas.

Although not mandatory, performance and application testing might also be an optional requirement of an 802.11 wireless survey. Depending on the purpose of the wireless network, different tools can be used, which is why the site survey interview and planning process is so important. Throughout the remainder of this chapter, we will also cover the variety of tools that may be used as part of your site survey arsenal.

Mandatory Spectrum Analysis

Before conducting the coverage analysis survey, locating sources of potential interference is a must. Unfortunately, many site surveys completely ignore *spectrum analysis* because of the high cost generally associated with purchasing the necessary spectrum analyzer hardware. Spectrum analyzers are frequency domain measurement devices that can measure the amplitude and frequency space of electromagnetic signals. Spectrum analyzer hardware can cost upward of $40,000 (in U.S. dollars), thereby making them cost prohibitive for many smaller and medium size businesses. The good news is that several companies have solutions, both hardware and software based, that are designed specifically for 802.11 site survey spectrum analysis and are drastically less expensive. Figure 16.1 depicts a 2.4 GHz hardware spectrum analyzer.

In order to conduct a proper 802.11 spectrum analysis survey, the *spectrum analyzer* will need to capable of scanning both the 2.4 GHz ISM band and the 5 GHz UNII bands. A company named Cognio sells a software-based solution that works with a special PCMCIA card. This software-based spectrum analyzer was designed specifically for 802.11 site surveys and can correctly identify specific energy pulses such as a microwave oven or cordless phone.

FIGURE 16.1   2.4 GHz spectrum analyzer

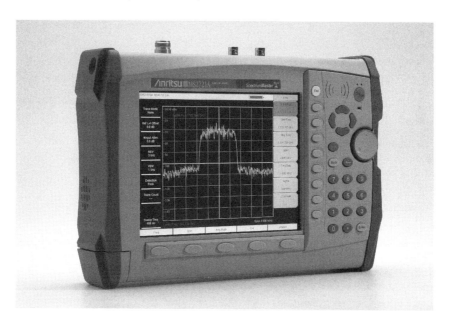

On the CD that accompanies this book is a live demo of the Cognio Spectrum Expert software. You will use this program to execute Exercise 16.1 using playback files of spectrum captures.

EXERCISE 16.1

Spectrum Analysis

In this exercise, you will use a demo program of Cognio Spectrum Expert to view sources of interference and simulate spectrum analysis.

1. The first step is to install the Cognio program that's included on this book's CD. Copy the file CognioDemoSetup.exe to your desktop. Click on the file and follow the default installation prompts.

2. Double-click the Spectrum Expert icon on your desktop. At the prompt, click the Screen Capture File button. Click the browse button and browse to an icon on your desktop called WiFi Demo.

3. From the main screen, click the Spectrum tab. Notice that the 2.4 GHz frequency space is very crowded.

4. From the main screen, click the Spectrum (2) tab. Notice that the 5 GHz frequency space is not as crowded.

5. From the main screen, click the Devices tab. Notice all the Wi-Fi access points as well as interfering devices.

6. Continue to maneuver through the program and familiarize yourself with the spectrum analyzer's features and capabilities.

So why is spectrum analysis even necessary? If the background noise level exceeds –85 dBm in either the 2.4 GHz ISM band or 5 GHz UNII bands, the performance of the wireless network can be severely degraded. A noisy environment can cause the data in 802.11 transmissions to become corrupted. If the data is corrupted, the cyclic redundancy check (CRC) will fail and the receiving 802.11 radio will not send an ACK frame to the transmitting 802.11 radio. If an ACK frame is not received by the original transmitting radio, the unicast frame is not acknowledged and will have to be retransmitted. If an interfering device such as a microwave oven results in retransmissions above 10 percent, the performance or throughput of the wireless LAN will suffer significantly. Wi-Fi data networks can handle a retransmission rate of up to 10 percent, but a Voice over Wi-Fi (VoWiFi) network needs to limit packet loss to a rate of 2 percent or less.

Interfering devices may also prevent an 802.11 radio from transmitting. If another RF source is transmitting with strong amplitude, an 802.11 radio can sense the energy during the clear channel assessment (CCA) and defer transmission. If the source of the interference is a constant signal, an 802.11 radio will continuously defer transmissions until the medium is clear. In other words, a strong source of RF interference could actually prevent your 802.11 client stations and access point radios from transmitting at all.

It is a recommended practice to conduct spectrum analysis of all frequency ranges, especially in the 2.4 GHz ISM band. The 2.4 to 2.4835 GHz ISM band is an extremely crowded frequency space. The following are potential sources of interference in the 2.4 GHz ISM band:

- Microwave ovens
- 2.4 GHz cordless phones, DSSS and FHSS
- Fluorescent bulbs
- 2.4 GHz video cameras
- Elevator motors
- Cauterizing devices
- Plasma cutters
- Bluetooth radios
- Nearby 802.11, 802.11b, or 802.11g WLANs
- Wireless Internet service providers (WISPs)

One of the first things you should determine during the site survey interview is the location of the microwave ovens. Microwave ovens typically operate at 800 to 1,000 watts. Although microwave ovens are shielded, they can become leaky over time. Commercial-grade microwave ovens will be shielded much better than a discount microwave oven that you can buy at many retail outlets. A received signal of –40 dBm is about 1/10,000 of 1 milliwatt and is considered a very strong signal for 802.11 communications. If a 1,000 watt microwave oven is even .0000001 percent leaky, the oven will interfere with the 802.11 radio. Figure 16.2 shows a spectrum view of a microwave oven. Note that this microwave operates dead center in the 2.4 GHz ISM band. Some microwave ovens can congest the entire frequency band.

Because of the extreme crowding of the 2.4 GHz ISM band, many enterprise deployments are switching to 802.11a equipment that transmits in the 5 GHz UNII bands. Switching to an 802.11a WLAN is often a very wise choice in the enterprise because the 5 GHz UNII bands are currently not very crowded and there are more choices on channel reuse patterns. Not nearly as many interfering devices exist, and there are just not many neighboring 802.11a networks that can potentially cause interference. Although there is much less interference currently present at 5 GHz as compared to 2.4 GHz, this will change over time. Just as everyone moved from 900 MHz to 2.4 GHz to avoid interference, the "band jumping" effect will also catch up with 5 GHz. Current potential sources of interference in 5 GHz UNII bands include the following:

- 5 GHz cordless phones
- Radar
- Perimeter sensors

FIGURE 16.2 Microwave oven spectrum use

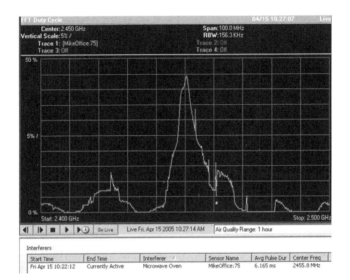

- Digital satellite

- Nearby 802.11a WLANs

- Outdoor wireless 5 GHz bridges

Although many devices can cause problems in both frequencies, one of the most common causes of interference will be other wireless LANs. Strong signals from other nearby WLANs can be a huge problem, especially in a multitenant building environment. You may need to cooperate with the neighboring businesses to ensure that their access points are not powered too high and that they are on channels that will not interfere with your access points. Once again, due to the proliferation of 2.4 GHz WLAN equipment, many businesses are now choosing to switch to 802.11a solutions.

After locating the sources of interference, the best and simplest solution is to eliminate them entirely. If a microwave oven is causing problems, consider purchasing a more expensive commercial-grade oven that is less likely to be a nuisance. Other devices, like 2.4 GHz cordless phones, should be removed and a policy should be strictly enforced that bans them. 5.8 GHz cordless phones operate in the 5.8 GHz ISM band, which overlaps with the upper UNII band (5.725 GHz to 5.825 GHz). Indoor use of 5.8 GHz phones will cause interference with 802.11a radios transmitting in the upper UNII band. If interfering devices cannot be eradicated in the 2.4 GHz bands, consider moving to the less crowded 5 GHz UNII bands. As stated earlier in this chapter, a Voice over Wi-Fi (VoWiFi) network needs to limit packet loss to a rate of 2 percent or less, meaning that a very thorough spectrum analysis of the 2.4 GHz ISM band is a necessity. Currently, Wi-Fi VoIP phones operate using High-Rate DSSS (HR-DSSS) technology and the radios therefore transmit in the very crowded 2.4 GHz ISM band. In the very near future, 802.11a VoWiFi phones will exist that transmit in the less crowded 5 GHz UNII bands. If your WLAN is being used for either data or voice or for both, a proper and thorough spectrum analysis is mandatory in an enterprise environment. It is important to make sure you know what your client devices are capable of before determining the spectrum to use. If all your client devices are restricted to using 2.4 GHz, then that may be your only option and you will need to be able to plan and engineer around the environment.

Mandatory Coverage Analysis

After conducting a spectrum analysis site survey, the next step is the all-important determination of proper 802.11 RF coverage inside your facility. During the site survey interview, capacity and coverage requirements are discussed and determined before the actual site survey is performed. In certain areas of your facility, smaller cells or co-location may be required due to a high density of users or heavy application bandwidth requirements. Once all of the capacity and coverage needs have been determined, RF measurements must be taken to guarantee that these needs are met and to determine the proper placement and configuration of the access points and antennas. Proper *coverage analysis* must be performed using some type of *received signal strength* measurement tool. These tools could be something as simple as the received signal strength meter in your wireless card's client utility, or they could be a more expensive and complex site survey software package. All of these measurement tools are discussed in more detail later in this chapter.

So how do you conduct proper coverage analysis? That question is often debated by industry professionals. Many site survey professionals have their own techniques; however, we will try to describe a basic procedure for coverage analysis. The first mistake that many people make during the site survey is leaving the access point radio at the default full power setting. A 2.4 GHz 802.11b/g radio transmitting at 100 mW will often cause interference with other access point coverage cells simply because it is generating too much power. Also, many legacy client cards have a maximum transmit power of 30 mW. The RF signal of a 30 mW client might not be heard at the outer edge of an access point's 100 mW coverage cell. A good starting point for a 2.4 GHz access point is 30 mW transmit power. After the site survey is performed, the power can be increased if needed to meet unexpected coverage needs, or it can be decreased to meet capacity needs. The hardest part of a coverage analysis site survey is often finding where to place the first access point and determining the boundaries of the first RF cell. The procedure outlined here is generally how this is achieved and is further illustrated in Figure 16.3:

1. Place an access point in the corner of the building with a power setting of 30 mW.

2. Walk diagonally away from the access point toward the center of the building until the received signal drops to -65 dBm. This is the location where you place your first access point.

3. Temporarily mount the access point in the first location and begin walking throughout the facility to find the −65 dBm end points, also known as cell boundaries or cell edges.

4. Depending upon the shape and size of the first coverage cell, you may want to change the power settings and/or move the initial access point. A good portion of a proper coverage analysis involves starting over and trying again.

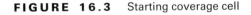

FIGURE 16.3 Starting coverage cell

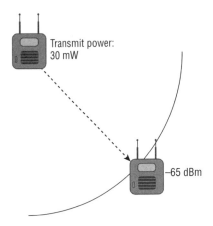

Once the first coverage cell and boundaries have been determined, the next question is where to place the next access point. The placement of the next access point is performed using a technique that's similar to the one you used to place the first access point:

1. Think of the cell boundary of the first access point, where the signal is –65 dBm, as the initial starting point, similar to the way you used the corner of the building as your initial starting point. From the first access point, walk parallel to the edge of the building, and place an access point at the location where the received signal is –65 dBm, as pictured in Figure 16.4.

2. Now walk away from this access point, parallel to the edge of the building, until the received signal drops to –65 dBm.

3. This is the farthest point to place the access point if you do not want cell overlap.

4. Using the distance from the previous access point and this location, the placement of this next access point should be about 15 to 20 percent (depending upon cell overlap requirements) closer to the previous access.

5. Move to that location and temporarily mount the access point and begin walking throughout the facility to find the –65 dBm end points, or cell boundaries.

6. Again, depending upon the shape and size of the first coverage cell, you may want to change the power settings and/or move this access point.

It is important to avoid excessive overlap because it can cause frequent roaming and performance degradation. The shape and size of the building and the attenuation caused by the various materials of walls and obstacles will require you to change the distances between access points to ensure proper cell overlap. After finding the proper placement of the second access point and all of its cell boundaries, repeat the procedure all over again. The rest of the site survey is basically repeating this procedure over and over again, effectively daisy-chaining throughout the building until all coverage needs are determined.

FIGURE 16.4   Second coverage cell

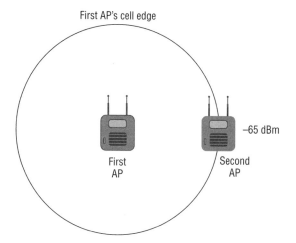

First AP's cell edge

−65 dBm

First
AP

Second
AP

The following cell edge measurements are taken during the site survey:

- Received signal strength (dBm), also known as received signal level (RSL)
- Noise level (dBm)
- Signal-to-noise ratio, or SNR (dB)
- Data rates

The received signal strength measurements that are recorded during a site survey typically depend upon the intended use of the WLAN. If the intent of the WLAN is solely coverage and not capacity, a lower received signal of −85 dBm might be used as the boundary for your overlapping cells. If throughput and capacity are issues, using a stronger received signal of −65 dBm is recommended. The SNR is an important value because, if the background noise is too close to the received signal, data can get corrupted and retransmissions will increase. The SNR is simply the difference in decibels between the received signal and the background noise, as pictured in Figure 16.5. Many vendors recommended a minimum SNR of 18 dB for data networks and a minimum of 25 dB for voice networks.

Some site survey professionals prefer to use the data rate measurements as opposed to the received signal strength measurements when determining their cell boundaries. The problem with using the data rate is that vendors have different receive signal strength indicator (RSSI) thresholds and different vendor cards will shift between data rates at different dBm levels. Cell design can be performed using one vendor's RSSI threshold values if the company deploying the WLAN intends to use just that one vendor's radios. If measurements are based on received signal levels (RSLs), then the WLAN surveyor can always go back and map different client cards and data rates without having to resurvey. A site survey using just data rates or a proprietary signal strength measurement threshold does not allow for any flexibility between vendors. Table 16.1 depicts the recommended minimum received signal and minimum SNR for a WLAN data network using one vendor's highly sensitive radio card.

FIGURE 16.5   Signal-to-noise ratio

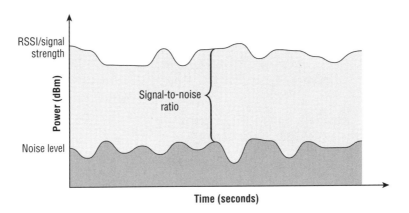

Most VoWiFi manufacturers require a minimum received signal of –70 dBm, therefore overlapping cells of –65 dBm is a good idea for VoWiFi wireless networks in order to provide a buffer. The recommended SNR ratio for a VoWiFi network is 25 dB or higher. Cell overlap of 15 to 20 percent will be needed and the separation of same channel cells should be 20 dB or greater. Figure 16.6 depicts the recommended coverage for a VoWiFi network.

 Although figures and drawings often depict the RF coverage as nice round symmetrical cells, the reality is that cell boundaries usually have an erratic shape that might resemble a starfish or or elements in a Pablo Picasso painting.

TABLE 16.1   WLAN Data Cell—Vendor Recommendations

Data Rate	Minimum Received Signal	Minimum Signal to Noise Ratio
54	–71 dBm	25 dB
36	–73 dBm	18 dB
24	–77 dBm	12 dB
12/11	–82 dBm	10 dB
6/5.5	–89 dBm	8 dB
2	–91 dBm	6 dB
1	–94 dBm	4 dB

FIGURE 16.6   VoWiFi cell recommendations

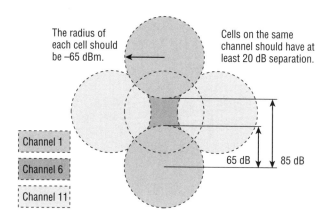

The radius of each cell should be −65 dBm.

Cells on the same channel should have at least 20 dB separation.

Channel 1
Channel 6
Channel 11

65 dB   85 dB

AP Placement and Configuration

As you have just read, coverage analysis also determines the proper placement of access points and power settings. When the site survey is conducted, all the cell edge measurements will be recorded and written on a copy of the floor plan of the building. An entry with the exact location of each access point must also be recorded. Next to the entry of each access point should be the transmission power level of the AP's radio card when the survey was conducted. The location of all the wiring closets will also be noted on the floor plan, and care should be taken to ensure that the placement of any access point is within a 100 meter (328 feet) cable run back to the wiring closet due to CAT5 cabling distance limitations.

Another very often overlooked component in WLAN design during coverage analysis is the use of semi-directional antennas. Many deployments of WLANs only use the manufacturer's default low gain omni-directional antenna, which typically has about 2.14 dBi of gain. Buildings come in many shapes and sizes and often have long corridors or hallways where using an indoor semi-directional antenna would be much more advantageous. Using a uni-directional antenna in areas where there are metal racks, file cabinets, and metal lockers can be advantageous because you can cut down on reflections. Using indoor semi-directional antennas to reduce reflections will cut down on the negative effects of multipath, namely the data corruption caused by the delay spread and inter-symbol interference (ISI). If data corruption is reduced, so is the need for retransmissions, thus the performance of the WLAN is enhanced by the use of semi-directional antennas in the correct situations. Figure 16.7 depicts the use of semi-directional antennas in a warehouse with long corridors and metal racks that line the corridors.

A good site survey kit should have a variety of antennas, both omni-directional and semi-directional. The best way to provide proper coverage in most buildings is to use a combination of both low gain omni-directional antennas and indoor semi-directional antennas together, as pictured in Figure 16.8.

FIGURE 16.7 Proper use of semi-directional antennas

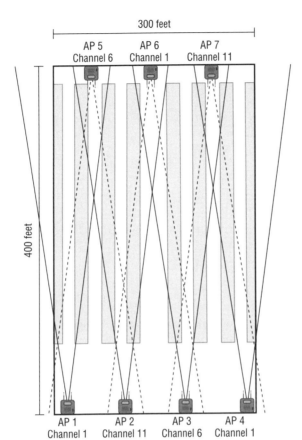

When a semi-directional antenna is used, recording the received signal strength, SNR, and noise level measurements is still necessary to find the coverage edges. The coverage area should closely resemble the radiated pattern of the semi-directional antenna. Simply record the signal measurements along the directional path and the edges of the directional path where the antenna is providing coverage.

Optional Application Analysis

While spectrum analysis and coverage analysis are considered mandatory during 802.11 wireless site surveys, *application analysis* is considered optional. Capacity planning is an important part of the site survey interview. Cell sizing or co-location can be planned and surveyed during the coverage analysis portion of the survey. Capacity testing using application analysis and throughput verification is not normally part of a standard site survey. However, tools do exist that can perform application stress testing of a WLAN. These tools may be used at the tail end of a site survey, but they are more often used during the deployment stage of the WLAN network. One company, IXIA, makes an 802.11a/b/g multistation emulation module and hardware device that can simulate multiple concurrent virtual wireless client stations. The virtual client stations can have individual security settings. Roaming performance can also be tested. The 802.11a/b/g multistation emulator works in conjunction with another component that can emulate hundreds of protocols and generate traffic bidirectionally through the virtual client stations. A great use of such a device could be to test the performance of a simulated wireless data network along with simulated wireless VoIP traffic.

FIGURE 16.8   Omni and semi-directional antenna combination

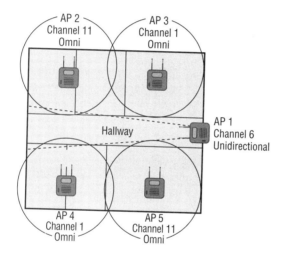

Site Survey Tools

Anyone who is serious about deploying wireless networks will put together a site survey toolbox with a multitude of products that can aid the site survey process. The main tool of course will be some sort of signal measurement software utility that interfaces with your wireless client card and is used for coverage analysis. Prepackaged site survey kits are often for sale on the Internet, but most site survey professionals prefer to put together their own kit. Indoor and outdoor site surveys are very different in nature, and we will discuss the different tools that are used in both types of surveys.

Indoor Site Surveys Tools

As stated earlier, a spectrum analyzer will be needed for locating potential sources of interference. Your main weapon in your coverage analysis arsenal will be a received signal strength measurement tool. This tool could be something as simple as the received signal strength meter in your wireless card's client utility, or it could be a more expensive and complex site survey software package. However, there are many other tools that can assist you when you are conducting the physical site survey. These are some of the tools that you might use for an indoor site survey:

Spectrum analyzer   This is needed for frequency spectrum analysis.

Blueprints   Blueprints or floor plans of the facility are needed to map coverage and mark RF measurements. CAD software may be needed to view and edit digital copies of the blueprints.

Signal strength measurement software   You'll need this for RF coverage analysis.

802.11 client card   This is used with the signal measurement software. It is a recommended practice to use the vendor client card that is most likely to be deployed.

Access point   At least one AP is needed, preferably two.

Battery pack   A battery pack is a necessity because the site survey engineer does not want to have to run electrical extension cords to power the access point while it is temporarily mounted for the site survey. Not only does the battery pack provide power to the access point, it also provides a safer environment because you don't have to run a loose power cord across the floor, and it makes it easier and quick to move the access point to a new location.

Binoculars   It may seem strange to have binoculars for an indoor sight survey, but they can be very useful in tall warehouses and convention centers. They can also be handy for looking at things in the plenum space above the ceiling.

Walkie-talkies or cellular phones   When performing a site survey in an office environment, it is often necessary to be as quiet and unobtrusive as possible. Walkie-talkies or cellular phones are typically preferred over yelling across the room. You must also remember that RF is three-dimensional and it is common for one person to be on one floor with the access point while the other person is on another floor checking the received signal.

Antennas   A wide variety of both omni-directional and indoor semi-directional antennas is a must in every indoor Wi-Fi site survey kit.

Temporary mounting gear   During the site survey you will be temporarily mounting the access point often high up just below the ceiling. Some sort of solution is needed to temporarily mount the AP. Bungee cords and plastic ties are often used as well as good old-fashioned duct tape. Some professionals will use a tripod and mount the access point on an extending mast. The tripod can then be moved within the building, thereby bypassing the need to temporarily mount the access point.

Digital camera   A digital camera should be used to record the exact location of the placement of the access point. Recording this information visually will assist whoever will do the final installation at a later date. Setting the date/time on the pictures may also come in handy when viewing the pictures later.

Measuring wheel or laser measuring meter   A tool is needed to make sure the access point will in fact be close enough for a 100 meter cable run back to the wiring closet. Keep in mind that a 100 meter cable run includes running the CAT5 cabling through the plenum. A measuring wheel or a laser distance measuring tool could be used to measure the distance back to the wiring closet. A measuring wheel is usually the better tool because the laser devices can often yield bad results.

Colored electrical tape   Everyone remembers the fable of Hansel and Gretel and how they used breadcrumbs to leave a trail to find their way home. The colored tape can be used to leave a trail back to where you want to mount the access points. Leave a small piece of colored electrical tape at the location where the access point was temporarily mounted during the site survey. This will assist whoever will do the final AP installation at a later date. A color scheme could even be used to track different channel frequencies: red for channel 1, green for channel 6, and blue for channel 11.

Ladder or forklift   Ladders and/or forklifts may be needed to temporarily the mount the access point from the ceiling.

When conducting a site survey, it is a highly recommended practice to use the same 802.11 access point hardware that you plan on deploying. Keep in mind that every vendor is different and implements RSSI differently. It is not advisable to conduct a coverage analysis survey using one vendor's access point and then deploy a completely different vendor's hardware. Many established site survey companies have put together different vendor site survey kits so that they can offer their customers several options.

Outdoor Site Survey Tools

Outdoor site surveys are conducted using either outdoor access points or mesh routers, which are the devices typically used to provide access for client stations in an outdoor environment. These outdoor Wi-Fi surveys will use most of the same tools as an indoor site survey but may also use a Global Positioning System (GPS) device to record latitude and longitude coordinates. Although outdoor 802.11 deployments can be used to provide access, usually a discussion of outdoor site surveys is about wireless bridging. Wi-Fi bridging exists at the distribution layer and is used to provide a wireless link between two or more wired networks.

An entirely different set of tools is needed for an outdoor bridging site survey, and many more calculations are required to guarantee the stability of the bridge link. In earlier chapters, you learned that the calculations necessary when deploying outdoor bridge links are numerous, including the Fresnel zone, earth bulge, free space path loss, link budget and fade margin. Other considerations may include the intentional radiator (IR) and equivalent isotropically radiated power (EIRP) power limits as defined by the regulatory body of your country. Weather conditions are another major consideration in any outdoor site survey, and proper protection against lightning and wind will need to be deployed. An outdoor wireless bridging site survey usually requires the cooperative skills of two individuals. The following list includes some of the tools that you might use for an outdoor bridging site survey:

Topography map   Instead of a building floor plan, a topography map that outlines elevations and positions will be needed.

Link analysis software   Point-to-point link analysis software can be used with topography maps to generate a bridge link profile and also perform many of the necessary calculations, like Fresnel zone and EIRP. The bridge link analysis software is a predictive modeling tool.

Calculators   Software calculators and spreadsheets can be used to provide necessary calculations for link budget, Fresnel zone, free space path loss, and fade margin. Other calculators can provide information about cable attenuation and voltage standing wave ratio (VSWR).

Maximum tree growth data   Trees are a potential source of obstruction of the Fresnel zone, and unless a tree is fully mature, it will likely grow taller. A chainsaw is not always the answer, and planning antenna height based on potential tree growth might be necessary. The regional or local agricultural government agency should be able to provide you with the necessary information regarding the local foliage and what type of growth you can expect.

Binoculars   Visual line of sight can be established with the aid of binoculars. However, please remember that determining RF line of sight means calculating and ensuring Fresnel zone clearance. For links longer than 5 miles or so, this will be almost impossible. A solid understanding of topography and earth bulge is necessary to plan a bridge link.

Walkie-talkies or cellular phones   802.11 bridge links can span many miles. Two site survey engineers working as a team will need some type of device for communicating during the survey.

Signal generator and wattmeter   A signal generator is used together with a wattmeter, also known as a Bird meter, to test cabling, connectors, and accessories for signal loss and VSWR. This testing gear is necessary for testing cabling and connectors before deployment. The testing gear should also be used periodically after deployment to check that water and other environmental conditions have not damaged the cabling and connectors.

Variable-loss attenuator   A variable-loss attenuator has a dial on it that allows you to adjust the amount of energy that is absorbed. These can be used during an outdoor site survey to simulate different cable lengths or cable losses.

Inclinometer   This is a device that is used to determine how high obstructions are. This is crucial when making sure that a link path is clear of obstructions

GPS   Recording the latitude and longitude of the transmit sites and any obstructions or points of interest along the path is important for planning.

Digital camera   You will want to take pictures of mounting locations, cable paths, grounding locations, indoor mounting locations, obstructions, and so on.

Spectrum analyzer   This should be used to test ambient RF levels at transmit sites.

Antennas and access points are not typically used during the bridging site survey. It is very rare that bridging hardware will be installed during survey since most times a mast or some other type of structure has to be built. If all the bridging measurements and calculations are accurate, then the bridge link will work. An outdoor site survey for a mesh network will require mesh APs and antennas.

On the CD that accompanies this book is a spreadsheet called LinkBudget.xls that will be used in Exercise 16.2 to calculate a link budget and fade margin. The CD also has a freeware software calculator courtesy of Times Microwave Systems. This calculator will be used in Exercise 16.3 to compute signal loss in different grades of coaxial cabling.

EXERCISE 16.2

Link Budget and Fade Margin

In this exercise, you will use a Microsoft Excel file to calculate a link budget and fade margin. You will need Microsoft Excel installed on your computer.

1. From this book's CD, copy the file LinkBudget.xls to your desktop. Open the Excel file from your desktop.

2. In row 10, enter a link distance of 25 kilometers. Note that the path loss due to a 25 kilometer link is now 128 dB in the 2.4 GHz frequency. In row 20, enter 128 for path loss in dB.

3. In row 23, change the radio receiver sensitivity to –80 dBm. Notice that the final received signal is now –69 dBm and the fade margin is only 11 dB. Try to change the various components such and antenna gain and cable loss to ensure a fade margin of 20 dB.

EXERCISE 16.3

Cable Loss Calculations

In this exercise, you will use the Time Microwave Systems attenuation calculator to see the dB loss per 100 feet for various grades of cabling.

1. From the enclosed CD, copy the file losscalc.zip to a temporary directory such as C:\temp. Unzip losscalc.zip to that same temporary directory.

2. From the temporary directory, double-click the file TMSAPHC.exe.

3. Under the product window, choose a grade of cable called LMR-1700-DB. In the frequency window, enter 2500, and in the length window, enter 200 feet. Click the Calculate button. Note that this grade of cabling is rated for 1.7 dB loss per 100 feet.

4. Under the product window, choose a lower grade of cable called LMR-400. In the frequency window, enter 2500, and in the length window, enter 200 feet. Click the Calculate button.

5. Note that this grade of cabling is rated for 6.76 dB loss per 100 feet.

Coverage Analysis

We have already discussed the many considerations of coverage analysis in an earlier section of this chapter. In the following sections, we will cover the three major types of coverage analysis site surveys: manual, assisted, and predictive. We will also discuss the software tools that can be used to assist you with all three of these types of coverage analysis surveys. Finally, we will discuss self-organizing WLAN technology that essentially is a real-time dynamic and adaptive RF coverage and capacity technology.

Manual

The most common method of coverage analysis is the old-fashioned manual site survey. *Manual coverage analysis* involves the techniques described earlier, which are used to find the cell boundaries. There are two major types of manual coverage analysis surveys:

Passive   During a *passive manual survey*, the radio card is collecting RF measurements, including received signal strength (dBm), noise level (dBm), signal-to-noise ratio (dB), and bandwidth data rates. The client adapter, however, is not associated to the access point during the survey, and all information is received from radio signals that exist at layer 1.

Active   During an *active manual survey*, the radio card is associated to the access point and has layer 2 connectively, allowing for low-level frame transmissions. If layer 3 connectivity is also established, Internet Control Message Protocol (ICMP) ping traffic is sent in 802.11 data frame transmissions. RF measurements can also be recorded during the active survey, and additional information such as packet loss and retransmission percentages can be measured since the client card is associated to a single access point.

Most vendors recommend that both passive and active site surveys be conducted. The information from both manual surveys can then be compared, contrasted, and/or merged into one final coverage analysis report. So what measurement software tools can be used to collect the data required for both passive and active manual surveys? There are numerous freeware site survey utilities, including NetStumbler, which is a freeware utility that is included on the CD that accompanies this book. NetStumbler can be used for a passive coverage analysis survey. Most Wi-Fi vendors' client card utility software at the very least comes with a passive survey tool that can be used to measure received signal strength and SNR. Many vendors' software client utilities will also include active survey capabilities like the Cisco client software pictured in Figure 16.9. Some handheld devices such as VoWiFi phones or Wi-Fi bar code scanners may have site survey capabilities built into the internal software that runs on the handheld device.

Many site survey professionals prefer working with the vendors' client card site survey software tools as opposed to newer dedicated coverage analysis applications. However, commercial RF site survey applications like the one pictured in Figure 16.10 have been gaining wide acceptance.

FIGURE 16.9   Passive/Active site survey utility

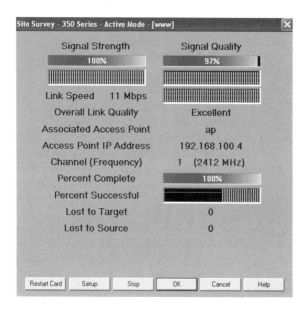

🌐 Real World Scenario

Can I Perform a Site Survey Using Built-in OS Client Utilities?

The most commonly used software interface for wireless client adapters is the Microsoft Wireless Zero Configuration (WZC) service that is built into Windows XP. The WZC currently does not have received signal strength reporting capabilities, nor does it have any other site survey features. The WZC may add site survey capabilities in later versions of the operating system, but until then other site survey tools will be needed.

FIGURE 16.10 Commercial coverage analysis application (AirMagnet Survey © Courtesy of AirMagnet, Inc.)

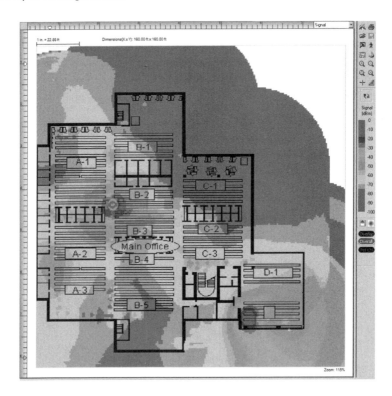

These commercial packages allow the site survey engineer to import a graphic of the building's floor plans into the application. A variety of graphic formats are usually supported and the floor plan typically must be to scale. The commercial application works with an 802.11 client radio and takes measurements in either a passive manual mode or an active manual mode. The site survey engineer walks through the building capturing the RF information while also recording their location on the graphic of the floor plan that is displayed in the software. The information collected during both active and passive modes can then be merged together and a visual representation of the RF footprints or coverage cells is displayed over the graphic floor plan. These commercial packages can also retain the information, which can be used for some offline modeling so the WLAN design engineer can create some "what-if" scenarios by changing channel and power settings. Commercial site survey applications can also assist somewhat in capacity planning in regard to data rates per cell and per VLAN. Floor plans for multiple floors can be loaded into the applications and 3D coverage analysis is often possible. For outdoor site surveys, GPS capabilities are included to log latitude and longitude coordinates. One vendor, Helium Networks, uses a hardware device with wheels as shown in Figure 16.11, to log the x- and y- coordinates on a grid for precise location RF measurements.

FIGURE 16.11   Helium Networks's SiteScout

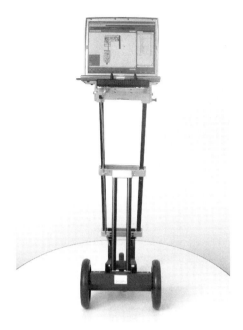

In Exercise 16.4, you will use a demo of a commercial site survey application called AirMagnet Survey. To properly execute Exercise 16.4, please download the software demo from www.airmagnet.com/products/demo-download.php.

EXERCISE 16.4

Manual Coverage Analysis

In this exercise, you will test-drive a commercial site survey software application called Air-Magnet Survey to simulate manual coverage analysis.

1. After downloading the AirMagnet Survey demo software, double-click on the executable file. Follow all the installation prompts.

2. From the Windows Start menu, under Programs, run the AirMagnet Surveyor Demo.

3. When prompted to open a sample project, click the Yes button.

4. In the top-left window of the program, choose PassiveSurvey1.svd. Click the Yes button and watch the demonstration.

EXERCISE 16.4 *(continued)*

5. Observe the colored heat maps that give a graphical representation of RF coverage areas.

6. In the top-left window of the program, choose `ActiveSurvey1.svd`. Click the Yes button and watch the demonstration.

7. In the top-left window of the program, choose `MergedPassiveActive.svd`. Click the Yes button and watch the demonstration.

8. Test-drive some of the other features on the bottom and right menu bars.

Assisted

Some WLAN switches and some centralized wireless network management system (WNMS) applications have the capabilities to conduct *assisted coverage analysis*. After the installation of access points, a centralized solution such as a wireless network management system (WNMS) or a WLAN switch scans the access point radio cards and collects the RF information, which is then used for visualization of coverage cells and for optimizing AP configurations such as channel and power settings. Most assisted solutions use the information gathered from the access point radio cards, but some solutions can also use a client radio to report information back to the centralized device during a client "walk-through" of the building. Assisted site surveys typically are used as a starting point before final deployment and are often used as a calibration or planning stage tool with WLAN switches. An assisted calibration process configures and reconfigures the access points based on analysis of all the collected RF data, as pictured in Figure 16.12. Most WLAN switch solutions that have assisted site survey capabilities also go to the next level and also offer dynamic Radio Frequency Spectrum Management (RFSM), which is discussed later in this chapter. Some system integrators bypass the site survey and install a grid pattern of thin access points. After the thin access points are installed, a wireless switch or wireless switches working together use some form of RFSM technology to dynamically adjust power and channel settings. The Wi-Fi switching architecture constantly monitors the environment and makes adjustments as needed. Although assisted site survey features are an excellent starting point prior to deployment, most professionals still recommend a manual site survey for validation.

FIGURE 16.12   Assisted site survey

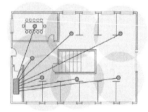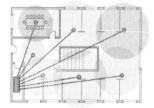

Predictive

The last method of RF coverage analysis uses applications that provide RF simulations and modeling design capabilities. *Predicted coverage analysis* is accomplished using an application that creates visual models of RF coverage cells, bypassing the need for actually capturing RF measurements. Projected cell coverage zones are created using modeling algorithms and attenuation values. One major switch vendor touts these modeling capabilities; however, most predictive coverage analysis tools are stand-alone software design applications.

Blueprints and floor plans often use vector graphic formats (`.dwg`, `.dwf`) and can contain layer information including the type of building materials that are used. Predictive analysis software supports both vector and raster graphics (`.bmp`, `.jpg`, `.tif`), allowing for the import of building floor plans. The WLAN design engineer will indicate in the software what materials are used in the floor plan. The predictive application already has attenuation values for various materials such as drywall, concrete, and glass programmed into the software. The software creates forecast models using the predictive algorithms and the attenuation information. The modeling forecast can include the following:

- Channel reuse patterns
- Coverage cell boundaries
- Access point placement
- Access point power settings
- Number of access points
- Data rates

Virtual access points are created and overlaid on the floor plan graphic. Multiple "what-if" scenarios can be created by changing the power settings, channel settings, or antenna type of the virtual access points, which can also be moved to any location on the floor plan. Predictive capacity analysis software vendors proclaim 85 percent accuracy in their modeling capabilities. Predictive applications are an excellent tool to use with blueprints of buildings that have yet to be built. It should be noted that entering the initial data for a predictive survey can be very time consuming; however, many site survey engineers have begun using predictive modeling software to cut down on the time needed for the actual site survey. A forecast model is first created with the predictive application and then the site survey engineer conducts a manual site survey to validate the projections. Predictive coverage analysis software can be a valuable tool, but a manual site survey is still necessary to confirm the coverage simulations.

On the CD that accompanies this book is a demo of a commercial site survey application called Ekahau Site Survey, which can be used for predictive analysis. You will use this program to execute Exercise 16.5.

EXERCISE 16.5

Predictive Coverage Analysis

In this exercise, you will test-drive a commercial site survey software application called Ekahau Site Survey to simulate predictive coverage analysis.

1. From this book's CD, double-click on the file Install_Survey_win32.exe. Follow all the installation prompts.

2. On your desktop, double-click the Survey icon. Click the No button when asked to install a new license.

3. On the menu bar, click the New Map icon, which is the second icon from the left. Click the Select button, browse to the CD, and click on the floorplan.jpg found on the CD. Click the Open button and then the OK button.

4. Click the AP icon and then click on the floor plan several times. This will place several virtual access points.

5. Click the Visualization tab on the bottom of the screen. Under View, choose several different simulations, including data rate, access point placement, and so on.

6. From Wall Type, choose different materials and place them on the floor plan. Notice the changes that take effect in the predictive analysis simulation.

Self-Organizing Wireless LANs

Could the need for manual site surveys ever be eliminated? Most site survey professionals would argue that a manual coverage analysis of some type will always be needed; however, dynamic RF technologies exist that could eliminate or drastically reduce the need for manual coverage analysis. Currently, software and hardware solutions already exist that provide *Radio Frequency Spectrum Management (RFSM)*, where a centralized device can dynamically change the configuration of thin or fat access points based on accumulated RF information gathered from the access points' radio cards. Based on the accumulated RF information, the centralized device controls the access points and adjusts their power and channel settings, dynamically changing the RF coverage cells. WLAN capacity needs can be also be addressed with RFSM, which utilizes dynamic load balancing of clients between the access points. When implemented, Radio Frequency Spectrum Management provides automatic cell sizing, automatic monitoring, troubleshooting, and optimization of the RF environment, which can best be described as a self-organizing wireless LAN. Wireless network management systems (WNMSs) can offer RFSM capabilities with fat access points, and WLAN switches or controllers offer RFSM capabilities with thin access points. Some hardware vendors are also using the client radio cards as scouts to collect RF information to be used in a RFSM environment.

One vender, AutoCell, takes a decentralized approach using a technology known as *swarm logic*. Much as with a swarm of bees, rather than deferring to a higher authority, radio cards establish collective intelligence and decentralize any decision making. Radio cards behave collectively with a higher-level intelligence to dynamically manage the RF environment. A radio card can sense the other radio cards' RF transmissions and dynamically make adjustments. All client radios and access point radios work together in a collective RF domain. Swarm logic technology can be integrated via software into any 802.11 radio device.

As defined under the 802.11h amendment, *transmit power control (TPC)* and *dynamic frequency selection (DFS)* are examples of RFSM technology. Currently all spectrum management technology is proprietary, but the 802.11k amendment could eventually define standards for 802.11 spectrum management. While most WLAN engineers still recommend manual site surveys, RFSM may have the potential to eliminate the majority of manual site surveys. Many WLAN engineers still prefer static WLAN design as opposed to a dynamic self-administering wireless LAN. Once standardization of RFSM technology is established, wider acceptance of RFSM will follow.

Summary

In this chapter, you learned the mandatory and optional aspects of a wireless site survey. Spectrum and coverage analysis surveys are always mandatory, while application and throughput testing are considered optional. We discussed the importance of locating potential sources of interference using a spectrum analyzer, and we defined all the steps necessary to conduct both a manual and passive coverage analysis site survey. This chapter also provided a discourse of all the tools necessary for either an indoor or outdoor site survey. We covered the three major types of coverage analysis as well as self-organizing WLAN technology. Conducting a well-defined and thorough wireless site survey will lay the foundation needed for proper WLAN design and WLAN management.

Exam Essentials

Define spectrum, coverage, and application analysis.   Understand why both spectrum and coverage analysis are considered mandatory and application analysis is usually optional.

Identify sources of WLAN interference.   Describe all of the various devices that are potential sources of interference in both the 2.4 GHz ISM and the 5 GHz UNII bands.

Explain RF measurements.   Be able to explain the procedure used while conducting coverage analysis and the different types of RF measurements recorded, including received signal strength and signal-to-noise ratio.

Understand AP placement and configuration.   Explain how AP placement, power, and channel settings are part of coverage analysis.

Identify all site survey tools.   Understand the difference between an outdoor and indoor site survey, and identify all the necessary tools.

Explain the three major types of coverage analysis.   Describe the differences between manual, assisted, and predictive site surveys, and explain self-organizing WLAN technology.

Key Terms

Before you take the exam, be certain you are familiar with the following terms:

active manual survey

application analysis

assisted coverage analysis

coverage analysis

dynamic frequency selection (DFS)

manual coverage analysis

passive manual survey

predicted coverage analysis

Radio Frequency Spectrum Management (RFSM)

received signal strength

Signal to Noise Ratio (SNR)

spectrum analysis

spectrum analyzer

swarm logic

transmit power control (TPC)

Review Questions

1. Name the mandatory requirements of an 802.11 wireless site survey. (Choose all that apply.)
   A. Application analysis
   B. Coverage analysis
   C. Throughput analysis
   D. Spectrum analysis
   E. Security analysis

2. Which potential regional weather conditions can adversely affect an outdoor wireless bridge link and should be noted during an outdoor site survey? (Choose all that apply.)
   A. Lightning
   B. Dew point
   C. Wind
   D. Cloud cover
   E. Thunder

3. Name the major types of coverage analysis site surveys. (Choose all that apply.)
   A. Assisted
   B. Self-organizing
   C. Manual
   D. Capacity
   E. Predictive

4. What type of spectrum management technology uses a decentralized approach to adjusting access point power and channel settings?
   A. Transmit power control
   B. Dynamic frequency selection
   C. Swarm logic
   D. RFSM
   E. GFSK

5. Which type of coverage analysis requires a radio card to be associated to an access point?
   A. Associated
   B. Passive
   C. Predictive
   D. Assisted
   E. Active

6. Which of the following tools can be used in an indoor site survey? (Choose all that apply.)

   A. Measuring wheel

   B. GPS

   C. Ladder

   D. Battery pack

   E. Microwave oven

7. Which of the following tools might be used in an outdoor site survey? (Choose all that apply.)

   A. Binoculars

   B. Access point

   C. Blueprints

   D. 802.11 bridge

   E. Yagi antennas

8. Name potential sources of interference in the 5 GHz UNII band. (Choose all that apply.)

   A. Microwave oven

   B. Cordless phones

   C. FM radios

   D. Radar

   E. Nearby 802.11b/g WLAN

9. Which of these measurements are taken during an indoor site survey? (Choose all that apply.)

   A. SNR

   B. dBi

   C. dBm

   D. dBd

10. Which of the following tools might be used in an outdoor bridging survey? (Choose all that apply.)

    A. Topology map

    B. Topography map

    C. Variable loss attenuator

    D. Radar gun

    E. Spectrum analyzer

11. Name the necessary calculations for an outdoor bridging survey under five miles? (Choose all that apply.)

A. Link budget

B. Free space path loss

C. Fresnel zone

D. Fade margin

E. Height of the antenna beamwidth

12. Name potential sources of interference that might be found during an 802.11g site survey. (Choose all that apply.)

A. Toaster oven

B. Nearby 802.11 FHSS access point

C. Plasma cutter

D. Bluetooth headset

E. 2.4 GHz video camera

13. Which of the following tools can be used in an indoor 802.11a/b/g site survey? (Choose all that apply.)

A. Multiple antennas

B. 902 to 928 MHz spectrum analyzer

C. Client adapter

D. Access point

E. Floor plan map

14. Mr. Williams is a site survey engineer who is planning to deploy a wireless switching solution with dual-radio, dual-frequency thin access points. The employees will be assigned to the 802.11a network and the guest users will be assigned to the 802.11b/g network. CCMP/AES encryption will be required for the employees, while the guest users will only use static WEP. Name the possible choices that Mr. Williams has for coverage analysis? (Choose the two best answers.)

A. Conduct a predictive site survey for the 802.11a network and an assisted site survey for the 802.11b/g network.

B. Install the thin access points in a grid and conduct an assisted site survey for both networks.

C. Conduct manual coverage analysis for the 802.11b/g network first and then conduct manual coverage analysis for the 802.11a network.

D. Conduct a predictive site survey for the 802.11b/g network and an assisted site survey for the 802.11a network.

E. Conduct manual coverage analysis for the 802.11a network first and then conduct manual coverage analysis for the 802.11b/g network.

15. Which of the following tools can be used for manual coverage analysis? (Choose all that apply.)

A. NetStumbler

B. Vendor client utility

C. Wireless Zero Configuration service

D. Client adapter

E. Commercial coverage analysis software

16. Which of the following tools may be found within an indoor site survey kit? (Choose all that apply.)

A. Digital camera

B. Colored electrical tape

C. Grid antenna

D. Access point enclosure unit

E. Temporary mounting gear

17. Mr. Turner is a site survey engineer who has to deploy eighty 802.11b/g autonomous access points in a warehouse with long corridors and metal racks. A WNMS appliance will be used to manage all the access points. Six hundred bar code scanners will be deployed throughout the warehouse using WPA2 Passphrase for security. Which is the most important site survey tool to ensure the best performance throughout the warehouse?

A. 802.11a/b/g multistation emulator

B. Directional antennas

C. Predictive analysis software

D. Security analysis software

E. All of the above

18. What access point settings should be recorded during manual coverage analysis? (Choose all that apply.)

A. Power settings

B. Encryption settings

C. Authentication settings

D. Channel setting

E. IP address

19. Which type of manual coverage analysis does not requires a radio card to be associated to an access point?

   A. Associated

   B. Passive

   C. Predictive

   D. Assisted

   E. Active

20. Which type of site survey uses modeling algorithms and attenuation values to create visual models of RF coverage cells?

   A. Associated

   B. Passive

   C. Predictive

   D. Assisted

   E. Active

Answers to Review Questions

1. B, D. Although often overlooked, checking for potential sources of RF interference is considered a mandatory requirement when conducting a site survey. Both spectrum analysis and visual inspection should be used to search for potential sources of interference. Coverage analysis involves certifying RF cell boundaries and is the main reason for a site survey. Application and throughput analysis are considered an optional requirement. The site survey interview will determine security expectations; however, security is not usually part of the site survey itself.

2. A, C. Lightning can cause damage to Wi-Fi bridging equipment and the network infrastructure equipment that resides behind the 802.11 bridges. Strong winds can cause instability between long-distance bridge links and a loss of RF line of sight. Potential weather conditions should be noted during the outdoor site survey. Proper protection against lightning, such as lightning arrestors and/or copper-fiber transceivers, must be recommended for deployment. In high wind areas, consider the use of grid antennas. Dew point, cloud cover, and thunder have no effect on an 802.11 outdoor deployment and therefore need not be considered during a site survey.

3. A, C, E. Manual site surveys are usually conducted for coverage analysis using a signal strength measurement tool. After the installation of access points, a centralized solution such as a WNMS or a WLAN switch can be used for an assisted coverage survey. Predictive analysis tools can create a model of RF coverage cells.

4. C. Radio Frequency Spectrum Management (RFSM) can be either centralized or decentralized. The 802.11h amendment defines TPC and DFS, which are forms of centralized spectrum management. Gaussian Frequency Shift Keying is a type of modulation. Swarm logic uses multiple radio cards to establish collective intelligence and decentralize decision making.

5. E. During an active manual survey, the radio card is associated to the access point and has layer 2 connectivity, allowing for low-level frame transmissions while RF measurements are also taken.

6. A, C, D. A measuring wheel can be used to measure the distance from the wiring closet to the proposed access point location. A ladder or forklift might be needed when temporarily mounting an access point. Battery packs are used to power the access point. GPS devices are used outdoors and do not properly work indoors. Microwave ovens are sources of interference.

7. A, B, D, E. Outdoor site surveys are usually wireless bridge surveys; however, outdoor access points and mesh routers can be deployed. Binoculars may be used to establish visual line of site during a bridge survey. Yagi antennas might be used in a short to medium bridge link. Blueprints are used during indoor surveys.

8. B, D. Cordless phones that operate in the same space as the 5 GHz UNII bands may cause interference. Radar is also a potential source of interference at 5 GHz. Microwave ovens and 802.11b/g WLANs transmit in the 2.4 GHz ISM band. FM radios use narrowband transmissions in a lower frequency licensed band.

9. A, C. The SNR is a measurement of the difference in decibels (dB) between the received signal and the background noise. Received signal strength is an absolute measured in dBm. Antenna manufacturers predetermine gain in either dBi or dBd values.

10. B, C, E. A topography map that outlines elevations and positions is needed for an outdoor site survey. A variable loss attenuator can be used during an outdoor site survey to simulate different cable lengths or cable losses. A spectrum analyzer is needed to locate potential outdoor sources of interference.

11. A, B, C, D. Outdoor bridging site surveys require many calculations that are not necessary during an indoor survey. Calculations for a link budget, FSPL, Fresnel zone clearance, and fade margin are all necessary for any bridge link.

12. B, C, D, E. Spectrum analysis for an 802.11g site survey should scan the 2.4 GHz ISM band. Bluetooth radios, plasma cutters, 2.4 GHz video cameras, and legacy 802.11 FHSS access points are all potential interfering devices.

13. A, C, D, E. Every indoor wireless site survey should use at least one access point and multiple antennas A client radio card will be needed for coverage analysis as well as a floor plan to record measurements. A spectrum analyzer is needed that sweeps the 2.4 GHz ISM band and 5 GHz UNII bands.

14. B, E. Most wireless switches have Radio Frequency Spectrum Management (RFSM) capabilities, and it is possible to bypass the manual site survey, deploy the access points in a grid, and perform an assisted survey, allowing the switch to automatically adjust the power and channel settings of the thin access points. If the survey was performed manually, the 802.11a coverage analysis should be done first because of shorter range due to the smaller size 5 GHz wavelength. When performing a site survey for dual-radio access points, perform the initial site survey for the technology that provides the smallest coverage area, in this case the higher-frequency 802.11a technology. The technology that provides the larger coverage area, in this case 802.11b/g, should be able to use the same access point location at a lower power setting to provide a similar coverage area as the 802.11a access points.

15. A, B, D, E. A client adapter will be needed to receive the signal from the access point during a manual survey. The software interface can be a freeware utility such as NetStumbler, the manufacturer's client utility, or a commercial application. The Microsoft WZC does not have a signal measurement tool.

16. A, B, E. Temporary access point mounting gear is a necessity. A digital camera and colored electrical tape may also be used to record the locations of AP placement. Grid antennas are used outdoors for long-distance bridge links. An access point enclosure unit is used for permanent mounting.

17. B. Multipath is the biggest concern in the warehouse, and directional antennas will be needed for the survey. Reflections down the long corridors and metal racks will create multipath performance issues that can best be addressed by using a directional antenna.

18. A, D. Wherever an access point is placed during a site survey, the power and channel settings should be noted. Security settings and IP address are not necessary.

19. B. During a passive manual survey, the radio card is collecting RF measurements, including received signal strength (dBm), noise level (dBm), signal-to-noise ratio (dB), and bandwidth data rates. The client adapter, however, is not associated to the access point during a passive survey.

20. C. Predicted coverage analysis is accomplished using an application that creates visual models of RF coverage cells, bypassing the need for actually capturing RF measurements. Projected cell coverage zones are created using modeling algorithms and attenuation values.

Glossary

4-way handshake   Under the 802.11i amendment, two stations (STAs) must establish a procedure to authenticate and associate with each other as well as create dynamic encryption keys through a process known as the 4-way handshake.

6 dB rule   Doubling the distance between a transmitter and receiver will decrease the received signal by 6 dB. Halving the distance between a transmitter and receiver will increase the received signal by 6 dB.

802.11g protection mechanism   In order for the 802.11b and 802.11g standards to coexist, the 802.11g stations enable 802.11g protection mechanism, also known as 802.11g protected mode. RTS/CTS or CTS-to-Self is used by the 802.11g stations to avoid interfering with the 802.11b stations.

802.11i   The 802.11i security amendment defines an enterprise authentication method as well as a method of authentication for home use. The 802.11i amendment requires the use of an 802.1X/EAP authentication method in the enterprise and the use of a preshared key or a passphrase in a SOHO environment. The 802.11i amendment also requires the use of stronger dynamic key management encryption methods. CCMP/AES encryption is the default encryption method, while TKIP/RC4 is the optional encryption method as defined by the 802.11i amendment.

802.1X   The 802.1X standard is a port-based access control standard. 802.1X provides an authorization framework that allows or disallows traffic to pass through a port and thereby access network resources. An 802.1X framework may be implemented in either a wireless or wired environment. The three main components of an 802.1X framework are the supplicant, the authenticator, and the authentication server.

absorption   The most common RF behavior is absorption. If a signal does not bounce off an object or move around an object, it will be absorbed to some extent by the object. Most materials will absorb some amount of an RF signal to varying degrees.

access   The access layer of the network is responsible for delivery of the traffic directly to the end user or end node. The access layer ensures the final delivery of packets to the end user. It is connected to the distribution layer, which is connected to the core.

access point   The CWNP definition is a half-duplex wireless device with switchlike intelligence. In reality, an access point is simply a hub with a radio card and an antenna. Access points must contend for the half-duplex medium in the same fashion that the client station radio cards do.

acknowledgment (ACK)   The ACK frame is one of the six control frames and one of the key components of the 802.11 CSMA/CA media access control method. Since 802.11 is a wireless medium that cannot guarantee successful data transmission, the only way for a station to know that a frame it transmitted was properly received is for the receiving station to notify the transmitting station. This notification is performed using an ACK. The ACK frame is a very simple frame consisting of 14 octets of information.

active gain   Active gain is usually the increase of a signal's amplitude caused by the use of an amplifier on the wire that connects the transceiver to the antenna. The amplifier is usually bidirectional, meaning that it increases the AC voltage both inbound and outbound. Active gain devices require the use of an external power source.

active manual survey   An active manual survey is a site survey method in which the radio card is associated to the access point and has layer 2 connectivity allowing for low-level frame transmissions. Layer 3 connectivity can also be established by generating ping traffic. RF measurements can also be recorded along with packet loss and retransmission percentages.

active mode   Active mode is the default power management mode for most 802.11 stations. When a station is set for active mode, the wireless station is always ready to transmit or receive data. Active mode is sometimes referred to as "continuous aware mode," and it provides no battery conservation. In the MAC header of an 802.11 frame, the Power Management field is 1 bit in length and is used to indicate the power management mode of the station. A value of 0 indicates that the station is in active mode. Stations running in active mode will achieve higher throughput than stations running in power save mode, but the battery life will typically be much shorter.

active scanning   In order for a station to be able to connect to an access point, it needs to first discover an access point. Active scanning is one of the methods that stations use to discover access points.

Ad-Hoc   The 802.11 standard defines three topologies known as service sets. One topology known as an independent basic service set (IBSS) involves direct communications between 802.11 client stations without the use of an access point. An 802.11 IBSS network is also known as a peer-to-peer network or an Ad-Hoc network.

Advanced Encryption Standard (AES)   The AES algorithm, originally named the Rijndael algorithm, is a block cipher that offers much stronger protection than the RC4 streaming cipher. AES is used to encrypt 802.11 wireless data using an encryption method known as Counter mode with Cipher Block Chaining-Message Authentication Code (CCMP). The AES algorithm encrypts data in fixed data blocks with choices in encryption key strength of 128, 192, or 256 bits.

all-band interference   All-band interference is RF interference that occurs across the entire frequency range that is being used. The term *all-band interference* is normally associated with frequency hopping spread spectrum (FHSS) communications that disrupt HR-DSSS and/or ERP-OFDM channel communications.

alternating current (AC)   An electrical current with a magnitude and direction that varies cyclically as opposed to direct current, the direction of which stays in a constant form. The shape and form of the AC signal—defined as the *waveform*—is what is known as a sine wave.

amplification   The increase of a signal's amplitude by the use of an external device.

amplifier   An RF amplifier takes the signal that is generated by the transceiver, increases it, and sends it to the antenna. An amplifier provides an overall increase in power by adding electrical energy to the signal, which is referred to as active gain. Unidirectional amplifiers perform the amplification in only one direction, either when transmitting or when receiving. Bidirectional amplifiers perform the amplification in both directions.

amplitude The height, force, or power of a wave.

Amplitude Shift Keying (ASK) Amplitude Shift Keying (ASK) varies the amplitude or height of a signal to represent the binary data. ASK is a current state technique, where one level of amplitude can represent a 0 bit and another level of amplitude can represent a 1 bit.

announcement traffic indication message (ATIM) A unicast frame that is used in an IBSS network when power save mode is enabled. If a station has buffered data for another station, it will send an ATIM frame to the other station informing it that it must stay awake until the next ATIM window so that it can receive the buffered data. Any station that either has buffered data for another station or has received an ATIM will stay awake so that the buffered data can be exchanged.

antenna An antenna provides two functions in a communication system. When connected to the transmitter, it collects the AC signal that it receives from the transmitter and directs, or radiates, the RF waves away from the antenna in a pattern specific to the antenna type. When connected to the receiver, it takes the RF waves that it receives through the air and directs the AC signal to the receiver.

antenna diversity Antenna diversity is when an access point has two antennas and receivers functioning together to minimize the negative effects of multipath. When the access point senses an RF signal, it compares the signal that it is receiving on both antennas and uses the antenna with the higher signal strength to receive the frame of data. This sampling is performed on a frame-by-frame basis, choosing whichever antenna has the higher signal strength.

antenna polarization Antennas radiate RF signals with the amplitude of the waves fluctuating either vertically or horizontally. The orientation of the antenna is referred to as either vertically or horizontally polarized.

application analysis Testing procedures that are used to determine how an application performs on the wireless network and how the application affects the wireless network. Tools exist that can simulate multiple concurrent virtual wireless client stations.

assisted coverage analysis An RF coverage analysis typically performed by a centralized Wireless Network Management System (WNMS) or a WLAN switch. The centralized device scans the access point radio cards and collects the RF information, which is then used for visualization of coverage cells and for optimizing AP configurations such as channel and power settings. Most assisted solutions use the information gathered from the access point radio cards; however, some solutions can also use a client radio to report information back to the centralized device during a client "walk-through" of the building.

association After a station has authenticated with the access point, the next step is for it to associate with the access point. When a client station associates, it becomes a member of a basic service set (BSS). Association means that the client station can send data through the access point and on to the distribution system medium.

association identifier (AID)   Any time a station associates to an access point, the station receives an association identifier (AID). The access point uses this AID to keep track of the stations that are associated and the members of the BSS.

attenuation   The decrease of amplitude or signal strength. Also known as loss.

attenuator   Attenuators are small devices about the size of a C-cell battery, with cable connectors on both sides. They absorb energy, decreasing the signal as it travels through. A variable-loss attenuator has a dial on it that allows you to adjust the amount of energy that is absorbed. Fixed-loss attenuators provide a set amount of loss.

authentication   Authentication is the verification of user identity and credentials. Users must identify themselves and present credentials such as usernames and passwords or digital certificates. More-secure authentication systems exist that require multifactor authentication, where at least two sets of different credentials must be presented.

authorization, authentication, and accounting (AAA)   AAA is a security concept. Authorization involves granting access to network resources and services. Before authorization to network resources can be granted, proper authentication must occur. Authentication is the verification of user identity and credentials. Accounting is tracking the use of network resources by users. It is an important aspect of network security, used to keep a paper trail of who used what resource and when and where.

authentication server (AS)   When an 802.1X/EAP solution is deployed, an authentication server validates the credentials of the supplicant that is requesting access and notifies the authenticator that the supplicant has been authorized. The authentication server will maintain a user database or may proxy with an external user database to authenticate user credentials.

authenticator   When an 802.1X/EAP solution is deployed, a device that blocks or allows traffic to pass through its port entity is known as the authenticator. Authentication traffic is normally allowed to pass through the authenticator while all other traffic is blocked until the identity of the supplicant has been verified.

autonomous AP   A term for the traditional access point. An autonomous access point contains at least two physical interfaces; usually an RF radio card and a 10/100BaseT port.

azimuth chart   The azimuth chart, labeled H-plane, shows the top-down view of the radiation pattern of the antenna.

bandwidth   Wireless communication is typically performed within a constrained set of frequencies known as a frequency band. This frequency band is the bandwidth.

Barker Code   A spreading/coding technique used by 802.11 cards.

basic service area (BSA)   The physical area of coverage provided by an access point in a BSS is known as the basic service area (BSA). Client stations may move throughout the coverage area and maintain communications with the AP as long as the received signal between the radios remains above RSSI thresholds. Client stations may also shift between concentric zones of variable data rates that exist within the BSA.

basic service set (BSS)   The 802.11 standard defines three topologies known as service sets. One topology, known as the basic service set (BSS), involves communications between a single access point and client stations that are associated to the access point.

basic service set identifier (BSSID)   The BSSID address is a 48-bit (6-octet) MAC address used as a unique identifier of a basic service set. In either a BSS or ESS topology, the BSSID address is simply the MAC address of a single access point. In an IBSS topology, the BSSID address is a virtual address.

Beacon management frame   One of the most important frame types. Commonly referred to as the Beacon. Beacons are essentially the heartbeat of the wireless network. They are only sent by the access point of a basic service set. Client stations transmit beacons only when participating in an IBSS also known as Ad-Hoc mode. Each beacon contains a time stamp, which client stations use to keep their clocks synchronized with the access point. Since so much of successful wireless communications is timing based, it is imperative that all stations are in sync with each other.

beamwidth   The measurement of how broad or narrow the focus of an antenna is. Beamwidth is measured both horizontally and vertically. It is the measurement from the center, or strongest point, of the antenna signal to each of the points along the horizontal and vertical axes where the signal decreases by half power (–3 dB). These –3 dB points are often referred to as half power points. The distance between the two half power points on the horizontal axis is measured in degrees, giving the horizontal beamwidth measurement. The distance between the two half power points on the vertical axis is also measured in degrees, giving the vertical beamwidth measurement.

Bluetooth   A short-distance RF technology defined by the 802.15 standard. Bluetooth operates using FHSS and hops across the 2.4 GHz ISM band at 1.600 hops per second. Older Bluetooth devices were known to cause all-band interference. Newer Bluetooth devices utilize adaptive mechanisms to avoid interfering with 802.11 WLANs.

Bridged Virtual Interface (BVI)   Autonomous access points contain at least two physical interfaces, usually an RF radio card and a 10/100BaseT port. The majority of the time these physical interfaces are bridged together by a virtual interface known as a Bridged Virtual Interface (BVI). The BVI is assigned an IP address that is shared by the two physical interfaces.

broadcast key   When an 802.1X/EAP solution is used with dynamic WEP encryption, a static key known as the broadcast key exists on the access point. The broadcast key is used to encrypt and decrypt all broadcast and multicast 802.11 data frames.

capacity   Proper network design entails providing the necessary coverage while trying to limit the number of devices connected to any single access point at the same time. This is what is meant by capacity.

carrier frequency   The nominal frequency of a carrier wave.

Carrier Sense Multiple Access with Collision Avoidance (CSMA/CA) Media access control method used by 802.11 networks.

Carrier Sense Multiple Access with Collision Detection (CSMA/CD) Media access control method used by 802.3 networks.

carrier signal If a signal is fluctuated or altered, even slightly, data can be properly sent and received. This modulated signal is now capable of distinguishing between 0s and 1s and is referred to as a carrier signal.

casual eavesdropping Casual eavesdropping is not considered malicious and is also often referred to as wardriving. Software utilities known as WLAN discovery tools exist for the purpose of finding open WLAN networks. Wardriving is strictly the act of looking for wireless networks, usually while in a moving vehicle. The most common wardriving software tool is a freeware program called NetStumbler.

channel reuse In order to avoid co-channel interference, a channel reuse pattern is necessary. Overlapping RF coverage cells are needed for roaming but overlap frequencies must be avoided. The only three channels that meet these criteria in the 2.4 GHz ISM band are channels 1, 6, and 11. Overlapping coverage cells therefore should be placed in a channel reuse pattern that minimizes co-channel interference.

Channel reuse patterns should also be used in the 5 GHz UNII bands. Due to the frequency overlap of channel sidebands, there should always be at least two cells between access points on the same channel. Also, it is a recommend practice that any adjacent cells use a frequency that is at least two channels apart and not use an adjacent frequency.

chips A series of bits that represent a single bit of data. To prevent confusion, the data is referred to as a bit and the series of bits are referred to as chips instead of bits.

chipping The process of converting a single data bit into a sequence of bits known as chips is often called "spreading" or "chipping."

chipset A group of integrated circuits designed to work together. Many 802.11 chipset manufacturers exist and sell their chipset technology to the various radio card manufacturers.

clear channel assessment (CCA) A process that determines if the medium is busy. This is performed prior to transmitting data.

client station A radio card that is not used in an access point is typically referred to as a client station. Client station radio cards are typically used in laptops, PDAs, scanners, phones, and many other mobile devices.

client utilities Software used to configure a wireless client card. The software interface will usually have the ability to create multiple connection profiles. Configuration settings of a client utility typically include the SSID, transmit power, security settings, 802.11e/QoS capabilities, and power management.

co-channel interference (CCI) Interference caused by overlapping coverage cells with overlapping frequencies.

co-location   Multiple access points placed near each other, where the RF signal from one AP could potentially affect the signal from another AP. 802.11 b and 802.11g APs are only capable of having three access points in the same area without causing interference.

Compact Flash   A peripheral expansion slot often found on handheld PDAs.

Complementary Code Keying (CCK)   A spreading/coding technique used by 802.11b cards to provide higher data rates (HR-DSSS).

contention window   After a station has waited while performing both virtual and physical carrier-senses, the station may contend for the medium during a window of time known as the contention window.

control frames   Control frames help to assist with the delivery of the data frames. They must be able to be heard by all stations; therefore, they must be transmitted at one of the basic rates. Control frames are also used to clear the channel, acquire the channel, and provide unicast frame acknowledgements. They contain only header information.

convolutional coding   A form of error correction. Convolutional coding is not part of OFDM but rather part of 802.11a and 802.11g. It is a forward error correction (FEC) that allows the receiving system to detect and repair corrupted bits. There are many levels of convolutional coding.

core   The high-speed backbone of the network. The goal of the core is to carry large amounts of information between key data centers or distribution areas. The core layer does not route traffic nor manipulate packets but rather performs high-speed switching. Redundant solutions are usually designed at the core layer to ensure the fast and reliable delivery of packets.

Counter mode with Cipher Block Chaining–Message Authentication Code (CCMP)   The default encryption method defined under the 802.11i amendment. This method uses the Advanced Encryption Standard (AES) cipher. CCMP/AES uses a 128-bit encryption key size and encrypts in 128-bit fixed-length blocks. An 8-byte Message Integrity Check is used that is considered much stronger than the one used in TKIP. CCMP/AES is the default encryption method defined by WPA2.

coverage   A wireless network design in which access points are configured with the power set to the maximum level to provide the largest coverage area possible.

coverage analysis   Determining the proper placement of access points, the transmission power of the access point radio card, and the proper use of antennas.

CTS-to-Self   A protection mechanism for mixed-mode environments. One of the benefits of using CTS-to-Self over RTS/CTS as a protection mechanism is that the throughput will be higher since there are fewer frames being sent.

data frames   Data frames carry the actual data that is passed down from the higher-layer protocols.

data privacy One of the key components of a wireless security solution. Data privacy is achieved by using encryption.

data rates Data rates are the transmission rates specified by the 802.11 standard and amendments, not actual throughput. Due to medium access methods, aggregate throughput is typically half or less of the available data rate bandwidth.

dBd The increase in gain of an antenna, compared to the signal of a dipole antenna. Another way of phrasing this is "decibel gain relative to a dipole antenna."

dBi The gain or increase of power from an antenna when compared to what an isotropic radiator would generate is known as decibels isotropic (dBi). Another way of phrasing this is "decibel gain relative to an isotropic radiator."

dBm Compares a signal to 1 milliwatt of power. dBm means "decibels relative to 1 milliwatt." Since dBm is a measurement that is compared to a known value, 1 milliwatt, then dBm is actually a measure of power.

deauthentication A notification frame used to terminate an authentication. Since authentication is a prerequisite for association, disassociation will also occur. Deauthentication cannot be refused by either party.

decibel (dB) Decibel is derived from the term *bel*. It is a measurement of the ratio between two powers: decibels = $10 * \log10(P_1/P_2)$

delay spread The delay between the reception of the main signal and the reflected signal.

deliverables The site survey information contained in the final report delivered to the customer. This can include spectrum analysis, RF coverage analysis, hardware placement and configuration, and application analysis.

delivery traffic indication message (DTIM) A special type of TIM that is used to assure that all stations are awake when multicast or broadcast traffic is sent.

denial of service (DoS) Any individual with ill intent can temporarily disable a Wi-Fi network by preventing legitimate wireless users from accessing network resources. Layer 1 and layer 2 attacks exist that can deny 802.11 wireless services to legitimate authorized users. 802.11 DoS attacks cannot be prevented, but they can be detected with the proper intrusion detection tools.

diffraction The bending of an RF signal around an object.

dipole antenna An antenna that consists of two elements. A half-wave dipole antenna consists of two elements, each $1/4$ of the wavelength long.

direct sequence spread spectrum (DSSS) A spread spectrum technology originally specified in the 802.11 standard. Provides 1 and 2 Mbps RF communications using the 2.4 GHz ISM band. DSSS 802.11 radio cards are often known as clause 15 devices.

disassociation   A notification frame used to terminate an association. A polite way of terminating the association. Disassocation cannot be refused by either party.

Distributed Coordination Function (DCF)   CSMA/CA is provided by DCF, which is the mandatory access method of the 802.11 standard.

distribution   The distribution layer of the network routes or directs traffic toward the smaller clusters of nodes of the network. The distribution layer routes traffic between VLANs and subnets.

distribution system (DS)   The DS is a system used to interconnect a set of basic service sets (BSSs) and integrated local area networks (LANs) to create an extended service set (ESS). The DS consists of a medium used for transport of traffic as well as services used for transport of traffic.

distribution system medium (DSM)   The DSM is a logical physical medium used to connect access points. Normally the DSM is an 802.3 Ethernet backbone; however, the medium can also be wireless or some other type of medium.

distribution system services (DSS)   The DS consists of system services built inside an access point usually in the form of software. The distribution system services are used to transport 802.11 traffic.

dwell time   A defined amount of time that the FHSS system transmits on a specific frequency before it switches to the next frequency in the hop set. The local regulatory body typically limits the amount of dwell time.

dynamic frequency selection (DFS)   Used for spectrum management of 5 GHz channels for 802.11a radio cards. The European Radiocommunications Committee (ERC) mandates that radio cards operating in the 5 GHz band implement a mechanism to avoid interference with radar systems as well as provide equable use of the channels. The DFS service is used to meet the ERC regulatory requirements.

dynamic rate switching (DRS)   Also known as dynamic rate shifting, adaptive rate selection, or automatic rate selection. A process that client stations use to shift to lower bandwidth capabilities as they move away from an access point and higher bandwidth capabilities as they move toward an access point. The objective of DRS is upshifting and downshifting for rate optimization and improved performance.

earth bulge   The curvature of the earth, which must be considered when installing long-distance point-to-point RF communications.

elevation chart   The elevation chart, labeled E-plane, shows the side view of the radiation pattern of the antenna.

endspan   Defined under the PoE standard as a switch with integrated power-supplying equipment, or more specifically a switch with a PSE (power sourcing equipment).

Enhanced Distributed Channel Access (EDCA)   As defined by the 802.11e amendment, Enhanced Distributed Channel Access (EDCA) is an extension to DCF. The EDCA medium access method will provide for the "prioritization of traffic" via the use of 802.1d priority tags.

enterprise encryption gateway   A specialty 802.11 device that provides for segmentation and encryption. The EEG typically sits behind several fat access points and segments the wireless network from the protected wired network infrastructure. Proprietary encryption technology using the AES algorithm at layer 2 is provided by the enterprise encryption gateway.

enterprise wireless gateway   A specialty 802.11 device used to segment autonomous access points from the protected wired network infrastructure. An EWG can segment the unprotected wireless network from the protected wired network by acting either as a router or a VPN endpoint and/or as a firewall.

equivalent isotropically radiated power (EIRP)   The highest RF signal strength that is transmitted from a particular antenna.

Erlang   Probabilistic traffic formulas use a telecommunications unit of measurement known as an Erlang. An Erlang is equal to one hour of telephone traffic in one hour of time.

evil twin attack   The evil twin attack, also known as wireless hijacking, occurs when a hacker disrupts communications between client stations and a legitimate AP. Client stations lose their connection to the legitimate AP and reconnect to the evil twin access point. The evil twin hijacks the client stations at layer 1 and layer 2, allowing the hacker to proceed with peer-to-peer attacks.

Extended Rate Physical–OFDM (ERP-OFDM)   Defined by 802.11g and used to enhance the 802.11b Physical layer to achieve greater bandwidth while remaining compatible with the 802.11 MAC. Used exactly as defined in the 802.11a amendment. Therefore, data rates of 6, 9, 12, 18, 24, 36, 48, and 54 Mbps are possible using OFDM technology. To maintain backward compatibility, the DSSS data rates of 1, 2, 5.5, and 11 are supported as well.

extended service set (ESS)   The 802.11 standard defines three topologies known as service sets. One topology, known as the extended service set (ESS), involves communications between multiple access points that share a network infrastructure. A ESS is two or more basic service sets that share a distribution system medium.

Extensible Authentication Protocol (EAP)   Extensible Authentication Protocol (EAP) is used to provide user authentication for an 802.1X port-based access control solution. EAP is a flexible layer 2 authentication protocol that resides under Point-to-Point Protocol (PPP).

fade margin   A level of desired signal above what is required.

fast secure roaming (FSR)   Proprietary solutions that provide fast and secure 802.11 roaming, which is needed to implement security and time-sensitive applications in a wireless network.

Federal Communications Commission (FCC)   The FCC is an independent United States government agency, directly responsible to the United States Congress. It was established by the Communications Act of 1934 and is responsible for regulating interstate and international communications by radio, television, wire, satellite, and cable. The FCC's jurisdiction covers all of the 50 states, the District of Columbia, and U.S. possessions.

Federal Information Processing Standards (FIPS)   In the United States, the National Institute of Standards and Technologies (NIST) maintain the Federal Information Processing

Standards (FIPS). The FIPS 140-2 standard defines security requirements for cryptography modules. The use of validated cryptographic modules is required by the United States government for all unclassified communications. Other countries also recognize the FIPS 140-2 standard or have similar regulations.

forward error correction (FEC)   A technology that allows a receiving system to detect and repair corrupted bits.

free space path loss (FSPL)   The loss of signal strength caused by the natural broadening of the waves, often referred to as beam divergence. RF signal energy spreads over larger areas as the signal travels farther away from an antenna, and as a result, the strength of the signal attenuates.

frequency   A term describing a behavior of waves. How fast the waves travel, or more specifically, how many waves are generated over a 1-second period of time is known as frequency.

frequency hopping spread spectrum (FHSS)   A spread spectrum technology that was first patented during World War II. FHSS was used in the original 802.11 standard and provided 1 and 2 Mbps RF communications using the 2.4 GHz ISM band. FHSS works by transmitting data using a small frequency carrier space, then hopping to another small frequency carrier space and transmitting data, then to another frequency, and so on.

Frequency Shift Keying (FSK)   Frequency Shift Keying (FSK) varies the frequency of the signal to represent the binary data. FSK is a current state technique, where one frequency can represent a 0 bit and another frequency can represent a 1 bit.

Fresnel zone (FZ)   An imaginary football-shaped area (American football) that surrounds the path of the visual LOS between two point-to-point antennas. Theoretically, there are an infinite number of Fresnel zones, or concentric ellipsoids (the football shape), that surround the visual LOS. The closest ellipsoid is known as the first Fresnel zone, the next one is the second Fresnel zone, and so on. If the first Fresnel zone becomes even partly obstructed, the obstruction will negatively influence the integrity of the RF communication.

functional policy   A functional security policy defines the technical aspects of wireless security. The functional security policy establishes how to secure the wireless network in terms of what solutions and actions are needed. A functional policy defines essentials, baseline practices, design, implementation, and monitoring procedures.

gain   Also known as amplification. Gain is the increase of amplitude or signal strength. The two types of gain are active gain and passive gain.

general policy   A general wireless security policy establishes why a wireless security policy is needed for an organization. The general wireless security policy defines a statement of authority, applicable audience, violating policy procedures, risk assessment, threat analysis, and auditing.

Generic Routing Encapsulation (GRE)   A process in which frames such as 802.11 frames are encapsulated in a packet, transmitted between two devices on a network, and then removed from the packet and forwarded.

grid antenna   A highly-directional antenna that resembles the rectangular grill of a barbeque, with the edges slightly curved inward. The spacing of the wires on a grid antenna is determined by the wavelength of the frequencies that the antenna is designed for.

hertz (Hz)   A standard measurement of frequency, which was named after the German physicist Heinrich Rudolf Hertz. An event that occurs once in 1 second is equal to 1 Hz. An event that occurs 325 times in 1 second is measured as 325 Hz.

hidden node   Hidden node occurs when one client station's transmissions are unheard by other client stations in the basic service set (BSS). Every time the hidden node transmits, there is a risk another station is also transmitting and a collision can occur.

highly-directional antenna   Strictly used for point-to-point communications, typically to provide network bridging between two buildings. Highly-directional antennas provide the most focused, narrow beamwidth of any of the antenna types. There are two types of highly-directional antennas: parabolic dish and grid antennas.

High-Rate DSSS (HR-DSSS)   The 802.11b 5.5 and 11 Mbps speeds are known as High-Rate DSSS, or HR-DSSS.

hop time   In a frequency hopping spread spectrum network, the amount of time it takes for the transmitter to change from one frequency to another.

hopping sequence   A predefined hopping pattern or set used in frequency hopping spread spectrum. The hopping sequence comprises a series of small carrier frequencies, or "hops." Instead of transmitting on one set channel or finite frequency space, an FHSS radio card transmits on a sequence of sub-channels called hops. Each time the hop sequence is completed, it is repeated.

hotspot   A free or pay-for-use wireless network that is provided as a service by a business.

Hybrid Coordination Function (HCF)   The 802.11e amendment defines enhanced medium access methods to support QoS requirements. Hybrid Coordination Function (HCF) is an additional coordination function that is applied in an 802.11e QoS wireless network. HCF has two access mechanisms to provide QoS: Enhanced Distributed Channel Access (EDCA) and Hybrid Coordination Function Controlled Access (HCCA).

Hybrid Coordination Function Controlled Access (HCCA)   As defined by the 802.11e amendment, Hybrid Coordination Function Controlled Access (HCCA) is similar to PCF. HCCA gives the access point the ability to provide for "prioritization of stations" via a polling mechanism. Certain client stations are given a chance to transmit before others.

independent basic service set (IBSS)   The 802.11 standard defines three topologies known as service sets. One topology, known as an independent basic service set (IBSS), involves direct communications between 802.11 client stations without the use of an access point. An 802.11 IBSS network is also known as a peer-to-peer network or an Ad-Hoc network.

Industrial, Scientific, and Medical (ISM)   The ISM bands are defined by the ITU-T in S5.138 and S5.150 of the Radio Regulations. Although the FCC ISM bands are the same as defined by the ITU-T, the usage of these bands in other countries may be different due to local regulations. The 900 MHz band is known as the Industrial band, the 2.4 GHz band is known as Scientific band and the 5.8 GHz band is known as the Medical band. It should be noted that all three of these bands are license-free bands and there are no restrictions on what types of equipment can be used in any of the three ISM bands.

The ISM bands are as follows:

902–928 MHz (26 MHz wide)
2.4000–2.4835 GHz (83.5 MHz wide)
5.725–5.875 GHz (150 MHz wide)

infrared   A communication technology that uses a light-based medium. Information about modern implementations of infrared can be found at the Infrared Data Association's website at www.irda.org.

Initialization Vector (IV)   The IV is utilized by the RC4 streaming cipher that WEP encryption uses. The IV is a block of 24 bits that is combined with a static key. It is sent in cleartext and is different on every frame. The effective key strength of combining the IV with the 40-bit static key is 64 bit encryption. TKIP uses an extended IV.

Institute of Electrical and Electronics Engineers (IEEE)   The IEEE is a global professional society with over 350,000 members. The IEEE's mission is to "promote the engineering process of creating, developing, integrating, sharing, and applying knowledge about electro and information technologies and sciences for the benefit of humanity and the profession."

International Organization for Standardization (ISO)   The ISO is a global, nongovernmental organization that identifies business, government, and society needs and develops standards in partnership with the sectors that will put them to use. The ISO is responsible for the creation of the Open Systems Interconnection (OSI) model, which has been a standard reference for data communications between computers since the late 1970s.

The OSI model is the cornerstone to data communications, and understanding it is one of the most important and fundamental tasks a person in the networking industry can undertake.

The layers of the OSI model are as follows:

Layer 1—Physical
Layer 2—Data-Link
Layer 3—Network
Layer 4—Transport
Layer 5—Session
Layer 6—Presentation
Layer 7—Application

intentional radiator (IR)   A device that intentionally generates and emits radio frequency energy by radiation or induction.

International Telecommunications Union Radiocommunication Sector (ITU-R)   The United Nations has tasked the ITU-R with global spectrum management. The ITU-R maintains a database of worldwide frequency assignments and coordinates spectrum management through five administrative regions.

The five regions are broken down as Region A (North and South America), Region B (Western Europe), Region C (Eastern Europe and Northern Asia), Region D (Africa), and Region E (Asia and Australasia).

Inter Access Point Protocol (IAPP)   Announcement and handover processes that result in how APs inform other APs about roamed clients and that define a method of delivery for buffered packets.

Internet Protocol Security (IPSec)   IPSec is a layer 3 VPN technology. IPSec can use RC4, DES, 3DES, and AES ciphers for encryption. It provides for encryption, encapsulation, data integrity, and device authentication.

inter-symbol interference (ISI)   A type of multipath interference caused by the difference in time between the primary signal and the reflected signals.

isotropic radiator   A point source that radiates signal equally in all directions. The sun is probably one of the best examples of an isotropic radiator. It generates equal amounts of energy in all directions.

keying method   When data is sent, a signal is transmitted from the transceiver. In order for the data to be transmitted, the signal must be manipulated so that the receiving station has a way of distinguishing 0s and 1s. This method of manipulating a signal so that it can represent multiple pieces of data is known as a keying method. A keying method is what changes a signal into a carrier signal. It provides the signal with the ability to encode data so that it can be communicated or transported.

last-mile   The term *last-mile* is often used by the telephone and cable companies to refer to the last segment of their service that connects the home subscriber to their network.

layer 3 roaming   Any roaming technology that allows mobile device users to move from one layer 3 network to another while maintaining their original IP address. While maintaining upper-layer connectivity is possible with these layer 3 roaming solutions, increased latency is often an issue.

lightning arrestor   A device that redirects (shunts) transient currents caused by nearby lightning strikes or ambient static away from your electronic equipment and into the ground. Lightning arrestors are used to protect electronic equipment from the sudden surge of power that a nearby lightning strike or static buildup can cause. The lightning arrestor is installed between the transceiver and the antenna.

line of sight (LOS)   When light travels from one point to another, it travels across what is perceived to be an unobstructed straight line, known as visual line of sight.

link budget The calculation of the amount of RF signal that is received minus the amount of signal required by the receiver.

lobes Even though the majority of the RF signal that is generated from an antenna is focused within the beamwidth of the antenna, there is still a significant amount of signal that radiates from outside of the beamwidth and from what is known as the antenna's side or rear lobes.

loss Also known as attenuation. Loss is the decrease of amplitude or signal strength.

malicious eavesdropping The unauthorized use of protocol analyzers to capture wireless communications is known as malicious eavesdropping and is typically considered illegal. Most countries have laws making it unlawful to listen in on any type of electromagnetic communications such as phone conversations. Unauthorized monitoring of 802.11 wireless transmissions is considered malicious and normally illegal. The most common target of malicious eavesdropping attacks is public access hotspots.

management frames A majority of the frame types in an 802.11 network. Used by wireless stations to join and leave the network. Management frames are not necessary on wired networks since physically connecting or disconnecting the network cable performs this function.

man-in-the-middle attack After successfully completing wireless hijacking, an attacker may use a second wireless card with their laptop to execute what is known as a man-in-the-middle attack. The second wireless card is associated with the original legitimate AP. The hacker bridges the second wireless card to the evil twin access point radio and routes all hijacked traffic right back to the gateway of the original network. The attacker can therefore sit in the middle and execute peer-to-peer attacks indefinitely while remaining completely unnoticed.

manual coverage analysis Determining the proper placement of access points, the transmission power of the access point radio card, and the proper use of antennas by performing a manual site survey. There are two major types of manual coverage analysis surveys: passive and active.

mesh networking A network environment where wireless mesh routers communicate with each other using proprietary layer 2 routing protocols, creating a self-forming and self-healing wireless infrastructure (a mesh) over which edge devices can communicate.

Message Integrity Check (MIC) TKIP uses a data integrity check known as the Message Integrity Check (MIC) to mitigate known bit-flipping attacks against WEP. The MIC is sometimes referred to by the nickname Michael.

Microsoft Point-to-Point Encryption (MPPE) MPPE is a 128-bit encryption method that uses the RC4 algorithm. MPPE is used with Point-to-Point Tunneling Protocol (PPTP) VPN technology.

midspan Defined under the PoE standard as a passthrough device with integrated power-supplying equipment. The midspan device does not regenerate the Ethernet signal and must not disrupt the Ethernet signal. Midspan devices can only send power over the unused twisted pairs on the Ethernet cable. A midspan solution will work with 10BaseT and 100BaseTX but not Gigabit Ethernet.

milliwatt (mW)   A unit of power equal to 1/1000 of a watt.

Mini PCI   A small form factor PCI expansion card. The mini PCI is a variation of the Peripheral Component Interconnect (PCI) bus technology and was designed for use mainly in laptops. A Mini PCI radio is often used inside access points and is also the main type of radio used by manufacturers as the internal 802.11 wireless adapter inside laptops.

mixed-mode   The default operational mode of most 802.11g access points. Support for both DSSS and OFDM is enabled, therefore both 802.11b and 802.11g clients can communicate with the access point.

Mobile IP   An Internet Engineering Task Force (IETF) standard protocol that allows mobile device users to move from one layer 3 network to another while maintaining their original IP address. Mobile IP is defined in IETF Request for Comments (RFC) 3344.

modulation   The manipulation of a signal so that the receiving station has a way of distinguishing 0s and 1s.

multipath   A propagation phenomenon that results in two or more paths of a signal arriving at a receiving antenna at the same time or within nanoseconds of each other.

Multiple Input Multiple Output (MIMO)   Any RF communications system that has multiple antennas at both ends of the communications link and being used concurrently.

near/far   A low-powered client station that is a great distance from the access point could potentially become an unheard client if other high-powered stations are very close to the access point. The transmissions of the high-powered stations can raise the noise floor to a higher level in which the lower-powered station cannot be heard. This scenario is referred to as the near/far problem.

network allocation vector (NAV)   A timer mechanism that maintains a prediction of future traffic on the medium based on duration value information seen in a previous frame transmission. When an 802.11 radio is not transmitting, it is listening. When the listening radio hears a frame transmission from another station, it looks at the header of the frame and determines if the Duration/ID field contains a Duration value or an ID value. If the field contains a Duration value, the listening station will set its NAV timer to this value. The listening station will now use the NAV as a countdown timer, knowing that the RF medium should be busy until the countdown reaches 0.

Newton's Inverse Square Law   This law states that the change in power is equal to 1 divided by the square of the change in distance.

noise floor   The level of background noise.

non-root bridge   Wireless bridges support two major configuration settings: root and non-root. Bridges work in a parent/child type relationship, so think of the root bridge as the parent and the non-root bridge as the child.

omni-directional antenna A type of antenna that radiates RF signal in all directions. The small rubber dipole antenna, often referred to as a "rubber duck" antenna, is the classic example of an omni-directional antenna and is the default antenna of most access points. A perfect omni-directional antenna would radiate RF signal like a theoretical isotropic radiator. Due to manufacturing limitations, a perfect omni-directional antenna cannot be made.

Open System authentication Open System authentication is the simpler of the two 802.11 authentication methods. It provides authentication without performing any type of client verification. It is essentially an exchange of hellos between the client and the access point.

Orthogonal Frequency Division Multiplexing (OFDM) Orthogonal Frequency Division Multiplexing is one of the most popular communications technologies, used in both wired and wireless communications. As part of 802.11 technologies, OFDM is specified in the 802.11a and 802.11g amendments and can transmit at speeds of up to 54 Mbps. OFDM transmits across 52 separate, closely and precisely spaced frequencies, often referred to as subcarriers.

oscillation A single change from up to down to up or a single change from positive to negative to positive. Also known as a "cycle."

oscilloscope A time domain tool that can be used to measure how a signal's amplitude changes over time.

Packet Binary Convolutional Code (PBCC) A modulation technique that supports data rates of 5.5, 11, 22, and 33 Mbps. Both the transmitter and receiver must support the technology to achieve the higher speeds. PBCC was developed by Alantro Communications, which was purchased by Texas Instruments. During the development of the 802.11g addendum, PBCC was adopted as an optional modulation technique.

panel antenna A type of semi-directional planar antenna designed to direct a signal in a specific direction. Used for short- to medium-distance communications.

parabolic dish antenna A highly-directional parabolic dish antenna that is similar to the small digital satellite TV antennas that can be seen on the roofs of many houses.

passive gain Passive gain is accomplished by focusing the RF signal with the use of an antenna. Antennas are passive devices that do not require an external power source. The internal workings of an antenna can focus the signal more powerfully in one direction than another.

passive manual survey When performing coverage analysis with a passive manual survey, the radio card is collecting RF measurements, including received signal strength (dBm), noise level (dBm), signal-to-noise ratio (dB), and bandwidth data rates. The client adapter, however, is not associated to the access point during the survey.

passive scanning In order for a station to be able to connect to an access point, it needs to first discover an access point. Passive scanning involves the client station listening for the Beacon frames that are continuously being sent by the access points.

patch antenna A type of semi-directional planar antenna designed to direct a signal in a specific direction. Used for short- to medium-distance communications.

PC Card   The PC Card Standard specifies three types of PC Cards. The three card types are the same length and width and use the same 68-pin connector. The thickness of the cards are as follows: Type I = 3.3 mm, Type II = 5.0 mm, and Type III = 10.5 mm.

PCMCIA   See Personal Computer Memory Card International Association.

peer-to-peer   See IBSS.

peer-to-peer attack   A wireless client station can attack the resources of any peer 802.11 client station in the same 802.11 service set. Peer-to-peer attacks can occur in any Ad-Hoc network or through any access point or Wi-Fi switch where client stations share an association. Wireless peer-to-peer attacks can be mitigated with a personal firewall on the client side or through the use of PSPF on the access point or Wi-Fi switch.

per session per user   After an EAP frame exchange where mutual authentication is required, both the AS and the supplicant now know information about each other due to the exchanging of credentials. This new-found information is used as seeding material or keying material to generate a matching dynamic encryption key for both the supplicant and the authentication server. These dynamic keys are generated per session per user, meaning that every time a client station authenticates, a new key is generated and every user has a unique and separate key. This dynamic session key is often referred to as the unicast key because it is the dynamically generated key that is used to encrypt and decrypt all unicast data frames. After the key is created, the AS delivers its copy of the unicast key to the access point. The access point and the client station now both have unique unicast keys.

Personal Computer Memory Card International Association (PCMCIA)   PCMCIA is an international standards body and trade association. The PCMCIA has over 100 member companies and was founded in 1989 to establish standards for peripheral cards and to promote interchangeability with mobile computers. A PCMCIA adapter is also known as a PC Card. A radio card can be used in any laptop or handheld device that has a PC Card slot. Most PC Cards have integrated antennas. Some cards only have external antenna connectors, while others have external antennas and external connectors.

phase   The relationship between two waves with the same frequency. To determine phase, a wavelength is divided into 360 pieces referred to as degrees. If you think of these degrees as starting times, then if one wave begins at the 0 degree point and another wave begins at the 90 degree point, these waves are considered to be 90 degrees out of phase.

Phase Shift Keying (PSK)   Phase Shift Keying varies the phase of the signal to represent the binary data. PSK is a state transition technique, where one phase can represent a 0 bit and another phase can represent a 1 bit. This shifting of phase determines the data that is being transmitted.

phased array antenna   An antenna system made up of multiple antennas that are connected to a signal processor. The processor feeds the individual antennas with signals of different relative phases, creating a directed beam of RF signal aimed at the client device. They are capable of creating narrow beams and transmitting multiple beams to multiple users simultaneously. Because of this unique capability, they are often regulated differently by the local RF regulatory agency.

physical carrier-sense   Performed constantly by all stations that are not transmitting or receiving data. Determines if a frame transmission is inbound for a station to receive or if the medium is busy before transmitting. This is known as the clear channel assessment (CCA).

Point Coordination Function (PCF)   An optional 802.11 medium access method that uses a form of polling. Although defined by the standard, the medium access method has not been implemented.

point coordinator   The polling device in an 802.11 PCF network.

point source   A point that radiates signal equally in all directions. The sun is one of the best examples of this.

point-to-multipoint   A wireless network configuration that has a central communications device such as a bridge or an access point providing connectivity to multiple devices such as other bridges or clients.

point-to-point   A wireless network configuration that connects only two devices together. This is typically a wireless bridge link.

Point-to-Point Tunneling Protocol (PPTP)   PPTP is a layer 3 VPN technology. It uses 128-bit Microsoft Point-to-Point Encryption (MPPE), which uses the RC4 algorithm. MPPE encryption is considered adequate but not strong. PPTP also uses MS-CHAP version 2 for user authentication, which is susceptible to offline dictionary attacks.

polarity   Wave polarity is defined as the position and direction of the electric field (E-field) as referenced to the surface of the earth. If an antenna element is positioned vertically, then the E-field is also vertical. Vertical polarization is when the E-field is perpendicular to the earth. If an antenna element is positioned horizontally, then the electric field is also horizontal. Horizontal polarization is when the E-field is parallel to the earth.

port-based access control   The 802.1X standard defines port-based access control. 802.1X provides an authorization framework that allows or disallows traffic to pass through a port and thereby access network resources. 802.1X defines two virtual ports: an uncontrolled port and a controlled port. The uncontrolled port allows EAP authentication traffic to pass through, while the controlled port blocks all other traffic until the supplicant has been authenticated.

Power over Ethernet (PoE)   A solution that can be used to power remote network devices over the same Ethernet cabling that carries data to the remote device. Using PoE to provide power to 802.11 access points is often a simpler and more cost-effective solution than hiring an electrician to install new electrical drops and outlets for every AP.

power save mode   An optional mode for 802.11 stations. A wireless station can shut down some of the transceiver components for a period of time to conserve power. The station indicates that it is using power save mode by changing the value of the Power Management field to 1.

Power Sourcing Equipment (PSE)   One of the two main components in a POE solution. Power is sent from the PSE to the PD over Ethernet cable. The Power Sourcing Equipment might be housed inside an inline switch or an injector. The PSE provides power for the connected device.

Powered Device (PD)   One of the two main components in a POE solution. Power is sent from the PSE to the PD over Ethernet cable. An example of a PD would be an access point. The Powered Device (PD) requires power from the PSE. The PD must be able to accept power through either the data pairs or unused pairs.

predicted coverage analysis   An RF coverage analysis method that uses an application that provides RF simulation and modeling design capabilities. Predicted coverage analysis is accomplished using an application that creates visual models of RF coverage cells, bypassing the need for actually capturing RF measurements. Projected cell coverage zones are created using modeling algorithms and attenuation values. Virtual access points are created and overlaid on the floor plan graphic. Multiple "what if" scenarios can be created by changing the power settings, channel settings, or antenna type of the virtual access points, which can also be moved to any location on the floor plan.

preshared keys (PSKs)   A method of distributing encryption passphrases or keys by manually typing the matching passphrases or keys on both the access point and all client stations that will need to be able to associate to the wireless network. This information is shared ahead of time (preshared) using a manual distribution method such as telephone, email, or face-to-face conversation.

probe request   An 802.11 management frame that is transmitted during active scanning. A client station that is looking for an SSID sends a probe request. Access points that hear the probe request will send a probe response, notifying the client of the access points' presence. If a client station receives probe responses from multiple access points, signal strength and quality characteristics are typically used by the client station to determine which access point has the best signal and thus which access point to connect to.

probe response   An 802.11 management frame that is transmitted during active scanning. After a client station sends a probe request, access points that hear the probe request will send a probe response, notifying the client of the access points presence. The information that is contained inside the body of a probe response frame is the exact same information that can be found in a Beacon frame with the exception of the traffic indication map (TIM).

propagation   The movement or motion of the RF waves through the air.

protection mechanism   A mechanism that allows the two technologies to coexist. The goal of the 802.11g "protection mechanism" is to prevent ERP-OFDM radio cards from transmitting at the same time as DSSS radio cards.

processing gain   The task of adding additional, redundant information to data. In this day and age of data compression, it seems strange that we would use a technology that adds data to our transmission, but by doing so, the communication is more resistant to data corruption. The system converts 1 bit of data into a series of bits that are referred to as chips.

Public Secure Packet Forwarding (PSPF)   PSPF is a feature that can be enabled on WLAN access points or switches to block wireless clients from communicating with other wireless clients on the same wireless segment. With PSPF enabled, client devices cannot communicate with other client devices on the wireless network. *PSPF is a term most commonly used by Cisco;* other vendors have similar capabilities under different names. PSPF is useful in preventing peer-to-peer attacks through an access point.

quality of service (QoS)   The attempt to prioritize and provide certain levels of predictable throughput along a shared access medium.

quality of service basic service set (QBSS)   An 802.11 basic service set that provides quality of service (QoS). An infrastructure QBSS contains an 802.11e-compliant access point.

Radio Frequency Spectrum Management   Software and hardware solutions that can dynamically change the configuration of thin or fat access points based on accumulated RF information gathered from the access points' radio cards. Based on the accumulated RF information, the centralized device controls the access points and adjusts their power and channel settings, dynamically changing the RF coverage cells.

range   The area or distance that an RF signal can provide effective usable coverage.

Rayleigh fading   Due to the differences in phase of the multiple paths, a combined signal will often attenuate, amplify, or become corrupted. These effects are sometimes called Rayleigh fading, named after British physicist Lord Rayleigh.

RC4   The RC4 algorithm is a streaming cipher used in technologies that are often used to protect Internet traffic, such as Secure Sockets Layer (SSL). The RC4 algorithm is used to protect 802.11 wireless data and is incorporated into two encryption methods known as WEP and TKIP.

reassociation   When a client station decides to roam to a new access point, it will send a reassociation request frame to the new access point. It is called a reassociation not because it is reassociating to the access point, but because it is reassociating to the SSID of the wireless network.

receive sensitivity   The amount of signal a wireless station must receive in order to distinguish between data and noise.

received signal strength   A measurement of the amount of signal received.

receive signal strength indicator (RSSI)   An optional 802.11 parameter with a value from 0 to 255. It is designed to be used by the hardware manufacturer as a relative measurement of the RF power that is received. The RSSI is one of the indicators that is used by a wireless device to determine if another device is transmitting, also known as a clear channel assessment.

receiver   The receiver is the final component in the wireless medium. The receiver takes the carrier signal that is received from the antenna and translates the modulated signals into 1s and 0s. It then takes this data and passes it to the computer to be processed.

reflection   One of the most important RF propagation behaviors to be aware of is reflection. When a wave hits a smooth object that is larger than the wave itself, depending upon the media, the wave may bounce in another direction. This behavior is categorized as reflection.

refraction   If certain conditions exist, an RF signal can be bent in a behavior known as refraction. Refraction is the bending of an RF signal as it passes through a medium with a different density, thus causing the direction of the wave to change. RF refraction most commonly occurs as a result of atmospheric conditions.

request to send/clear to send (RTS/CTS)   A mechanism that performs a NAV distribution and helps to prevent collisions from occurring. This NAV distribution reserves the medium prior to the transmission of the data frame. RTS/CTS can be used to discover hidden node problems. RTS/CTS is one of the two protection mechanisms used in mixed-mode environments.

residential wireless gateway (RWG)   A very fancy term for a home wireless router. The main function of a residential wireless gateway is to provide shared wireless access to a SOHO Internet connection while providing a level of security from the Internet. These SOHO Wi-Fi routers are generally inexpensive yet surprisingly full featured.

RF shadow   The area directly behind an RF obstruction. Depending upon the change in direction and velocity of the diffracted signals, the area of the RF shadow can become a dead zone of coverage or still possibly receive degraded signals.

roaming   The ability for the client stations to transition from one access point to another while maintaining network connectivity for the upper-layer applications.

robust security network (RSN)   A robust security network (RSN) is a network that only allows for the creation of robust security network associations (RSNAs). An RSN utilizes CCMP/AES encryption as well as 802.1X/EAP authentication.

robust security network associations (RSNAs)   As defined by the 802.11i security amendment, two stations (STAs) must establish a procedure to authenticate and associate with each other as well as create dynamic encryption keys through a process known as the 4-way hand-shake. This association between two stations is referred to as a robust security network association (RSNA).

rogue access point   A rogue access point is any wireless device that is connected to the wired infrastructure but is not under the management of the proper network administrators. The rogue device acts as a portal into the wired network infrastructure. Because the rogue device has no authorization or authentication security in place, any intruder can use the open portal to gain access to network resources.

role-based access control (RBAC)   Role-based access control (RBAC) is an approach to restricting system access to authorized users. The three main components of an RBAC approach are users, roles, and permissions. Separate roles can be created such as the sales role or the marketing role. Individuals or groups of users are assigned to one of these roles. Permissions can be defined as firewall permissions, layer 2 permissions, layer 3 permissions, and bandwidth permissions and can be time based. The permissions are then mapped to the roles. When wireless users authenticate via the WLAN, they inherit the permissions of whatever roles they have been assigned to.

root bridge   Wireless bridges support two major configuration settings: root and non-root. Bridges work in a parent/child type relationship, so think of the root bridge as the parent and the non-root bridge as the child.

rule of 10s and 3s   Provides approximate values when performing RF math calculations. All calculations are based upon the following four rules:

> If you add 3 to the dBms, you must multiply the mWs by 2.
> If you subtract 3 from the dBms, you must divide the mWs by 2.
> If you add 10 to the dBms, you must multiply the mWs by 10.
> If you subtract 10 from the dBms, you must divide the mWs by 10.

scattering   Scattering can most easily be described as multiple reflections. Scattering can happen in two different ways. The first type of scatter is on a smaller level and has a lesser effect on the signal quality and strength. This type of scatter may manifest itself when the RF signal moves through a substance and the individual electromagnetic waves are reflected off the minute particles within the medium. Smog in our atmosphere and sandstorms in the desert can cause this type of scattering.

The second type of scattering occurs when an RF signal encounters some type of uneven surface and is reflected into multiple directions. Chain-link fences, tree foliage, and rocky terrain commonly cause this type of scattering. When striking the uneven surface, the main signal dissipates into multiple reflected signals, which can cause substantial signal downgrade and may even cause a loss of the received signal.

sector antenna   A special type of high-gain, semi-directional antenna that provide a pie-shaped coverage pattern. These antennas are typically installed in the middle of the area where RF coverage is desired and placed back to back with other sector antennas. Individually, each antenna services its own piece of the pie, but as a group all of the pie pieces fit together and provide omni-directional coverage for the entire area. A sector antenna generates very little RF signal behind the antenna (back lobe) and therefore does not interfere with the other sector antennas that it is working with.

Secure Digital (SD)   A peripheral expansion slot often found on handheld PDAs.

semi-directional antenna   A type of antenna that is designed to direct a signal in a specific direction. Semi-directional antennas are used for short- to medium-distance communications, with long-distance communications being served by highly-directional antennas.

service set identifier (SSID)   The SSID is a network name used to identify an 802.11 wireless network. The SSID wireless network name is comparable to a Windows workgroup name. The SSID can be made up of as many as 32 characters and is case sensitive.

Shared Key authentication   The more complex of the two 802.11 authentication methods. Shared Key authentication uses WEP to authenticate client stations and requires that a static

WEP key be configured on both the station and the access point. In addition to WEP being mandatory, authentication will not work if the static WEP keys do not match. The authentication process is similar to Open System authentication but includes a challenge and response between the AP and client station.

short interframe space (SIFS)   A short gap or period of time that is used during the transmission of data.

signal-to-noise ratio (SNR)   The SNR is the difference in decibels between a received signal and the background noise. The SNR is an important value because, if the background noise is too close to the received signal, data can get corrupted and retransmissions will increase.

site survey   A process performed to determine RF coverage, potential sources of interference, and the proper placement, installation, and configuration of 802.11 hardware.

slot time   A period of time that differs between the different spread spectrum technologies. It is a large enough time to allow for receive-to-transmit radio turnaround, MAC processing, and clear channel assessment (CCA) detect.

small office, home office (SOHO)   A common reference to the office environment of self-employed people, satellite employees, or an environment in which someone is likely to bring work home with them.

software defined radio (SDR)   A future technology that will be able to dynamically switch across a wide range of frequency bands, transmission techniques, and modulation schemes so that a single radio could replace multiple products.

spectrum analysis   Locating sources of interference in the 2.4 GHz ISM and 5 GHz UNII bands is considered mandatory when performing an 802.11 wireless site survey. Using a spectrum analyzer to determine the state of the RF environment within a certain frequency range is known as spectrum analysis.

spectrum analyzer   Spectrum analyzers are frequency domain measurement devices that can measure the amplitude and frequency space of electromagnetic signals. A spectrum analyzer is a tool that should always be used to locate sources of interference during an 802.11 wireless site survey. Spectrum analyzers are also used for security purposes to locate layer 1 denial of service attacks. Most spectrum analyzers are stand-alone devices, but distributed solutions exist that can be used as layer 1 intrusion detection systems.

splitter   A splitter takes an RF signal and divides it into two or more separate signals. Only under an unusually special or unique situation would you have a need to use an RF splitter.

spread spectrum   Spread spectrum transmission uses more bandwidth than is necessary to carry its data. Spread spectrum technology takes the data that is to be transmitted and spreads it across the frequencies that it is using.

station (STA)   The main component of an 802.11 wireless network is the radio card, which is referred to by the 802.11 standard as a station (STA). The radio card can reside inside an access point or be used as a client station.

supplicant   When an 802.1X/EAP solution is deployed, a host with software that is requesting authentication and access to network resources is known as the supplicant.

swarm logic   Swarm logic is when 802.11 radio cards establish collective intelligence and decentralize any decision making in a BSS. Client stations behave collectively with a higher-level intelligence to dynamically manage the RF environment. A client station can sense the other client stations' RF transmissions and dynamically make adjustments. All client radios and access point radios work together in a collective RF domain.

system operating margin (SOM)   The calculation of the amount of RF signal that is received minus the amount of signal required by the receiver.

Task Group   Various 802.11 task groups are in charge of revising and amending the original standard that was developed by the MAC Task Group (MAC) and the PHY Task Group (PHY). Each group is assigned a letter from the alphabet, and it is common to hear the term "802.11 alphabet soup" when referring to all the amendments created by the multiple 802.11 task groups. Quite a few of the 802.11 task group projects have been completed and amendments to the original standard have been ratified. Other 802.11 task group projects still remain active and exist as draft amendments.

Temporal Key Integrity Protocol (TKIP)   TKIP is an enhancement of WEP encryption that addresses many of the known weaknesses of WEP. TKIP starts with a 128-bit temporal key that is combined with a 48-bit Initialization Vector (IV) and source and destination MAC addresses in a complicated process known as per-packet key mixing. TKIP also uses sequencing and uses a stronger data integrity check known as the Message Integrity Check (MIC). TKIP is the mandatory encryption method under WPA and is optional under WPA2.

throughput   A measurement of the amount of user data that successfully traverses the network over a period of time.

topology   The physical and/or logical layout of nodes in a computer network.

traffic indication map (TIM)   The traffic indication map (TIM) is used when stations have enabled power save mode. The TIM is a list of all stations that have undelivered data buffered on the access point waiting to be delivered. Every beacon will include the AID of the station until the data is delivered.

Transition Security Network (TSN)   An 802.11 wireless network that allows for the creation of pre-robust security network associations (pre-RSNAs) as well as RSNAs is known as a transition security network. A TSN supports 802.11i defined security as well as legacy security such as WEP within the same BSS.

transmit power control (TPC)   Part of the 802.11h amendment. TPC is used to regulate the power levels used by 802.11a radio cards. The ERC mandates that radio cards operating in the 5 GHz band use TPC to abide by a maximum regulatory transmit power and are able to alleviate transmission power to avoid interference. The TPC service is used to meet the ERC regulatory requirements.

transmitter   The initial component in the creation of the wireless medium. The computer hands the data off to the transmitter, and it is the transmitter's job to begin the RF communication.

unicast key   A dynamically generated WEP encryption key that is generated per session per user is often referred to as the unicast key. Unicast keys are used to encrypt and decrypt all unicast 802.11 data frames.

unit of comparison   Units of measure that provide comparative measurements, not absolute measurements. Decibel is an example of a unit of comparison.

unit of power   Units of measure that provide absolute measurement values, not relative or comparative measurements. Watt is an example of a unit of power.

Unlicensed National Information Infrastructure (UNII)   The IEEE 802.11a amendment designates data transmissions within the frequency space of the 5 GHz UNII bands. The 802.11a amendment uses three groupings or bands of UNII frequencies, often known as the lower, middle, and upper UNII bands. These three bands are also known as UNII-1 (lower), UNII-2 (middle), and UNII-3 (upper). All three of these bands are 100 MHz wide, which is a useful fact when trying to remember their frequency ranges. The commonly used UNII bands are as follows:

UNII-1 (lower) is 5.15–5.25 GHz
UNII-2 (middle) is 5.25–5.35 GHz
UNII-3 (upper) is 5.725–5.825GHz

virtual AP   A major wireless switching provider has a system know as a virtual AP. A virtual access point solution uses multiple access points that all share a single BSSID MAC address. Because the multiple access points advertise only one single virtual MAC address (BSSID), client stations believe they are connected to only a single access point, although they may be actually roaming across multiple APs.

virtual carrier-sense   When an 802.11 radio is not transmitting, it is listening. When the listening radio hears a frame transmission from another station, it looks at the header of the frame and determines if the Duration/ID field contains a Duration value or an ID value. If the field contains a Duration value, the listening station will set its NAV timer to this value. The listening station will now use the NAV as a countdown timer, knowing that the RF medium should be busy until the countdown reaches 0.

virtual local area networks (VLANS)   Virtual local area networks (VLANS) are used to create separate broadcast domains in a layer 2 network and are often used to restrict access to network resources without regard to physical topology of the network. In a WLAN environment, individual SSIDs can be mapped to individual VLANs and users can be segmented by the SSID/VLAN pair, all while communicating through a single access point.

virtual private network (VPN)   A private network that is created by the use of encryption, tunneling protocols, and security procedures. VPNs are typically used to provide secure communications when physically connected to an insecure network.

Voice over IP (VoIP)   Voice over Internet Protocol. The transmission of voice conversations over a data network using TCP/IP protocols.

Voice over Wi-Fi (VoWiFi)   Any software or hardware that uses voice over IP communications over an 802.11 wireless network is known as VoWiFi. Because of latency concerns, VoWiFi requires QoS mechanisms to function properly in an 802.11 BSS.

voltage standing wave ratio (VSWR)   VSWR is a numerical relationship between the measurement of the maximum voltage along the line (what is generated by the transmitter) and the measurement of the minimum voltage along the line (what is received by the antenna). VSWR is therefore a ratio of impedance mismatch, with 1:1 (no impedance) being optimal but unobtainable and typical values from 1.1:1 to as much as 1.5:1. VSWR military specs are 1.1:1.

VPN wireless routers   VPN wireless routers have all of the same features that can be found in a SOHO wireless router, along with providing secure tunneling functionality in addition to 802.11 layer 2 defined security capabilities. Supported VPN protocols may include PPTP, L2TP, IPSec, and SSH2.

wardriving   Wardriving is the act of looking for wireless networks, usually while in a moving vehicle. Software utilities known as WLAN discovery tools exist for the purpose of finding open WLAN networks. The most common wardriving software tool is a freeware program called NetStumbler.

watt   A basic unit of power, named after James Watt, an eighteenth-century Scottish inventor. One watt is equal to 1 ampere (amp) of current flowing at 1 volt.

wavelength   The distance between similar points on two back-to-back waves. When measuring a wave, the wavelength is typically measured from the peak of a wave to the peak of the next wave.

wave propagation   The way in which the RF waves move—known as wave propagation—can vary drastically depending on the materials in the signal's path. Drywall will have a much different effect on an RF signal than metal.

Wi-Fi Alliance   The Wi-Fi Alliance is a global, nonprofit industry trade association with over 200 member companies. The Wi-Fi Alliance is devoted to promoting the growth of wireless LANs (WLANs). One of the Wi-Fi Alliance's primary tasks is to ensure the interoperability of WLAN products by providing certification testing. During the early days of the 802.11 standard, the Wi-Fi Alliance further defined the 802.11 standard and provided a set of guidelines to assure compatibility between different vendors. Products that pass the Wi-Fi certification process receive a Wi-Fi Certified certificate.

Wi-Fi Multimedia (WMM)   The Wi-Fi Alliance maintains the Wi-Fi Multimedia (WMM) certification as a partial mirror of 802.11e QoS amendment. WMM currently provides for traffic prioritization via four access categories.

Wi-Fi phishing attack   After completing a wireless hijacking attack at a hotspot, a hacker may also use web server software and captive portal software to perform a Wi-Fi phishing attack. Once client stations have been hijacked to an evil twin access point, they are redirected to a login web page that looks exactly like a hotspot's login page. The hacker's fake login page will request a credit card number from the hijacked user. Phishing attacks are very common on the Internet and are now appearing at Wi-Fi hotspots.

Wi-Fi Protected Access (WPA)   Prior to the ratification of the 802.11i amendment, the Wi-Fi Alliance introduced Wi-Fi Protected Access (WPA) certification as a snapshot of the not-yet-released 802.11i amendment, supporting only the TKIP/RC4 dynamic encryption key management. 802.1X/EAP authentication was required in the enterprise and passphrase authentication in a SOHO environment. After 802.11i was ratified, the Wi-Fi Alliance introduced WPA2. WPA2 is a more complete implementation of the 802.11i amendment and supports both the CCMP/AES and TKIP/RC4 dynamic encryption key management. 802.1X/EAP authentication is required in the enterprise and passphrase authentication in a SOHO environment.

Wired Equivalent Privacy (WEP)   WEP is a layer 2 encryption method that uses the RC4 streaming cipher. The original 802.11 standard defined 64-bit WEP as the default encryption method. 64-bit static WEP uses a 24-bit Initialization Vector and a 40-bit static key. WEP encryption has been cracked and is not considered a strong encryption method.

wireless distribution system (WDS)   Although the distribution system (DS) normally uses a wired Ethernet backbone, it is possible to use a wireless connection instead. A wireless distribution system (WDS) can connect access points together, using what is referred to as a wireless backhaul.

wireless hijacking   Wireless hijacking, also known as the evil twin attack, occurs when a hacker disrupts communications between client stations and a legitimate AP. Client stations lose their connection to the legitimate AP and reconnect to the hacker's access point. The hacker AP hijacks the client stations at layer 1 and layer 2, allowing the hacker to proceed with peer-to-peer attacks.

Wireless Internet service provider (WISP)   WISPs deliver Internet services via wireless networking. Instead of directly cabling each subscriber, a WISP can provide services via RF communications from central transmitters. WISPs often use wireless technology other than 802.11 allowing them to provide wireless coverage to much greater areas. Service from WISPs is not without its own problems.

wireless intrusion detection system (WIDS)   A WIDS is a client/server solution that is used to constantly monitor for 802.11 wireless attacks such as rogue APs, MAC spoofing, layer 2 DoS, and so on. WIDS usually consist of three components: a server, sensors, and monitoring software. Wireless intrusion detection uses policies and alarms to properly classify attacks and alert administrators to potential attacks.

wireless intrusion prevention system (WIPS)   A WIPS is a wireless intrusion detection system (WIDS) that is capable of mitigating attacks from rogue access points. WIPS use spoofed deauthentication frames, SMNP, and proprietary methods to effectively render a rogue access device useless and protect the network backbone.

wireless LAN bridge   A very common nonstandard deployment of 802.11 technology. The purpose of bridging is to provide wireless connectivity between two or more wired networks.

A bridge generally supports all the same features that a fat access point possesses; however, the purpose is to connect wired networks and not to provide wireless connectivity to client stations. Although bridge links are sometimes used indoors, generally they are used outdoors to connect the wired networks inside two buildings.

wireless local area network (WLAN) The 802.11 standard is defined as a wireless local area network technology. Local area networks provide networking for a building or campus environment. The 802.11 wireless medium is a perfect fit for local area networking simply due to the range and speeds that are defined by the 802.11 standard and its amendments. The majority of 802.11 wireless network deployments are indeed local area networks (LANs) that provide access at businesses and homes.

wireless metropolitan area network (WMAN) A wireless metropolitan area network provides coverage to a metropolitan area such as a city and the surrounding suburbs. The wireless technology that is typically associated with a WMAN is defined by the 802.16 standard. The 802.16 standard defines broadband wireless access and is sometimes referred to as Worldwide Interoperability for Microwave Access (WiMAX).

Wireless Network Management System A central point of management to configure and maintain as many as 5,000 fat access points. A Wireless Network Management System can be either a hardware appliance or a software solution.

wireless personal area network (WPAN) A wireless computer network used for communication between computer devices within close proximity of a person. Devices such as laptops, personal digital assistants (PDAs), and telephones can communicate with each other using a variety of wireless technologies. Wireless personal area networks can be used for communication between devices or as portals to higher-level networks such as a local area network (LAN) and/or the Internet. The most common technologies used in wireless personal area networks are Bluetooth and infrared.

wireless wide area network (WWAN) A wireless computer network that covers broad geographical boundaries but obviously uses a wireless medium instead of a wired medium. Wireless wide area networks typically use cellular telephone technologies. Data rates and bandwidth using these technologies are relatively slow when compared to other wireless technologies such as 802.11. However, as cellular technologies improve, so will cellular data transfer rates.

wireless workgroup bridge (WGB) A device that provides wireless connectivity for wired infrastructure devices that do not have radio cards. The radio card inside the wireless workgroup bridge associates with an access point and joins the basic service set (BSS) as a client station. This provides fast and quick wireless connectivity for wired devices through the association the WGB has with the access point. Because the WGB is an associated client of the access point, the WGB does not provide connectivity for other wireless clients. It is also important to understand that only the radio card inside the WGB can contend for the 802.11 wireless medium and the wired cards behind the WGB cannot contend for the half-duplex RF medium.

Wireless Zero Configuration (WZC) service   The most widely used client utility is an integrated operating system client utility, more specifically known as the WZC service utility that is enabled by default in Windows XP.

WLAN controller   Also known as a wireless switch, WLAN controllers provide AP management, user management, RF Spectrum planning and management, layer 2 security, layer 3 security, captive portal, VRRP redundancy, WIDS, and VLAN segmentation. Another major advantage of the WLAN switch model is that most of the switches support some form of fast secure roaming, which can assist in resolving latency issues often associated with roaming.

WLAN mesh router   Wireless mesh routers communicate with each other using proprietary layer 2 routing protocols, creating a self-forming and self-healing wireless infrastructure (a mesh) over which edge devices can communicate.

WLAN switch   Also known as a wireless controller, WLAN switches provide AP management, user management, RF Spectrum planning and management, layer 2 security, layer 3 security, captive portal, VRRP redundancy, WIDS, and VLAN segmentation. Another major advantage of the WLAN switch model is that most of the switches support some form of fast secure roaming, which can assist in resolving latency issues often associated with roaming.

WMM–PS (Power Save)   The Wi-Fi Alliance oversees the WMM–PS (Power Save) certification, which uses 802.11e mechanisms to increase the battery life via advanced power saving mechanisms.

WMM–SA (Scheduled Access)   The Wi-Fi alliance maintains the proposed WMM–SA (Scheduled Access) certification, which is contention free access, based on 802.11e HCCA mechanisms.

yagi antenna   A type of semi-directional antenna designed to direct a signal in a specific direction. Used for short- to medium-distance communications.

Index

Note to the reader: Throughout this index **boldfaced** page numbers indicate primary discussions of a topic. *Italicized* page numbers indicate illustrations.

Numbers & Symbols

Q

Y

Z

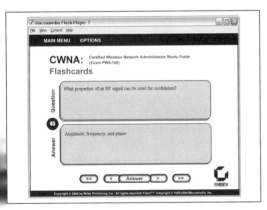

Wiley Publishing, Inc.
End-User License Agreement